THE CAPITALIST MANIFESTO

THE CAPITALIST MANIFESTO

*The Historic, Economic and Philosophic Case
for Laissez-Faire*

Andrew Bernstein

University Press of America,® Inc.
Lanham · Boulder · New York · Toronto · Oxford

**To Regina Milano,
Who Made It All Possible**

Contents

Acknowledgements

Many people necessarily helped to bring about a book of this scope. Thanks go to BB&T for helping to fund the writing of this book

Robert Tracinski, publisher and editor of *The Intellectual Activist*, provided excellent editorial criticism, helping to improve the book in innumerable ways.

Special thanks go to Dr. John Ridpath, whose editorial feedback greatly improved the content of the manuscript.

That hard-driving entrepreneur, Carl Barney, President of College America, supported this project in more ways than he realizes. Above all, whenever I need inspiration, I think of capitalism's noblest feature, the phenomenon of the "self-made man." The individual who perfectly embodies it is the man who has integrated hard-nosed business judgment with a heart of gold: Carl Barney.

Dr. Eric Daniels, Visiting Assistant Professor of History at Duke University's program for Values and Ethics in the Marketplace, helped with the research and with his vast knowledge of American history. Jason Rheins, a graduate student in the Philosophy Department at the University of Pennsylvania, Sherri Tracinski, Mark Kormes, Alan Wachtel, Lucy Fake, and Neil Erian, Adjunct Professor of Philosophy at the State University of New York at Purchase, all assisted ably with the research.

Richard Salsman, CFA, President and Chief Market Strategist of

InterMarket Forecasting, provided helpful feedback regarding technical issues of economics.

The great Tamara Fuller provided help simply by showing how much is still possible in a relatively-free society.

Robert Begley, founder of the New York Heroes Society, also did this, and more: he did excellent and arduous work proofreading the manuscript. Damian Begley ably performed the difficult task of compiling the book's Index.

My firebreathing literary agent, Holly White, who is puzzled that there are those who regard "no" as an answer, has aided this project in ways too numerous to mention. My dear friends, Robert and Amy Nasir, have been extremely generous with their time and energy in helping to bring this project to fruition.

My sister, Aline, like our mom, always believed in me and, knowing the constancy of her soul, always will. My beautiful daughter, Penelope Joy, gives her daddy hope that mankind's future may yet be brighter than its past.

Above all, towers my wife, to whom this book is justly dedicated. Lovely Regina, those cynics who bleat that brains and beauty stand in inverse proportion to each other, never knew you.

Introduction: The Great Disconnect

Here are the most important facts:

The capitalist revolution began in Great Britain in the late-18th century. Since that time, the capitalist nations have been the freest countries of history. In Western (and now parts of Eastern) Europe, in the United States, in Japan, Hong Kong and the other Asian Tigers hundreds of millions of human beings are guaranteed freedom of speech, of religion, of intellectual expression, of assembly, and of voting. Men are free there to earn and to own property – their own homes, farms and land. They are free to start their own businesses and to retain the profits that they earn. A hallmark of capitalism is a rule of law that protects private property, safeguards investments and enforces contracts. The fundamental moral principle upon which capitalism is based is that individuals have inalienable rights and that governments exist solely to protect those rights. Capitalism requires the limiting of governmental power to maximize the freedom of the individual.

Capitalism, the system of individual rights, has brought increased freedom to men all over the world. In Europe, capitalism ended feudalism, the dictatorship of the aristocracy. In America, the principle of individual rights impelled the British colonists to throw off the rule of the monarchy and establish history's freest nation – and the logic of the country's founding principles led, in less than a century, to the abolition of slavery, a practice that existed everywhere in the world through all of history, and one still practiced widely today throughout the non-capitalist world. In post-World War II Japan, under America's influence, a semi-capitalist, vastly freer society replaced the military dictatorship that preceded it. In Hong Kong, Taiwan and South Korea, the freedom of their capitalist or semi-capitalist systems enabled those countries (or colonies) to become havens for millions of refugees fleeing Communist oppression.[1]

More broadly, it is to the capitalist nations across the globe that immigrants come, millions of them, both historically and currently, often fleeing political and/or religious persecution in their homelands. They come on rafts to the United States from Cuba. By the millions and for 15 years, the Vietnamese "boat people" fled for their lives from Communism – and today, more than 1.6 million of them have found freedom, mostly in the West. Muslims seeking religious and political freedom flee to the Western capitalist nations from all over the Islamic world. And, of course, for more than 150 years, America has been the hope and the chosen destination of persecuted peoples from around the globe, including from Ireland, Jews from Eastern Europe, Sicilians suppressed by the 19th century remnants of aristocratic rule, and Chinese and Koreans oppressed by the Communists.[2]

Finally, the Western capitalist nations, by inflicting military defeat on the Fascists, and political-economic defeat on the Communists, eliminated the scourge of totalitarianism from large parts of the earth, bringing greater freedom to hundreds of millions of human beings in Japan, Germany, Italy, Eastern Europe and Russia.

Capitalism is the system of freedom.

Freedom leads to dramatic economic results. The "great laboratory" of capitalist West Berlin side-by-side with communist East Berlin provided the most vivid example — West Berlin, a modern, prosperous commercial center, East Berlin so destitute and squalid that, by 1989, the rubble remained from World War II battles four decades earlier. The striking truth is that the capitalist nations are the wealthiest countries of history. For example, famine, the scourge of all non-capitalist societies, past and present, has been wiped out in the West. There has never been a famine in the history of the United States. Has there ever been one in any capitalist country? The author does not know of any.[3]

Regarding the empirical correlation between economic freedom, i.e., capitalism and prosperity: the Heritage Foundation and the *Wall Street Journal* jointly publish an annual survey examining the degree of economic freedom in the world. Its title is the *Index of Economic Freedom.* "The story that the Index continues to tell is that economically freer countries tend to have higher per capita incomes than less free countries…The more economic freedom a country has, the higher its per capita income is." The editors organize 155 countries into four categories, which are, in ascending order – repressed, mostly unfree, mostly free and free. "Once an economy moves from the mostly unfree category to the mostly free category, per capita income increases nearly four times." The mostly free countries, including Japan, Taiwan, Canada, Poland and Sweden, have an average per capita income of greater than $11,000. Additionally, the per capita income among free countries is, on average, almost double that of the mostly free countries. The free countries, including the United States, Great Britain, Hong Kong and Singapore show an average per capita income of greater than $21,000.[4]

Capitalism is the system of wealth.

But under statism, conditions are diametrically opposite. Many political systems have ruthlessly suppressed the rights and lives of individuals. Feudalism, military dictatorships, theocracies, National Socialism (Nazism) and Communism are merely several examples. What these and other such systems share in common is the denial of individual rights. These are the anti-capitalist systems in which the individual is forced to live and die for the state. The horrors of such lack of freedom are historically and currently manifest.

Under feudalism, for example, the common man – the overwhelming preponderance of mankind – was suppressed by the *ancien regime*. Heretics were often burned at the stake; countless women were condemned to death for practicing "witchcraft;" the serfs were tied to the land and possessed few rights; and the most advanced thinkers were persecuted – Galileo's forced recantation under threat of torture was merely the most notorious such case.

In the 20th century, statism reached its most virulent form. The National Socialists plunged the world into the most catastrophic war of history and butchered 25 million innocent victims in a 12-year reign of terror. The Communists were just as prolific in their commitment to brutality, establishing in Russia, China, Cambodia, North Korea and elsewhere totalitarian regimes that murdered a numbing 100 million victims in 80 years.

In Africa, oppressive dictatorships and ghastly tribal slaughters are the norm. In Sudan, the Islamic regime currently holds tens of thousands of blacks in slavery. In Rwanda, Hutu "militia" in 1994 hacked to pieces 800,000 victims, mostly members of the Tutsi tribe. In Somalia, endless, bloody warfare rages between rival warlords. In Zaire, the dictator, Mobutu, bankrupted the economy, pushing countless individuals into starvation by embezzling billions of dollars. In Zimbabwe, the Marxist dictator, Mugabe, stole the land from commercial farmers with the inevitable result: famine for millions of people. The shocking truth is that more than 225 years after the American Revolution, freedom is virtually unknown around the globe.[5]

Statism – the subordination of the individual to the state – leads inevitably to the most hideous oppression.

Further, just as the freest nations, i.e., the most capitalist ones, are the wealthiest – so the most repressed countries are the most destitute. For example, according to one economist, Angus Maddison, feudal Europe and its aftermath was as miserably poor as is commonly believed.

The Great Disconnect

Economic growth was non-existent during the centuries 500-1500 — and per capita GDP rose by merely 0.1 percent per year in the centuries 1500-1700. In 1500, the estimated European per capita income was roughly $215; in 1700, roughly $265.[6]

In the 20th century, China under Mao suffered massive famine that killed anywhere from 20 to 43 million individuals – and hundreds of millions subsisted on less than a dollar a day. Also under the Communists, conditions were similar in North Korea and worse in Cambodia. The Soviet Union and its slave states of Eastern Europe were miserably poor by Western standards. The repressive dictatorships of Africa are countries where per capita living standards are measured in hundreds – not thousands – of dollars. Across the globe, the oppressed nations of Asia, South America and the Middle East are unspeakably poor.[7]

For example, the *Index of Economic Freedom* shows that the repressed nations –·including Cuba, Iran, Iraq (under Saddam Hussein) and North Korea – have an average per capita income around $2800. The mostly unfree countries – including Russia, Saudi Arabia, Egypt and Brazil – possess an average per capita income of approximately the same. This means that the freer countries – the semi-capitalist and capitalist nations – enjoy per capita incomes from four to ten times as great as those in the non-capitalist world.[8]

Additionally, it must be pointed out that the unfree nations of the world have per capita incomes as high as $2800 for primarily one reason: the enormous aid they receive in various forms from the West, especially the diffusion of American technology. Without investment, loans, aid, technical training and supplies, etc., from the capitalist nations, the unfree countries would subsist in vastly worse misery than they already do. As merely one example, without massive food shipments from the West, an incalculable number of human beings would starve to death in the endless famines that recur in the unfree countries, from Ethiopia to North Korea to Zimbabwe.[9]

Statism – in all its forms – is the system of appalling destitution.

The facts show that capitalism is the system of freedom – and that it creates wealth. The facts similarly show that statism is the system of repression – and that it causes poverty. Capitalism is the system of freedom and prosperity. Its antithesis – statism in any form – is the system of oppression and destitution. Despite these facts, however, widespread antagonism toward capitalism exists; and generally from among society's most educated members – Humanities professors, writers, artists, journalists, teachers, clergymen and politicians.

Anti-capitalist intellectuals and writers present a constellation of related criticisms. They hold that capitalism creates inequalities of income, that it exploits the workers and the impoverished, that it supplants spiritual values with materialism, and that it leads to imperialism and war. Successful businessmen, according to their view, accumulated fortunes largely by means of fraud and peculation. Such accusations come alike from socialists and conservative defenders of the current mixed economies, from secularists and religionists, from Marxists and from Catholic clergymen, from Jews and from Muslims.

Marx and Engels, for example, wrote: "The bourgeoisie [the practitioners and supporters of capitalism]…has left remaining no other bond between man and man than naked self-interest and callous 'cash payment'…In one word, for exploitation veiled by religious and political illusions, [the bourgeoisie] has substituted naked, shameful, direct, brutal exploitation."[10]

Pope Paul VI in the encyclical, Populorum Progressio, claimed: "But it is unfortunate that on these new conditions of society a system has been constructed which considers profit as the key motive for economic progress, competition as the supreme law of economics, and private ownership of the means of production as an absolute right that has no limits and carries no corresponding social obligation." The Pope went on to state that "a certain type of capitalism has been the source of excessive suffering, injustices and fratricidal conflicts whose effects still persist."[11]

Such "liberal" modern American historians and writers as Charles Beard, Richard Hofstadter and Matthew Josephson routinely denigrated leading industrialists and capitalists, arguing that Cornelius Vanderbilt, John D. Rockefeller, Andrew Carnegie, J.P. Morgan, et al., built their careers by "exploiting workers and milking farmers, bribing Congressmen, buying legislatures, spying upon competitors, hiring armed guards, dynamiting property, [and] using threats and intrigue and force."[12]

The system of freedom and wealth is repeatedly and savagely attacked by many intellectuals and other highly educated individuals — worse, by men and women claiming to be "liberals," humanists, lovers of man, i.e., the very individuals who should function as the protectors and preservers of human life. There is an enormous disconnect between the facts of capitalism's nature and history – and the evaluation of these by many "progressive" writers and the millions whose thinking they influence. The facts of capitalism's nature and history are not unknown. Certainly the educated critics are well aware of them. Capitalism's enemies are simply unimpressed. Why? What is responsible for the great disconnect?

The reason is that the objections to capitalism are not based on factual grounds – and all the evidence in the world establishing the freedom and prosperity of those living under capitalism will not influence the system's critics to the slightest degree. The criticisms are motivated solely by moral and philosophical theories.

Since long before capitalism's 18th century inception, moral theories antagonistic to egoism and profit-making have been dominant. From its birth, therefore, capitalism was an intellectual anomaly: a great boon to human prosperity that was unsupported, even opposed, by men's dominant moral and philosophical codes. Hence the tragic historical spectacle of capitalism providing abundance for the first time for untold millions while sustaining repeated intellectual blows from its moral and philosophical enemies — from thinkers who claimed to care about mankind.

For example, socialists – whether of a Marxist or non-Marxist variety – insist that it is an individual's moral obligation to sacrifice himself for the state. Capitalism, they accurately point out, is not founded on principles of self-sacrifice. Rather, capitalism rests on an egoistic moral code – on the inalienable right of each and every man to his own life. The freedom that capitalism offers an individual to pursue his own personal, selfish happiness is, to socialists, anathema. To them, individual rights and political-economic freedom are appalling because they follow logically from an egoistic moral code that they regard as evil.

As a further example, modern egalitarians seek equality of income. But, contrary to their wishes, the freedom of the capitalist system will always lead to enormous disparities of income, because, in fact, individuals are not equal. They are not equal in talent, they are not equal in initiative, they are not equal in capacity to satisfy customer demand. Left free, some individuals will cure cancer, some will make the baseball Hall of Fame, some will drop out of school, some will work in the local grocery store, some will refuse to work and sponge off of families, friends and private charities.

The enormous general prosperity of the capitalist countries – the ability of capitalism to inherit widespread poverty and then proceed to create a vast middle class – does not and will not begin to impress egalitarians. The principle of economic equality – not universal prosperity – is their moral god. Consequently, they admire the "equal" destitution of Cuba's citizens and repudiate the unequally-shared wealth of America. To them, it is morally superior if everybody subsists roughly equally on $1,000 annually and morally inferior if some possess millions while others live on "merely" $15,000 or $20,000 or $30,000. Rational men prefer to earn $15,000 in a country where others are millionaires to $1,000 in a country where others are equally poor. But egalitarians loathe the economic inequalities necessitated by the freedom of the capitalist system.

Finally, to a devout religionist, such as contemporary Islamists, what matters the earthly riches and comforts enjoyed by those in the capitalist countries? To them, all that matters is salvation in a higher world. If Allah repudiates the secularism, selfishness and materialism of capitalism, if such a life leads to eternal damnation, then the religionist must abjure it, even seek to annihilate it. Islamic terrorists, after all, did not destroy the towers of the World Trade Center simply because they were tall buildings. For years, they targeted those buildings because they were the nerve center of the world financial markets, located in the Wall Street area of New York City, the world's commercial center. Those towers were, in terms both practical and symbolic, at the heart of global capitalism – and this is exactly why they were destroyed.

Too often, freedom's supporters have limited themselves to responses that demonstrate capitalism's unparalleled ability to increase men's prosperity. While true and important, such defenses miss the essence of the criticism. It is as if a great dialogue regarding the most momentous issues held across a span of centuries has been conducted at cross purposes. The critics argue on moral grounds; the supporters on economic grounds. The critics, wedded to a moral code of self-sacrifice, are oblivious to capitalism's practical success. The supporters, equally wedded to such a code, are morally disarmed against the onslaught of their antagonists — and are reduced to the citation of empirical facts and figures. The supporters, unable to break free of the conventional creed urging selflessness, have too often regarded capitalism's inherent pursuit of self-interest as a guilty secret, akin to an unsavory skeleton in a family closet.

It is time to come out of the closet.

For two centuries, capitalism has cried out for its supporters to finally embrace the code of rational egoism as an undiluted virtue of which to be proud. That will be an important part of this book. The torrent of facts showing capitalism's practical superiority will be presented within a philosophical framework showing that capitalism is the only moral system for human beings.

Two intellectual tasks must be accomplished in order to establish capitalism as the ideal social system. The first is to factually document the enormous practical benefits to man's life wrought by capitalism. These are the tasks of history and economics. The second is the job of philosophy: to show that morality arises only because of the factual requirements of man's life on earth, i.e., the concepts "good" and "evil," "right" and "wrong," are based in the facts of human nature, specifically in the objective requirements of human survival and prosperity. Only when the good is shown to be that which promotes man's life will it be possible to understand and appreciate the enormous moral virtue embodied in capitalism's unparalleled ability to do precisely that. All codes upholding human sacrifice must be exposed as anti-life, therefore, anti-good, i.e., immoral. When the philosophical job is accomplished, then and only then will men have the moral code by means of which to properly evaluate capitalism's stunning, life-giving success.

The tragic spectacle of capitalism's life-promoting achievements evaluated by means of moral philosophies woefully unequipped to understand or appreciate them will finally, after 200 years, end. Part One of this book performs the practical task. In examining capitalism's essence, its predecessors, and its earliest days, it provides sufficient factual evidence to establish the system's historic achievements and to refute the common misconceptions that have been fostered about its nature and its past. The data presented are illustrative of the moral-philosophical theories of egoism, individualism and man's mind as his means of survival — theories that are later identified and articulated as the intellectual foundation upon which capitalism rests.

Part Two — the book's most important section — is dedicated to the philosophical task: the explanation of the rational moral theories necessary to understand capitalism's nature and achievements — and to finally assess them properly. After two centuries, the great disconnect between facts and evaluation will mercifully be brought to an end. The book's thesis will be clear: capitalism is the only moral political-economic system because it alone embodies the rational principles upon which human survival and prosperity depend.

Part Three refutes the chronic moral accusations levelled against capitalism — that it is responsible for war, imperialism and slavery. It shows that, on the contrary, capitalism and the moral principles on which it is based represent the antidote to these horrors that have long afflicted mankind — and, conversely, that statism and the moral principles on which it is based bear causal responsibility for them.

Part Four is devoted to explaining the essential reason that capitalism is economically superior to any form of socialism or statism more broadly. The writings of the great economists both explain the workings of a free market and validate it as the only means by which to create widespread prosperity. That economics is relegated to the end of this book, therefore, represents no slap at the economists. Quite the contrary, for to a significant degree they have done their job superbly. It is time for the moralists and philosophers to do theirs.

Finally, the Appendix applies the moral principles elucidated in the book to the important and long misunderstood topic of the "Robber Barons." When evaluated from the standpoint of a rational code of ethics that upholds the requirements of man's life as the standard of morality, the enormous productivity of Carnegie, Rockefeller, Hill, Harriman, et al., stamps them as productive geniuses who were enormous benefactors of the human race. Originally, this chapter was included in Part One but needed to be cut because of space limitations. But the topic was too important to be removed from the book, so was included in its present form.

The overall goal of rational cognition in any field is to reduce a vast complexity of phenomena to a principle(s) that explain it. For example, consider the quest of the Pre-Socratic philosophers to explain the teeming multiplicity of nature in terms of a single material principle — whether water, air or Anaximander's "boundless." The Greeks called it "finding the one in the many." Regarding the enormity of capitalism's success, both morally and practically, in different centuries, on far-flung continents, involving a hundred issues, the explanatory principle that will emerge is: capitalism is par excellence the system of liberated human brain power. This principle will recur throughout the book.

The moral and philosophical theories presented in this book are grounded fully in the revolutionary intellectual work of Ayn Rand — and the reader is strongly encouraged to read her seminal novel, *Atlas Shrugged*, as well as her non-fiction works, *The Virtue of Selfishness* and *Capitalism: The Unknown Ideal.*

This book is written for the rational mind anywhere and anytime, whether the reader is a professional intellectual or an intelligent layman. It seeks to make the case for individual rights and freedom in terms intelligible to all rational men.

This book is in full, one-hundred percent support of capitalism, and repudiates all forms of the initiation of governmental force, whether in the economic or personal affairs of innocent men. As such, the presentation is neither balanced nor open-minded, if "open-minded" means the belief that all opinions hold equal cognitive weight — for they do not. Rather, the book is objective. It is open exclusively to facts and to rational argumentation. It is because of its objective method that its content is relentlessly pro-capitalist, for no facts exist and no rational arguments can be adduced to show the superiority of statism.

The author has a proudly selfish stake in promoting capitalism. As an American — though a teacher — he is rich, as are all Americans by both historic and current non-capitalist standards of wealth and poverty. Since capitalism is the only system capable of creating universal prosperity, he recognizes that his ongoing wealth depends on its continued existence.

All readers who seek to preserve their own wealth — or more urgently, to earn wealth and economically rise — should recognize a similar selfish stake in understanding and promoting the content of this book.

A final point is that many of the great men in the history of freedom and capitalism are heroes — and this book is written by an unabashed hero worshipper.

Part One: History

1: What is Capitalism?

A proper understanding of capitalism is sorely lacking among current politicians, intellectuals and even the American people, who generally support it. In order to gain such understanding, it is helpful to start with a true story that reveals the spirit, the sense of life, the emotional stance and outlook that characterizes capitalism. Then it will be possible to comprehend the deeper principles it embodies and the intellectual causes that give rise to it. The political principles of capitalism will be presented in this chapter; the moral and philosophical principles that validate it in Part Two.

In the early 19th century, Robert Fulton, the inventor of the steamboat, held a legal monopoly granted by the state of New York to run all steamboat traffic in that state. The state-enfranchised monopoly legally prevented competition from entering the field, thereby keeping prices artificially high to the detriment of the customers, who detested the monopoly.

But in early 19th century America, men believed in their inalienable rights as free U.S. citizens, and did not bow compliantly to arbitrary government authority. In 1817, a New Jersey businessman hired twenty-three-year-old Cornelius Vanderbilt (1794-1877) to ferry passengers between New Jersey and New York City in a direct challenge to the monopoly's power. For the next six years, a cat-and-mouse game ensued between the monopoly and its challenger, with the young Vanderbilt at the epicenter of the struggle.

Cornelius was "a big-bodied, husky, black-eyed lad" who performed superbly all the physical activities of a vibrant young man living near the sea. "He would swim farthest in the surf and row farthest out to sea," and was a daring horseman as well.[1]

Vanderbilt hoisted a flag on the masthead of his boat, the Bellona, reading "New Jersey must be free!" and for sixty consecutive weekdays in 1817 eluded capture by authorities who sought to arrest him and confiscate his vessel. To the delight of the passengers who loved his lower-priced service, he used "every possible trick or subterfuge to avoid capture." He hid near the gangplank, then scurried off when police officers boarded so their papers could not be served. He constructed a secret closet in which to hide, so when law officers boarded him in the bay they found only a young woman steering the boat, whom they questioned to the taunts and derision of the other passengers.

One day Vanderbilt was caught on a New York wharf in broad daylight, arrested and sent to Albany to answer contempt of court charges before the magistrate. An insolent Vanderbilt produced a paper showing that for that day only his boat had been hired by Daniel D. Tompkins, Vice-President of the United States, and had a legal right to enter New York. Vanderbilt returned triumphant to the New York City waterfront, where he was acclaimed for outsmarting the monopoly.

On the premise of "if you can't beat him, hire him," the monopoly offered him substantially more money to captain their largest vessel on the Hudson, but Vanderbilt, who looked forward to the day he could operate independently, refused.[2]

The upshot was that in 1824, the Supreme Court – in the famous case of Gibbons vs. Ogden – declared the Fulton monopoly illegal, ruling that the states did not have the authority to regulate interstate commerce.

The break-up of the state-franchised monopoly led to a burst of technological innovations in the steamboat industry. With the market open and profit possible, entrepreneurs rushed in with new ideas, including tubular boilers rather than expensive copper ones and a cheaper fuel – coal – to replace cordwood. As costs dropped, steamboat companies were able to lower their fares.

Starting his own company, Vanderbilt proceeded to run steamboats at reduced rates all over the Northeast. He lowered the standard three-dollar fare on the New York to Philadelphia route to one dollar. He charged six cents a trip and provided free meals on the New Brunswick to New York run and, in competition with the Hudson River Steamboat Association, lowered the standard New York to Albany fare from three dollars to one, then to ten cents, then to nothing, making profit exclusively from the sale of food and drink on board. When he moved his cost-and-price-cutting practices to the New England routes, he succeeded in slicing the New York City to Providence fare from eight dollars to four and then to one, prompting the *New York Evening Post* to bestow on him the title of "the greatest practical anti-monopolist in the country." Commodore Vanderbilt's fortune was made in open competition on a free market, without government aid or franchise, to the immense betterment of his customers.[3]

The dashing, swashbuckling nature of Vanderbilt's activities, akin to those of a commercial buccaneer, has never been lacking among entrepreneurs and captures what can be thought of as the sense of life or emotional ethos of capitalism. Capitalism is driven by bold, risk-taking entrepreneurs, and the Vanderbilt saga displays the essence of their spirit. The term "entrepreneur" was coined by the French economist Jean-Baptiste Say, who was one himself, opening and operating a successful cotton manufacturing plant in the north of France in the first decades of the 19th century. The term literally means "undertaker," i.e., one who undertakes new tasks, but because of the often daring, pioneering nature of such activities it was originally translated "adventurer."[4]

One economist argues that entrepreneurs bring about a "creative response" in society, that by originating some product or service "that is outside of the range of existing practice" they foster a heightened awareness of life's more expansive possibilities. Such a creative response can be of historic proportions – as with Henry Bessemer's invention of a revolutionary steelmaking process – or of less monumental significance – such as Thomas Lipton's original idea of selling tea in pre-packaged bags. Many inventors have become entrepreneurs, of whom Thomas Edison is only the most famous example. But the development of inventions and new technologies is not necessary to the process. Entrepreneurs are individuals who recognize new ideas and opportunities, and who "get things done."

Because of entrepreneurial innovation, a capitalist society is never stationary, but makes continuous advances. Automobiles replace horses and buggies and electric lights triumph over gas lamps. New firms with original ideas and innovative products cut into the market share of corporate giants – as Apple did with IBM and Amazon with Barnes and Noble. Such a process of innovation and dynamic entrepreneurship enables capitalism to be an ongoing, never-ending revolution, incessantly moving toward progress.[5]

But what is the essence of the capitalist system in literal, not emotional, terms? What are the principles that explain and give rise to the "can do" optimism of capitalism's great inventors, innovators and entrepreneurs, the joyous confidence that enables them to make technological and industrial breakthroughs that create better lives for both themselves and millions of customers?

The Philosophical Essence of Capitalism

The view of capitalism widespread in the world today is that it is an economic system in which production is controlled by the men of capital. Such a theory constitutes a definition by non-essentials and is far too narrow to permit a proper understanding. Human beings must understand the nature of freedom, the principle of individual rights and the role that the rational mind plays in man's life. All of this is indispensable to understand capitalism and to appreciate the magnitude of its achievements.

The primary issue regards the moral principle upon which capitalism is based. Novelist-philosopher Ayn Rand identified the fundamental question that forms the essence of any social system.

Does a political-economic system respect individual rights? she asked—or, what comes to the same thing: does it ban the initiation of force from human relationships? The question can be asked in an alternative formulation: Is a human being a sovereign individual who owns his life, mind, effort and its products—or is he a slave to society, who can control his life, dictate his thinking and expropriate his property?

The fundamental issue is merely: Is man free? Capitalism is the only system that truthfully answers: Yes.

"Capitalism is a social system based on the recognition of individual rights, including property rights, in which all property is privately owned."[6]

The principle of individual rights is capitalism's essence, its fundamental distinguishing characteristic.

The deeper moral principles embodied in capitalism's nature—regarding the proper beneficiary of values (i.e., of those things that are good), the means by which values are gained, and the standard by which they are judged—are the subject of Part Two. But in this context, the nature of individual rights, and the relationship between rights and politics, must be made clear.

The concept of "rights" links the principles of personal morality to those guiding an individual's relations with others; it is a moral concept that protects each and every individual in his dealings with other men. The concept of "rights" provides a connection between an individual's moral code and a society's legal system. "Individual rights are the means of subordinating society to moral law."[7]

For centuries, philosophers have examined and debated the nature of rights—what they are, what role they play in life, who possesses them. But in the 20th century, Ayn Rand provided an analysis that revolutionized men's understanding of this critical principle.

"A 'right' is a moral principle defining and sanctioning a man's freedom of action in a social context." The one fundamental right is an individual's right to his own life. Since life requires a process of self-sustaining and self-generated action, a right to life means the freedom to take all the actions necessary for a rational being to achieve fulfillment and happiness.

Simply put, a man's rights protect his freedom of action. They restrict other men from physically interfering with, compelling or coercing him.

"Thus, for every individual, a right is the moral sanction of a positive—of his freedom to act on his own judgment" in pursuit of his own happiness. Regarding others, his rights impose on them only a negative obligation—to refrain from violating his rights.[8]

Men often understand that an individual's life belongs to him and cannot be disposed of by society, but fail to grasp that his property must similarly belong to him and be protected against confiscation by society. In fact, men cannot live without an inalienable right to own property. "The right to life is the source of all rights—and the right to property is their only implementation. Without property rights, no other rights are possible. Since man has to sustain his life by his own effort, the man who has no right to the product of his effort has no means to sustain his life. The man who produces while others dispose of his product, is a slave."[9]

Only other men can violate an individual's rights and only by initiating force against him. Whether a force wielder is a private criminal or a government official, whether he initiates force directly in the form of physical violence or indirectly in the form of fraud, this is the sole means of preventing men from acting on their own judgment in pursuit of their well-being. If men are to be free—free to use their minds in seeking their own happiness—it is the initiation of force that must be banned. "Freedom, in a political context, has only one meaning: the absence of physical coercion."[10]

When men are free, they can use their minds to advance their goals and further their lives. They are free to think, to write, to speak; free to write novels and compose symphonies, study science and mathematics, make life-promoting breakthroughs in medicine, agriculture and technology, start their own businesses, run their own farms; and free to plan out their educations, their careers, their relationships, their day-to-day lives.

Both private individuals and the government are potential violators of a man's rights. Private individuals who initiate force are criminals, and men form governments to protect themselves from these. But the government holds a legal monopoly on the use of force in a given geographical region—and, consequently, constitutes the gravest potential danger to an individual's freedom.

A dictatorial government is a far worse threat to men than is a common criminal. It is not merely that murderous tyrants like Adolf Hitler, Joseph Stalin, Mao Tse-tung and Pol Pot killed vastly more innocent victims than did thugs like Al Capone and John Gotti. It is that the authority of the state enables them to commit the most heinous atrocities with unquestioned legal sanction. Within their own borders, dictators are sovereign brutes against whom their victims have no legal recourse. It is against the government that men's freedom needs to be most urgently protected. It is appropriate in this regard to remember George Washington's famous warning that, "Government, like fire, is a dangerous servant."

A right is a moral principle applicable only in a social setting.

The Capitalist Manifesto

Robinson Crusoe, alone on his desert island, has no need and no use of such a concept. Men can derive great advantages from living in human society—education, love, family, friendship, a division of labor economy and many other benefits. But if men do not respect an individual's rights, if they initiate force against him, then society stops being a boon and commences being a hazard.

A man is vastly better off alone on a desert island than living in Hitler's Germany or Stalin's Russia, because he is at least free on the island to use his mind to confront the problem of survival in the face of physical nature. There are no evil men using brute force to apprehend him and construct camps for his confinement or extermination. For society to fulfill its promise as a potential boon to a man, it must respect his rights to life and property; more, it must protect them.

Without the principle of individual rights there exists no moral constraint preventing social intercourse from degenerating into the rule of brute force. Human society then devolves into either murderous tyrannies of a Nazi or Communist ilk, or the incessant violence of lawless chaos warned of by the English philosopher, Thomas Hobbes, and perpetrated recently in such countries as Lebanon, Somalia and Rwanda. To reiterate: "Individual rights are the means of subordinating society to moral law."

For men to be free—for them to be able to live as rational beings—the initiation of force must be banned from human life. This is just as true of governmental force as of its private use. The use of force must be legally limited to retaliation against those who start it. Men must form a government to protect themselves from private criminals, and formulate a written Constitution with a Bill of Rights to protect themselves from the government. The Constitution must legally outlaw the initiation of force by the leaders and agents of the state, as well as by private citizens. Capitalism requires, as a matter of moral principle, a universal ban on the initiation of force.

What is Capitalism?

Unfortunately, the U.S. Constitution, for all of its superb virtue, failed to fully accomplish this. The government retained, in a variety of forms, the legal power to initiate force against American citizens, and this is why their freedoms are gradually eroded.

Simply stated, the government must establish a system of criminal justice that protects innocent men from those who initiate force and fraud. Criminals must be punished severely. Thieves, swindlers, rapists, murderers, etc., must be dealt with harshly by the state. This includes successful and wealthy businessmen if and only if they commit acts of criminal wrongdoing such as fraud. But the ban on the initiation of force must not be limited to private action; it must be applied to the government, as well. Above all, if individual freedom is to be protected, it is the government that must be constitutionally shackled.

Capitalism requires that the government protects the rights and the freedom of its citizens, not itself violate that freedom. So, for example, the military of a capitalist society must be exclusively on a volunteer basis; there must be no draft. The government must not be granted the power to ban consenting adults from the use of cigarettes, alcohol or drugs, from indulging in pornography or prostitution, from engaging in a thousand acts that may be irrational or self-destructive, but which – crucially – do not initiate force or fraud against others. A consenting adult in a free society must have the legal right to choose actions that threaten his own life; he must be legally restricted from only those actions that threaten the health and lives of others.

Further, the government must protect the right of honest men to own guns, it must protect the freedom of a dying individual to seek medical assistance to end his life painlessly, and it must protect the right of a physician to provide that help. It is a logical contradiction to claim that individuals have the moral and legal right to direct their own lives – but only as long as they make the decisions that conform to the wishes of the majority or the government.

Similarly, in the economic realm the government must protect the unrestricted right of profit-seeking individuals to engage in the production and voluntary exchange of goods and services. Such productive activities are virtuous, because they create wealth and promote man's life on earth. They are not immoral and certainly not criminal. As such, they are not to be controlled or restricted by the state.

Near the end of Ayn Rand's *Atlas Shrugged*, one of the heroes – a judge – proposes to add a clause to the Constitution, making it more consistent with its basic commitment to individual liberty: "Congress shall make no law abridging the freedom of production and trade." Related to this, the government must be legally prohibited from the coercive re-distribution of income; it must not be allowed to rob the productive to provide for the unproductive. All charity in a capitalist society must be voluntarily undertaken by private individuals and organizations.[11]

Ayn Rand explained the point this way: "America's founding ideal was the principle of individual rights...The rest—everything that America achieved, everything she became, everything 'noble and just,' and heroic...was the logical consequence of fidelity to that one principle." The first result was the achievement of political freedom—of an individual's freedom from physical coercion by the state. The second was the logical application of such political freedom to economics: the system of capitalism.[12]

In both the economic realm and the area of personal morality; in every aspect of life—including education, career, investments, love, family, friendship, politics, religion, entertainment, etc.—a consenting adult must be left free to follow his own judgment. As long as he does not initiate force or fraud, the government must respect and protect his right to do as he will.

One consequence of the narrow, misconceived definition of capitalism is the inability to comprehend the role played by the rule of law. The rule of law is fundamental to capitalism. The courts must protect all manifestations of individual rights, including property rights and the sanctity of contracts. They must protect honest men from thieves and criminals of every variety, whether they commit fraud or overt acts of physical coercion, whether they are private individuals or government bureaucrats.

This is an especially urgent point in the early 21st century when former Communist nations seek to move to a capitalist system without first instituting the rule of law. Whether in states of the former Soviet Union or in Albania or elsewhere, if gangsters control significant elements of an economy, it will be impossible to protect property rights and enforce contracts. Legitimate businessmen will then be intimidated (or killed), private investment will be withheld, and the attempt to implement a free economy will founder. Any hope to create a capitalist system rests on the antecedent requirement of establishment of the rule of law. In the absence of this, all such attempts are doomed to fail.

The fundamental point cannot be sufficiently emphasized: "Capitalism is a social system based on the recognition of individual rights, including property rights, in which all property is privately owned."[13]

The Empiricist Fallacy

A system that consistently protects individual rights, that legally prohibits any initiation of governmental force, has never existed. The northern states of the United States in the 19th century were the closest to a laissez-faire form of government that mankind has come. But even there, federal and state authorities often retained the legal power to coercively regulate industry and trade—and to abridge individual rights in other forms. The historical systems commonly referred to as "capitalist" were, in fact, uniformly mixed economies, i.e., systems combining clashing elements of freedom and statism, individual rights and governmental initiation of force. A consistent, non-contradictory implementation of the principle of individual rights necessitates laissez-faire; anything other or less is not capitalism. It is central to a proper understanding of capitalism that its philosophical essence be distinguished from the flawed historical attempts to implement it.

A related misunderstanding is the belief that the actions and principles of individual capitalists are necessarily representative of the nature of capitalism. It might as well be argued that the murderous activities of Hitler and Stalin are necessarily representative of the nature of government (they are representative of the nature of statism). The unfortunate and generally overlooked truth is that capitalists are often neither supporters nor practitioners of capitalism. Businessmen frequently violate the principles of capitalism. They often yelp for tariffs and other protectionist restrictions; seek monopolistic governmental franchises; look for subsidies and corporate bailouts; clamor for anti-trust legislation and other legal constraints to be imposed on their competitors. On a regular basis, they call for governmental initiation of force to violate the rights of both their actual and prospective competitors.[14]

To take one example: that some businessmen support tariffs (or trade barriers) does not make it a policy congruent with capitalist principles— nor would that change even if all businessmen favored protectionism. Honest individuals and companies have the moral right to trade freely with other honest individuals or companies regardless of the specific nationalities involved. No consensus of businessmen could alter the nature of tariffs—that they involve governments forcing foreign producers to pay a tax on their exports—and thereby impose higher prices on those who choose to buy imported goods. Similarly, that these same individuals oppose international free trade does not mitigate, much less negate, that free trade is a direct consequence of the moral principles that constitute the essence of capitalism. What is or is not capitalistic is a matter of political, economic and, above all, moral principles, not of the beliefs, actions or policies of specific capitalists.

What is Capitalism?

The confusion of the history of capitalism (or the actions of capitalists) with the system's fundamental nature is an example of what may be termed the Empiricist Fallacy. Such a cognitive error involves treating the historical facts, rather than the philosophical essence of a political/cultural phenomenon as the deepest, most significant level of its explanation. In order to properly assess the nature and impact of capitalism, the Empiricist Fallacy must be scrupulously avoided. Historical data must be carefully distinguished from philosophical essence, and the latter used to gain a deeper understanding of the former.

The Influence of the Enlightenment

The ideal of individual rights – including the right to property – on which America was founded first became dominant during the Enlightenment. The 18th century period in Western culture was an era stressing reason, science, progress and the rights of man. In science, the ideas of Isaac Newton (1642-1727), and in philosophy, those of John Locke (1632-1704) were widely influential. A point too rarely grasped by both freedom's critics and its supporters is that to understand the origins and nature of capitalism it is necessary to study the Enlightenment. Capitalism was born during this period, and Enlightenment principles compose its essence.

Locke's *Two Treatises of Civil Government*, published in the 1690s, argued that human beings have inalienable rights that they are born with, that belong to them simply by virtue of being men. Chief among these are the rights to life, liberty and property. It follows then that a foremost moral responsibility of all is to leave other men free to live their lives and dispose of their property without interference. "The State of Nature has a Law of Nature to govern it, which obliges every one: And Reason, which is that law, teaches all Mankind...that being all equal and independent, no one ought to harm another in his Life, Health, Liberty or Possessions."15

Locke's ideas were widely studied and admired on the other side of the Atlantic. "...a succession of thinkers [during the Enlightenment] developed a new conception of the nature of government. The most important of these men and the one with the greatest influence on America was John Locke. The political philosophy that Locke bequeathed to the Founding Fathers is what gave rise to the new nation's distinctive institutions." Such writers, patriots and statesmen of America's Revolutionary Period as John Adams, Samuel Adams, Thomas Jefferson, James Madison and Thomas Paine (among others) applied Locke's ideas to the specific circumstances of England's North American colonies, helping to found the new republic on the principle of the rights of man.[16]

But the essence of the Enlightenment, and of its influence on the new nation, was its uncompromising commitment to man's faculty of reason. For this, the 18th century *philosophes* owed much to Newton. It is not merely the birth of the principle of individual rights during this period that is important. As will be seen, capitalism rests fundamentally upon the reverence for the reasoning mind that is the hallmark of Enlightenment thought and culture.

Prior to Newton, some of the laws governing nature had been identified by such scientists as Copernicus, Kepler, Galileo and others. But the great English scientist took man's knowledge to a higher level. "If the character of so intangible a thing as light could be discovered by playing with a prism, if, by looking through a telescope and doing a sum in mathematics, the force which held the planets could be identified with the force that made an apple fall to the ground, there seemed to be no end to what might be definitely known about the universe." Newton, to be sure, built on the achievements of his predecessors, but to his 18th century adherents it appeared that he had "with one almost incredible intellectual effort, compelled nature to order."[17]

The European thinkers of the Enlightenment were not reticent in expressing their admiration for such a genius and his prodigious accom-

plishments. Voltaire, extolling Newton's distinctively intellectual achievements, called him the "greatest man who ever lived." He wrote: "If true
greatness consists of having been endowed by heaven with powerful
genius, and of using it to enlighten both oneself and others, then a man
like M. Newton (we scarcely find one like him in ten centuries) is truly
the great man, and those politicians and conquerors…are generally nothing but celebrated villains."

The Sage of Ferney was not alone in this estimate. Alexander Pope,
in a famous couplet wrote: "Nature and Nature's Laws lay hid in Night.
God said, Let Newton be! and All was Light." Edmond Halley, the
English astronomer whose support was instrumental in the publication
of Newton's *Principia*, commented on its greatness that "it is not lawful
for mortals to approach divinity nearer than this." The Italian legal
philosopher, Beccaria, "was delighted to hear his friends calling him 'little Newton;'" the French philosopher, d'Alembert, as well as Thomas
Jefferson, hung the scientist's portrait in their studies. "All of
them…included him in their trinity of the greatest men in history."[18]

By the turn of the 18th century, British universities were already
teaching the new ideas, and the *Principia* went through eighteen editions
prior to 1789. "When Newton, crowned with honors and offices, died in
1727, his funeral was a national event, observed with forms usually
accorded only to royalty." A steady stream of books, lectures and courses
were offered seeking to explain his theories to the intelligent layman. The
success of one such mid-eighteenth century text, Benjamin Martin's *A
Plain and Familiar Introduction to the Newtonian Philosophy in Six
Lectures*, which went through five editions in fifteen years, is representative of the level of popular interest.[19]

Newton's achievements were the culmination of more than a century of scientific and mathematical advance, and as such were both representative of and inspirational to their age. He, his followers, and the predecessors on whom they built showed the men of the 18th century that

man's unaided reason was fully capable of understanding nature's laws. He demonstrated that the physical universe was intelligible, that if men renounced prejudice and superstition, and committed themselves to observation and rationality there was nothing in the world beyond their comprehension. And the Enlightenment thinkers learned the lesson well.

The triumph of natural science imbued the educated men of the day with confidence that the formerly intractable problems of life would finally yield to the power of man's mind. One 20th century commentator on the Enlightenment stated: "The pitiless cycles of epidemics, famines, risky life and early death…the treadmill of human existence – seemed to be yielding at last to the application of critical intelligence." Eighteenth century Europe saw the development of technology, industry and medicine capable of growing greater amounts of food, providing cheap manufactured goods and curing diseases. Based on these advances, both man's standard of living and his life expectancy rose, and "the word 'innovation,' traditionally an effective term of abuse, became a word of praise." Reason, science and technology began to transform the Western world, so that, "the self-assurance of natural scientists, merchants, public servants – and philosophers – was not the boasting that conceals impotence; it was a rational reliance on the efficacy of energetic action."[20]

Locke wrote that the human mind was capable of contriving inventions "to shorten or ease our labors" and to produce commodities that would make life more convenient and enjoyable. Voltaire, in his enthusiasm for English culture, argued that it was the greater liberty of the English, their commitment to free inquiry and religious toleration that made possible both their intellectual and economic advances. "'Reason' became a potent word of praise, rather like 'science,'" and everywhere superstition and blind conformity to the ignorant ways of the past were giving way to men's growing enlightenment.

Beliefs in astrology and alchemy declined "precipitously." Voltaire, in writing about the widespread belief in the curing power of a king's touch, said: "When reason arrives, that sacred fashion will disappear." It did, and he was correct. The period's leading thinkers held that "reason is the same for all thinking subjects, all nations, all epochs, and all cultures." Because of such confidence in the cognitive efficacy of man's mind, "perhaps no other century is so completely permeated by the idea of intellectual progress as that of the Enlightenment." Such "prosperity of reason in the eighteenth century" led men to significant practical advances.[21]

Perhaps the crowning testimonial to man's mind in this era was the compilation of the *Encyclopedie*, a compendium of virtually the total sum of human knowledge to that time. Denis Diderot, the engine primarily responsible for driving it to completion, edited thousands of articles; he chased all over Paris, commissioning authors, prodding and cajoling, exhorting them to continue; and he employed his vast erudition to himself write countless entries, ranging over an eclectic tangle of topics from "intolerance" to "boa constrictors." Persecuted by both the aristocracy and the Church for his unbending commitment to the cause of the free-thinking mind, earlier imprisoned, suffering through the intimidation and resignation of his co-contributors, Diderot nevertheless clawed forward through two decades of unremitting toil, and in 1765 saw the encyclopedia's final volume published.

This ode to knowledge and the new science, which Diderot considered the favorite among his Herculean efforts, referring to it as "a labor that has been the torment of my life for twenty years," frightened and infuriated supporters of faith, tradition and the *ancien regime*, but over the years and the centuries (in conjunction with its successors) proceeded to enlighten millions. In concert with Samuel Johnson's *Dictionary*, published in England in 1755, it signaled the dawn of an era: knowledge was no longer reserved for the aristocrats and the clergy, and its advance would not be halted by prohibitions of state or church; it was now directed to all those of intelligence and curiosity, wherever they were to be found, without regard to birth, class or caste. To a significant degree, the

Encyclopedie was financed by the emerging middle-class, and it represented their declaration of intellectual independence from the aristocracy and the Church. "Man is born to think for himself," Diderot had written, and the *Encyclopedie* facilitated exactly that.[22]

The spirit and achievements of the Enlightenment are perhaps best represented in the work of Georges-Louis Leclerc, Comte de Buffon (1707-1788). Though of noble birth and made Comte de Buffon by Louis XV, his life was devoted to science, not to politics. "The thirty-six volumes of Buffon's *Histoire Naturelle* (1749-85), which appeared during his lifetime, supplemented by eight volumes published (1788-1804) after his death, *covered every subject in nature from man and birds to cetaceans, fishes and minerals.*" Buffon observed, examined and factually described extensive aspects of nature, both animate and inanimate. Though a practicing Catholic, he sought natural causes for the world of nature he dearly loved. Buffon was tactful in dealing with the Church, but nevertheless claimed that the earth was vastly older than the religious belief of his day allowed and argued for a constantly-and-slowly-changing earth. Nature, he claimed, was not a finished product, but underwent ceaseless processes of change, an idea that helped pave the way for the theory of evolution in the next century.

Though fluent in Latin, Buffon wrote his empirical, encyclopedic work in French, seeking successfully to bring knowledge of natural facts and of scientific method to the literate common man. "For the first time in publishing history, books of popular science were best sellers." In the spirit of the age, Buffon not only immensely advanced the cause of scientific inquiry, he did so with the explicit conviction that knowledge was power, that it was not reserved for the aristocratic elite, but that it would bring practical benefit to mankind.[23]

The significance of these books was that they were written for commoners. Implicit in their writing was the recognition that commoners have minds, that these minds could be cultivated, and that the educated common man could and would be a potent force for positive change in the world. Even the accomplished historian, Carl Becker, though he had difficulty distinguishing the leading Enlightenment thinkers from medieval philosophers, acknowledged that the achievements of Locke, Newton and the other exemplars of the new observation-based rationalism made accessible to the common man a deeper understanding of the world of nature. He wrote: "Here was nature all about...revealing, to the eyes of common men, no less than to the learned, those laws that imposed on all things their reasonable and beneficent...commands."[24]

The Enlightenment glorification and liberation of everyman's mind – its completion of a task Western man had begun in the Renaissance and the Age of Reason – would bear ripe fruit in the practical as well as in the theoretical realm. In the 18th and 19th centuries, such common men as James Watt, Edward Jenner, George Stephenson, Samuel Morse, Cyrus McCormick, Thomas Edison, et al., would prove quite uncommon as innovative thinkers who created the steam engine, the smallpox vaccine, the locomotive, the telegraph, the reaper and the electric lighting system, respectively. Based on the newly-and-fully-unleashed brainpower of commoners, mankind would accelerate its tortuous upward path out of ignorance and misery, inching forward at first, but then striding more confidently toward technological, industrial, economic, agricultural and medical advance.

The English colonies of North America were to play a key role in this drama of human progress. Here, too, in the 18th century, commitment to observation, common sense and reason in opposition to blind faith and acceptance of tradition became increasingly entrenched.

Benjamin Franklin, born in 1706, a true son of the Enlightenment, was a scientist, inventor, astute common-sense thinker and extraordinary statesman. Long interested in science and its applications, he found a method to reduce the smoke from chimneys and, in the 1740s, invented the Franklin stove, which produced greater heat while using less fuel. In

1747, he began his famous experiments with electricity. He subscribed to the theory that lightning was an electrical phenomenon, devised a means of proving the claim, and, eventually, invented the lightning rod. This resulted, of course, in far fewer homes and other buildings burning down in fires caused by lightning. For his scientific accomplishments, he received an honorary degree from Oxford University. Franklin, as other Enlightenment thinkers, was keenly aware that scientific advance must be made practical, that benefits to human life must proceed from it. The consequence of such an aspiration were the Technological and Industrial Revolutions initiated during the 18th century.

"God helps them that help themselves," Franklin wrote in *Poor Richard's Almanack*, expressing his code of self-reliance; and, through the famous maxim, "Early to bed and early to rise, makes a man healthy, wealthy and wise," *Poor Richard* influenced generations of Americans seeking wealth by honest effort.[25]

In a similar view, Thomas Jefferson expressed the spirit of the American Enlightenment in a famous letter to his nephew, Peter Carr: "Fix reason firmly in her seat, and call to her tribunal every fact, every opinion. Question with boldness even the existence of a God; because, if there be one, he must more approve the homage of reason, than that of blindfolded fear." Jefferson lived out his philosophy of rationality, which swore eternal hostility to "every form of tyranny over the mind of man." He was an architect, who designed his estate at Monticello, and later, the campus of the University of Virginia; the inventor of the dumbwaiter, a swivel chair and an improved plow; an exquisitely-gifted writer in whose *Declaration of Independence* the Lockean philosophy of individual rights received its most elegant literary expression; the author of *Notes on the State of Virginia*, a highly respected piece of scientific writing, which included important observations regarding agriculture, climate, geography and natural history.

Jefferson was also a lawyer – a student of the Greek and Latin classics

What is Capitalism?

– a prolific reader whose 6500-volume library formed the basis of the Library of Congress – a legislator responsible for the statute separating state and church in Virginia, protecting freedom of religion – and, in correspondence with his colleague, James Madison, an uncompromising advocate of a bill of rights for the fledgling republic. Additionally, Jefferson's friend and fellow freedom fighter, the Marquis de Lafayette, wrote the French *Declaration of Rights* for that country's new constitution, drawing heavily on the *Declaration of Independence*.[26]

Thomas Paine, the author whose pamphlets and essays, notably *Common Sense* and *The American Crisis*, earned him the title "pen of the American Revolution," could be more fundamentally designated "popular spokesman of the American Enlightenment;" for his commitment to the inviolate sovereignty of man's mind was as complete as any thinker's of that era, and his lucid writings the most accessible to the layman. In his dedication to *The Age of Reason*, he wrote: "The most formidable weapon against errors of every kind is reason. I have never used any other, and I trust I never shall." Through both the political controversies of *Common Sense* and his later *The Rights of Man*, and the deeper philosophical conflicts aroused by *The Age of Reason*, Paine remained committed to his creed. A Deist who embraced God but repudiated faith, miracles and revelation, Paine refused to surrender his mind or his conclusions though the storm of controversy that descended upon him from the citadels of religious orthodoxy caused this hero of the Revolution to die in poverty and relative obscurity in 1809. "My own mind is my own church," he declared in *The Age of Reason*, and if such independence of judgment brought him general disapprobation, it won from his fellow spirit, Jefferson, in 1801 the highest praise. "It will be your glory to have labored, and with as much effect as any man living," stated the then President of the United States."[27]

Nor did the 18th century *philosophes* flinch from the logical though controversial political conclusions of their principles. If man was a rational being, they argued, he was preeminently capable of self-government, and must be free from tyranny of all kinds. Locke, the Enlightenment thinkers held, had established in his *Essay Concerning Human Understanding* that all human knowledge, regardless of complexity or technicality, originated ultimately in ordinary sense experience, and not in innate ideas or divine revelation. That being the case, the knowledge required for right living took no specialized expertise, no cultivated capacity to interpret Holy Scripture or explicate principles deeply embedded in the human mind. It took rather observation of nature and the application of rational intelligence, which were capacities possessed by every individual. Consequently, traditional claims of clergy, aristocrats, kings and royal scholars to either divinely-inspired knowledge or a divine right to rule that superseded the minds and rights of commoners were unfounded. In this regard, the *Encyclopedie*, that compendium of knowledge for all intelligent men regardless of class or social rank, was the perfect expression of the *philosophes'* most cherished epistemological and political principles. The era of individual thought and individual liberty was at hand. Free minds required free political institutions, among them notably the rights to freedom of speech, freedom of the press and freedom of religion.

Further, if man was a rational being, and not an impulse-riddled creature, inexorably driven by lascivious urges and sinful, fleshly desires, as the Calvinists held – a claim with which the influential political philosopher Thomas Hobbes, albeit in a secular form, more or less agreed – then he required no all-powerful authority, whether transcendent or worldly, to curb his passions and enforce his obedience to moral law. Men could be left free to pursue their private gain, because there was no need to fear or prohibit the self-interested activities of rational – as opposed to irrational – men.

One contemporary philosopher makes the point succinctly: "The potency and value of man the rational being means the potency and value of the individual who exercises his reason." Therefore, man the individual – man the rationally thinking individual – had self-discipline, moral worth and an inviolable right to his own life. The individual, not the aristocracy, the Church, the king or the state, was now seen to be the unit of social value. A government existed to serve its individual citizens, not, as formerly thought, the other way around. "Throughout history the state had been regarded…as the ruler of the individual – as a sovereign authority…an authority logically antecedent to the citizen and to which he must submit. The Founding Fathers challenged this primordial notion. They started with the premise of the primacy and sovereignty of the individual." As Locke had written, and Jefferson later affirmed, individuals had certain inalienable rights, among which are, according to the provisional constitution of New Hampshire in 1766, "the enjoying and defending of life and liberty; acquiring, possessing and protecting property; and in a word, of seeking and obtaining happiness."[28]

Not surprisingly, the 18th century European *philosophes*, celebrating man's mind and rights as they did, looked on the American Revolution and the establishment of the American republic with unmitigated appreciation. "The splendid conduct of the colonists, their brilliant victory, and their triumphant founding of a republic were convincing evidence, to the *philosophes* at least, that men had some capacity for self-improvement and self-government, that progress might be a reality instead of a fantasy, and that reason and humanity might become governing rather than merely critical principles." The enlightened thinkers of Europe looked to America for hope, inspiration and a model upon which to base freedom in their own lands. "The liberty that the Americans had won and were guarding was not merely an exhilarating performance that delighted European spectators and gave them grounds for optimism about man; it was also proving a realistic ideal worthy of imitation." Britain's former North American colonies, longtime students of advanced European culture, were now, united into a new and free country, themselves becoming a teacher. "The American Revolution converted America from an importer of ideas into an exporter. What it exported was, of course, mainly itself, but that was a formidable commodity – the program of enlightenment in practice."[29]

The only economic system logically correlative to such political liberty was and is a free market. If men have a right to their own lives – and are not the chattel of state or church – including the right to pursue their own happiness, then it follows that they must possess the right to own the product of their intellectual and bodily effort, and to exchange their work and its products voluntarily for whatever other goods they desire. Capitalism is freedom – and this involves freedom of the marketplace fully as much as freedom of the mind.

Such leading thinkers of the European Enlightenment as John Locke and Adam Smith understood the importance of the rights to private property and the pursuit of profit. In a famous passage, Locke argued that when a man puts forth his effort to transform the raw materials of nature into finished products – such as using the wood of trees to construct a cabin or to build furniture – the end result belongs to him, and he can dispose of it as he sees fit. "Every man has a property in his own person. This nobody has any right to but himself. The labor of his body and the work of his hands…are properly his. Whatsoever he removes out of the state nature has provided, and left it in, he has mixed his labor with, and joined to it something that is his own, and thereby makes it his property."[30]

Similarly, Adam Smith (1723-1790) as fully of the Enlightenment in his thinking as in his lifespan, advocated a system of "natural liberty." In his masterwork, *The Wealth of Nations,* he revolutionized the science of modern economics. On grounds of economic utility and – to some degree – the rights of man, Smith endorsed economic liberty – the rights of individuals to compete freely and peacefully, free of coercive interference from the government. In arguing against state-imposed apprenticeships and licensing requirements, for example, in favor of the unfettered rights of workers to enter a field, and of employers to hire them, Smith echoed the teachings of Locke. "The property which every man has in his own labor, as it is the original foundation of all other property, so it is the most sacred and inviolable...and to hinder him from employing this [labor] in what manner he thinks proper without injury to his neighbor, is a plain violation of this most sacred property. It is a manifest encroachment upon the just liberty of both the workman, and of those who might be disposed to employ him." For the government to coercively restrict a man's entry to a profession is a policy "as evidently...impertinent as it is oppressive."[31]

Though inconsistent, Smith supported liberty – including religious freedom – in many specific instances. For example, in discussing the restrictions England placed upon manufacturing in her North American colonies, he wrote: "To prohibit a great people...from making all that they can of every part of their own produce, or from employing their stock and industry in the way that they judge most advantageous to themselves, is a manifest violation of the most sacred rights of mankind." The arbitrary power of aristocrats, kings and government-supported monopolies had to give way before the right of the common man to pursue his rational self-interest by means of production and exchange in a competitive marketplace, largely free of coercive state interference. "Natural liberty includes...the right to buy goods from any source, including foreign products, without the restraints of tariffs or import quotas." Stated simply, this means that liberty, of its very nature, involves international free trade. Further, it also includes the right to seek work in whatever occupation a person wants and wherever desired – and to offer wages in accordance with whatever the market will bear, and to accept or reject such wages. Such freedom, Smith was confident, would lead to increasing wealth for all; it would result in "universal opulence which extends itself to the lowest ranks of the people."[32]

Today, the intellectual heirs of Locke and Smith claim that the

Enlightenment program of reason and freedom embodied in modern capitalism has abundantly fulfilled this promise. Capitalism's critics, on the other hand, argue that its offer of freedom is a chimera, and that its wealth has been largely achieved by exploiting workers, the poor and the Third World. Whose understanding is accurate? What has been the result of the Enlightenment philosophy in action?

In order to answer these questions, we must examine the beginnings of capitalism in its full historical context. Conditions of life prior to the advent of capitalism must be understood. Then only can the ability of capitalism to provide widespread prosperity be judged.

Summary

The distinguishing characteristic of capitalism is the moral principle of individual rights, which means: universally banning the initiation of physical force from human life. Men require a government to protect them from private criminals and a written Constitution with a Bill of Rights to protect them from the government.

Although such a system has not yet existed in a fully consistent form, the northern states of the United States came closest to this ideal during the 19th century. It is a fallacy to confuse the philosophical essence of capitalism with the imperfect historical attempts to implement it.

Capitalism was born during and of the essence of the Enlightenment's commitment to the mind and rights of the individual common man. Though by no means fully consistent, leading 18th century thinkers on both sides of the Atlantic often recognized the efficacy of the independent reasoning mind and were led to the logical conclusion that individual thinking beings had the capacity and the right to govern their own lives.

2: The Pre-Capitalist Political-Economic Systems

Today, in Western society, we take capitalism and its achievements for granted. The industrialization, the inventiveness, the technological progress so characteristic of the capitalist system are all around us. We drive to work or school in our cars, flood our homes with electric light, warm them against winter's cold with gas, oil or electric heat, cool them in the summer with air conditioning, write on the personal computer, shop on the Internet, fly comfortably to distant places on jets, wash clothes and dishes with electrical appliances and take advantage of modern conveniences in countless additional ways. More fundamentally, we often take for granted our rights as free men – our right to freedom of thought and speech, to freedom of religion, to own property or start our own business, etc.

But what of the societies that have not implemented capitalism – what are they like? What are the living conditions there? Do the non—capitalist political-economic systems have the same freedom and living standards? The first place to look in answer is to the conditions that existed immediately prior to the birth of capitalism in the late 18th and early 19th centuries.

Anti-capitalist intellectuals have long glorified the life of the workingman in the pre-industrial era. They speak glowingly of a lost "Golden

Age," prior to the development of the factory system, in which the workers lived happily in freedom and prosperity. Friedrich Engels, the Communist writer and collaborator of Karl Marx, says that "their standard of life was much better than that of the factory workers today [1845.] They were not forced to work excessive hours; they themselves fixed the length of the working day and still earned enough for their needs." He claims that they had leisure for play and recreation, engaging in sports with their neighbors – "bowls and football" – which contributed to their physical health and vitality. If children helped their parents work, it "was only an occasional employment and there was no question of an eight-or twelve-hour day." In the absence of child labor, Engels continued, "workers' children were brought up at home...Children grew up in idyllic simplicity and in happy intimacy with their playmates."[1]

Engels is hardly the only writer describing the happy circumstances of pre-industrial workers. The influential British historians, J.L. and Barbara Hammond, wrote that prior to the Industrial Revolution "the worker was in all senses a free man"; he controlled the course of his own life, and generally, was happier in 1760 than in 1830. "In the medieval village all over Europe, here as elsewhere, the normal man had certain rights...The domestic worker was not like the modern...worker...He was not hopelessly and despairingly poor. He had some say in his own life: he could go out and dig in his garden or smoke as he pleased." He had land of his own, the Hammonds claimed, and was not reduced to the destitute condition in which all he could do was sell his labor.[2]

Richard Oastler, a fervent 19th century critic of capitalism, argued that everyone was better off spiritually and materially in the Middle Ages than in the industrial era. Oastler, a tireless campaigner on behalf of a government-required 12-hour and later a 10-hour working day in the factories, claimed in evidence to a Parliamentary committee that child labor in England in his time was as bad or worse than slavery. He claimed that under the domestic manufacturing system prior to the advent of the large factories, "it was the custom for the children...to mix learning their trades with other instruction and with amusement." They had but "a little work to do, and then some time for instruction, and they were generally under the immediate care of their parents."[3]

The 19th century British writer, William Cooke Taylor, treated such anti-capitalist "reformers" with savage irony. People entered the factory (or imagined they did) – he said – and saw the young workers. They thought "how much more delightful would have been the gambol of the free limbs on the hillside; the sight of the green mead with its spangles of buttercups and daisies; the song of the bird and the humming of the bee." Such, they claimed, was the lot of these children prior to the era of industrial capitalism.[4]

The anti-capitalist writers do not stop there. They go on to claim that the factory system developed by the early capitalists of the late 18th and early 19th centuries lowered the workers' living standards, causing widespread poverty and misery. The Industrial Revolution "fell like a war or a plague" on the workers, stated the Hammonds. It allegedly crammed men, women and children into the mills under unsanitary conditions, and forced them into long hours of inhuman toil in exchange for pitiably low wages. "Surely never since the days when populations were sold into slavery did a fate more sweeping overtake a people than the fate that covered the hills and valleys of Lancashire and the West Riding with the factory towns..."

Engels was likewise adamant in his belief that industrialization lowered the living standards of English workers. The capitalists' introduction of machinery into the productive process "leads to unemployment...the greater the technical improvement the greater the unemployment." Any advance in mechanization "affects a number of workers in the same way as a commercial crisis and leads to want, distress and crime." He asserted: "In the existing state of society improvements in machinery can only be detrimental to the interests of the workers, and are often extremely so.

Every new machine brings with it loss of employment, want and suffering."[5]

Many of the anti-capitalist reformers drew their information (and inspiration) from the Sadler Report of 1832. Michael T. Sadler, a member of Parliament from Leeds and a close friend of Oastler, sought to gain Parliamentary passage of a bill limiting the work day to ten hours, and to that end Parliament commissioned him to investigate the conditions in the factories. His report was filled with "stories of brutality, degradation and oppression." According to Sadler's published account, the child laborers were starved and beaten sometimes into deformity, and generally subsisted in the most miserable conditions. His report presented "a dreary picture of cruelty, misery, disease, and deformity among the factory children," and this picture was generally accepted as accurate. Summarizing the viewpoint of the critics (with which he does not agree), one economist wrote: "The factory system reduced the free worker to virtual slavery; it lowered his standard of living to the level of bare subsistence."[6]

The early critics of capitalism reached two conclusions: the first that the workers' living conditions were generally satisfactory in the pre-capitalist era, and the second that the factory system of the capitalists lowered those living standards significantly. The truth, however, is that both claims are egregiously false.

The Destitution of Pre-Capitalist Europe

Prior to the advent of industrial capitalism (in roughly the 1760s) the lot of the English working class was generally miserable. Utter destitution was rampant, literal starvation not uncommon and the country was overrun with paupers. "There was, in point of fact, widespread poverty of the most abject kind in England and other countries of 18th century Europe." It is difficult for men in the industrial West today to conceive of the kind of poverty that was widespread in pre-capitalist Europe. By a test employed in Lyons, France, in the 17th century, poverty was reached when daily income was less than the daily cost of minimum bread requirement – in other words, when a person could not make enough money to buy a crust of bread. A quarter to half the population of 17th century England subsisted near or below this line of destitution.

If the U.S. Bureau of Labor Statistics were to today employ a similar standard of poverty, Americans below the poverty line would be those making $18 a month, or $216 a year. England had such a problem with penniless vagrants that in 1547 Parliament passed a law that "they should simply be sent into slavery;" revoking it two years later only because the legislature was unable to decide whom such forced labor should serve. It is staggering to Westerners today, but this was the condition of a large portion of the pre-capitalist European population.[7]

Many hardships in post-Medieval, pre-Industrial Europe were caused by a continuous absence of scientific, technological and medical knowledge. But government controls of the economy exacerbated the widespread poverty and generalized misery. The acronym GECAT, short for Guilds – Enslavement – Corn Laws – Alcohol – Taxes, can be created to illustrate merely some of the government's harmful policies.

The laws restricting the practice of numerous trades to members of guilds (professional organizations holding legal monopolies) and imposing requirements of lengthy periods of apprenticeship often made it impossible for poor workers, though possessing marketable skills, to make a living. Adam Smith argued against such laws in the 1700s, but their history extended back for centuries. Two hundred years earlier (and before) "those who...sought an entrance into industry, found their way barred by stringent guild restrictions or exorbitant fees." Both years of apprenticed, unrecompensed labor and professional entrance fees were, of course, exactly what the poor could least afford.[8]

Another problem was that the practice of serfdom continued into the post-Medieval period, ending in western Europe only in the 15th and

16th centuries (although its gradual phasing out began somewhat earlier in England.) Under serfdom, a peasant was legally tied to the land, owed military service to his lord, and was subject to the power of judge, jury and executioner invested in his single authority. "The feudal nobleman...for all practical purposes...was the local government: he combined in his person the powers of policeman, judge, and lawmaker. His workers were legally prohibited from leaving his estate...he derived his income in his capacity as a virtual slave owner and as a tax collector." Serfs did possess specific legal rights, and the lords were under certain limited obligations to them. Nevertheless, as a form of enforced involuntary servitude, serfdom bore some moral resemblance to slavery.[9]

The deleterious economic consequences of this institution should be apparent. By effectually enslaving peasants and tying them to the land it undercut the establishment of a mobile labor force. It formed an integral component of a militarist system responsible for endless wars and destruction. Above all, by granting to peasants only minimal opportunities for private ownership and profit seeking, serfdom vastly undercut the incentive to agricultural production. To a significant degree, the feudal system contributed to the near all-encompassing destitution existing at the birth of the modern era. Even in England, where serfdom was virtually eradicated by the late-14th century, it left a legacy of oppression and poverty against which men struggled for centuries. As cited above, the economist, Angus Maddison, estimated a European per capita income of $215 in 1500 and of $265 in 1700.[10]

Further, in the early days of the Industrial Revolution the British government imposed the Corn Laws, i.e., high tariffs on imported grain after the Napoleonic Wars, designed to "protect" the English landowners. The artificially high food prices brought about by such protectionism were especially onerous for the poor who, above all others, benefited from the lower prices provided by free trade in grain and other foodstuffs.

Additionally, governmental policy contributed significantly to mass death from alcoholism among the poor in the early 18th century. The English historian, M. Dorothy George, has provided a detailed picture of London life prior to the Industrial Revolution. It is not a pretty sight. "In the middle of the [18th] century there was one fact which stood out with terrible clearness...that the deaths in London greatly exceeded the births..." In the first half of the century, burials outnumbered baptisms by an order of roughly three to two; in the three years from 1740 through 1742 the ratio was better than two to one. In 1741, London saw 32,169 burials, while it had only 13,571 baptisms in 1742. According to the best figures available at the time, the London death rate was 1 in 25 in 1700, 1 in 20 or 21 in 1750, 1 in 35 between 1797 and 1801, 1 in 38 from 1801 to 1811 and 1 in 40 in 1821. The London mortality rate shows a marked decline as the 18th century progressed past its midpoint and on toward the 19th.[11]

What were the cause(s) of the high death rate in the first half of the century – and of its diminishment in the second half? Dr. George, following a commonly held belief of the 18th century itself, claimed that a significant causal factor of the high mortality rate in the first half of that century was the copious consumption of hard liquor by the poor. Gin was plentiful and cheap at that time largely because of the policies of the government. The sale of grain was a major source of income for the landowning class – who were often aristocrats – and the distilling industry, a new trade at that time, was an important buyer of that grain. "Such considerations could not be disregarded by an eighteenth-century Parliament. Everything was done to promote the production and consumption of spirits." For example, the Mutiny Act of 1720 lifted from "retailers who were also distillers" of a specific kind "the burdensome obligation to have soldiers quartered upon them."[12]

The consequences were devastating. "Gin-drinking was essentially a disease of poverty. Gin was so cheap, so warming and brought such forgetfulness of cold and misery. It was a passion among beggars and the inmates of workhouses and prisons…the typical gin-drinkers were the poorest and most wretched of the community, their poverty a cause as well as a result of their craving for gin…" According to one physician of that time, greater than one-eighth of all deaths among people older than twenty years occurred "prematurely through excess in spirit-drinking." Further, one witness of that era wrote about "the sickly state of such infants [born to gin-drinking mothers] who with difficulty pass through the first stages of life and live very few of them to years of manhood…" The children of such parents who did survive were often "starved and naked at home…forced to beg while they are children, and as they grow up learn to pilfer and steal."[13]

Another factor contributing to the poverty and misery was the ubiquitous taxes imposed by kings and nobles. The hovels of the poor in London and elsewhere were health hazards of the highest order – and one of the reasons was the tax on windows first levied in 1696, repeatedly stiffened, and repealed only in 1851. Predictably, the duty caused many windows to be boarded up, restricting the flow of fresh air and sunlight into houses, especially those of the poor who could least afford to pay. Dark, dank, airless spaces, of course, bred germs.[14]

GECAT is a convenient acronym by means of which to remember the harmful consequences of guilds, enslavement, corn laws, Alcohol and taxes – but the effects of the specifically feudal form of statism in the early modern era were more widespread than merely these. For example, the dominant economic theory of mercantilism involved strict governmental regulation of the national economy, designed to accumulate gold and silver bullion, stimulate domestic industry, maximize exports and minimize imports. The theory held that wealth was money, i.e., that a country's wealth was measured in terms of the bullion in its national treasury. When wealth was defined in these terms, and not in widespread access to inexpensive goods, then pauperism and famine among the masses were not viewed as indications that a country was poor.

The tariffs and trade barriers, the guilds and state franchised monopolies, the enforced apprenticeships and restrictions on the labor market, the costly wars, the oppressive taxes – the full feudal/mercantilist system – combined to severely undercut industry and general living standards. But this was not generally held to be a bad thing – not until the Enlightenment, anyway, and especially Adam Smith.[15]

But there were other factors in addition to the excessive drinking of gin that contributed to the high mortality rate in London. The dirt, the filth, the lack of adequate sanitation, the consequent diseases, and the dearth of medical knowledge and supplies so characteristic of pre-industrial societies were ubiquitous in London of that era. All of these contributed to the staggering infant mortality rate. In the most terrible years of the 18th century's first half, "over 74 percent of the children born in London died before they were five…" The numbers were even worse for the parish children, the orphans, foundlings and abandoned children of the poor brought up in government workhouses or put out to nurse by the local authorities. According to one social reformer of the day, "the parish infant poor's mortality may be…80 or 90 or…upon those received under twelve months old, 99 percent." The Foundling Hospital, established in the 1740s to relieve such horrors, shows an "improvement" – "only" 724 of the 1384 children admitted during its first fifteen years of operation perished in childhood. But immediately after, as its rate of admission rose, its death rate rose as well; so that during its almost four-year period of open admission, "14,934 children were taken in of whom only 4,400 lived to be apprenticed."[16]

The dwellings of the numberless poor were often ramshackle "tenements of the most wretched description…These places are most of them very old and very slightly built, frequently with boards held together by iron hoops…" The collapse of buildings with the consequent burial and death of their occupants was commonplace. "When a messenger ran into a City tavern with an urgent piece of news, the instant supposition (in

1718) was that he had come to warn the inmates that the house was falling." Improvements came only slowly. Samuel Johnson in 1738 remarked that London was a town in which "falling houses thunder on your head."[17]

The hovels of the poor in London and elsewhere were health hazards of the highest order. The tax on windows was only one reason. Sanitation was primitive and sewage much the same. In many parts of London, people simply threw their garbage into the street to rot or molder, and be eaten by pigs and stray dogs. There were outhouses and cesspools instead of sewers; excrement was carried off by cart to be dumped beyond the city limits, but was sometimes poured covertly into the Thames. "The Field Lane district was intersected by the filthy channel of the Fleet ditch (called in 1722 'a nauseous and abominable sink of nastiness') into which the tripe dressers, sausage makers and catgut spinners…flung their offal." The city had extensive "filthy tide ditches," called by an anonymous writer, possibly Defoe, "those most loathsome…byplaces."[18]

Overcrowding was severe, and dirt, garbage and filth ubiquitous. A London physician reported that three to eight individuals of differing ages often slept in the same bed, and it was common for those of the lower class to "not put clean sheets on the bed three times a year." In cases where there were no sheets, blankets went perpetually unwashed. Windows, of course, were few; the air, consequently, was not merely bad, but often filled "with putrid excremental effluvia from a vault at the bottom of the staircase." The houses were made of wood, not uncommonly rotting, and "infested with all kinds of vermin." One historian concluded: "From a health point of view the only thing to be said in their favor was that they burned down very easily."[19]

Burn they did. On Sunday September 2nd, 1666, a fire started in the bakery of Thomas Farynor on Pudding Lane near the banks of the Thames. "Fires were a fact of life in London, a cheek-by-jowl infinity of timber-framed buildings ensured that this was so…" and though at first the Lord Mayor responded contemptuously that "a woman could piss it out," it was tragically not to be. Filled with wooden houses and severely overcrowded conditions, possessed of only primitive firefighting equipment and methods, London blazed like the slums of Hell. The fire raged unabated for 5 days. When the Great Fire of London finally ran its course on Thursday, September 6th, an area of one-and-a-half miles by one-half mile lay in ashes. "Over 13,000 houses had been destroyed, eighty-nine churches were rubble, forty-four livery halls were ash, and 100,000 people faced a cold, homeless winter."[20]

Only the year before, London had suffered an outbreak of plague that had killed some 70,000 residents, almost 15 percent of the city's population. The English naval administrator, literary figure and accomplished rake, Samuel Pepys, witnessed both catastrophes. He stayed courageously at his post throughout the agonizing months of plague, when other officials retired to the country – and, upon realizing the fire's severity, he rushed to the King to gain permission to tear down houses as a firebreak. Pepys recorded firsthand observations in his now-famous Diary. "Every day sadder and sadder news of [the plague's] increase. In the City died this week 7496; and of them, 6102 of the plague. But it is feared that the true number of the dead this week is near 10,000 – partly from the poor that cannot be taken notice of through the greatness of their number..."[21]

Regarding the Great Fire, he observed, "But Lord, what a sad sight it was to see the whole City almost on fire – that you might see it plain at Woolwich, as if you were by it...the fire being spread as far as I could see it...The Exchange a sad sight, nothing standing there of all the statues or pillars...Thence homeward, having passed through Cheapside and Newgate-market, all burned..." If there was any consolation, it was that the fire also destroyed large numbers of rats, fleas and other vermin, possibly providing London relief from further plague.[22]

Nor were these isolated catastrophes. There had been a previous

Great Fire of London in 1086, which destroyed large parts of the city, resulting in a death toll of 3,000. In 1189, with "the memory of two comparatively recent, devastating fires in mind, the London sheriff ordered that stone walls...be built between adjoining wooden houses..." Obviously, the measures were insufficient (or went unobeyed) for destructive conflagration remained a perennial problem. One reason was because roofs were often thatched with straw. "Thatched roofs had formidable drawbacks...above all they caught fire. Yet even in London they prevailed."

Plague, similarly, was a tragedy of incessant recurrences. Plague closed all London theaters between 1592 and 1594, leaving a young, poor William Shakespeare the free time to write *Venus and Adonis* and *The Rape of Lucrece*, as well as to begin his celebrated sonnets. The 1593 outbreak killed approximately 18,000 in London, mostly in the rat-infested slums around the docks. Between 1348 and 1665, there were repeated outbreaks of plague; thirty epidemics between 1351 and 1485 alone, twelve of them occurring on a nationwide scale. "Between 1543 and 1593 England suffered from plague in twenty-six years." A major epidemic in 1563 also killed roughly 18,000 in London, motivating a thirty-year-old Queen Elizabeth to remove to Windsor, where she had constructed a gallows upon which to execute any resident of London foolhardy enough to attempt a visit.

Nor were conditions different in other parts of Europe. Bubonic plague devastated the Continent in the years after 1347, wiping out an estimated twenty-five million of Western Europe's population of about eighty million. In the 16th century alone, epidemics struck in 1509, 1514, 1526, 1560 and 1576. In the 1720s, it ravaged Marseilles and other areas of Southern France. In Italy, the famous Church of Santa Maria della Salute in Venice was built as a shrine to the Virgin Mary in gratitude for relief from a plague that killed 47,000 in that city alone between the years 1630-31. Indeed, Venice was struck by epidemics of plague twenty-one times between 1348 and 1630; Paris twenty-two times between 1348 and 1596; and Barcelona seventeen times between 1457 and 1590.[23]

But relief from the all-encompassing, abysmal poverty would have to wait for the coming of the industrial age. In the 18th century and for one to two centuries prior, London conditions were especially wretched for the sizable population of Irish immigrants. In such neighborhoods, it was possible to find greater than 700 people living in 24 small homes, sometimes with three or four families per room, and with 100 pigs roaming the court. According to a report of the time, "the place was never cleansed, people were afraid to enter it for fear of infection..." There were few children, because of "the great want of care taken of them in infancy...not only many die, but a great proportion of them that live are crippled and crooked and very unhealthy."[24]

Conditions in Ireland were abysmal. Long after industrialization occurred in England, the Irish economy remained largely based in tenant farming and beset by the problem of absentee landlords. The results of the British conquest, the continuing repressive policies of the English government and an agrarian economy of an essentially feudal nature combined in Ireland, ensuring rampant destitution and frequent starvation. By conservative estimate, tens of thousands died of starvation in the 1740s, anticipating the worse famine to come a century later. "The dire poverty of the early nineteenth century Irish may be indicated by their average life expectancy of 19 years – compared to 36 years for contemporary American slaves – and the fact that slaves in the United States typically lived in houses a little larger than the unventilated huts of the Irish and slept on mattresses, while the Irish slept in piles of straw."[25]

European conditions of life had been even worse prior to the late 17th and early 18th centuries. In the Middle Ages, sanitation and living conditions among the English poor were dismal by modern standards. "Street cleaning defeated the authorities of every medieval town...house-

holders persisted in dumping refuse and sewage in the streets, and allowing their animals and poultry to foul public thoroughfares at will. Few
people concerned themselves if dead animals lay about unburied for
days…The channel which ran down the middle of most streets became
an open sewer…" Drinking water often came from such streams as the
Walbrook, the Fleet and the River Thames, "the ultimate destination of
most of London's garbage and sewage."

In other countries, the way of life was similar. "In the Middle
Ages…all refuse, including human excreta, was thrown into the street."
In Paris in the 1300s every form of waste was hurled from the window
with the cry of "Watch out for the water!" In Edinburgh, where there
were no privies, this enchanting practice continued until well into the
18th century. Under such unsanitary conditions, diseases such as cholera,
typhoid and dysentery could flourish; and in the 14th century, the Black
Death, spread by the fleas that infest rats, killed more than one million
human beings in England alone, greater than one-third of the country's
population.[26]

During the reign of Elizabeth I in the 16th century, the combined
population of England and Wales was no more than two-and-a-half to
three million – meaning that in two centuries the population was barely
able to equal what it had been prior to the Black Death – and the population density was as sparse as that of European Russia in the 19th century. Industrial development at that time actually lagged behind other
European nations, and England was relatively poor. Begging was a common occurrence, and according to a contemporary observer, the poor "lie
in the streets, in the dirt as commonly is seen…and are permitted to lie
like dogs or beasts without any mercy or compassion showed them at all."
Perhaps for many that didn't help, it was from no lack of good will, but
from a lack of means.[27]

Under the Stuarts and the Cromwell Protectorate of the 17th century, the desperate conditions of the English poor did nothing to improve.

The Pre-Capitalist Political-Economic Systems

Those fortunate enough to gain employment in cottage industries at least generally had enough to eat, but little else. Fuel and clothing, as well as shelter, were in short supply. One foreign observer of the period noted: "These English have their houses made of sticks and dirt..." The poverty line, as discussed above, was defined at the starvation level, and a full 8 percent of the populace subsisted there at the best of times, many more during periods of depression. Tragically, for hundreds of thousands existing chronically at the starvation level, there were depressions in the 1620s, in the early 1640s, in 1659 and later. The private charity that existed after the dissolution of the monasteries often went for relief of the poor, who "were constantly harassed by epidemics, wretched housing and hygiene, and by unwanted children..."[28]

Although historians differ regarding its extent, they agree that death by famine was prevalent in Europe in the centuries leading up to the Industrial Revolution, including in England. Andrew Appleby, a leading researcher of the period, wrote: "In 1587-88, 1597 and 1623, the northwestern English counties of Cumberland and Westmoreland were struck by famine. In those years, thousands of people starved..." It is likely that with edible food unobtainable, the poor ate the bark from trees and "unripe grain, roots, grass, and the intestines and blood of animals that had been slaughtered as food for the better-off." Fatality from starvation must be understood broadly enough to include death from intestinal disorders induced by eating such unsuitable foods, as well as "pure" starvation, in which "caloric intake is reduced to the point where bodily functions slowly cease..."

Although it is possible that starvation among the English poor was too common "to elicit any comment," conditions were even worse in other parts of Europe. A French 1662 report stated: "Famine this year has put an end to over ten thousand families...and forced a third of the inhabitants...to eat wild plants." Another commentator said: "Some people ate human flesh." Even accounting for exaggeration, the situation was grim. In the same era another writer claimed: "The people of Lorraine...are reduced to such extremities that, like animals, they eat the grass in the meadows...and are as black and thin as skeletons."

In Germany, "famine was a persistent visitor to the towns and the flatlands." In Scotland, the "Lean Years" of 1697-1703 saw widespread crop failure and harrowing suffering. "No one knows how many died during the famine...but they probably numbered in the tens of thousands," a sizable percentage of the population in a country with fewer than two million inhabitants. In the same period, a horrific tragedy struck Finland. "If one wants to measure the catastrophes of history by the proportion of victims claimed, the 1696-7 famine in Finland must be regarded as the most terrible event in European history. A quarter or a third of the Finnish population disappeared at that time."[29]

In the early 18th century, on the eve of the Industrial Revolution, what is striking is how little the lot of the masses had improved since the Middle Ages, i.e., in 600 years. As cited above, it is estimated that per capita income did not grow at all in the thousand years from 500 to 1500 and per capita GDP grew by an annual average rate of merely 0.1 percent between 1500 and 1700. An estimated European per capita income in the range of two or three hundred dollars during the 16th and 17th centuries is roughly comparable to living standards in the starving Third World nations of today. Indeed, "Third World Europe" was significantly poorer; for while Africa today—the world's most destitute region—benefits to some degree from electric lights, telephones, automobiles, airplanes, and modern medical and agricultural technology, the Europeans of 400 years ago had no access to such advances, for their invention came only centuries later. Most of this centuries-long stagnation was due to ignorance and a general lack of knowledge.[30]

The Role of Feudalism

But feudalism and its legacy bore a heavy culpability for that, too. For the medieval system, by denigrating the common man, caused the overwhelming preponderance of human minds to be unvalued, undeveloped and unused. How many potential Isaac Newtons, John Lockes, Voltaires, Denis Diderots, Thomas Jeffersons, Benjamin Franklins, James Watts, Thomas Edisons, Alexander Graham Bells, Andrew Carnegies, et al., were compelled to live in utter bondage, slaving away as manual laborers in the manorial fields – or, at the very least, threatened with imprisonment, torture, even execution if their radical ideas clashed with the precepts of king, aristocracy or clergy?

Diderot, for example, was imprisoned for his ideas, as was Voltaire for writings mistakenly ascribed to him by the *ancien regime*. D'Alembert, the great scientist and writer, was intimidated into temporarily severing his connection with the *Encyclopedie*. Galileo was threatened with torture and Giordano Bruno burned at the stake because their thinking clashed with the beliefs of the Church. Further, these examples occurred in the 17th and 18th centuries, in the post-Renaissance period when commitment to the independent reasoning mind was growing. The suppression had been far more comprehensive in earlier centuries when "heretics," including such serious intellectual challengers as the Arians, the Pelagians and the Manicheans, were often brutally suppressed. The advances in philosophy, literature, science, technology, inventiveness and industrialization – the means by which men rose from ignorance and privation – were impossible in an era whose greatest minds were subordinate to dictates of state and church.[31]

But the intellectual forces supporting the mind, science and freedom against strict obedience to the *ancien regime* had been gathering momentum since the Renaissance. The men of the 18th century had seen the historical evidence: after all, Michelangelo had not been an aristocrat, nor had Leonardo. Nor were Galileo, Shakespeare, Descartes, Milton, Locke, Newton or numerous other geniuses. Such facts supporting the efficacy and potential stature of the common man could not be overlooked. The

Enlightenment's leading thinkers, building on their inheritance from the Renaissance and the Age of Reason, recognized the latent power and validity of everyman's mind and succeeded in sweeping away centuries of aristocratic and clerical prejudices, eventually unleashing countless millions to use their minds, seek an education, think, innovate and advance. Finally, during the Enlightenment and of its essence, liberated human brain power would bring the beginning of relief from centuries of suffering.

Summary

A number of anti-capitalist historians and writers have argued that the industrial system of capitalism generally lowered the workers' living standards from what had been tolerable levels in the pre-industrial era. This is arrant mythology.

Prior to the industrial revolution, living standards in Europe were generally as low (or lower) than in the poorest regions of the Third World today. Famine, filth, plague and extreme destitution were the norm and had been for centuries.

The tyrannical system of the *ancien regime*, by suppressing the minds and rights of commoners, undermined the means by which men could make the scientific, technological and industrial advances necessary to ameliorate the tragic conditions of their lives.

3: The Enlightenment and the Industrial Revolution

The political/economic system that would shortly bring freedom and prosperity to the masses was created as an integral component of the Enlightenment's commitment to applied reason as the means of delivering practical progress.

The *philosophes* and the leading thinkers of the 18th century recognized that the commercial spirit of capitalism and the new social order it promoted were vital parts of their agenda for the advancement of mankind. Characteristically, they endorsed industry and the work ethic as noble virtues. Joseph Addison stated these ideals eloquently in *The Spectator*, the publication whose influence as the "arbiter of elegance" for Europe's 18th century literary and intellectual tastes was vastly greater than its brief life span. "There are not more useful members in a commonwealth than merchants," he wrote enthusiastically, because they create wealth, provide productive employment and engage in the peaceful trade which knits "mankind together in a mutual intercourse of good offices...Sloth," he reminded his readers, "has ruined more nations than the sword."

Voltaire, in his passion for progress and English liberalism, echoed these sentiments. "Enter the London stock exchange," he argued in his *Lettres Philosophiques*, and you witnessed a place "more respectable than many a court," for here men of all races and religions harmoniously and without bigotry engaged in mutually beneficial trade. Voltaire praised the reasonableness of business, which not only raised the general standard of living but awarded men offices based on merit, not on birth or religion, and whose voluntary commercial relations between nations promoted peace. Who is more useful, Voltaire queried in effect, an aristocrat or powerful government official, whose accomplishments consisted primarily of mastering "all the intricacies of courtly ritual" – or "the merchant who sends his ships across the seas and enriches his country?"

The Enlightenment thinkers, sick to heart after centuries of unrelieved human want and suffering, yearned for practical results above all. David Hume may have been an arch-skeptic regarding theoretical knowledge, and as such a fundamental opponent of the period's deepest premises, but even he – one of Adam Smith's dearest friends – recognized the immense practical benefits of the new capitalist order. Men of business, Hume believed, were "one of the most useful races of men." Samuel Johnson, perhaps speaking a trifle tongue-in-cheek, was nevertheless earnest when he claimed that "a man is seldom so innocently employed as in making money." Arthur Young, a well-educated, widely-traveled English writer, stated in response to a Frenchman's astonishment that Young's travels were not publicly subsidized: "Everything is well-done in England, except what is done with public money." Young's reply may be taken as representative of the new spirit of laissez-faire in opposition to the prevailing mercantilist doctrines of government interventionism.[1]

The *philosophes* and the major thinkers of the 18th century generally recognized that the pacific nature of business and voluntary exchange made it a moral, as well as a practical system. Men who manufactured goods and traded to mutual advantage were creative – and in bringing goods and services into existence, they earned the wealth they gained. In this peaceful and widely-beneficial acquisition of wealth, the capitalists contrasted with plunderers, who won riches, power and "glory" by force of bloody arms. "Master butchers," Diderot contemptuously termed conquerors. Voltaire regarded as great men those whose energies benefited human life, not those "who sack provinces." The superb novelist, Henry Fielding, scorned the "sackers of towns, the plunderers of provinces, and the conquerors of kingdoms." "I cannot conceive why he that has burned cities, wasted nations, and filled the world with horror and desolation should be more kindly regarded by mankind than he who died in the rudiments of wickedness..." proclaimed the normally dispassionate Dr. Johnson. It was their love of mankind, and their fervent desire to finally elevate humanity to its proper stature after centuries of ignorance, privation and degradation that motivated the 18th century thinkers to embrace the peaceful, productive businessman and to repudiate the brutal, rapacious conqueror.[2]

Similarly, Adam Smith, whose work on economic theory in his fifties would provide a systematized body of rational principles explaining and validating the productive activities of profit-seeking capitalists, was a leading Scottish *philosophe*, a Professor of Moral Philosophy for ten years at the University of Glasgow. His *Theory of Moral Sentiments* (1759) was based on his lectures, and received public acclaim; it was largely an analysis of moral psychology that examined the origin and role of "sympathy" in human life. Smith was of the heart of Scottish Enlightenment culture, belonging to virtually every elite intellectual circle of his day, including the Poker Club (named after the fire poker because club members stirred things up), the Oyster Club and the Select Society, groups of Scotland's most learned men who met over good food and strong drink to discuss controversial topics. Tellingly, the name of the group which succeeded the Select Society in 1763 was the Edinburgh Society for Encouraging Arts, Sciences, Manufactures and Agriculture in Scotland. Smith made the trip to Edinburgh regularly for sundry intellectual gatherings; and though a Glaswegian, the man who more than any other placed economic science and free market theory on the intellectual map, was also on the editorial board of the famed literary journal, the *Edinburgh Review*. The combinations of moral philosophy and economics, literary art and business theory, intellectual achievements and support of manufacturing were of the essence of Smith's mental life.[3]

Though many of the *philosophes* accepted God's existence and were more ambivalent than hostile regarding religion, the Enlightenment philosophy was essentially one of secular rationalism. The era's thinking was secular in its belief in the supreme importance of this world and of life in it, as contrasted with otherworldliness and an emphasis on the hereafter. A correlative of secularism was the theory of metaphysical naturalism – recognition of the lawfulness of nature (including human nature), of its inherent orderliness which possessed no need of magical or supernatural intervention. The thinkers of the day were committed to rationalism – as opposed to any form of irrationalism – which involved confidence in the reasoning mind, and of especial importance, "confidence in private judgment, as distinguished from reliance on the dogmatic authority of others." Deism, the theory that God created the world to run in accordance with immutable natural laws that required no further divine intervention, was widely held by the *philosophes*. Such a theory was, of course, largely consistent with metaphysical naturalism.

Recognizing that the accomplishments of Newtonian science were made possible only by the new observation-based rationalism, and desirous to apply this methodology to all fields, thereby revolutionizing them in service of progress, the *philosophes* knew their intellectual and political foes: "all dogmatic claims to authority on the part of the Churches, and of [claims to] the 'divine right' of Kings…"[4]

If humanism – the conviction that man and his life on earth are the paramount values of a proper moral philosophy – was the guiding tenet of the day, then the *philosophes* had provided their own marching orders: the miserable human existence of the previous centuries had to be ameliorated. If human advancement, enrichment and happiness were the ends, then science, technology and industry were the indispensable means.

In the 1770s, the *Encyclopedia Britannica* announced that "the discoveries and improvements" wrought by the period's leading inventors and industrialists "diffuse a glory over this country unattainable by conquest or dominion." That glory, of course, was rational, because inventiveness undilutedly promoted man's life on earth whereas conquest and empire came at a high cost in bloodshed and misery. Even Samuel Johnson – often a critic of Enlightenment culture – expressed a grudging note of admiration for the era's bustling productivity and increasing prosperity when he half-heartedly grumbled that "the age is running mad after innovation; all the business of the world is to be done in a new way." [5]

Not surprisingly, many of the period's leading businessmen were themselves inventors and/or scientists – or were fully caught up in the Enlightenment spirit of scientific research designed to bring material progress and prosperity. The Scots took the lead in this regard.

The Heroes of the Scottish Enlightenment

The Scottish Enlightenment had a galvanizing effect on British industry. Scotland's primary schools, her universities and her philosophical-literary-scientific societies led the way in promoting the scientific spirit and its application to practical affairs at a time when at Oxford and Cambridge the torch of scientific inquiry and innovative thinking "burnt dim." Unlike these famous English schools, which were then closed to all but members of the Church of England, the great Scottish centers of learning at Glasgow and Edinburgh were open to Dissenters, the best thinkers among whom flocked there. Many of Great Britain's most active minds taught and studied there, including at the great medical school and sister hospital at Edinburgh, founded in 1725 and 1736 respectively.

The University of Edinburgh medical school implemented the cognitive method of Newtonian science and became an unsurpassed training ground not merely for physicians, but for scientists and engineers, as well. Throughout 18th century Scotland – in Glasgow, in Edinburgh, in Aberdeen – men of genius took up the Enlightenment cause and carried it forward as if it were their personal banner, applying the new and ruling principle of the age: to marry the theoretical to the practical, the scientific to the industrial, the intellectual to the entrepreneurial.[6]

But the struggle for enlightenment had been fierce. Early in the 18th century, Scotland had been divided by two cultural antipodes between which it had to choose. The old Scotland had been a society embodying the feudal obligations of tenants to their lords and in which the Kirk – the national church – held repressive power over books, the arts, and culture more broadly. Large segments of the population, particularly in the Highlands, were herders, even hunter-gatherers, who subsisted in a poverty exceeded only by their ignorance. The Highlands had been largely a warlike society of violence and authoritarianism – clannish, rural, backward and disdainful of productive enterprise.

The new Scotland aspired to the Enlightenment ideal, upholding secular rationalism and the rights of the individual. It embraced the greater freedom of British Parliamentarianism and rejected the "divine rights of kings." It stood for capitalism, the rising middle class, an emphasis on education and enlightenment, an industrious work ethic and repudiation of the warrior-plunderer code – and, as a consequence, growing urbanization and prosperity.

In the rebellion of 1745, this conflict came to a head. The Jacobite advocates of the Old Order supported Bonnie Prince Charlie's attempt to reinstate the Stuart monarchy on the English throne while the Whig advocates of the New Order remained loyal to the English government and resisted the usurping efforts of the Young Pretender. The British Army's crushing of the uprising at Culloden – and the ensuing disarming and harsh punishment of the savage Highland clans – settled the matter forever.

The new Scotland – desperate to throw off the repression and destitution of its feudal past – eagerly embraced the Enlightenment ideals. "The years after 1745 witnessed an explosion of cultural and economic activity all across Scotland." Samuel Johnson, visiting in 1773, remarked that Scottish progress had been "rapid and uniform." He added archly: "What remains to be done they will quickly do, and then wonder, like me, why that which was so necessary and so easy was so long delayed." Also in the 18th century's second half, Horace Walpole, son of the former British prime minister, openly acknowledged: "Scotland is the most accomplished nation in Europe." Across the Channel, Voltaire concurred: "It is to Scotland that we look for our ideas of civilization."[7]

A prime example of such advance was James Watt (1736-1819), the representative inventor of the age. Watt, who perfected Thomas Newcomen's steam engine, thereby creating "the work engine of the Industrial Revolution," grew up "surrounded by the paraphernalia of seagoing Glasgow," a largely self-taught man. He was instrument maker for the University of Glasgow, where he amazed the professors with his knowledge and mental powers. "I saw a workman, and expected no more," said one, John Robison, later Professor of Natural Philosophy at the University of Edinburgh, "but was surprised to find a philosopher." Though receiving no formal education, Watt possessed boundless self-confidence. "He believed he could fix, or make, anything," and proved it once when – though fully ignorant of music, and unable to distinguish one note from another – he nevertheless blithely accepted an order from the Masonic Lodge of Glasgow to build a pipe organ. For several weeks he studied the philosophical theory of music, and "found that science would be a substitute for his want of ear." He learned about organs, selected the materials, designed the plans and built them himself, a small one first for the chemist, Joseph Black, then the large one for the Lodge. Musicians often admired the quality of his organs.

Watt was an exemplar of the brimming can-do optimism of the period. William Hutton, the printer at Birmingham, England and local historian, stated in 1780 that, "Every man has his fortune in his own hands." At around the same time, Thomas Paine, across the sea in North America, proclaimed in his *Common Sense* that, "We have it in our power to begin the world over again...The birthday of a new world is at hand." Watt and his peers of the Scottish Enlightenment, determined to transfigure what was in all likelihood the poorest country of Europe, lived out this credo of audacious, world-transforming creativity – what one scholar aptly termed Western man's "recovery of nerve" – to the full.[8]

Watt was no mere paragon of mechanical tinkering; he was a careful student of the properties and power of steam. He was friend, assistant and pupil to one of the era's leading scientists, Joseph Black (1728-1799), professor of chemistry, medicine and anatomy at the University of Glasgow. Black, who isolated and gave a detailed account of the chemical activity of carbon dioxide, discovered the principle of latent heat in about 1761, and three years later was able to measure its quantity in steam. Watt, Black, John Robison – who later helped design, edit and contribute to the *Encyclopedia Britannica* – and other University thinkers had already been examining the properties of steam for years when, on a walk early in 1765, Watt hit on the idea of separate condensation, which permitted his engine to generate a constant motion.

"Nature has its weak side," Watt said, "if only we can find it." That, of course, was the task of science. To transform the principles of theoretical science into useful technology was "the job of the engineer – and his business sidekick, the entrepreneur." Watt would later make a well-deserved fortune on his invention – and such a combination of brilliant science and profitable entrepreneurship was not uncommon among enlightened Scots. "Watt was perfectly comfortable with the idea that his scientific expertise, like his machine, should be used to make a profit."

Black himself had dedicated a good deal of his chemical expertise and

effort to upgrading methods of bleaching employed by local linen manufacturers. Further, Black's own teacher, William Cullen, who revolutionized the teaching of medicine at the University of Edinburgh in the
1760s, had initiated "the bleaching agent project" when teaching anatomy previously at Glasgow. "When [Cullen] moved to Edinburgh in
1755, he was a distinguished figure not only in the field of medicine, but
also in what might be called industrial science." Similarly, Watt's first
partner in the production of steam engines, Dr. John Roebuck, was a
practicing physician (Edinburgh trained) and a chemist, an inventor who
created the lead-chamber process for manufacturing sulphuric acid, and
a wealthy industrialist who owned ironworks at Carron and coal mines at
Borrowstoness. "This was, again, very typical of the Glasgow
Enlightenment's fusion of the practical and the theoretical."

Additionally, James Hutton, an early pioneer of geology, was a
Scottish scientist who studied medicine at Edinburgh, and who, along
with such luminaries as Adam Smith and Joseph Black, was a leader of
that city's "enlightened intellectual elite." Hutton, who originated the
modern theory of the evolution of the earth's crust, who maintained that
the earth was much older than previously believed, and whose pioneering ideas – presented in his two volume 1795 book, *Theory of the Earth*
– caused a controversy among some biblical scholars, was also a chemical
manufacturer who earned "considerable wealth" from his innovative
process of synthesizing ammonium chloride.

Hutton – the geologist-manufacturer – and Black – the chemist-
industrial consultant dined every Sunday evening at an Edinburgh tavern
with Adam Smith – the moral philosopher-economist. The three friends
represented a microcosm of the Scottish Enlightenment: science, philosophy and rational inquiry in general placed in service of industrialization
and life-enhancing progress.[9]

In France, Diderot encouraged a union of theoretical and practical
thinkers to overcome the "resistance of nature" in order to serve man's

life, and nowhere is this exhortation more fully incorporated than in Watt's innovations. The steam engine – "the decisive invention of the Industrial Revolution – is simply a superb illustration of Diderot's ideal; it is unthinkable without the work of [17th century English scientist, Robert] Hooke and Newton, and without the work of contemporary scientists all over Europe."[10]

Numerous luminaries of Scotland's Industrial Revolution were medical men, including Cullen – Adam Smith's personal physician – Black, Roebuck and others. "The two fields resembled each other. The hallmarks of Scottish medicine were close clinical observation, hands-on diagnosis, and thinking of objects such as the human body as a system – not so different from the practical approach of engineers such as James Watt."[11]

Scottish engineers also helped revolutionize Britain's transportation system during the 18th century, a vital function for an economy rising out of poverty by means of industry and trade. "The state of the roads in England was abominable until the late 18th century." They were generally little more than muddy ruts, often impassable. The most efficient method of travel was to walk, and moving goods was best done by pack horse. Conditions in Scotland were even worse. Roads in the Highlands barely existed, and local roads were so bad that in wet weather "horses sink to their bellies, and carts to their axles." This began to change in the 1790s.[12]

The engineer, John McAdam (1756-1836), devised a new method of road building. Traveling the breadth of Great Britain, he inspected virtually every by-way in the country in the course of tramping 30,000 miles. McAdam used crushed stones and gravel to inexpensively improve roads, finding that the weight of wagon wheels and horses' hooves would "compact the layers of stone to form a firm hard surface – a macadam surface." The macadamized roads were soon in use all over Britain, expediting land travel and transport immensely. (A later innovation not used by McAdam bound road surfaces with tar – a surface known as tarmacadam or tarmac for short.) The improved roads cut travel time from London to Edinburgh from ten days to less than two – and the journey from Edinburgh to Glasgow that formerly took Adam Smith a-day-and-a-half was now done in four-and-a-half hours.

John Rennie (1761-1821), was another superb Scottish engineer who made significant contributions to Britain's burgeoning transportation industry. Though his father was reckoned among the best farmers in the neighborhood of East Lothian, it must be remembered that this estimate was in accordance with the standards of 18th century Scottish agriculture, which subsisted in "an incredibly backward state, compared with either England or even Ireland…" Frequently, the mechanically-talented young Rennie played truant and spent his time working at a millwright's shop near his home, where he was eventually employed for two years during which time he learned the trade. The prodigy soon exhausted the knowledge of both his teachers and his employer, and eventually worked his way through the University of Edinburgh, supporting himself as a millwright during the months that classes were not in session. At Edinburgh, Rennie studied with both Joseph Black and John Robison, where the great Robison recognized Rennie's talents and masterfully oversaw his education in the natural sciences.

Years later, when Rennie was firmly established as a superb engineer, Robison visited him at his London home. The professor had agreed to write the articles on Mechanics for the celebrated third edition of the *Encyclopedia Britannica*, and desired insight from Rennie, which the latter gratefully provided, enabling Robison to write with greater knowledge of the practical details of engineering. The flow of knowledge between experts in theoretical science and masters of practical construction and industry was reciprocal during the Scottish Enlightenment.

It was Robison who recommended Rennie to his old friend James Watt when Watt and his partner, Matthew Boulton, sought an engineer to construct Albion Mills, the new, state-of-the-art flour mill that would employ the most powerful steam engines that Watt had yet built. Though, tragically, the mills later burned to the ground never to be rebuilt, the superb work performed by Rennie did not go unnoticed, helping to launch him on a spectacular career that later produced both the Waterloo and New London Bridges across the Thames, the London and East India Docks, the Plymouth Breakwater, several harbors and numerous other construction projects.[13]

It was yet another extraordinary Scot, the engineer, Thomas Telford (1757-1834), who created Britain's modern transportation system. Telford, known as the "Father of Civil Engineering," made roadbuilding into a science. He recognized the need of a level line of construction, and built the London to Holyhead road, now the A5, with its superb suspension bridge spanning the Menai Straits.[14]

Even by the exalted standards of the day, Telford was an exceptional man. His father, a shepherd in Glendenning, died shortly after his birth, and his widowed mother reared him in crushing poverty. He was literally born in a hovel consisting of four mud walls and a thatched roof. To be able to eat, he apprenticed with a local stonemason, but still learned to read, write and do mathematics. Later, he worked as a mason in Edinburgh and London. "Long after he made his fortune…Telford was crossing Waterloo Bridge (built by…John Rennie)…and he pointed to Somerset House…saying, 'You see those stones there: forty years since I hewed and laid them, when working on that building as a common mason.'"

But it was as a builder of canals that Telford would reach his greatest achievements. "Canal mania" gripped Britain in the late 18th and early 19th centuries, for water transport was the quickest and cheapest means of shipping heavy goods, including coal. Just prior to Telford's day, James Brindley (1716-1772) had constructed several of the important early canals.

Brindley, an Englishman born into rural poverty, worked as a laborer until about 17 years old, and in 1733 was apprenticed to a village millwright. "By sheer native intelligence and determination (for he received so little instruction from his master that when his apprenticeship ended he could neither read nor write) Brindley mastered his craft..." In the 1760s, Brindley built a canal to carry coal from the Duke of Bridgewater's pits at Worsley to the still-small city of Manchester. Brindley proposed the innovative method, as then unused in England, of carrying the canal on aqueducts over instead of through the rivers standing in its path. Though many people mocked Brindley's conception as "the dream of a madman," he carried it through to such successful completion that the growing commerce enabled Manchester's population to double over the next thirty years. The canal brought numerous products – among them lime, coal and manure – to the landowners in proximity, and enabled them to get their produce to market. "No longer was the weekly convoy of one hundred and fifty pack-horses needed to carry Manchester goods...for export..."

Brindley also built the Grand Trunk Canal, linking the Trent to the Mersey, and both to the Severn, three of Britain's main rivers. The Grand Trunk not only enabled Josiah Wedgewood, the innovative pottery manufacturer, to ship supplies and finished products to and from his works at Etruria; it also opened vast new communication and transportation throughout England "by uniting the navigation of the three rivers which had their termini at the ports of Liverpool, Hull, and Bristol, on the opposite sides of the island." This opened up industries leading to the great economic development of the previously-impoverished English hinterlands. In all, Brindley "laid out almost four hundred miles of canals in a network all over England."[15]

However, it was in the achievements of Telford that the period of canal building reached its zenith. Telford, who taught himself the principles of architecture and proceeded to build churches, castles and prisons, designed two vast aqueducts for his Ellesmere Canal linking the Mersey, the Dee and the Severn, then the most ambitious canal ever built. One of them, spanning the Dee at Pont Cysylltau (which means "great crossing") introduced a cast iron trough on "lofty masonry piers" and represented a significant feat of engineering. The aqueduct "rose 127 feet above the Dee River, on a one-hundred-foot raised bank, with an iron trough carrying boats and barges along a nearly quarter-mile span. Two hundred years later it is still…in use." The Scottish novelist, Walter Scott, called it, "the most impressive work of art he had ever seen."

The Caledonian Canal, running through the Scottish Highlands, connected the Atlantic Ocean to the North Sea and took Telford fifteen years to build. His survey of the project agreed on all important points with that turned in almost thirty years earlier by his friend, James Watt. Its construction cut through sixty miles of the Great Glen, with more than twenty miles of canals and locks, and represented enormous engineering challenges that had to be met. One was that the elevation between Loch Eil and Loch Lochy changed by ninety feet in a distance of under eight miles, inducing Telford to design a flight of eight gigantic locks to rise up the hillside, which he dubbed "Neptune's Staircase." But that was not all. He and thousands of his workers had to dredge existing lochs, cut new channels, excavate countless thousands of tons of dirt and create a harbor for the ships using the canal. With its 110 foot width, it was truly epic in proportion. Further, Telford built over one thousand bridges, "often in glens where no bridge had ever existed before."

It is rare in history that a single individual has done as much to promote the progress of a previously-undeveloped area as Telford did in the Scottish Highlands. Now gone were the Lean Years at the turn of the 18th century in which tens of thousands died of famine in Scotland.

A problem was that the Caledonian project was government run and financed, and consequently ran way over budget. "Almost all of the money came from the British government, for what was the first public inland waterway project in the nation's history." Generally, however, the British of the 18th century had the good sense to let private enterprise build their infrastructure and to keep their government out of it. "Unlike the Continental despotisms, British governments were conducted on laissez-faire principles as a rule. They were not in business to create transport systems – that was for the local authorities or private enterprise."

Nevertheless, though the prodigious Canal was not a commercial success, it was more than a stupendous engineering triumph that later served as the model for the Suez Canal; for it opened to trade for the first time the previously remote and wild areas of the Scottish Highlands. Regarding Telford's overall accomplishments, suffice it to say that 75 percent of "his enormous output" is still effectively functioning today, 200 years later.[16]

Telford vigorously supported free enterprise, and explicitly regarded his work as promoting progress and capitalism. "I admire commercial enterprise," he stated. "It is the vigorous outgrowth of our industrial life. I admire everything that gives it free scope, as wherever it goes, activity, energy, intelligence – all that we call civilization – goes with it." But money was only a means to an end for Telford, "who wrote poetry, and good poetry" for much of his life. The goal – as for most of the great entrepreneurs – was to create works of enduring value that were positive and life-promoting, to live productively, to build, to act in accordance with the same creative drive in the material realm that inspired mankind's greatest artists and theoretical scientists in the spiritual.

Though Telford regularly charged low fees and considered money but a secondary value, independence was important: he earned and invested sufficiently to maintain his London house in comfort. When he died in 1834, his savings amounted to some 16,600 pounds sterling, a relatively significant sum in those days, much of which was bequeathed to an engineering institute, Scottish libraries and such poet friends as Robert Southey and Thomas Campbell. The destitute shepherd's son from

Glendenning, in death as in life, devoted himself to the cultivation of the mind. Regarding Telford's specific achievements, one historian concludes: "It was a life's work that flowed from a bottomless reservoir of creativity and self-confident energy."[17]

But the conduit between Enlightenment principles and the British Industrial Revolution was not limited to the leading Scottish minds of the day. There were numerous kindred spirits in England who sought to implement theoretical knowledge in the realm of practical inventiveness in service of industrial progress; and a select number of them centered in Birmingham, where James Watt moved to perfect and manufacture his steam engine.

The Lunar Society of Birmingham

In the 18th century's second half, at the Enlightenment's height, a diverse array of scientific, technological and manufacturing talent gathered in the area of Birmingham, England that is perhaps matchless in the history of industry. Watt, in his new partnership with Matthew Boulton, owner of the Soho Engineering Works, found a mind that was brilliantly able regarding issues of engineering and applied science. Further, Boulton, already well-established in business, employed "the craftsmen Watt needed to make the valves and other delicate parts of the engine." Their partnership earned large sums of money manufacturing the steam engine and, in Enlightenment fashion, was not only dedicated to furthering both scientific understanding and its practical applications, but to doing so as a means of creating wealth and promoting prosperity. Watt and Boulton were integral members of an extraordinary group of physicians-scientists-inventors-entrepreneurs who met regularly to further the related causes of research, technology and industry.

The Lunar Society of Birmingham, so-called because it met at the time of the full moon when its light most brilliantly illuminated the still-primitive roads, was at its zenith in the late 1770s and 1780s. Its list of members reads like a Who's Who of 18th century British scientific and industrial talent. In addition to Watt and Boulton, the group included Erasmus Darwin, one of England's most able physicians (Edinburgh-trained), an inventor, botanist, poet, all-around original and innovative mind, and grandfather of Charles Darwin (who, like his grandfather, similarly studied medicine at Edinburgh.) Another superb physician, William Withering, was a member, an outstanding researcher who introduced the use of digitalis into medical practice, a medication allowing successful treatment of the then fatal ailment edema or dropsy, and constituting a revolution in the history of cardiac care. Withering, also Edinburgh-trained, rivaled Darwin as the leading provincial physician of his day, and like his competitor, later became noted for his botanical studies.

Josiah Wedgewood, the innovative maker of pottery, could not be overlooked in any group, however exalted. Wedgewood, based on extensive experimentation, created earthenware pottery for common use that was of the quality of the expensive, celebrated service he made for Catherine the Great of Russia (except for the hand-painted decorations), which the poor man could purchase at roughly a shilling a piece. "In time that is what transformed the kitchens of the working class in the Industrial Revolution"…and is what made Wedgewood a wealthy man. He also designed a new method of measuring the high temperatures in the kiln – by means of "a…sliding scale of expansion in which a clay test-piece moved" – thereby advancing the techniques used to resolve that ancient and difficult problem. Wedgewood was, it should be noted, Charles Darwin's other grandfather.

Further, the chemist, James Keir, made significant contributions to the group. Keir, who also studied medicine at Edinburgh (and who was nephew to James Lind, the Edinburgh-trained Scottish physician who discovered the cure for scurvy) translated the Frenchman Macquer's advanced Dictionary of Chemistry, thereby making "a significant contribution to the chemical studies of his time." He became part owner of a glassmaking firm, served as a consultant to Boulton, and supplied the Soho firm with glass tubing for thermometers. Later, Keir opened the Tipton Chemical Works, which "grew to a chemical plant equal in size to any in England at the time…" and which produced a new metallic alloy which had been developed by Boulton and Keir jointly. Keir's life illustrated vividly the overall intent of Lunar Society members to "make a practical use of scientific knowledge…" meaning "to make some discovery by which [a man] might increase his fortune."

Not to go unmentioned in this circle of extraordinary men was Dr. William Small, a Scot who studied medicine at the University of Glasgow, and who became Professor of Natural Philosophy and Mathematics at the College of William and Mary in Virginia, where his teachings so inspired the young Thomas Jefferson, who was his "daily companion," that the future President of the United States remarked that Small's influence "fixed the destinies of my life." Small introduced the lecture method in Virginia, contributed to what later became the new science curricula of the United States, and procured for William and Mary the best collection of scientific apparatus in America. Small was a friend of Benjamin Franklin's, and upon his return to England, a friend and family physician to Boulton and a scientific advisor to Watt and Boulton whose "role in the development of the steam engine industry…[was] too significant for him to have remained entirely unstudied." Small was widely loved for his "benevolence and profound sagacity," and while at Birmingham took out several patents for improvements of clocks.

But it was when Joseph Priestley moved to Birmingham in 1780 that the Lunar Society reached its apogee. Priestley, chemist par excellence, Unitarian minister, radical free thinker and friend of Benjamin Franklin was one of the great minds of his or any age. It was Priestley who isolated and described several gases, including oxygen, as well as ammonia, nitrous oxide, sulfur dioxide and carbon monoxide. Encouraged by

Franklin, whom he met in London in 1766, Priestley conducted experiments in the new field of electricity, and wrote his *The History of Electricity* the next year.

An innovative thinker in religion, as well as in science, he wrote *History of the Corruptions of Christianity* in 1782, a book officially burned in 1785. Tragically, in 1791, due to strong backlash against the French Revolution, which Priestley openly supported, an enraged mob burned to the ground the religious radical's home, his laboratory and his library. (The destruction of Priestley's home during the Birmingham Riots was painted by Exted, a student of Hogarth's, who drew the scene on the spot.) Devastated, Priestley left Birmingham and, three years later, England, moving to revolutionary America, where he spent the rest of his years writing. Priestley was a firm supporter of the "Enlightenment belief that science and technology underlay material advance and were moved forward by freedom." He wrote: "It will soon appear that Republican governments, in which every obstruction is removed to the exertion of all kinds of talent, will be far more favorable to science, and the arts [that is to technology], than any monarchical government has ever been."

During his decade in Birmingham, Priestley served as scientific adviser to Wedgewood; as he had been for years to his brother-in-law, the innovative English iron magnate, "Iron Mad" John Wilkinson, who pioneered the use of cast iron, who was among the first to build iron boats and bridges, and whose foundry produced most of the machine parts for the firm of Boulton and Watt. In 1774, Wilkinson had patented a process for boring cannon that he adapted to boring cylinders for Watt's engines with a new and matchless degree of accuracy. (Wilkinson acquired his colorful nickname "because he firmly believed that anything could be made of his metal...he had an iron desk and an iron bed and kept an iron coffin propped up in his office to persuade others to place orders." Wilkinson's will was also reputed to be as hard as iron and he possessed "a temper as hot as his furnaces" – but it was his new boring machine that "finally made the [steam] engine viable.")

The relationship between the great scientist, Priestley – "the father of pneumatic chemistry" – and the industrialists/inventors composing the rest of the Lunar Society was a microcosm of the Enlightenment's ideal of the close working relationship between theoretical reason and the progressive forces of inventiveness and industrialization. Priestley "was no 'pure' scientist to be horrified with a suggestion that his work be turned to use...The mixing of science, applied science, and technology in Lunar activities found a supporter in Priestley" – and, "as an industrial research organization, [the Lunar Society] found in him also a paid consultant."

So many of the Lunar men were either Scots or educated at the University of Edinburgh — the cradle of the Scottish Enlightenment — that it is no exaggeration to claim "that at times it would seem as though Birmingham itself was an intellectual colony of Scotland."[18]

The Continuing Advance of the Era

Enlightenment scholar, Peter Gay, pointed out that though from a current vantage point, 18th century technology was primitive and living conditions horrifying, the educated men of the day saw "life getting better, safer, easier, healthier, more predictable – that is to say, more rational – decade by decade." This emphatically included the inventions, the machinery, the factory system and the division of labor – all of which contributed significantly to the immensely-increased productivity of the day.[19]

Part of this progress was the medical advance of the era, to which students of the University of Edinburgh's medical school contributed significantly. For example, William and John Hunter were innovators in various branches of medicine. More than anyone, William transformed obstetrics from a primitive field into a "scientifically precise discipline" — and his brother wrought similar advances in dentistry; indeed, he "first coined the terms incisor, bicuspid and molar for describing teeth."

The historian, Arthur Herman, points out, "The Hunters were bona fide figures of the Scottish Enlightenment." Both Adam Smith and Edward Gibbon attended William's lectures — and John treated Smith, as well as diagnosing David Hume's fatal ailment. One of John Hunter's most able English students, Edward Jenner, discovered a treatment for smallpox, one of history's most lethal killers, and was a prime mover in the medical breakthrough of vaccinations.[20]

The Edinburgh medical school implemented the new scientific methodology of the age: it emphasized a Newtonian observation-based rationalism – a reverence for facts, knowledge and critical thought in contrast to the authoritarian dogmas of the past. One philosopher describes Newton's cognitive method: "The procedure is thus not from concepts and axioms to phenomena, but vice-versa. Observation produces the datum of science; the principle and law are the object of the investigation."

Such a reason-oriented, unprejudicial outlook and spirit contributed to the religious freedom of the Scottish universities and helped attract to them many of Great Britain's most brilliant minds. Without this realization, it will be inexplicable to current scholars – as opposed to merely astonishing – how many outstanding engineers and scientists (not just physicians) studied medicine at the University of Edinburgh in the subsequent century, a list that includes Charles Darwin. *The University of Edinburgh, especially its medical school, became a fountainhead of the Scottish Enlightenment, including its Industrial Revolution, because of its superlative emphasis on the new cognitive method of Newtonian science.*[21]

It is of the utmost importance to bear in mind that the pre-Enlightenment eras had neither the rational, secular philosophy nor the practical knowledge and wealth that was its effect to concern themselves with sanitizing towns, improving personal hygiene and upgrading factory (or general working) conditions. The filth, disease, famine and early death of previous periods were too overwhelming, too all-pervasive for there to be any hope of amelioration. It was only in the 18th century, after human knowledge of the principles of rational philosophy and science had greatly advanced, that there arose belief in the capacity of man to significantly – even vastly – improve his living conditions. In this regard, the technological and industrial revolutions, and the medical advances, were inseparable from the great burst of self-confidence that occurred during the 18th century. Locke both contributed to and was representative of the new attitude. In expounding on the possibilities opened by the beckoning field of applied science – on the potential for inventions, medical breakthroughs and life-enhancing creations – he concluded: "for such discoveries as these the mind of man is well fitted."

Men saw the rational mind transfiguring the physical world all around them. Although the beginnings of the railway age belong to the early 19th century – not to the 18th – the continued influence of Enlightenment principles and attitudes was unmistakable. For one thing, the new mode of transport relied heavily on Watt's steam engine, that quintessential integration of scientific theory and practical innovation.

Richard Trevithick, a Cornish blacksmith and wrestler – and an exceedingly inventive man – was an early creator of the locomotive. In the first years of the 19th century, Trevithick, applying Watt's creation to the problem of locomotion, introduced a high-pressure engine capable of serving as a "mobile power pack." In London, in 1808, he demonstrated his new steam locomotive, Catch-me-who-can, charging one shilling for passengers to ride around a circular track. But it was George Stephenson, the poor grandson of a Scot who settled in northern England, who earned the title, "Father of the Railroad."

Like Telford, Stephenson came from a family of shepherds, though his father was a coal miner. In his youth, he had little or no education, and at age eighteen could neither read nor write. But he was in love with the steam engine, and there was little in the mines that he couldn't fix.

He was one of the inventors of the miner's safety lamps, and in the 1820s built a series of locomotives, the first of which, Blucher, could pull a 30-ton load up a slight incline at four miles per hour.

Recognizing the importance of education, Stephenson sent his young son, Robert, to a school he could reach only by riding 10 miles a day on a donkey. The father learned to read and write, and took lessons from his son on the latter's return in the evening. Together, they studied volumes of science and technology. Together, also, they designed dozens of advanced steam engines, each an improvement on the last, and revolutionized transportation in the 1820s. (To complete his formal education, Stephenson sent Robert to the University of Edinburgh, where he studied natural philosophy, mineralogy and chemistry under several outstanding professors.)

During this period, a group of businessmen desired to construct a railroad to link the cities of Manchester and Liverpool, thereby providing safe, cheap shipping, reducing the time from 36 hours by canal to 5 or 6 hours. Overcoming fierce resistance from the canal interests and their government supporters, the railroad men went ahead, and offered a prize of 500 pounds sterling for the best locomotive. The "Rainhill Trials" took place on October 6th, 1829, with the Stephenson's entry, Rocket, competing against four other contestants. The Trials lasted several days, and were held in front of ten thousand spectators. Rocket vanquished the field by "averaging 14 miles per hour over 60 miles, and it weighed less and consumed less coal than any of the others." On the 15th of September, 1830, the Liverpool and Manchester Railway opened, possessing by that time eight steam locomotives. The railroad saved Manchester manufacturers thousands of pounds sterling; it offered extensive passenger service as well, and "in due course...would lead to standardized time [schedules]." Not surprisingly, railways began to spread. In all, Robert Stephenson, superbly carrying on his father's work, designed and supervised construction of some eighteen hundred and fifty miles of railway before his death in 1859.[22]

George Stephenson, like Brindley, Rennie, Telford and so many others was a self-made man who rose from poverty undreamed of in today's capitalist nations to a superb success. The historian, Paul Johnson, notes the irony in the belief that the Industrial Revolution was a period of increasing suffering for the workingman. "In fact, it was the age, above all, in history of matchless opportunities for penniless men with powerful brains and imaginations, and it is astonishing how quickly they came to the fore. Capitalists...were anxious to recognize, promote and reward talent."

But it is not astonishing at all when two related points are realized: 1. the innovativeness required by industrial development made it in the capitalists' rational self-interest to reward mental ability wherever they found it. 2. *the Industrial Revolution and capitalism were distinctively Enlightenment phenomena.*[23]

The Enlightenment belief in the mind and the rights of everyman had undercut aristocratic and class prejudices, proclaiming the truth that the common man could be quite uncommon, making it possible for penniless commoners of talent and initiative to rise under the new system of political/economic freedom. Capitalism, the political/economic system of the Enlightenment, gave both birth and currency to that most noble phrase: "the self-made man." The phenomena of the self-made – and initially poor – common man is merely one illustration of the broader principle that capitalism is the system of the mind; for the Enlightenment's glorification and liberation of human intelligence, regardless of the birth status or class background of an individual, was the fundamental cause of the era's ability to make such spectacular progress in applied science, medicine, technology, industry and business. An individual's mind and his initiative counted, not his birth or social class.

This truth was even more applicable in England's North American colonies. Though the soon-to-be United States was still largely untamed wilderness – and lacked the great libraries, universities and intellectual salons of Europe – the spirit and values of the Enlightenment took deep root there. For America also lacked a hereditary aristocracy, a governmentally-recognized church, internecine feudal and monarchical wars, and other European statist institutions that suppressed the common man. Consequently, from its earliest days, it was a society of, for and by commoners, the nation unequalled in history for legally unleashing the brain power of everyman.

The Enlightenment's Beneficent Impact in America

Benjamin Franklin, for example, was the fifteenth child of his father, Josiah Franklin, a chandler by trade; and young Benjamin — who grew to be the greatest American scientist of the age and the toast of Europe's leading minds — began making candles and soap at age ten.[24]

Franklin brilliantly typified the practical-minded spirit of the common man acutely aware of the misery in which his ilk had lived and died for centuries. He wrote: "What signifies Philosophy [a broad term then that included science] that does not apply to some use?" Franklin was confident that "genuine science would ultimately yield useful results." He pursued this goal by developing a plan for colonial cooperation to promote the sciences, realizing that by such intellectual endeavors Americans would increase their power "over matter, and multiply the conveniences or pleasures of life." According to one historian, Franklin felt "chagrined" until he found some practical use for the knowledge gained from his experiments with electricity. In this he succeeded admirably, for his suggestion of the lightning rod made in *Poor Richard's Almanack* was soon taken up with beneficial results.[25]

Franklin's improvements to the fireplace and his invention of the Franklin stove were likewise implementations of the age's boundless confidence that "science could be applied to the improvement of the material conditions of life." Societies of the colonies' most advanced thinkers sprang up – the American Society for Promoting and Propagating Useful Knowledge, the American Philosophical Society, the Virginia Society for Promoting Useful Knowledge – all dedicated, in various forms, to the utilitarian application of scientific advances. In 1787, the American inventor, John Fitch, though rebuffed in his quest for aid from the American Philosophical Society, built "the first successful steamboat," and shortly after ran one on a "commercial schedule between Philadelphia and Burlington." Indeed, Fitch had a steamboat running on the Delaware River in August of 1787 while the Constitutional Convention met in Philadelphia. It was simultaneously a perfect integrating moment and a harbinger of things to come. For by the turn of the 19th century, the American Enlightenment would create the beginnings of a second transformation equally momentous as the American Political Revolution – the American Industrial Revolution.[26]

Eli Whitney, though a devout Puritan antagonistic to such leading Enlightenment figures as Jefferson and Paine, embodied in his practical inventiveness the period's central commitment to applied rationality. Whitney fired several of the first shots of the American Industrial Revolution. The budding inventor, born into poverty on a farm in rural Massachusetts in 1765, honed his technical skills on the primitive farm equipment available to him. At age 18, he decided to attend college, and with his father's help and six years of preparation, he worked his way through Yale as an engineer, graduating at age 27.

Though most famous as the inventor of the cotton gin (1793), an ingenious contrivance that vastly increased the production of cotton, Whitney's greatest contribution to the manufacturing process was his innovative conception of mass production. When he signed a contract with the U.S. government to supply 10,000 muskets, he realized that the way to achieve manufacturing efficiency on a vast scale was by means of interchangeable parts, by introducing uniformity and standardization "on a scale never before imagined." Though Whitney's specific efforts to mass produce muskets met with mixed results, by the mid-19th century his "American System" had enabled the United States to become an industrial giant, churning out "standardized products mass-produced by machine methods including doors, furniture, and other woodwork, boots, shoes, plows, mowing machines, wood screws, files, nails, locks, clocks, small arms, nuts, bolts – the list was endless." In less than a century, Whitney – a quiet fiend who lived for his work, who drove his assistants as hard as himself and who sometimes chased them to bring them back after they'd fled – had helped transform his country from an agrarian backwater into one that surpassed Great Britain as the world's leading industrial producer.[27]

If capitalism is the political/economic system of the Enlightenment, then the United States is the nation of its fullest expression. Though only some of the advances of 19th century science – in the field of electricity, for example – were incorporated into America's inventive achievements, and most of her leading inventors were not versed in scientific theory, they were nevertheless brilliant practical thinkers, engineers in many cases, men who superbly applied whatever deeper principles they had grasped.

In Europe, the Enlightenment spirit was undercut from the first by entrenched social institutions and defeated ultimately by the rise of 19th and 20th century philosophical irrationalism. Though America too was susceptible to and damaged by such subsequent European intellectual trends as Marxism, Existentialism and post-Modernism – all attacking the mind's importance, whether by upholding materialism or overt irrationalism – the Enlightenment spirit had caught deep hold in the New World. The American people throughout their history and to this day, though battered in recent decades by a flood of environmentalist anti-science, anti-technology claims, still hold to the central animating principle of the Enlightenment: *rational intelligence, including in the fields of applied science and technological/industrial development, will significantly improve human life on earth.* It is the fundamental source of the nation's superb "can do" practical success.

The technological and industrial revolutions did not end in 1850 or at any time. More recent advances such as electricity, telephones, automobiles, air travel, personal computers, the Internet, etc., have made men's lives incomparably easier and more comfortable than those of their ancestors. The innovations made possible by rational intelligence have enabled men to achieve vastly higher living standards than in any previous historical period.

In 1776, at the dawn of the Industrial Revolution, Matthew Boulton spoke proudly to Johnson's biographer, the gifted Scottish writer, James Boswell: "I sell here, sir," the industrialist said, "what all the world desires to have – Power." Boulton's exultant words could and should be the motto of industrial capitalism; for the faint hints of Bacon's famous maxim that "Knowledge is Power" are both discernible and accurate: knowledge, obviously, *is* power – to create or destroy – and if promoting human well-being is the good, all the more cherished in the midst of centuries of brain-numbing misery, then Watt and Boulton – and the inventors and entrepreneurs of the Industrial Revolution more broadly – used their power to create enormous value, thereby bringing superlative, unprecedented good.[28]

From the beginning of the 19th century, Western man's standard of living and life expectancy have risen almost continuously. Industrial capitalism has created wealth and innovations undreamed of by men prior to the late 20th century, giving rise to a vast middle class and enabling the "poor" to live at a level unobtainable even by royalty a mere two centuries ago. But first the new political/economic system had to confront the abysmal destitution it inherited from centuries of feudalism. Capitalism's critics claim that the advent of the Industrial Revolution was not a boon for all members of society, that it created worse hardships for the working class and for the poor. What is the truth regarding such accusations?

What was capitalism's track record regarding the creation and spread of wealth in the days of its infancy?

Summary

The British Industrial Revolution will not be fully understood or appreciated until it is seen as an integral aspect of the Scottish Enlightenment. Leading Scottish intellectuals were early technologists-industrialists and/or major supporters of industry because they held fast to the central Enlightenment insight that human life would be fundamentally bettered by the unleashed brain power of the liberated common man.

This conviction took deep root in America, the first true modern homeland of the common man, and the 18th century achievements of such geniuses as Franklin were mere preludes to the unprecedented material advances the world's freest nation would reach in the subsequent century. (See Chapter Five)

4: The Industrial Revolution Brings Advance

Numerous thinkers have pointed out that the Industrial Revolution was, in fact, an evolution, as are all dramatic changes in human life. But to understand this, human beings must realize more than that industrialization gradually started before 1760 and that it is an ongoing process that will never cease as long as man's mind remains free. They must recognize above all that its positive impact on human life has, indeed, been revolutionary. To the everlasting credit and advancement of the English and the Scots (and eventually, the progress of all of mankind) the Industrial Revolution – for all practical purposes – began in the world's freest country of the time: Great Britain.

The beginnings of the factory system, with its unparalleled ability to create an abundance of consumer products inexpensively, did not arise in a cultural vacuum. It was an integral part of the advances in science and technology made during the preceding centuries and accelerating during the 18th century Enlightenment. Industrialization is the application to economics – to the production of material goods required by man's life – of the most advanced scientific and technological knowledge available in an era. This principle was as true of industrialization's early days as it is today.

It was and remains the full Enlightenment program – of rational, critical thought applied to a wide range of practical concerns, including sanitation, medicine and agriculture, as well as manufacturing – that has been so beneficial to human life. Industrialization can only be understood when seen as a vital and inseparable part of the Enlightenment project for improving man's life on earth. This topic, too often left undiscussed by both capitalism's supporters and its critics, needs to be studied.

The Big Bang of the Industrial Revolution

A vast increase in output of manufactured goods requires greater power – and the invention of the steam engine was vital in this regard. Thomas Newcomen (1663-1729), an English blacksmith, improved earlier steam-powered water pumps and in 1712 erected a steam engine at the Dudley Castle mine. The Newcomen engine represented a significant advance of the time and was soon successfully pumping water out of mines across Europe. "Newcomen's engine had a profound impact on the coal-mining industry. It provided power to pump water from the deepest mines and opened up seams that had previously been unworkable because of flooding."

But as late as the 1750s, it "still wasn't obvious that steam power was the way forward for all needs." The Newcomen engine was "inefficient compared with the best possible use of steam," because, as James Watt soon realized, the condensing of steam in its cylinder wasted the preponderance of energy produced. In the 1760s, after much careful thought, Watt hit upon his idea of separate condensation that would revolutionize the power industry of the 18th century. Watt's partnership with Matthew Boulton of the Soho Manufacturing Works of Birmingham facilitated, in the 1780s, his inventing and manufacturing a double-action rotative steam engine, "a momentous event" in the history of technology.

The application of the Watt and Boulton steam engine to the manufacture of textiles in 1785 constituted the "Big Bang of the Industrial

The Industrial Revolution Brings Advance

Revolution," adding enormous power to the already-increasing mechanization of the production of cotton clothing. In 1733, John Kay had invented the flying shuttle, "an improvement to looms that enabled weavers to weave faster." But, due to slow communications and Kay's lack of entrepreneurship, the device did not catch on until the 1750s, at which time it "fuelled the search for a faster method of spinning."

In answer to this need, James Hargreaves, in the mid-1760s, created the "spinning jenny," a machine (named after his wife) by which a worker could spin at first six or seven – but later up to eighty – threads at once. Richard Arkwright's frame of 1768 or 1769 produced a stronger thread suitable for both weft and warp. "Unlike the jenny, the frame required, for its working, power greater than that of human muscles, and hence from the beginning the process was carried on in mills or factories." In 1771, Arkwright established a large factory driven by water power in which he soon employed roughly 600 workers. Such advances, in addition to Samuel Crompton's 1779 invention of the "mule" – a cross breed of the jenny and the frame that produced a yarn capable of making all kinds of textiles – and Arkwright's innovative method of carding by cylinders, ensured that the future of textile production would be mechanized, rather than hand-driven, and conducted predominantly in factories, not in the domestic settings of the older cottage industries.

The results of such innovations were stupendous. In 1765, half a million pounds of cotton had been spun in England, all by hand. By 1784, 12 million pounds were spun, all by machine. In 1785, the powerful Watt and Boulton steam engines were first applied to spinning by rollers, and in the 1790s steam power was used to drive the mules. Production increased to the point that by 1812 the supply of cotton yarn was so enormous that its price had dropped to a mere 10 percent of what it had been previously. "By the early 1860s the price of cotton cloth…was less than 1 percent of what it had been in 1784, when the industry was already mechanized. There is no previous instance in world history of the price of a product in potentially universal demand coming down so fast. As a result, hundreds of millions of people, all over the world, were able to dress comfortably and cleanly at last."[1]

The machine-driven, steam-powered, large-scale factories produced vastly more cotton clothes than the hand weavers of the cottage industries. This is true of mechanized factories in general: whether they manufacture automobiles, refrigerators, televisions or one of a thousand other products, the factories churn out goods far more readily than can the old-fashioned hand-made methods of home industries. Economically, the result of such an increased supply tends to be lower prices.

The law of supply and demand predicts that as supply of a good increases relative to demand for it, its price tends to fall. From shoes to apples to cell phones—if supply of a commodity diminishes relative to demand, the competition among buyers tends to bid up its price; if supply increases relative to demand, the competition among sellers tends to reduce its price. With more goods available and prices declining, human beings achieve a higher standard of living.

Historically, the factory system began with the cotton clothing industry; but it didn't end there. Gradually, by the mid-19th century Britain became "the workshop of the world," with leading industries in iron and then steel, coal and railroading. The vastly increased production did not merely lower prices for goods made of iron or steel, for heating and cooking fuel, or for goods shipped across country – but also, through international trade, brought greater quantities of "sugar, grain, coffee and tea for the people at large." The lower prices achieved through such increased production and availability of consumer goods meant rising real wages for British workers.[2]

Economists distinguish between nominal and real wages. Nominal pay is wages measured in terms of how much money a man makes. Although it is generally better to make more money than less, the point, in itself, is trivial. For even if a man earns a million dollars an hour, he is still poor if it costs him a trillion dollars for a loaf of bread (as was virtually the case during the hyper-inflation in Weimar Germany during the 1920s.) Real pay, on the other hand, is wages measured in terms of purchasing power, i.e., in terms of what and how much a man can buy with his income. "Real wages [are] the goods and services the worker can buy with his money wages…The higher are wages relative to prices, or equivalently, the lower are prices relative to wages, the more can the worker's money wages buy." The most important point regarding wages is not how high they are, but how high they are relative to prices.[3]

Economic theory predicts that an increasing supply of goods tends to promote falling prices. The British Industrial Revolution resulted in vast increases in the supply of consumer goods. Therefore, the British in general should have grown wealthier, and as part of such economic progress real wages should have risen steadily for the workers of this period. Indeed, this is exactly what occurred.

Economic Progress

Regarding economic growth, one historian points out that "the rate of growth of industrial output between 1782 and 1855 was 3 to 4 percent per annum…over the same period the annual rate of growth of population varied from 1.2 to 1.5 percent."

Such industrial growth in early 19th century Britain bears out the estimates of contemporaries that "average real income doubled" in the period between 1800 and 1850. Mid-20th century estimates by economic historians also indicate a near doubling of British average real income for this period. Indeed, in comparison to conditions in 1800 "average per capita income had already increased fifty percent by 1830."[4]

Because of technological and industrial advances the British population was better fed during this period than it was previously. Average wheat yields, for example, rose from 25 bushels per acre at the time of Waterloo to 47 bushels by the early 1850s.

Additionally, due to growing political pressure from the Anti-Corn Law League, headed by Richard Cobden, John Bright and other supporters of free trade, the Corn Laws were finally repealed in 1846. The lifting of these tariffs on imported grain was accompanied during the same decade by the reduction of the duties on meat, butter, cheese and other foodstuffs. International free trade – the commitment to eliminate tariffs and trade barriers between countries, and to respect the rights of individuals and companies to trade unrestrictedly – is a key component of a free country's proper foreign policy. In its early days in Britain, the policy of free trade led to an increased supply of food with its consequent reduced prices.[5]

Further, due to agricultural innovations and upgraded transportation facilities – including improved roads and the construction of first canals and later railroads – meat became part of the diet of average Englishmen in the first half of the 19th century. The railroads, as well as steamships and such "technical innovations" as "the development of deep-sea trawling," contributed to an increased consumption of fish throughout England, as well. "The conclusion...is unquestionably that the amount and variety of food consumed increased between 1800 and 1850."[6]

Contrary to a long tradition of pessimist writers regarding the impact of the Industrial Revolution, these economic benefits were emphatically extended to the working class and to society's poorest members. Empirical research performed by leading economic historians show significant economic gains by virtually all British workers of this period.

By the turn of the 20th century, the findings of statistics-minded historians were already starting to overturn the claims of the pessimists (in some cases before those claims were written.) The work of such thinkers as A.L. Bowley, G.H. Wood and, later, J.H. Clapham showed that, although the handloom weavers, stubbornly clinging to their craft, suffered in increasingly agonizing poverty, the general financial trend for England's working class was clearly upward. "For every class of urban or industrial labor about which information is available…wages had risen markedly during the intervening sixty years [between 1790 and 1850.] For the fortunate classes, such as the London bricklayers or compositors, they had risen well over 40 percent, and for urban and industrial workers in the mass, fortunate and unfortunate, perhaps about 40 percent."[7]

Presumably, the further back one goes in time, the sketchier the statistical information becomes. Nevertheless, there is some evidence indicating working class pay increases dating to the Industrial Revolution's earliest days.[8]

The critics of capitalism who follow the teachings of Marx often make the error of believing that a worker, because he sells his labor to an employer, is therefore not working for himself in any sense. That he works for his employer who hopes to significantly profit, in part from his labor, is clear. But what is often missed is that he receives more than his wages in return. Because the system of mass production creates an abundance of goods inexpensively, his wages purchase an increased amount of food, coal, clothing, etc. He and his family consequently have more to eat, newer and cleaner clothes to wear and more fuel with which to heat their homes and cook their food. Increased production has its counterpart in a generalized increased consumption, including by the workers. In an important sense, he works for himself – for his own gain and betterment.[9]

The great Austrian economist, Ludwig von Mises, pointed out: "The outstanding fact about the Industrial Revolution is that it opened an age of mass production for the needs of the masses. The wage earners are no longer people toiling merely for other people's well-being [as on a feudal manor or as an unpaid apprentice.] They themselves are the main consumers of the products the factories turn out. Big business depends upon mass consumption."[10]

Given the truth of these claims, it is not surprising that more recent research using an expanded data base shows significant gains by virtually all types of workers for this era. Overall improvement for the period stretching from 1781-1851 show an average real wage gain in excess of 60 percent for farm workers, over 86 percent for blue collar workers and more than 140 percent for all workers, including white collar ones. "The evidence suggests that material gains were even bigger after 1820 than optimists had previously claimed..."[11]

One leading current expert on the period writes: "After a prolonged stagnation, blue-collar workers' real wages doubled between 1810 and 1850. This is a far larger increase than even past optimists had announced...Unless new errors are discovered, the debate over real wages in the early nineteenth century is over: the average worker was much better off in any decade from the 1830s on than in any decade before 1820. The same is true of any class of worker" analyzed in this extensive study. Though researchers tend to be cautious regarding generalizations from their findings, at least one economist now claims the evidence is "overwhelming" that workers' real wages rose as a result of Britain's Industrial Revolution. Because of this, the "hardships faced by the workers at the end of the Industrial Revolution [extreme though they were by current standards] cannot have been nearly as great as those faced by their grandparents" or by their earlier ancestors.[12]

Additionally, it must always be remembered that England fought a long and costly war against first Revolutionary and then Napoleonic France during this period. The British did not merely fight Napoleon and his "Continental System" on land and on sea, they helped subsidize various coalitions of European states against him. In significant part, the wealth and power generated by Britain's industrial might was responsible for its victory, but contrary to some people's belief, war is not good for a country's general standard of living.

During war, manufacturers produce weapons and ammunition at the expense of consumer goods; large quantities of food and other goods are necessary to supply the armed forces; and men who would otherwise be productively employed are now fighting and dying, often by the thousands. Consequently, domestic shortages, higher prices and rationing are frequent occurrences during wartime, even in wealthy nations. Britain, for example, during the Napoleonic Wars, experienced "shortages of timber, bricks, glass" and "difficulties [in] obtaining foodstuffs from abroad."

Also (though the French Wars were not fought on British soil), in general warfare destroys large amounts of property, including farms, homes and factories. Such capital assets not only have to be rebuilt, depriving men of the additional goods they might otherwise have created with the same effort, but they are denied the food and consumer goods that those farms and factories would have produced all along.

To put it simply, wars are about destruction; productive, prosperity-generating activity is about construction. By far, the greatest tragedy of war is its callous, inhumane slaughter of human life, but it is also an economic disaster; for some of society's most potentially-productive individuals are often idealistic young men, who, believing in the justice of their cause, fight and die in the conflict. Given mankind's endless warfare, it is impossible to calculate how many potential Carnegies, Rockefellers or Gates' might have been killed as youths, not to mention budding geniuses of other fields. It is therefore understandable that England's greatest economic gains for its citizens in general and for its workers came after 1820; for by then its factory system was more highly developed than in the Industrial Revolution's earliest days, and the factories were producing consumer goods to a far greater degree than weapons of war.

Nobody knows how much British production was shifted from consumer goods to military hardware by the protracted struggle (from 1793-1815 with brief interspersed periods of peace) but, as one example, in 1781 "Iron Mad" John Wilkinson supplied iron pipes for the construction of waterworks, "but during the war he and his fellow iron-masters were making cannon, not pipes." Even in the cotton industry, it was only "after the end of the French war [that] the pace of development quickened." In 1813, there were approximately 2,400 power looms in England; but by 1820, there were 14,000 and by 1833 about 100,000. Great Britain's burgeoning industrial might was largely free to concentrate on goods of mass consumption only after Napoleon's final defeat.[13]

More recently, some researchers have conceded the significant rise in real wages, but have argued that "per capita income growth in Britain was slow during the Industrial Revolution." As two economists claim, "per capita consumption of desirable goods shows no significant improvement before the mid-1840s." But even if this last claim is true, the question is "slow growth" – by what standard? The factory system began in roughly the 1770s; the Watt and Boulton steam engines were applied to the process of cotton spinning in 1785; but the growth of consumer-oriented manufacturing was interrupted by the war and became extensive only after 1815. This is why the greatest rise in real wages occurred after 1820. If per capita consumption increased significantly only after 30 years of industrial growth, by what historical standard can that be considered "slow"? For centuries prior to the Industrial Revolution, millions of the British poor had subsisted in unrelieved squalor.

During the early 19th century, for the first time, significantly improved living conditions for the mass of the British population became possible. Even if it had taken British capitalism not 30 years but a full century to raise general living standards, that would still represent an unprecedented historical achievement. Neither the pre-capitalist societies prior to Britain's Industrial Revolution nor the non-capitalist societies of the Third World in the present and recent past ever matched or could hope to match such a monumental accomplishment. Capitalist Britain achieved in mere decades what non-capitalist societies cannot do in centuries. As the same economists point out: "Growth in per capita income was far higher after the Industrial Revolution than before it."[14]

Further, per capita consumption figures need to be understood in relation to the significant growth of savings in the era. "After the establishment of savings banks in 1817 deposits increased to 14.3 millions [pounds sterling] by 1829, and to almost 30 millions by 1850..." These savings were largely the accumulation of wage earners. For example, there were 14,937 depositors of the Manchester and Salford Savings Bank in 1842: 3,063 were domestic servants, 3,033 were children whose parents saved for them, 2,372 were tradesmen, clerks, warehousemen, porters, artists and teachers, and 6,469 were laborers and industrial workers. Rising per capita income was reflected in more than increased consumption by members of the working class; it was shown by their growing ability to save.[15]

But it is insufficient to understand merely that Britain grew significantly wealthier during this period and that the mass production of her factory system was the economic cause of it. It is necessary to identify the deeper philosophical reasons for such advance.

Man-Made Power

The technological and industrial revolutions have been ongoing over at least the last 250 years. Recent technological advances have enabled men to achieve vastly higher living standards than ever before. For example, because of the power gained first from steam, then from electricity and internal combustion – derived from the burning of coal or petroleum or from splitting the atom – human beings today can, by the simple pushing of buttons, flicking of switches and turning of keys, flood their houses with light, communicate with people around the globe by phone, fax or e-mail, travel in comfort and safety in air-conditioned cars or planes or watch on television news events or athletic competitions occurring on the other side of the globe. "As the result of industrial civilization, not only do billions more people survive, but in the advanced countries they do so on a level far exceeding that of kings and emperors in all previous ages..."

The economist, George Reisman, points out that human beings have added man-made power to the paltry strength of human muscles and draft animals, power far greater than that found ready-made in nature in the form of wind and rushing or falling water. "This man-made power, and the energy released by its use" is the fundamental cause of our higher living standards, and is the result of advances in both theoretical and applied science and in technology. Man-made power is fundamentally human brain power applied to the specific issue of energy production.[16]

It was the vastly increased application of mind power in the form of then state-of-the-art technology that was the fundamental cause of Britain's dramatic economic growth during the Industrial Revolution. Industrialists of that era gradually introduced steam engines and power looms, canals and railroads, and numerous other technical advances. "The new mills of the post-war years were driven by steam instead of by water; improvements were made year after year in the mule and the spinning frame; the power loom was steadily taking the place of the less-efficient hand loom." Progress was similarly made in the field of coal mining. The use of iron tubbing and cast-iron rails, for example, made it possible to mine deeper and more economically. Ventilation in the mines was improved and, gradually, illumination. The steady evolution in the use of coke rather than charcoal in the smelting process resulted in greatly increased production of iron, which in turn encouraged building of every kind. Human brain power was transfiguring British life.[17]

Sanitation and Hygiene

The leading thinkers of the era also made significant progress in the fields of sanitation, sewage and hygiene, resulting in important health benefits and a rising expectancy of life.

Knowledge regarding sanitation, waste disposal and hygiene was scant prior to the Enlightenment, and improved only gradually over the 300 years between 1700 and the present. The problem of sewage mixing with drinking water is an old one that even in the 21st century plagues many countries of the non-industrialized world. Most people in the capitalist nations today do not realize that prior to the late 19th century it was often not safe to drink the water in their countries. The difficulty of obtaining clean drinking water was one reason that people on both sides of the Atlantic often consumed copious amounts of alcohol.

Historians of the period have written: "In Northern Europe and North America they drank beer, and in Southern Europe, wine. In London, beer was now brewed in industrial quantities." In England, even charity children were given beer. "Enormous quantities of spirits were drunk in the United States in the late 18th and still more in the 19th century, when people had more money." Spirits were generally bottled at 80 proof, and "during the 1830s the per capita consumption of absolute alcohol in America was calculated at 7.1 gallons annually." "Hence the name for America, the 'Alcohol Republic.'"[18]

The creation of a soft-drinks industry in the 19th century was, in part, a response to this problem. In the 1780s, a German-born Swiss citizen and amateur scientist named Jacob Schweppe perfected a process for carbonating water that cleansed it of dangerous impurities and duplicated the properties of sparkling spring water. With several partners, he founded a firm in Geneva to mass-produce his new soda water, and in 1792 in partnership with his daughter, Colette, established a plant in England.[19]

By 1807 soda water was being sold in draught and in bottles in the U.S.; "it was listed in the *US Pharmacopoeai* of 1820 as a 'medicated water,'" and by 1830 flavored syrup had been added. The next year a patent was issued for a machine enabling carbonated drinks to be sold across the counter, and the American drug store soda fountain was born. Schweppe's advance made possible both John Styth Pemberton's creation of Coca-Cola in 1886 – and Caleb D. Bradham's invention of "Brad's Drink" in the 1890s, a name he soon changed to Pepsi-Cola because he thought it could cure dyspepsia.[20]

In England, cleaner water came only gradually. Iron pipes, a product of the Industrial Revolution that enabled the introduction of iron water mains between 1756-60, were an improvement. Iron water mains became general only between 1810 and 1820. But the jointing was still defective, permitting contaminated surface water to seep into the pipes. Sewer and water mains, both defective, often ran near each other, and it was not infrequent for sewage to ooze into the water mains. It was only in the second half of the 19th century that the problem of adequate jointing was solved and new methods of waste detection devised.[21]

In 19th century London, much of the water came from the Thames, which still had so much sewage dumped into it that "the windows of the Houses of Parliament could never be opened because of the stench…" Unfortunately, this problem was not new. As one historian of the period put it: "Filth of every imaginable description accumulated indefinitely in the unpaved streets and in all available space and was trodden into the ground…the horrible conditions of the early 19th century towns were not a result of the new order but a terrible relic of the old."[22]

The problem of clean drinking water was finally solved in the Western nations in the late 19th century. In the 1870s and 1880s, Dr. Robert Koch, the German scientist who founded modern medical bacteriology, and other researchers established that germs existing in water were the causes of such fatal diseases as cholera and often of typhoid.[23]

After the Civil War, the United States became a leader in the science of water treatment, and by 1908 American water works were using chlorine as a disinfectant. Cholera and typhoid – major killers throughout history, including the 1832 and 1848 New York City cholera epidemics that caused the deaths of 8,000 people – were thereby eradicated from American life by the 1920s. The purifying capacity of chlorine was known as early as 1800, but the development of reservoirs with their attendant cleansing facilities and a vast delivery network of pipes required a great deal of money, as well as technical expertise. "Only as American cities and towns grew and prospered could they afford such an effort to protect their drinking water."

Tragically, in the non-industrialized nations of the world, the availability of such treated and clean drinking water is practically non-existent, causing widespread epidemics. According to the World Bank, in the 1990s fully one billion people had no clean drinking water, and in 1990 alone, over three million children under the age of five died from cholera, typhoid and chronic dysentery.[24]

The quest for upgraded human living standards was apparent not only in the quest for clean drinking water, but also in regard to improved personal hygiene. Well into the 19th century most people did not bathe regularly. This changed slowly in the industrial era, and the gradual introduction of soap, hot water boilers, toothpaste, etc., facilitated the drive toward cleanliness.[25]

Several contemporary economists point out the myriad ways in which technological and industrial development have cleansed the environment of the modern Western world, making it incomparably safer than it was for our ancestors. The cotton mills of the early Industrial Revolution, for instance, made possible an array of inexpensive clothes. The new cotton garments could be washed, and because they were manufactured in abundant supply their shortened life expectancy brought about by repeated washings was not a problem. By contrast, the woolen clothes that preceded the cheaper cotton ones could not be washed for two reasons: they shrunk – and, existing in short supply, they were expensive. Consequently, washing or any other process that shortened their life expectancy imposed serious financial burdens on the poor. As a direct result of the new cotton mills the poor wore cleaner clothes, with the health benefits that followed from living with reduced numbers of lice, germs and other vermin.[26]

The human body today is incomparably cleaner than it was in pre-industrial societies, because private, profit-seeking companies manufacture a wide variety of cleansing agents, including bath soap, toothpaste, mouth wash, shampoo, toilet tissue and others. When William Procter and James Gamble became business partners in 1837 in Cincinnati, for example, their soap manufacturing company already had 14 other soap and candle makers in the city with whom to compete. In 1879, James Norris Gamble, son of the founder and a trained chemist, developed an inexpensive white bath soap of high quality that the company named Ivory. By 1890, Procter and Gamble was selling more than 30 different types of soap, including detergent for washing clothes.

In the meantime, Fred Maytag of Maytag Washers had come out with the "Hired Girl," the first mechanically powered washing machine, in 1909. By 1923, Maytag, originally an Iowa-based firm manufacturing farm machinery, had dropped all other products but washers, and had popularized its advertising slogan, "Dirty clothes know no season."[27]

By the late 19th century, American capitalism, under the influence of the advancing knowledge of the day, had become a dynamo of effective sanitary and personal hygiene products. The Standard Sanitary Manufacturing Company, one of the firms later consolidated to form American Standard, pioneered the use of many plumbing improvements at the turn of the 20th century, including the one-piece toilet.

Related to this, in 1879, Clarence and Edward Irvin Scott started a pushcart paper jobbing business in Philadelphia based on their pooled $300.00 savings. Soon realizing that the development of indoor plumbing was the trend of the future, the Scotts chose to concentrate their paper company on the production of bathroom tissue. In 1907, Scott Paper Products – based on insight gained from a defective roll of paper, one too heavy and wrinkled to be used as toilet tissue – introduced the first paper towels to be used for household cleansing.[28]

In 1873, the soap company founded decades earlier by immigrant, William Colgate, introduced Colgate Dental Cream in a jar, and in 1896, packaged it in the collapsible tubes still used today. In later years, such toothpaste manufacturers as Colgate continued to research the product, and introduced fluoride into the compound to protect the teeth against decay, a significant step forward in dental hygiene. Related to this, when the Lambert Pharmaceutical Company of St. Louis introduced an antiseptic mouthwash in 1880, they named it "Listerine," in honor of the great British medical man and champion of antiseptic medical practices, Joseph Lister.

Like their bodies, people's houses today are cleansed with soaps, disinfectants and vacuum cleaners that did not exist in the pre-capitalist eras. Although men in the industrial age's early days had just begun to recognize the health benefits of cleanliness and still lacked the products to promote it, it was the Enlightenment philosophy and the Industrial Revolution it spawned that gradually made both possible. Historically, capitalism and industrialization are the great practical cleansing agents of mankind.[29]

It is reasonable to assume that the improvements in sanitation, hygiene and the beginning of the application to medicine of the new empirical method contributed to the period's declining death rate. "Between 1740 and 1820 the death-rate [of England] fell almost continuously – from an estimated 35.8 [per thousand] for the ten years ending in 1740 to one of 21.1 for those ending in 1821." Further, the evidence, though sketchy, points to a steady decline in the British child mortality rate during the late 18th and early 19th centuries. Presumably, some part of that decline is attributable to improved hygienic conditions and the drives toward first inoculation, and later, vaccination.[30]

Rising Life Expectancy

Based on these economic, sanitary and medical improvements, it is not surprising that the average life expectancy of Britain rose. For example, in 1541, the English life expectancy was 33.75 years. It rose and fell thereafter within a limited range – but in 1761, on the eve of the

Industrial Revolution, it was still merely 34.23 years. It had increased, on average, less than .5 of one year in greater than two centuries. By contrast, in 1811, it was 37.59; in 1851, it had climbed to 39.54; and in 1871, to 41.31. During the Industrial Revolution, the average expectancy of life increased by greater than seven years in the course of just over a century. By the turn of the 19th century, the trend was clearly upwards. "It is clear that a steady advance begins just after the turn of the 19th century, and accelerates after about 1871-5."

The pre-industrial period could generate only minor fluctuations in life expectancy, averaging in the mid-to-high 30s, but the Industrial Revolution created a sustained upward movement. "People lived longer because they were better nourished and sheltered, and cleaner, and thus were less vulnerable to infectious…diseases…that were peculiarly susceptible to improved living standards." The industrial era initiated a gradual but steady march upward regarding English life expectancy, which is currently 74.7 years on average for men and 80.2 for women. "It took thousands of years to increase life expectancy at birth from just over 20 years to the high 20s. Then in just the past two centuries, the length of life…in the advanced [i.e., industrialized] countries jumped from less than 30 years to perhaps 75 years."

These significant gains are further augmented by the realization that they were achieved during a period of steady population shift from rural areas to large towns. In 1670, only 13.5 percent of the English population lived in towns numbering residents of greater than 5,000. But by 1770, the figure stood at 21 percent, and by 1801, at 27.5 percent. Bearing in mind that towns always had a higher mortality rate than the countryside, "the fact that the average aggregate life-expectancy increased by about six years between c. 1680 and 1820 is therefore remarkable."[31]

Based on the advances in industry and manufacturing, in transportation, in sanitation and personal hygiene, the general death rate and the child mortality rate fell while the birth rate rose. The result, of course, was a spectacular rise in Britain's population. In 1771, England's population was 6,447,813 and growing slowly; since 1541, it had never reached a growth rate above 5.79 percent per 5-year period (which it reached only once), and it had seven such time periods in which population actually declined. As a benchmark, in 1671 its population had been 4,982,687, which means it grew by roughly a third in the century prior to the Industrial Revolution.

But in 1871, after close to 100 years of industrialization, the country's population was a staggering 21,500,720; it more than tripled in the first century of the industrial era, consistently reaching growth rates exceeding 6 percent (and sometimes reaching 7 and even 8 percent) for virtually every 5-year period of the 19th century up to 1871. Consumer goods necessary for the sustenance of life were now produced in vastly greater quantities and the early 19th century beginning of a sustained rise in real wages meant that parents could support their children at a higher standard of living.[32]

Recognition that the per capita standard of living rose in England in the midst of this explosion of population is perhaps the greatest tribute that can be paid to the extraordinary productivity of industrial capitalism. It undoubtedly would have still constituted a great achievement if per capita consumption had merely remained steady while the population rocketed upward. For researchers to refer to per capita growth of consumption as "slow" in such circumstances is to drop the full context in which it occurred and to fail to grasp the historic meaning of the phenomenon: capitalism, even in its infancy, refuted the Malthusian notion that population growth inevitably outstrips productivity.

Tragically, Malthus was and remains correct regarding all pre-capitalist and non-capitalist systems, where abysmal destitution and literal starvation remain the norm. But in such capitalist societies as Hong Kong, where, in the late 20th century, population density was 185 times greater than that of the U.S., an extremely large population relative to area is no danger to living standards, because the rates of productivity are so high.[33]

The Enlightenment principle of critical intelligence applied in a context of political-economic freedom with the goal of raising the human standard of living and life expectancy led as fully to the revolutions in sanitation, hygiene and medicine as it did to the similar revolutions in technology, industry and manufacturing. The Industrial Revolution and the sanitary-hygienic-medical advances were offspring of the same intellectual parent – and delivered the same salutary result.

A summary of the above points shows that by the 19th century's first half England was experiencing rising real wages, increasing life expectancy and "slow" growth of per capita living standards amidst an explosion of its population. The Latin legal phrase comes to mind, *res ipsa loquitur* – "The thing speaks for itself."

Child Labor

But the aspect of the Industrial Revolution's early days that is especially criticized by anti-capitalist historians is the use of child labor. The British historian, E.P. Thompson, for example, in his scholarly 1963 book *The Making of the English Working Class*, agrees with the Hammonds and the earlier pessimists. He states that, "there was a drastic increase in the intensity of exploitation of child labor between 1780 and 1840, and every historian acquainted with the sources knows that this is so." Child labor during this period, he concludes, "was one of the most shameful events in our history." Professor Thompson proceeds, as did numerous pessimist historians before him, to recount a series of grisly stories and anecdotes regarding the conditions and treatment of children in the factories. But numerous scholars express serious doubts regarding the reliability of such anecdotal evidence.[34]

For one thing, many of these anecdotes date from the Sadler Committee, established by Parliament in 1832, which presented such a depressing tale regarding the factory children. The American economist,

Clark Nardinelli, however, pointed out that Sadler's colleague, Richard Oastler (and others) handpicked witnesses and coached them regarding their answers to Sadler's questions, ensuring that Sadler received the anti-factory responses he sought. Further, the British historian, W.H. Hutt, reminded readers that Sadler's witnesses did not testify under oath, a serious defect given the religious convictions of the day. Even Engels criticized the report of the Sadler Committee, describing it as containing in large part, "the most distorted and erroneous statements."[35]

But the argument supporting capitalism does not depend on these depressing accounts being false (and some of them, presumably, are true.) The logical error, so often committed, lies in ripping a phenomenon out of its historical context and analyzing it independently of the causal factors that gave rise to it. The employment of children in the factories cannot be understood apart from the conditions of childhood and child labor in the periods leading up to the Industrial Revolution. That conditions in the factories were ghastly by current standards – and that young children employed there worked exhaustingly long hours – is not to be questioned. But it must be recognized that prior conditions were worse – significantly so – and that the factory system was an important and necessary step in improving the conditions of life for English children.

The horrendous, virtually ubiquitous poverty of pre-capitalist England has already been documented. As an economic necessity, children were put to work at a very young age, as they still are today all over the non-capitalist world. The conditions of life and work were abysmal by current standards.

The worst conditions were for foundlings, orphans and abandoned children. Countless people subsisted at or near the starvation level, and for them a child was an intolerable financial burden whose support could not be undertaken. Such children over the years and centuries, by the tens of thousands, were left to the tender mercies of the poor houses. The poor houses were, in a phrase, chambers of horrors.

If the father of a bastard was known, he was forced to pay a one-time fee for the parish – the local civil authority – to take the child off his hands. Often the parish officers dissipated the money in feasting – a practice called "saddling the spit" – then shunted the infant along with a tiny fee to a parish nurse, who generally permitted the baby to die of neglect. "The terrible mortality among infants entrusted to parish nurses encouraged parish officers to assume that the cost of maintenance would be small…" Such children, if and when they survived, "lived only…to swell the numbers of vagrants and beggars."[36]

Regarding starvation in the non-capitalist, agrarian areas, the 19th century British writer, William Cooke Taylor, stated: "we have seen children perishing from sheer hunger in the mud hovel, or in the ditch by the wayside." He stressed that agricultural laborers subsisted in the most abject poverty relative to the factory workers.

Compare Taylor's observations to the accounts offered by distinguished modern historians of existence prior to the capitalist era. "It is difficult for those living in the industrialized countries of the 20th century to imagine hunger and famine. People literally died of hunger, and it was not unusual to find men dead at the roadside, their mouths full of grass and their teeth sunk in the earth." Or: "Famine recurred so insistently for centuries on end that it became incorporated into man's biological regime and built into his daily life. Dearth and penury were continual and familiar, even in Europe…famine only disappeared from the West at the close of the eighteenth century, or even later."[37]

In response to such tragic loss of life among the poorhouse children, the authorities in the early 18th century established workhouses for the abandoned children to provide a minimum of industrial training. The workhouses aimed at being a kind of primitive factory. In the better ones, the children lived thirty or forty in a ward under the charge of a nurse, bunking two to a bed. They began work at 7 in the morning, "twenty under a mistress, to spin wool and flax, knit stockings," etc. This continued until 6 in the evening, with a break from noon until 1 for lunch and play. Some perfunctory attempt at education was sometimes included. Some children earned a halfpenny a day, some a penny, some four pence. More often, however, the nurses were "dirty and decrepit," and children slept six to eight in a bed.[38]

Before the age of 14, the parish children were apprenticed, essentially sold by the state to a master in exchange for a fee. The master took the apprentice and all of the apprentice's earnings until the younger man reached age 24. The Elizabethan Statute of Apprentices prohibited any man from working in a profession without having served at least a seven-year apprenticeship. Such an abrogation of the freedom of commerce was, of course, strenuously opposed by Adam Smith in *The Wealth of Nations*, and would eventually be wiped out by the Enlightenment commitment to individual rights, but this feudal legacy continued throughout most of the 18th century.

Terms were even worse for the parish children, whom the state sold into at least a 10-year period of indentured servitude. In his early years, the workhouse child belonged to the state; in his teen years, to his master. He possessed but few rights. The results of such a system were predictable.

"The master may be a tiger in cruelty, he may beat, abuse, strip naked, starve or do what he will to the poor innocent lad, few people take notice, and the officers [of the state] who put him out the least of anybody." The horror stories of the apprentice system, especially regarding the workhouse children, are extensive. These include frequent cases of poor masters murdering the indentured apprentices whose subsistence they could not afford.[39]

As the first factories came into existence, the practice of selling workhouse children into bondage continued. The early factories, prior to the development of steam energy, relied on water power, and were therefore constructed alongside country streams. It was difficult to attract a labor force to such remote, out-of-the-way areas. At the same time, poorhouse officials, especially in London, were desperate to free themselves from financial responsibility for the orphaned children under their jurisdiction. The government officials sent these children to the mills, per their traditional policy; the children were "bound by these officials into long terms of unpaid apprenticeship in return for bare subsistence." The first legislative act applied to factory children, the Apprentice Bill of 1802, was passed to protect just these unpaid, virtually enslaved apprentices.[40]

It must be stressed that government officials sending or selling human beings into involuntary servitude is many things, but capitalism is not one of them. The essence of capitalism, as described in Chapter One, is respect for individual rights and a consequent legal ban on the initiation of coercion. Only the government has the power to legally force men into involuntary servitude; no private individual or corporation, without such government backing, has that power.

The guild system, the legally enforced apprenticeships, the coerced binding of children into unpaid servitude – these are characteristics of feudalism that still remained in English society. "When feudalism reigned, men, women and children were indeed 'sold' at auction, forced to work long hours at arduous manual labor…This was the system of serfdom, and the deplorable system of parish apprenticeship was a remnant of Britain's feudal past." The growth of capitalism, with its principles of individual rights and limited government, would, in time, wipe out these feudal legacies.[41]

One, though by no means the only, superlative achievement of capitalism regarding child labor is that its creation of a free labor market ended the odious practice of apprenticeship. Eventually, as shall be seen, capitalism ended the age-old need for children to work at all.[42]

Regarding free labor, conditions were better. The free labor market, in protecting a man's liberty to choose an occupation and seek employment, was an embodiment of the principle of individual rights and the

Enlightenment spirit. Under capitalism, factory owners were free to offer jobs, and workers were free to accept or reject them. This included parents and their children.

The cotton mills, where the advancing technology increased the productivity of labor, were the largest employers of children. The young had performed many of the same tasks in the cottage industries at home, but now the power of machinery was added to the power of human effort. "The result was an increase in the productivity of child labor..." and an increase in real wages. In short, factory workers using power looms had far greater output than cottage weavers using handlooms; consequently, their earnings were higher.[43]

Finally, though factory hours were long, much of the work was physically undemanding, so that children could easily perform it. The most common job children performed in factories was known as "piecing," tying together loose strands of thread when the machine broke them. The work no doubt was repetitious and boring, and many children were on their feet for long hours, but compared to the grueling agricultural jobs many children held – such tasks as weeding, stone-picking and potato planting – factory work was physically light and far less exhausting. Indeed, children not as physically robust as their peers, but who nevertheless needed to work, were able to gain employment in the cotton factories precisely because of the physical lightness of the work there.[44]

As with children's agricultural work, the work in the cottage industries was generally conducted under worse conditions than those in the factories. For example, girls in the pillow lace and straw plait trades started work at four or five years of age, worked long hours habitually scrunched into cramped physical positions in overcrowded, poorly ventilated and often poorly lit cottages. Discipline was characteristically harsh: "some mistresses insisted upon the neck and arms being kept bare, so that the children could be 'slapped more easily'" – and since those mistresses received higher income who got the most work out of the girls, the plait schools generally contained "formidable looking sticks." The chronically poor posture required for the work had a harmful impact on the children's physiques; the intricate work under poor lighting on their eyes; and the unhygienic cottages on their health: "tuberculosis was a particular enemy of the young lacemakers." But farm laborers in some areas expected their daughters to go into these cottage trades as a matter of course, because the families needed the income.[45]

On a free labor market, where a diminishing but still significant poverty was widespread, parents and their children by the tens of thousands chose factory work over jobs in the fields or cottage industries. The reasons are obvious: higher pay for physically less demanding work. The reason for both was the introduction and use of what was then state-of-the-art technology, machinery which simultaneously lightened the workers' labor and boosted their productivity.

If work in the factories was not ideal, the other options available to those "who voted with their feet for factory work" were significantly worse. The factories attracted workers because of, not in spite of, the level of their wages – because wages were "well above the poverty level, and better than anything available elsewhere to an impoverished agricultural population." The most important point, generally ignored by the anti-capitalists, is: "the low wages, long hours, and oppressive discipline of the early factories are shocking in that the willingness of the inarticulate poor to work on such terms [and by the tens of thousands] bespeaks, more forcefully than the most eloquent words, the even more abysmal character of the alternatives they had endured in the past" – and of the other options available to them in the present. One anti-capitalist writer even states that the workers were "forced into the factories by the lure of higher wages." He is correct at least regarding the higher wages. "That factory workers received higher wages than either agricultural laborers or workers in domestic industry there can be no doubt."[46]

Finally, it was only the wealth created by roughly a century of capitalism that ended the age-old necessity for children to work. The percentage of child labor in the textile mills had been declining for decades prior to the years 1835-38, the period in which inspectors began to enforce the Factory Act passed by Parliament in 1833. The figures bear this out. In 1816, children under the age of 10 constituted 6.8 percent of the cotton industry's labor force, but by 1835 a mere 0.3 percent. Children under the age of 13 were an estimated 20 percent of the labor force in 1816, and but 13.1 percent in 1835. Similarly, there was a decline of those under the age of 18 in those years from 51.2 percent of the labor force to 43.4.

One reason for this was advancing technology. The advent of steam power meant that manufacturers no longer needed to locate near out-of-the-way streams for water power, but could now build in towns, reducing the difficulty of attracting an adult labor force, and thereby obviating the need for apprenticed workhouse children. Further, it must be remembered that the primary task of children in the factories was to piece together broken threads. But "as technological change led to improved machines there was less waste and fewer broken threads...and the relative demand for child labor decreased."[47]

But, eventually, it was the rising standard of living that led to the elimination of the practice. Real wages increased slowly and gradually throughout the Industrial Revolution, more rapidly after the conclusion of the Napoleonic Wars. As real income rose, parents made enough money to support their families, and children no longer needed to work. "The supply of children...was unambiguously decreasing as rising family incomes induced families to keep children out of the labor force until later ages."

After many centuries of child labor due to the destitution and stagnation of the feudal system, capitalism in scarcely one hundred years stamped out the necessity of that practice. Children no longer had to work to survive. "The emancipators and benefactors of those children were not legislators or factory inspectors, but manufacturers and financiers." Their capital accumulation and investments in machinery led to a steady rise in labor's productivity, to an abundance of inexpensive manufactured goods and to increasing real incomes. Removing the financial necessity for it was capitalism's second great achievement regarding child labor.[48]

In economic terms, capitalism ended both the demand for, and the supply of, child labor. Steam power made it possible to attract an adult labor force while improved machinery eliminated the primary tasks performed by children. Such developments caused diminished demand for child labor in the factories. At the same time, rising real wages among the workers made it unnecessary for children to work, thereby greatly decreasing the supply of children seeking jobs.

As a final point, child labor exists all over the non-capitalist world today. "Millions of children worldwide work in hazardous, poor conditions." The response in Western countries is often to seek to ban products made by child labor. But economist Kaushik Basu points out: "Many poor families depend on their children's incomes and send their children to work out of need rather than malice." In brief, the poor countries of the world are currently in the exact situation England was in prior to the Industrial Revolution and the development of capitalism.[49]

The author and his wife help to support a little girl in Tanzania through Childreach, one of numerous charity organizations attempting to aid children throughout the Third World. The Childreach literature abounds with heartbreaking true stories, such as that of a six year old girl who labors in the fields from dawn until sundown, receiving only a slice of bread and thirty-five cents a day. Or of a thirteen year old African orphan who can't go to school because he must work a plot of land in order to support both himself and his nine year old brother. Such societies are not merely in a pre-capitalist stage of development, but more fundamentally, are in a pre-Enlightenment stage. Only capitalism can eradicate such crushing poverty that necessitates child labor. But capitalism, as a political/economic system, is not fundamental; it is dependent on the intellectual and cultural principles discussed in Chapter One.[50]

Capitalism is, in fact, the only system that did or could raise workers' real wages to first eradicate destitution and then to create prosperity. But its critics accuse it of impoverishing the workers. Similarly, capitalism is the only system that did or could eradicate child labor, but its critics accuse it of exploiting children. Given the historical and contemporary records of capitalism, feudalism and socialism – the widespread abundance created by the first, and the miserable poverty by the latter two – the critics voice accusations in polar opposition to the truth. In critiquing the only political/economic system capable of eradicating the ills they decry, capitalism's antagonists speak volumes about the inability of their philosophy to comprehend and explain reality; they say nothing about capitalism.

An Error of Logic

The economist, Angus Maddison, writing in the 1980s, described the progress wrought in the leading capitalist nations – the United States, Great Britain, Japan, Australia, et al. – since 1820.

> In the past 160 years, the total product of the sixteen countries considered here has increased sixty-fold, their population more than four-fold, and their per capita product thirteen-fold. Annual working hours were cut from 3,000 to less than 1,700, which means that labor productivity increased about twenty-fold. Life expectation doubled from about thirty-five to over seventy years. I call this the 'capitalist epoch' because its main engine of growth has been the acceleration of technical progress, with capital formation as the major instrument by which it was exploited to increase output.[51]

Such facts show that there are serious errors in the thinking of capitalism's critics. One of these is the failure to examine the rise of capitalism in its full historical context. The critics of the factory system look at the workers toiling for low wages, and become indignant at the capitalist who pays them. They accuse him of exploitation. But the full truth is that these workers eagerly sought such work because it represented a significant advance in their living standard – and, in more than a few cases, it meant the difference between life and starvation.

There are two important facts regarding the industrial working class of this era. One is that it was poor. The other is that its living standard was gradually rising. The first is capitalism's inheritance from feudalism. The second is its own achievement. Capitalism's critics are guilty of a logical fallacy: they drop historical context. No event or phenomenon can be understood outside of the causal factors that give rise to it. The impoverished condition of the working class of this era is the direct result of the feudal system. To ignore this is to sweep aside the facts of its genesis. To then accuse capitalism of causing the poverty – while in the very act of eradicating it – is to commit both a historical error and a profound injustice.

The close correlations in the world today between freedom and prosperity — and between statism and destitution — were discussed above. Still, capitalism's enemies currently assail it as a system oppressive to the workers and the poor. They attack Asian factories affiliated with such American companies as Nike and The Gap as "sweatshops." The anti-capitalist agitators criticize Nike for paying Vietnamese workers an average daily wage of $1.60. Such an amount of money is truly miserable by the standards of modern capitalist countries. But what is it relative to the alternatives open to these workers elsewhere in their Communist, socialist or feudal economies?

According to the World Bank, in 1998 more than 278 million people in East Asian countries subsisted on less than a dollar a day.

Communist Vietnam is down at the bottom of the list regarding prosperity. If a 260-day work year is assumed, then $1.60 per day adds to $416.00 per year, significantly above the $250.00 per year income that many in Bangladesh, Vietnam and other countries subsist on. No wonder Nike has no difficulty attracting workers into its employ. It is paying wages quite a bit higher than what is available to these laborers elsewhere in the oppressive feudal or Communist societies in which they live.

But no such hypothetical calculation needs to be taken as the final word. The actual facts of Vietnamese living conditions redound even more greatly to capitalism's credit – for the minimum wage there averages out to $134 annually while Nike's workers receive on average $670. In Indonesia, Nike's subsidiaries pay an average of $720 annually in contrast to the minimum wage which totals $241. "In the poorest developing countries, someone working for an American employer draws no less than eight times the average national wage." Further, foreign companies in the poorest countries pay their workers, on average, twice what the corresponding native firms pay.

The difference, of course, is the technology made possible by the greater capital invested by American and other Western firms, which raises the productivity of each worker. Similarly, the more modernized plants of the American companies translate to better and safer working conditions. Technology and industrial mechanization – the achievements of the minds of men made possible by freedom – are raising living standards in 21st century Asia just as they did in 18th century Europe.[52]

The real problem in Third World countries is not that Western companies "exploit" their workers – they do not; it is that indigenous dictatorial regimes – whether communist, socialist, theocratic, feudal or military – oppress their own citizens. The moral imperative is not to pressure Nike, et. al., into "better treatment" of its employees; it is to overthrow the communist, theocratic or military despots and establish capitalism, the only system that respects the rights of the individual.

The Capitalist Manifesto

The "Asian Tigers"—Japan, Hong Kong, Taiwan, South Korea and Singapore—are important examples. In the post-World War II period, these nations, often under America's guidance and/or protection, moved toward capitalist or semi-capitalist political-economic systems. As a result, these became comparatively the freest and wealthiest nations of Asia—most likely in the history of Asia. (See Chapter 11.)

The parallel between the pre-capitalist European economies of the 18th century and the pre-capitalist Asian economies of the 20th and 21st centuries is striking. In both, state-dominated economies led to destitute conditions or worse. In both, capitalists opened factories to which workers flocked because the wages offered were significantly higher than what was otherwise available to them. In both, the factory system was denounced by anti-capitalist writers as "exploitative." Regarding both, capitalism's critics are guilty of the logical fallacy of context-dropping. If they were truly concerned with helping the poor, they would criticize the statist political systems responsible for causing the poverty. They would not attack the germinating capitalism that begins to relieve it.

Voting With Their Feet

Related to this, it is necessary to understand the common practice known as people "voting with their feet." Marxist intellectuals and politicians (and other opponents of capitalism) typically do not like this practice for the simple reason that people generally vote for things that Marxists do not think they should vote for – such things as freedom, capitalism and prosperity. Looking back over recent history from early in the 21st century, it is apparent how many poor immigrants "voted" to emigrate to America (or other capitalist nations), escaping from Marxist regimes and sundry dictatorships, including heartbreaking attempts to float on doors and various unseaworthy "craft" from Cuba to Florida.

Poor parents and children voting for the factories over work in the fields and cottages are examples of the same principle: human beings rationally assess the alternatives open to them and then volitionally opt for that which best serves their lives and furthers their goals. Sometimes these rational decisions are made under terrible external circumstances that include severe poverty. Nevertheless, it is "choice," it is "freedom," it is "rational self-interest." But Marxists call it "exploitation."[53]

The philosophical point is that human beings have rational faculties or minds of their own – and that destitution does not invalidate their capacities to think or choose or to make informed decisions. For example, countless millions of starving (not to mention actually exploited and oppressed) people have made the rational, life-enhancing decision to emigrate to freer lands. Being poor means that one has no money, not that one has no brains. That most people desire to live well, and recognize political/economic freedom as a necessary condition of satisfying such a desire is precisely the reason that totalitarian states close their borders. The Fascist/Communist despots recognize that rational men and women by the millions – poor, starving and oppressed – would otherwise choose to flee. And still, despite armed borders and the murder of emigrants, the victims of totalitarianism continue to rationally choose escape and freedom.

Most human individuals do not suffer from the tragic ailment of brain damage. Consequently, they themselves – not an external authority – are preeminently suited to decide what is best for them. That tens of thousands of poor parents and children in England in the early days of the Industrial Revolution chose the factories over alternative forms of employment demonstrates only that in their judgment the factories were the best – or perhaps the least objectionable – place for children to work. The economic facts bear out their assessment. This exact point is true of poor workers seeking jobs in factories owned by American companies in Third World countries today. Understandably, all of these individuals, not Marxist intellectuals, knew (and know) what was (and is) best for them.

The Capitalist Manifesto

Two related conclusions must be persistently stressed: 1.) capitalism and the Industrial Revolution were integral components of the Enlightenment's commitment to applied rationality as the means of promoting practical improvements in man's life on earth; 2.) it was this full Enlightenment program that constituted (and continues to constitute) a revolution in human life.

It is because capitalism is the system of the Enlightenment that, in the 19th century, the world's leadership in applied science and industrialization shifted from Great Britain, the mother of the Enlightenment, to the United States, the child born of that mother. The child, upon reaching young maturity, launched a skyrocket of exploding advances that fulfilled its Enlightenment origins and promise. That child, in the post-Civil War period, became the most progressive nation of history.

Summary

The British Industrial Revolution led to higher real wages for British workers; and rising living standards, declining mortality rates and increased life expectancies for the British population in general. Additionally, the rising real wages finally put an end to the need for child labor that had persisted for centuries under the pre-capitalist systems.

Anti-capitalist writers commit the fallacy of dropping historical context when they blame the excruciating poverty of the Industrial Revolution's early days on the new-born capitalist system. They further fail to understand the volitional nature of human beings as manifested in the phenomenon of individuals repeatedly "voting with their feet" for various aspects of capitalism.

5: The Inventive Period

The hallmark of a capitalist society is a principled commitment to freedom — an across-the-board protection of individual rights. Has such a society ever existed in human history? Not yet — but mankind came close to achieving this ideal in the United States of the late 19th century. This period — from the 13th Amendment ending slavery in 1865 until the growing influence of the so-called Progressives early in the 20th century, in which the government accelerated its policy of restricting and regulating productive businesses — is the freest period of the freest country in history.

In 1902, Attorney General Knox, acting under the orders of President Theodore Roosevelt, announced a federal case designed to break up the Hill-Morgan-Harriman super trust, the Northern Securities Company. Though James J. Hill pointed out that his railroads had greatly helped to open up the economic development of the Northwest and carried freight at the lowest rates, the Supreme Court disregarded such facts, ruling in 1904 that Northern Securities stood in violation of the Sherman Anti-Trust Act and had to be broken up. The Northern Securities Case, as a landmark application of the Sherman Act and, more broadly, of Progressive anti-free market principles, can be seen symbolically as the end of the era of almost unfettered capitalism in the United States. The movement toward statism, toward increased government regulation and control of productive men and their activities, accelerated after this.

But in the years between the end of the Civil War and the turn of the 20th century, the legal initiation of force was at a historic all-time low, certainly in the northern states. Given recognition of the mind's role in promoting advance, and of its non-negotiable need of freedom, one would predict a torrential outpouring of creative achievements. What, in fact, was the practical result of such freedom?

The 19th century in America was the single greatest era of technological and industrial advance in history. Americans of this period invented the telegraph, the reaper and the sewing machine. They created skyscrapers, perfected the suspension bridge, controlled typhoid and yellow fever, invented the camera, the phonograph, the electric light, the motion picture projector and, early in the 20th century, the television. Innovative Americans revolutionized transportation by commercializing the automobile and inventing the airplane. They created vast industries in steel and oil and constructed a transcontinental railroad. In manufacturing, they developed the method of mass production that brought modern inventions to millions. These advances greatly raised the country's standard of living – and, eventually, large areas of the world.

The world center of technological progress and industrial development shifted from Great Britain to the United States in the final third of the 19th century. In effect, although the technological and industrial revolutions were born in Britain, they reached their full fruition in America.

An Extraordinary Outpouring of Genius

A brief survey of the period makes clear its extraordinary achievements. For example: Thomas Edison's (1847-1931) contributions are legendary. His first great creation was the quadruplex telegraph in 1874, an improvement on Samuel Morse's (1791-1872) telegraph, which was itself a superlative innovation of 19th century America. The quadruplex permitted multiple messages to be sent in the same direction simultaneously over the same wire.

Edison continued his extraordinary career with the invention of the phonograph (1877), the incandescent light (1879), the electric power plant (1882), the motion picture camera (1893), the storage battery (1909) and numerous other devices. He also coordinated movies with phonographic sound to create the world's first "multi-media" presentation. This greatest of all inventors, a productive fiend, once said of himself that he had worked 18 hours a day for 45 years. When he was age 75, his wife cut down on his work time – she only permitted him to work 16 hours a day. Once, Edison was asked by a prospective employee regarding pay and working conditions. Imagine the reaction of a 21st century union leader to Edison's answer: "We don't pay anything and we work all the time." But great though Edison's contributions were, he was by no means alone in exemplifying the scientific, technological and industrial genius of the period. He had numerous comrades.[1]

Alexander Graham Bell (1847-1922) invented the telephone in 1876, a device that would soon revolutionize the field of communications. Bell, a Scottish immigrant who taught at his father's school for the deaf in Boston, applied for a patent a scant two hours before rival inventor, Elisha Gray, on February 14th, 1876. Though the invention was lauded later that year at the Philadelphia Centennial Exposition by no less a scientist than William Thomson (later Lord Kelvin), the newly organized Bell Telephone Association struggled financially. Sixteen months after Bell's invention, there were a mere 778 telephones in use. Discouraged, the inventor and his backers approached Western Union with an offer to sell for $100,000, but the corporation refused. "What use could this company make of an electrical toy?" the firm's president snorted. Two years later, Western Union would have gladly paid $25,000,000 for the patent rights.

Edison's invention of the carbon microphone, "which greatly increased the volume of sound transmitted," was only one of the subsequent innovations that contributed to the development of modern telephone technology. (In England, Edison's version of the telephone was known as "the shouting telephone," because of its greater volume and clear articulation.) It took almost 40 years, but in 1915 the first transcontinental telephone line was completed. Bell in the East spoke to his old research assistant, Thomas Watson, on the West Coast. He repeated his by-then famous first words over the telephone: "Mr. Watson, please come here. I want you." Watson replied: "It would take me a week now." Bell's invention was making possible instantaneous global verbal communication.[2]

In less than a decade following the telephone's creation, the distinctively American architectural form of the skyscraper was born in Chicago. One practical factor giving impetus to the new mode of construction was the catastrophic Chicago Fire which raged between October 8th and 10th of 1871, burning 18,000 buildings to the ground. The bustling town on the shores of Lake Michigan was only further energized by the disaster. The Midwestern metropolis has been described as "the only great city in the world to which all of the citizens have come for the avowed purpose of making money." Appropriately, commercial Chicago then saw "architects descend on the stricken city from all directions," for large areas had to be completely rebuilt and tall buildings could be hugely profitable in "big, concentrated commercial city centers."

The problem of elevators had already been solved by Elisha Graves Otis, whose earlier invention of a safety device removed the hazard from ascent and descent. Otis established a factory in Yonkers, New York and in 1861 patented and manufactured his steam elevator. The problem of creating inexpensive steel for construction was solved by Andrew Carnegie, whose vast production was based on enormous new economies of scale. Carnegie employed "larger plants, greater economies, the regular replacement of older equipment by the newest – costing less to operate – and new methods." These innovations in steel manufacturing made towering steel-frame structures affordable to build.

The brilliant engineer, William Lebaron Jenney (1832-1907) erected the 10-story Home Insurance Company Building in 1884-85 – with steel girders supplied by Carnegie – the first "building of true skyscraper design or 'cage construction,'" earning him the designation "father of the skyscraper." The renowned architect Louis Sullivan (1856-1924) worked briefly for Jenney and best represented Chicago's phoenix-like rise from the ashes: in the years from 1887-95, his office received 90 important commissions, including the 10-story Chicago Auditorium Building in which he decided to house his own office. The exuberantly confident American spirit created the term "skyscraper," as well as its concrete reality; a January 13, 1889 article in the Chicago Tribune was entitled "Chicago's Skyscrapers."[3]

During the years that steel and concrete buildings tall enough to "scrape the sky" were conceived – and at a time when Trinity Church was still the tallest structure in New York City – John Roebling (1806-1869) perfected the design of suspension bridges and began his masterpiece – the Brooklyn Bridge. Roebling, a German immigrant who had studied philosophy with Hegel at Berlin, founded a Trenton, New Jersey factory manufacturing iron wire, which later became the first American firm to produce steel wire rope. He was an inventor, as well as an engineer, and "designed every piece of machinery in [his] mill." Known to friends and acquaintances as a "man of iron," he worked inexhaustibly, never owned himself beaten, regarded illness as "a moral offense" and refused to rest. "In all his working life John Roebling had never been known to take a day off." He earned a fortune from the company that he created "from nothing" – he was a millionaire in the 1860s – and built bridges and aqueducts across the northeast.

Tragically, Roebling died as a result of an accident that occurred at the outset of the Brooklyn project, but his son, Washington, and daughter-in-law, Emily Warren Roebling, carried the monumental undertaking to fruition. It took the entire decade of the 1870s and cost Washington Roebling years of suffering from a severe case of caisson's disease and a nervous disorder, but by 1883 the epic struggle had been won and the world's biggest, longest, busiest suspension bridge was opened to traffic. Fittingly, much of the wire used in the bridge's construction, as well as in the later George Washington and Golden Gate Bridges, was manufactured by John Roebling's Sons, the company established by the bridge's designer. (The firm also supplied "nearly all [the] cable" used by the Otis Elevator Company, contributing to the great age of skyscraper construction. The company held "the first rank...as manufacturers of wire rope," earning millions for Roebling's sons. Washington Roebling's "own estate would be approximately $29 million.")

The bridge greatly expedited traffic across the East River between the two growing cities of Brooklyn and New York, handling 37,000 people daily by the time it was a year old and half a million per day 25 years later. Today, 120 years after its completion, the refurbished bridge carries more than 121,000 cars and trucks a day. According to the engineers who maintain it, with normal maintenance the great bridge will last another century. But, they say, if parts are replaced from time to time – "it will last forever."[4]

Roebling's achievement with the Brooklyn Bridge is famous, but today we rarely hear mentioned many of the innovative thinkers who invented life-enhancing devices and thereby carried mankind to a new level of prosperity. During the 1830s, for example, Cyrus McCormick (1809-1884) invented an improved reaping machine in Virginia. McCormick was unrelenting. When Virginia farmers showed little interest in his machine, he canvassed the midwest with greater success. When sales of his reaper were slow, he introduced new marketing methods, including warranties and public demonstrations of his product. "When the Great Chicago Fire demolished his huge factory, he ordered a new and larger one built even before the cinders were cool." He opened a temporary factory office the following day, and followed this shortly with temporary manufacturing facilities. McCormick was hardly the only manufacturer working on improved farming equipment, but his career is an excellent example of the increasing "technologization" of American farming with its consequent higher yield and lower price of foodstuffs for all Americans.[5]

Elias Howe (1819-1867) invented the sewing machine and – after years of litigation – grew rich on the royalties from his patent. Charles Goodyear (1800-1860) pioneered the process of vulcanization that made rubber useful. Unfortunately, he was a dreamer regarding monetary affairs, who lavishly spent borrowed money and occupied a Parisian debtor's prison for awhile. He lived in an attic surrounded by "pots of white lead, rubber, shellac and miscellaneous chemicals." Becoming hopelessly smeared with gum and chemical stains, he "clothed himself from head to toe in his experimental rubber." Somebody gave a famous description of him at this time: "If you meet a man who has on an Indian rubber cap, stock, coat, vest and shoes, with an Indian rubber money purse without a cent of money in it, that is he." In 1852, his lawyer, the great Daniel Webster, helped him win a patent infringement case before the U.S. Circuit Court in New Jersey, and he began to make a modicum of money. But his profligacy was incurable and he died owing $200,000. Nevertheless, his process was instrumental in the development of automobile tires, and his name justly became widely known.[6]

Isaac Merritt Singer (1811-1875), inventor and sometime actor, improved Elias Howe's sewing machine in 1850. Exhausted after days and nights of steady effort, Singer and his financial backer tested his prototype, which failed. "Sick at heart," Singer and his friend Zieber walked back to the cheap hotel room they shared. But in the course of conversation, it struck Singer that he had neglected to adjust the tension on the needle thread. They hurried back to the shop, adjusted the machine, and tried again. It worked perfectly.

The Capitalist Manifesto

The Singer sewing machine was an enormous success, for its inventor was equally innovative as a businessman, introducing such practices as installment buying, advertising campaigns and service with sales. His improved machine made possible the manufacture of inexpensive clothing for millions, and provided productive employment for untold numbers of penniless immigrants.

Singer conducted a messy, even bizarre, personal life in which he simultaneously had a legitimate family with the wife who left but never divorced him, a second with a woman who believed she was his common-law wife, and two other separate illegitimate families under assumed names. It is more than an irony that a man who conducted his personal life so irrationally – a cad who deceived and used women shamelessly – invented a machine that raised the standard of living of millions, especially women. For in his professional life as an inventor and entrepreneur, Singer was representative of the Enlightenment rationality that so imbued this era of innovativeness, a real-life illustration of the moral principle that a man's pursuit of his rational self-interest benefits others. [7]

In the mid-19th century, the American entrepreneur, Cyrus Field (1819-1892) directed one of the epic struggles of the modern era: the 13-year battle to lay the trans-Atlantic telegraph cable. Field, who had been so successful in the paper business that he had retired after nine years at age 33, set up the New York, Newfoundland and London Telegraph Company; and although Peter Cooper, builder of the first American steam locomotive, was president, and Samuel Morse – the telegraph's inventor – vice-president, "Field was the driving force of the enterprise."

From the beginning, the endeavor was plagued with disruptions: violent storms scattered the company's ships, the cable repeatedly snapped, the U.S. Civil War intruded on commercial construction, Field's warehouse burned and his company went bankrupt. Forty times, Field crisscrossed the Atlantic, "when such crossings took the better part of a month and were far from comfortable." In 1865, the owners of the gargantuan *Great Eastern*, designed by the pioneering engineer, Isambard Kingdom Brunel – and five times the size of any previous ship – "made Field a sporting offer: Let Field use the ship as a cable layer. If she failed, there should be no charge for her use; if she succeeded, the syndicate should receive $250,000 in cable stock." Though the mammoth vessel performed admirably, a defective piece of cable caused it to snap after fully two-thirds had been successfully laid. Finally, in 1866, after 12 million dollars and repeated misfirings, Field and his crew succeeded in laying the transoceanic cable, making possible quick telegraphic communication between Europe and North America.[8]

George Westinghouse (1846-1914), a young man by the time Field achieved his goal, introduced numerous inventions in various fields, but concentrated on the railroad industry. Before the age of 20, he created the "railroad frog," an invention that permitted trains to switch tracks. His most famous advance was the air brake, invented around 1866, which became a standard feature on all trains. At the time, the greatest railroading problem was stopping trains efficiently, the lack of an effective means of which caused many accidents. Westinghouse conceived his idea while reading a magazine story regarding the use of compressed air to bore a tunnel in Switzerland. But at first, the air brake was not taken seriously. "The idea was called 'foolhardy,' earning young Westinghouse the nickname 'Crazy George.' The brake was termed 'impossible,' 'unsound' and 'nonsense.'" Nobody was interested in funding the 20-year-old's innovation, not even his own father, who advised him to find a more practical line of work. Eventually, a friend, Ralph Baggaley, provided sufficient funding to outfit a locomotive and four cars with air brakes. Railroad officials examined the new device, but for months nothing happened. Finally, W.W. Card, Superintendent of the Steubenville Division of the Panhandle Railroad liked what he saw and convinced his superiors to schedule a test run – provided Westinghouse assumed all expenses and accepted all the risk.

The Capitalist Manifesto

On the day of the test, Westinghouse, Baggaley and Card all boarded the train. Incredibly, despite the railroad's measures to keep the track clear, as the train emerged from the Grant Hill Tunnel in Pittsburgh a wagon two blocks ahead blocked the line. The horses reared in fright, throwing the driver to the track. "Crazy George's" brake was applied, and the train stopped a bare four feet from the terrified driver. The train's passengers, some of whom were bruised and angry from the jolting they'd received, raced outside to see what had happened. When they realized the truth, their anger turned to congratulations. The "absurd" and "unsound" invention had worked. Subsequently, Westinghouse, Baggaley and Card met with prominent railroad officials; the result was the formation of the Westinghouse Airbrake Company, with Westinghouse as President, Baggaley as Vice-President and Card as General Agent. This story is but one example illustrating the truth of Austrian economist Joseph Schumpeter's claim that capitalism is driven forward by daring, risk-taking entrepreneurs.[9]

Westinghouse developed hundreds of innovations, acquired more than 400 patents, founded the Westinghouse Electric Company in 1886 and, together with the Croatian immigrant Nikola Tesla (1856-1943), pioneered the use of alternating current (AC) power in the United States. Tesla invented the AC induction generator in the 1880s, the first practical motor powered by alternating current. He sold the patent to Westinghouse, who put it to commercial use in the first major AC power plant built at Niagara Falls in 1895. Westinghouse hired Tesla, and together they demonstrated that alternating current was able to generate electrical power over great distances more economically than the direct current favored by Edison. Because American capitalism provided the freedom to compete, the superior power system won out, even against Edison's established name and great reputation. Westinghouse himself became a millionaire (from the air brake) before he was thirty, and went on to earn a vast fortune from his inventions and the manufacturing companies he originated.[10]

Likewise, during this period George Eastman (1854-1932) forever changed photography with the invention of a new type of camera, the Kodak. Several years after young George's father died in 1862, he left school at age 14 to work full-time as an insurance firm's messenger boy for three dollars a week. He studied accounting at night and by age 19 the company hired him as a junior clerk. But photography soon replaced accounting as his first love. What started as a hobby shortly became a vocation and obsession, and Eastman turned his mother's kitchen in their Rochester, New York home into a laboratory, where he experimented through the long nights after work, seeking an innovative method of dry-plate photography. "Upon leaving the bank each day he carried on experiments from 3 P.M. until breakfast. Mornings, his mother found him asleep on the floor."

In 1884, he patented the first film in roll form to prove practical. In 1888, he revolutionized photography by introducing his Kodak camera, a portable box camera that eliminated the need for expensive, bulky equipment. "In 1900, Eastman introduced the product that forever established Kodak's presence in the public imagination: the Kodak Brownie camera. Selling for one dollar each, the [small and convenient] Brownie could be afforded by almost anyone. As the new century dawned, the poor young man from Rochester was a millionaire many times over, and the leader of an industry that would transform the modern world."[11]

On the eve of the 20th century, America's technological advances were only beginning. Though Charles and Frank Duryea of Illinois, who built their first car in Massachusetts in 1893, are often credited as inventing the automobile, engineers in Germany and France had been experimenting with gas powered cars for several years before that. But it was Henry Ford who made the new means of transportation commercially viable.

The Capitalist Manifesto

On the morning of June 4, 1896, Ford (1863-1947), a machinist at the Detroit Electric Company, battered down the brick wall of his rented garage with an axe and drove out his first car, a hand-built product of seven years of working nights. Others, of course, had already built and run cars, but Ford began the Ford Motor Company in 1903 and made the automobile a commercial reality. Though at that time, the auto was a mere plaything of the rich – Woodrow Wilson scornfully termed it the "new symbol of wealth's arrogance" – Ford was determined to cut its manufacturing cost and sell cars to middle class Americans. He succeeded, and soon millions of Americans drove automobiles.[12]

That same year of 1903, Wilbur (1867-1912) and Orville (1871-1948) Wright, two bicycle mechanics from Dayton, Ohio, who were self-educated regarding the principles of aeronautical engineering, accomplished the first controlled, powered flight of a heavier-than-air vehicle at Kitty Hawk, North Carolina. Starting in the summer of 1899, the Wrights had been studying aeronautics intensively – poring over Octave Chanute's *Progress in Flying Machines* and other books – and experimenting with flying devices. Both the automotive and aviation ages dawned in early 20th century America as a direct outgrowth of the achievements of the late 19th. As historian Charles Beard observed of America in the decades between 1865 and 1900: "Nearly every year between the close of the civil conflict and the end of the century witnessed some signal achievement in the realm of applied science."

In 1909, 24-year-old Clinton Peterkin proposed to Wilbur the formation of an American Wright company to manufacture Wright Flyers. Peterkin, whose first job was as a 15-year-old office boy for J.P. Morgan, initially convinced his former employer to invest. (Morgan later discreetly withdrew when he "learned that the other stockholders feared they would be overshadowed if that mighty mogul of twentieth-century finance sat on the board of directors.") The Wright Company was incorporated on November 22, 1909 with offices on Fifth Avenue in New

York City and manufacturing plant in Dayton, Ohio. In October of 1915, Orville (Wilbur died of typhoid in 1912) sold the company to a group of eastern capitalists for $1.5 million, took a consulting job with the company for $25,000 annually, and devoted himself again to aeronautical research.[13]

A little research provides an endless number of stories of inventive men. Charles Steinmetz (1865-1923), a German immigrant, went to work for General Electric (a firm based on Edison's pioneering work) as its first director of research and development and, in the 1890s, pioneered both the spread of electrical networks and the rise of the corporate research lab. Willis Carrier (1876-1950) realized, as he stood in a Pittsburgh train station one night in 1902, that air could be dried by saturating it with water, to induce condensation. He built his first air conditioner that year.

Robert Goddard (1882-1945), in 1899, had a vision of space flight while sitting in a tree, and devoted his life to that goal. Years later, he shot off the world's first liquid-fueled rocket, and eventually his rockets reached 8,000 feet. All later achievements of the space age are based on his work. Edwin Howard Armstrong (1890-1954), was fascinated by radio from childhood. He built a 125-foot-tall antenna in the front yard of his parents' home in Yonkers, New York, and went on to invent the continuous-wave transmitter and the superheterodyne circuit. Today, Armstrong, who was "a noted professor of engineering at Columbia University and a recognized genius in electronic circuitry," is acknowledged as the creator of FM radio.[14]

A few years later, in 1906, a baby was born to a Mormon family in a single-room log cabin in rural Utah. It was a home lacking electricity, radio and telephone. Yet that child, Philo T. Farnsworth, when 14 years of age, noted the straight, parallel lines of furrows in a hayfield and "envisioned a system of scanning a visual image line by line and transmitting it to a remote screen." He went on to invent the image dissector tube, making possible the first all-electronic television technology, but unfortunately, because of the Depression and World War Two, his patent expired before its successful commercialization and he made little money.

Farnsworth's chief rival was David Sarnoff (1891-1971), a brilliant, hard-nosed Jewish immigrant, who by age 10 – because of a father ailing from tuberculosis – had to rise at 4 am and deliver Yiddish-language newspapers by "running along the rooftops of the...tightly packed tenement buildings" of New York's Lower East Side. Sarnoff clawed his way to the top of corporate America as President of the fledgling Radio Corporation of America – and through the heyday of radio he kept his eyes fixed on the future, financially supporting, in the depths of the Depression, RCA's pioneering research in the field of television. "Only Sarnoff had the breadth of vision to see that control of television would rely on more than the creation of the best camera tube." He understood that content was as important as equipment and founded NBC.[15]

No survey of innovative American thinkers at the turn of the 20th century, no matter how brief, could be adequate without discussion of the man who revolutionized the field of agricultural science: George Washington Carver (1861-1943). Though born a slave in Missouri, orphaned as a baby when his mother was kidnapped by nightriders during the Civil War, and plagued with a sickly constitution as a child, he overcame unimaginable obstacles to gain an education. He was hired by Booker T. Washington of the Tuskegee Institute for $125 a month in 1896 and worked there for 47 years, repeatedly rejecting proffered increases in salary, answering: "What would I do with more money? I already have all the earth."

He developed a new type of cotton – Carver's Hybrid – but is best known for pioneering peanuts and sweet potatoes as leading crops. He also invented hundreds of plant-based products, taught methods of soil improvement and, by means of his discoveries, induced southern farmers – white and black – to grow crops other than cotton. Carver "was among the first to see...that in everything that grew was locked the chemical magic that men could forge to their use, not for food alone" but for industrial products as well.

In 1940, Carver, a lifelong bachelor, contributed all of his money to the founding of the George Washington Carver Foundation at the Tuskegee Institute for purposes of scientific research. His achievements, impossible if the feudal-agrarian slave system had continued, illustrate not merely that liberty is necessary for intellectual advance – but, more subtly, that capitalism provides a culture of dynamic innovativeness that stimulates superlative creativity, including by men who seek their reward in forms other than the monetary.[16]

America was a confident young nation – some would say cocky – and none more certain of his own ability than the man who epitomized American inventiveness: Thomas Edison. Mark Twain captured the swaggering spirit of the era. His Connecticut Yankee stated: "I could make anything a body wanted – anything in the world, it didn't make any difference what; and if there wasn't any new-fangled way to make a thing, I could invent one – and do it as easy as rolling off a log."[17]

That, in addition to their advances, these revolutionary thinkers made many errors is not to be doubted. This is certainly true of the great Edison, who, besides being dead wrong regarding the AC vs. DC "war of the currents," spent years and millions of his own dollars futilely attempting to extract iron ore from marginal deposits. The latter venture cost Edison all of the money he had made on his inventions up to that time – and prompted one scholar to remark about him that "no man was so right about so many fundamental things and so wrong about so many others." But the outstanding point regarding Edison and the others is not their errors – all men make these – but their exemplary accomplishments. They wrought technological advances that made America the most progressive and prosperous country in the history of the world.[18]

The Capitalist Manifesto

Errors of the Anti-Capitalist Historians

But what of the intellectuals? How do historians assess this era of unprecedented creativity in applied science and industrialization? Do they celebrate – or even recognize – the life-enhancing, indeed revolutionary, nature of the period? Unfortunately, they do not. Employing another Mark Twain quote – this time a negative one – American historians characteristically refer to the post-Civil War period as the "Gilded Age," as if there were something corrupt in America's rise to wealth. One writer refers to the era as the "Great Barbecue," to which only a privileged, exploitative few were invited. Often, these same historians have dubbed the major businessmen of the era "robber barons," as though their fortunes were gotten by fraudulent means.

For example, Richard Hofstadter, one of the most accomplished of American historians, accepted and perpetuated the rapacious view of 19th century American business. "Under the competitive capitalism of the 19th century," he wrote, "America continued to be an arena for various *grasping* and creative interests." In a chapter entitled, "The Spoilsmen: An Age of Cynicism," Professor Hofstadter acknowledged that the country at this time was preeminently in the hands of business entrepreneurs and then proceeded to claim: "The industrialists of the Gilded Age were...parvenus and they behaved with becoming vulgarity; but they were also men of heroic audacity and magnificent exploitative talents – shrewd, energetic, aggressive, rapacious, domineering, insatiable. They directed the proliferation of the country's wealth, they seized its opportunities, they managed its corruption..."[19]

In the same intellectual vein is Matthew Josephson's influential book, *The Robber Barons.* Josephson, an American writer and biographer, began his study of the great American capitalists with the following quote from Bacon: "There are never wanting some persons of violent and undertaking natures, who, so they may have power and business, will take it at any cost." In the 1962 Foreword to his 1934 book, he stated that then current attempts to revise the Hofstadter-Josephson view, so that the capitalists were depicted as creators, rather than plunderers of wealth, recalled "the propaganda schemes used in authoritarian societies, and the 'truth factories' in George Orwell's...1984." The book's content was more of the same.

Predictably, to Josephson, inventors and innovators, when mentioned at all, were not heroic men of genius, but had simply taken from the "reservoir of knowledge which is the general property of human society" – and who themselves were generally "used and flung aside by men of ruse and audacity who had shown gifts for the accumulation of capital..." Simply put, his view was that inventors expropriated to themselves numerous small advances made by many common men, and were then themselves expropriated by the wealthy capitalists, who profited hugely from the new creations, leaving the inventor "displaced," rarely able to "win the full fruits of his invention." (All of this from a man who authored an admiring – and, in fairness – excellent biography of Thomas Edison – and who, consequently, should have known better.)[20]

Professor Hofstadter wrote blandly and unquestioningly, as if he could imagine no alternative to this view, that the captains of industry did their work "cynically;" and that "exploiting workers...milking farmers, bribing Congressmen, buying legislatures..." was their standard mode of procedure. He took it as self-evident that the leading entrepreneurs of the period stole their wealth. He treated graft and corruption as if these were the dominant essence of the age. Not surprisingly, then, Thomas Edison was not deemed worthy of inclusion in his chapter on late 19th century America. Nor was George Westinghouse. Nor was George Eastman. The Wright Brothers were not mentioned. Nor was Henry Ford. Nor was Alexander Graham Bell. Endless claims were made regarding the "rapacity" with which the industrialists strove for money and power. But the inventions – and the brilliant minds that created them – the new products, the innovations, the mass production of inexpensive consumer goods, the rising living standards of the period, none of these were worthy of his notice.

Did one of the most accomplished experts on American history forget that although the U.S. population grew enormously during the 19th century – including the arrival of millions of penniless immigrants from Ireland, Sicily and Eastern Europe – the average American per capita income doubled between the ratification of the Constitution and the outbreak of the Civil War – and then doubled again between the end of the Civil War and the start of World War I? Did it simply slip his mind that American wage rates were more than double those in Europe, at a time when laissez-faire generally ruled in the U.S. and was being legislated out of existence across the Atlantic? Evidently so.[21]

But the facts are clear regarding America's extraordinary economic growth. In 1790, there were roughly four million people living in the United States; by 1860, the population was 31 million; and by 1900, 84 million. One economist wrote: "This rise in population, enormous as it was, was actually outstripped by increases in output of goods and services to such an extent that the rising output per head of population came to be a thing taken for granted by Americans." Increasing production of goods and services meant greater supplies, diminishing prices and the widely rising living standards for which America became justly famous.[22]

In fairness to Professor Hofstadter, he was writing about American political, not business history. But this did not prevent him from depicting post-Civil War business history as essentially unscrupulous.

Professor Hofstadter and the other historians of this school are profoundly, egregiously, tragically mistaken. The inventors, innovators, entrepreneurs and industrialists of the period created a vast array of new products and methods; their productivity wrought great prosperity in the United States; their fortunes were abundantly earned. The designation "Gilded Age" does not merely miss the essence of the era, it distorts and contradicts it. Inventiveness was the dominant characteristic of the age;

it must be acknowledged and celebrated. From now on, the era must be glorified for what it was. It was the Inventive Period. If Germany is the land of poets and philosophers, as has often been stated, then the United States is the land of inventors and innovators.[23]

No one has understood this vital point as well as Ayn Rand. "Throughout the centuries there were men who took first steps down new roads armed with nothing but their own vision. Their goals differed, but they all had this in common: that the step was first, the road new, the vision unborrowed…" Though their inventions, innovative methods and groundbreaking theories were often opposed by society, "the men of unborrowed vision went ahead. They fought, they suffered and they paid. But they won." In no country is this as true as in the United States. In no era was this as real as during The Inventive Period.[24]

There is a reason that Professor Hofstadter and his ilk pay scarce attention to the inventors and innovators of capitalism's greatest period, why they virtually ignore many of the most creative minds of history. To them, the mind has little or no creative role in the vast production of wealth achieved by capitalism. According to Hofstadter, the American people "grew mighty in the world on their great resources in coal, metals, oil, and land." Metals, oil and land — material stuff — not the inventive mind, made America rich.

What of the fact that without innovative thinkers, the potential uses of raw materials go unrecognized, and the coal, iron and oil remain just so much glop and ooze in the ground – as indeed they did for all the centuries that nomadic tribes roamed the North American continent? Not important. What of the countries that combine(d) equally great natural resources with abysmal poverty – such as the former Soviet Union or most African nations today? Not to be considered. What of the societies that combine(d) less (and in some cases virtually no) natural resources with great wealth – such as Hong Kong, Japan and even England? Insignificant. What of trading for natural resources, offering for them ideas, inventions and high-tech products, such as the United States can do for oil? Not part of the picture. Ironically, most modern intellectuals – theoretically men of the mind – have little or no understanding of the mind's role in the creation of wealth. This is one important reason that it is impossible for them to appreciate capitalism.[25]

Again, Ayn Rand was the thinker with the clearest understanding of these facts.

> If you want to prove to yourself the power of ideas...the intellectual history of the nineteenth century would be a good example to study. The greatest, unprecedented, undreamed of events and achievements were taking place before men's eyes...I am speaking of the industrial revolution, of the United States and of capitalism...The creative energy, the abundance, the wealth, the rising standard of living for every level of the population were such that the nineteenth century looks like a fiction-Utopia...If life on earth is one's standard of value, then the nineteenth century moved mankind forward more than all the other centuries combined.
>
> Did anyone appreciate it? Does anyone appreciate it now? Has anyone identified the causes of that historical miracle?[26]

What made possible this extraordinary outpouring of creativity and innovativeness? What are the causal factors underlying and giving rise to such dynamic and seemingly endless inventiveness? What factor prevalent in 19th century American society was responsible for the Inventive Period? The answer should be obvious: America was and remains the nation of the Enlightenment.

The Underlying Causes of the Inventive Period

The Inventive Period

That period's commitment to the practical efficacy of reason was a foundational principle of the new republic, one that to the present day informs numerous American institutions. The more obviously practical an endeavor, the more vociferously enthusiastic was American support. For example, although the Humanities always flourished in the new country in the creation of a superb national body of literature and other forms, it was in the fields of theoretical and applied science, technology and industry that the American genius achieved its full flowering. The Americans recognized the practical value of applied science in the way the Greeks recognized philosophy. The American commitment to the material improvement of human life by means of applied mind power has never been equalled by any other civilization. It is one key to understanding the unprecedented standard of living reached in the United States.

The other, related key is political-economic freedom. A cultural commitment to applied thought obviously necessitates an equal commitment to the freedom of the thinkers applying their thought. America's pioneering minds were free to conceive new ideas, to experiment and invent, to develop new products and methods, to start their own companies, to bring their new products to the marketplace, to convince the customers that the new ways were superior to the old, and to make a fortune. It was the freedom of 19th century American society that enabled it to become a seething hotbed of revolutionary ideas and products, all leading toward higher living standards and increased success and happiness for countless millions of human beings.

These original thinkers would be subordinated to the government in a different type of system – be it feudal, socialist, Fascist, Communist, etc. They would not be free to experiment, create, invent or market new products. They would have to apply for permission to the King, the feudal baron, the commissar, the military dictator or the regulatory bureaucrat. One problem is that now two people – the entrepreneur and the political authority – must agree that the unproven idea is worth trying.

When airplanes have never flown, when skyscrapers have never stood, when electrical power plants have never lighted a city, people tend to be afraid of such things. The more men who must approve the development of the untried, the more likely that it will remain untried. Two experts in the history of technology, speaking of its growth in the West, make the point this way: "The first condition of this proliferation was that the innovations did not require the assent of governmental or religious authorities."[27]

More fundamentally, entrepreneurs and officials of a coercive regime have opposing interests. The entrepreneur gains by upsetting the status quo – e.g., by filling the roads with automobiles, where previously there had been only horses and buggies, etc. But a statist official has a vested interest in retaining his power over men. Since the status quo includes his political control, whatever new development threatens the current state of affairs potentially undermines his authority. If he recognizes merit in the entrepreneur's proposal, he sees that it will bring increased prosperity to the citizens, e.g., owning an automobile raises a man's standard of living. But the more prosperous an individual, the more control he has over his own life – and the less likely he will be to obey an external authority. The statist official, forced to choose between progress and his own power, invariably chooses power. This is why no state-dominated society has ever approximated 19th century America in terms of scientific, technological and industrial advance – and why none ever will.

The deepest reason that statists stifle innovation is that inventors and entrepreneurs are independent thinkers, just as surely as are writers, artists and philosophers. Minds capable of inventing electric light, designing the first skyscraper or creating and operating vast steel, oil or software companies are capable of questioning the moral rectitude of the statist's regime. Independent thinkers do not obey. Dictators of all degrees – from Hitler to petty bureaucrats – recognize this, and seek to stifle independent thinkers. For example, observe the multitude of political prisoners in every dictatorship of history, men whose only "crime" was to think. Freedom is fundamentally freedom of the mind.[28]

The Inventive Period is the most vivid historical example of Ayn Rand's historic identification that the mind's fullest functioning requires the legal protection of individual rights.

When a society holds a general commitment to reason, it will value freedom as a means of safeguarding the mind's unrestricted functioning. When the men of the mind are protected from the initiation of force, they will carry mankind to advances both revolutionary and undreamed of by prior generations. The 19th century is an eloquent illustration of this principle. America, the freest country of history, rose the highest. Great Britain, the second freest, rose the second highest. The other countries of Western Europe gradually swept away the suppression of the *ancien regime*, established a degree of freedom surpassed only in America and Britain, and rose higher than any nation other than these. Conversely, the non-Western countries, lacking an Enlightenment influence, remained autocracies, ruled by kings, emperors or tribal chiefs. These regions scarcely rose at all.

The spirit of the Enlightenment imbues capitalism and provides its essence: Free minds, free men, free societies, free markets, free trade.

The Great Disconnect Rears its Ugly Head

The fundamental error of virtually all of capitalism's critics, and too many of its supporters, is their failure to understand this absolutely essential point: Capitalism is the revolution, the liberation of creative human mind power from centuries of feudalism and other forms of statism. The subsequent socialist onslaught against capitalism constitutes a statist counterrevolution against the mind, led fittingly by Marx and his heirs, philosophical materialists who deny the mind's value (even its existence) and exalt manual labor — the functions of the body — as the source of economic production. It is because of its unleashed brain power that capitalism raised, and continues to raise, workers' real wages and living standards. It is also the reason that capitalism eradicated child labor. The capitalist revolution performed, and continues to perform, a miracle in the life of the common man while its critics putter about on its fringes debating whether its results have been good or bad. Because they are witless regarding capitalism's fundamental nature and cause, they are intellectually unequipped to recognize the immensity of its effects.

An endless succession of facts can be adduced to demonstrate the enormity of capitalism's practical benefit to men's lives. But at a certain point, the evidence must be considered overwhelming and the conclusion established. The preceding chapters have chronicled capitalism's all-too-rarely studied history. They have shown the integrity of capitalism's founders and practitioners — the unbreached devotion to inventiveness and progressive innovations demonstrated by the great thinkers and entrepreneurs responsible for individual rights, free enterprise and the Industrial Revolution. Neither the high-minded moral character of capitalism's heroes nor the incalculable advances achieved by their work can any longer be doubted. The conclusion of Part One must be: capitalism, in the brief span of two centuries, has brought greater improvement in the material conditions of men's lives than have the statist regimes of all preceding centuries combined.

The disturbing specter of the Great Disconnect is then perceived with greater clarity. Capitalism is condemned solely because it counters mankind's prevailing moral code. But if the facts of capitalism's life-giving benevolence oppose men's dominant moral code, then it is time to challenge that code.

Summary

Late-19th century America was the greatest historical center of advance in applied science, technology and industry. The two related causes were the influence of the Enlightenment commitment to reason, science, progress, and the resultant freedom of men to think and act on their conclusions.

The leading American historians who cling to the "Gilded Age" myth of this era utterly fail to recognize the creative role of the mind in the rise of capitalism. Indeed, when capitalism's achievements are studied, the contrast they form with the anti-capitalists' evaluations points directly to the true culprit: the irrational moral code underlying and giving rise to anti-capitalist political theory.

Part Two: Philosophy

6: The Nature of the Good

The history of capitalism provides ample evidence from which to induce the moral and philosophical principles that form the intellectual foundation of the system.

Here is the meaning of the achievements of the Enlightenment, the Industrial Revolution and the Inventive Period: If and when the advancement of human life on earth is held to be the ruling concern, men are superbly able to accomplish it. The attainments of those centuries show that the reasoning mind is the principal means by which such advancement is gained. They indicate that productiveness is a major moral virtue. Finally, to the surprise of some, they show that egoism—the theory urging a man's pursuit of his rational self-interest—is an unsurpassed force for good.

The explication and validation of these principles will be the task of the next three chapters.

The Conventional Moral Code

These principles have often, even generally, been opposed by modern intellectuals. Most of the leading philosophers of the past two centuries did not critique or even question the deeply entrenched ethical beliefs of mankind. They were content to accept the principle that a man must live for his brothers (altruism)—and its political corollaries: that society as a whole is pre-eminent over the individual, who owes it unremitting service (collectivism)—and that the government must be granted the legal power to enforce an individual's social obligations (statism).

Typical of the post-Kantian history of moral philosophy is a relentless assault on the theory that a man should properly be the beneficiary of his own actions (egoism)—and on *its* political corollaries, the creed that a man has an inalienable right to his own life and is not the slave of society (individualism) — and that the government's sole legitimate function is to protect an individual's rights (capitalism). Indeed, the altruist-collectivist-statist axis utterly dominates moral and political theory of the past 200 years.

The profoundly influential German philosopher, Immanuel Kant, was so extreme an advocate of duty, of renunciation of self-interest as the criterion of virtuous action, he claimed that if a man desired to perform the action commanded by duty, he could never be certain that his action was morally pure, i.e., that it was not selfish, hence immoral. To be certain of the moral worth of his act, it must be performed in defiance of his personal desires. This was true even of a duty to preserve one's own life. "But if adversities and hopeless sorrow completely take away the relish for life, if an unfortunate man...wishes for death, and yet preserves his life without loving it and from neither inclination [desire] nor fear but from duty—then his maxim has a moral import," i.e., his motivation is morally pure.

Though subsequent thinkers disagreed with Kant on a thousand specifics, they generally agreed that virtue required a full divorce of morality and self-interest. "The absence of all egoistic motivation is, therefore, the criterion of an action of moral worth," taught German philosopher Arthur Schopenhauer.[1]

The American philosopher, John Dewey, admired the moral code of the Soviet Union (which he visited in 1928), especially its effect on education. Unlike American educators, Dewey believed, their Soviet counterparts were not hampered in the quest for social change by "the egoistic and private ideals and methods inculcated by the institution of private property, profit and acquisitive possession."

Dewey's colleague, the Progressive educator, George Counts, also visited the Soviet Union during the Stalin era. Counts similarly bemoaned the individualism and selfishness of American society and admired Soviet teaching methods. Activity in Soviet schools, he enthused, "is activity with a strongly collectivistic bias," and: "individual success is completely subordinated to the ideal of serving the state and through the state the working class."[2]

Nor was devotion to altruism and collectivism limited to moral philosophers and educators. The eminent American historian, Charles Beard, in his essay, "The Myth of Rugged Individualism," wrote in the Depression year of 1931: "The cold truth is that the individualist creed...is principally responsible for the distress in which Western civilization finds itself." Beard, arguing in support of socialism, stated: "The task before us, then, is not to furbish up an old slogan, but to get rid of it, to discover how much planning is necessary, by whom it can best be done."[3]

The logic of the anti-capitalist thesis is clear. If, in his personal life, a man has unchosen obligations to others—indeed, if the essence of virtue is to provide selfless service for those others—then, in the consideration of social issues, the needs of the public as a whole (others on a grand scale) take precedence over an individual's own values, and it is morally imperative that the government be legally empowered to coerce those recalcitrant individuals too selfish to discharge their social responsibilities.

For decades now, even centuries, Western man has been inundated with an intellectual onslaught railing against self-interested action and individualism. The extent to which most professional intellectuals of the past century have embraced the altruist-collectivist-statist axis in philosophy is unimaginable to the average American, who shares none of these premises. For example, in a recent interview, Harvey Klehr and John Earl Haynes, two American historians who have written carefully researched accounts of the involvement by American Communists in Soviet espionage, were asked regarding the denial of Communism's horrific crimes by many anti-capitalist historians. Their answer revealed a remarkable depth of insight:

> Many of those you speak of live in a different reality from that of the rest of us. Psychologically, they do not see what you see. They see the present and the past through a special lens. *What is overwhelmingly clear to them is an imagined future collectivist utopia* where antagonisms of class and race have been eliminated...poverty does not exist and social justice reigns...and an economy planned by people like themselves has produced economic abundance...You look at Soviet history and see the Gulag, the executions of the Terror, the pervasive oppression... Psychologically, the leftists you speak of see little of that. They see a Communist state that articulated their vision of the future and which sought to destroy the societies and institutions they hated. They cannot see the horror that communism actually created.[4]

Nor, on such moral premises, can they see the life-giving abundance that capitalism actually created.

Until the 20th century, these premises were not challenged by any thinker able to provide a systematic rational alternative. Nietzsche, for example, originated sharp, effective criticism of altruism, which he termed the "slave morality," but he was an enemy of reason and beyond his often brilliant polemics had little positive moral guidance to offer men.

But at the same time, by the 20th century, a vast amount of historical data had accumulated regarding both the mind's role in human life and the contrasting practical effects of the two opposing moral-political systems—egoism-individualism-capitalism and altruism-collectivism-statism.

The Fundamentals of Ethics

The exponents of capitalism wrought the extensive progress in freedom and living standards described above. The anti-individualist, collectivist backlash against the revolutionary individualism and freedom of the 19th century originated in post-Kantian Germany, led by the philosophers, G.W.F. Hegel and Karl Marx. In the 20th century, followers of their theories created the two most virulent statist regimes of history—Communist Russia and National Socialist Germany. The extreme to which individuals were compelled to sacrifice for the state in these two societies made them exact antitheses of the United States. The inevitable results of these dictatorships were enslavement, genocide and war. Both of these regimes denied men the right to their own lives and their own minds, and consequently were no match for the capitalist West. One succumbed, the other collapsed—and the truth regarding collectivism was revealed. The historical evidence necessary to identify the role of the mind in man's life, and man's necessity of freedom, was now fully available, if there could only arise a mind great enough to comprehend its meaning

Such a mind did arise. It belonged to Ayn Rand.

Not surprisingly, Ayn Rand (1905-1982), born in Czarist Russia, was educated under the Communists but chose to live under the capitalists. She defected to the United States in 1926, where she lived the rest of her life. It took an individual (real name, Alisa Rosenbaum) born under one form of statism, raised under another, and who was an American by conscious choice and conviction, to finally identify the revolutionary moral and philosophical principles validating the intellectual foundations of capitalism. To do so, she went to the fundamental issues of moral philosophy.

Ayn Rand re-conceived the foundations of morality in light of the achievements of the Industrial and American Revolutions.

The field of morality—or ethics—deals with questions of right and wrong, good and bad, what men should and should not do. But what makes some action or individual good or evil? Similarly, what makes a political-economic system just or unjust? If capitalism—or any other element of human life—is to be morally judged, to be evaluated as good or evil, then men need to identify what constitutes virtue or vice, right or wrong. They need a criterion or yardstick by means of which to assess such qualities. For example, if a man held that working hard and supporting himself by honest effort was good, most human beings would doubtless agree. But what makes it good? Is it God's will—or society's judgment—or each individual's belief for himself? Alternatively, is there some immutable fact of reality, some law of nature, that requires productive work of men – some fact, not the will or whim of some being or group of them?

The question regards a possible fundamental fact of reality that underlies and gives rise to men's concepts of good and evil – it involves the relationship between facts and values, i.e., between facts and that which men consider valuable, right, proper, good.

Ayn Rand raised the questions: "Is the concept of value, of 'good or evil' an arbitrary human invention…unsupported by any facts of reality – or is it based on a metaphysical fact, on an unalterable condition of man's existence?" Is ethics based solely in subjective whim – whether individual, social or divine – or is it grounded in hard objective fact? Is the field of morality merely a matter of taste, like dessert, varying from group to group or individual to individual – or is it, properly understood, a science, providing solid, fact-based principles to guide human behavior? Asked simply: what is the relationship between values and facts?[5]

The Scottish philosopher, David Hume, in a famous passage,

inquired if an "ought" proposition could be derived from an "is" proposition, i.e., if judgments of good and evil, of what men ought and ought not to do, could be based on matters of fact. His answer was an unqualified "no." For example, Hume might argue that though it is true that man has a rational mind which education enhances, the claim "education is good" does not logically follow. Hume's point is that although he can observe an individual studying, gaining knowledge, applying it, etc., he cannot observe the "good" or the "rightness" in any of these actions; neither can he observe the "bad" or the "wrongness" in the actions of those who abjure intellectual development. He concluded that there was no evidence upon which to assert a positive relationship between facts and values.

This has been a dominant form in which the question has been raised and answered. The majority of thinkers throughout history have held that there is no positive relationship between values and facts. These philosophers argued that matters of right and wrong are decided by somebody's will – be it God's, Society's or an individual's for himself; that the laws and the facts of nature are irrelevant to the questions of good and evil.

Ayn Rand identified that most of the leading moral philosophers of history have construed ethics as a discipline dominated by irrational whim. One school, the religionists, held that "God's will" was the standard of good and evil—while modern thinkers have generally offered nothing more than a secularized version of religion, arguing that the "will of the people" is the source of right and wrong. Others, recognizing the authoritarianism inherent in both the religious and social approaches, claimed that the good is what each individual wills for himself. But conspicuously absent in all three historical schools of ethics are facts, reason, logic. Ethics has been predominantly a matter of whims and arbitrary decrees. The ultimate question is: are values objective? Or phrased alternatively: is there a factual basis for moral judgments?[6]

To answer this affirmatively, ethics must be examined from a fresh perspective. To sweep aside the errors of the past and to make a new start, it is necessary to begin at the beginning. In the field of morality, the first questions to be answered are: What are values? What role do they play in man's life? Why do human beings need them? All subsequent quotes and paraphrasings in the philosophy section are from the work of Ayn Rand or that of her leading student, philosopher Leonard Peikoff.

Ayn Rand defined "value" as that which one acts to gain and/or keep. The existence of values presupposes a being that requires such things and is able to attain them—a being capable of pursuing specific ends in the face of an alternative. Where no alternatives exist, she wrote, no goals, no ends, no values are possible.

The essence of Ayn Rand's revolutionary ethics lies in her identification of the relationship between values and the nature of living beings.

There is but one basic alternative in reality, she argued, and it applies only to living beings. Inanimate matter cannot be destroyed; it changes its forms, but it does not and cannot cease to exist. But life is not unconditional. Organisms face a constant alternative: the matter of life and death. Any organism must initiate and sustain an ongoing series of actions to remain alive. If it fails to find or grow food, build shelter, etc., it will die. Its chemical constituents remain in existence, but its life is irretrievably gone. "It is only the concept of 'Life' that makes the concept of 'Value' possible. It is only to a living entity that things can be good or evil."[7]

The issue of good or evil arises in the world only because certain actions sustain the life of an organism – and others harm or kill it. For example, men can imagine a universe devoid of life forms, a world of rock and sun and sea, but no living beings. In such a universe, Ayn Rand argued, there would be no such thing as good or evil, no values or valuing – the phenomenon as such would not arise. For what could harm or benefit the wind? Or the tides? Or a rock or a grain of sand? What could be good for it – or ill? The rational answers to all such questions are: not applicable. There are no courses of action for such inanimate objects or processes to pursue that would improve their existence, and none that could undermine it.

But for a plant, an animal, a man, conditions are fundamentally different. If a plant fails to dig its roots into the soil by means of which to gain chemical nutrients – it dies. Similarly, if a lion cannot hunt to gain the meat it needs—or if human beings do not succeed in building shelter from winter and the elements—they will perish. Living beings—and only living beings—have to attain certain ends in order to sustain their existences. Consequently, it is a profound error to hold that a man being stabbed and the knife piercing his body are similar kinds of entities merely because each is a collection of atoms in motion. Put simply, one of these entities can lose his life; the other is incapable of it. In this sense, living beings are destructible—but matter as such is not. One of these two can become inanimate—but the other already is.[8]

The basis of Ayn Rand's ethics is this fundamental, irreducible, factual distinction between living and non-living entities. To remain in – or to exit – the realm of existence is the fundamental alternative faced by all living beings and only by them. This alternative between existence and non-existence is the pre-condition of valuing as such. If a being did not face such an alternative, it could not pursue goals or values of any kind.[9]

To concretize her point, Ayn Rand introduced the idea of an immortal, indestructible robot, "which moves and acts, but which cannot be affected by anything, which cannot be changed in any respect, which cannot be damaged, injured or destroyed." Such a creature, she argued, would be a value-less being; for it, nothing could be good or evil, because nothing could harm or promote its existence. "Such an entity would not be able to have any values; it would have nothing to gain or to lose; it could not regard anything as for or against it, as serving or threatening its welfare, as fulfilling or frustrating its interests. It could have no interests and no goals."[10]

Consequently, such a being is incapable of taking any course of action. It may be confronted by alternatives – but none lead it to purposeful action. There is no reason for it to choose one alternative as distinct from another, because the fundamental alternative that gives rise to values is absent. "There is no 'to be or not to be.'" The need to take action applies only to a being who possesses two characteristics: the potential to be destroyed—and the ability to prevent it. The ultimate goal of preserving its life makes possible all other goals.

For example, without the constant alternative of life or death, the robot could not enjoy a good meal – for being indestructible, it has no need of nutrition. Nor could it relax by watching a movie. Relax from what? Relaxation is a necessity for beings who work to sustain their lives. But this being has no concern about the sustenance of its existence. Values exist solely to sustain life. Where there is no need to sustain life, there can be no values – no good and no evil.

"Only the alternative of life vs. death creates the context for value-oriented action, and it does so only if the entity's end is to preserve its life. By the very nature of 'value,' therefore, any code of values must hold life as the ultimate value."[11]

Ayn Rand's robot example was an illustration from a negative stand-point, showing the processes that an indestructible, inanimate being could not perform. It is possible to argue for the same conclusion from a positive standpoint, as well, by showing the processes that a destructible, animate being must perform (if it is to sustain its life). The existence of a bird, for example, though far simpler than that of a man, involves a series of activities it must successfully perform in order to remain alive. Externally, above all, it must learn to fly; it must hunt the worms or other food it requires; it must find the sticks or twigs it needs to build its nest; on the ground, it must be ceaselessly alert to elude cats or other preda-tors; etc. Further, internally, its digestive, respiratory, circulatory systems, etc., must function without impairment. If any of these processes (or others) go awry, its life can be terminated. If, for example, it relaxes its vigilance for one moment as it hunts for worms, it can become the hunted and itself be killed. This is an example of merely one kind of living being from among thousands. Universally, the continuous series of actions that must be successfully performed for the purpose of sustaining life constitutes the sole basis for the existence of values.

No organism can choose the necessities of its survival. These are determined by reality – by the organism's nature, by the essence of the kind of being that it is. In the case of any organism, the goals that it must attain and the processes that it must perform, are pre-set by nature: the requirements of its life are the fundamental fact that necessitate the ends it must reach and the steps it must take. What it is determines what it should do.

The maintenance of life requires a ceaseless process of self-sustaining action – whether to eat, to find or build shelter, to carry on involuntary life-support functions, etc. The goal of such activities, the ultimate value to be attained, is an organism's own life.

An ultimate value is the final goal toward which all actions are but necessary steps or means. A final value provides the standard or criterion by reference to which any lesser goal is appraised. "An organism's life is its standard of value: that which furthers its life is the good, that which threatens it is evil."[12]

This is the revolutionary identification that has finally, after 2500 years of the history of philosophy, tied values—and by that means, ethics—to facts. Morality is now a science, a field of objective, rational, fact-based analysis; it is no longer a matter of will or whim or desire – whether social or personal.

Ayn Rand's answer to Hume and the other philosophers who argue that no positive relationship can be established between values and facts is that the nature of living beings necessitates the existence of values.

Therefore, moral principles are established by reference to the facts of reality. "The fact that a living entity is, determines what it ought to do." This represents a proper understanding of the relationship between "is" and "ought."[13]

What, then, is the standard of moral value, the objective measuring rod by reference to which something may be evaluated as good or evil? The standard of value of Ayn Rand's ethics—the standard by which one judges what is good or evil—is man's life, or: that which is required for man's survival qua man. "Since reason is man's basic means of survival, that which is proper to the life of a rational being is the good; that which negates, opposes or destroys it is the evil."[14]

To express Ayn Rand's point simply: all that which objectively promotes man's life, the life of a rational being – whether a nutritious meal, an education, a love relationship, the construction of skyscrapers and cities, the invention of labor-saving devices, cures for diseases, etc. – is the good. All that which objectively harms or destroys human life—whether poison, a blow to the head, the physical destruction of skyscrapers and cities, the forcible prevention of education, religious-racial-or-political persecution, etc.—is the evil.

What has been so far established is that values—and, consequently, all judgments of good and evil—come into existence only because living beings need to reach certain goals in order to sustain their lives; and that without life—its nature and its requirements—the concepts of "value" and of "good and evil" would have no rational meaning. Since values exist only to serve life, the objective requirements of life are the standard by means of which all existents are evaluated.

The Validation of Egoism

A second critical moral principle follows logically: if values come into existence only to sustain life, then living beings must achieve values. Each one of them should, properly, seek those values its nature requires for the advancement of its own life. This provides a rational answer to one of the major questions of moral philosophy: who should be the beneficiary of values? The question is generally stated: who should be the beneficiary of an individual's actions? There are essentially two possible answers—the individual himself—or others.

Ayn Rand's answer is a straightforward derivation from her fundamentals: an individual himself should benefit from his actions. Egoism— each individual's pursuit of his own self-interest—is the only proper moral code.

Several points must be made to establish egoism. The first can be stated simply: if values come into existence only to sustain life, who or what is alive? Only particular things exist in general, and only individuals live. This is abundantly clear at the non-human level of life. A plant digs its roots into the soil and turns its leaves toward the sun to gain the chemical nutrients and sunlight it needs to sustain its life. A bird must fly to further its survival. A plant or an animal: "as a living entity, each necessarily acts for its own sake; each is the beneficiary of its own actions." These organisms necessarily, automatically and non-volitionally pursue the values that their lives require.[15]

In *The Fountainhead*, the novel's hero, Howard Roark, makes this point clearly: "We can divide a meal among many men. We cannot digest it in a collective stomach. No man can use his lungs to breathe for another man. No man can use his brain to think for another. All the functions of body and spirit are private. They cannot be shared or transferred." Just as there is no collective stomach engaged in digestion—only many individual ones—so there is no collective organism whose survival depends on value achievement; there are only many individual ones, and the life of each one is sustained only by reaching those goals its nature stipulates.[16]

Properly understood, egoism is a corollary of man's life as the standard of moral value: since values exist solely to promote life, each living being must pursue and gain the values its sustenance demands. Plants and animals have no choice regarding their pursuit of values. They do so automatically by a pre-programming hard-wired into their nature. "Plants and animals do not have to decide who is to be the beneficiary of their actions." They often fail in their pursuit of values and die – but they are incapable of repudiating the quest for values that their lives depend on. Humans are the sole beings who must pursue values by choice.[17]

Human beings can choose between, for example, nutritious food and poison, between education and ignorance, between medical care and neglect of an ailment, etc. They can make the fundamental choice between life and death – and, similarly, the choice between policies that promote life and those that promote death. Indeed, throughout history and to this day, men have often chosen self-destructive, suicidal courses of action. Because of this, "man must choose to accept the essence of life. He must choose to make self-sustenance into a fundamental rule of his voluntary behavior. The man who makes this choice is an 'egoist.'

"'Egoistic,' in the Objectivist view, means self-sustaining by an act of choice and as a matter of principle."[18]

According to Objectivism, to be an egoist in the proper and highest sense of that term is a significant achievement. It involves a consistent and unbreached commitment to the values upon which a man's life as a reasoning being depends. Because life requires the attainment of values, because good and evil come into existence only because of this fundamental fact, it follows that the essence of moral virtue is value achievement, i.e., it involves the attempt of each individual to further his own life. Virtue is egoistic.

The heroes of the Enlightenment and the Inventive Period are perfect examples of egoism. The issue goes far deeper than that James Watt, Thomas Edison, Alexander Graham Bell, et al., made well-deserved fortunes from their creative work. It is even more than that they pursued the work they loved and, consequently, lived passionately and joyously. These are important and legitimate aspects of egoism. But the fundamental point is that—at least at an implicit level—they recognized that their advances were in accordance with the survival requirements of man's life and dedicated themselves to their full development. They lived the rationally creative lives proper to men. This is the essence of egoism.

Properly conceived and implemented, egoism is a profoundly and uniquely benevolent force in human life—and the great heroes of capitalism make the clearest examples. It is only because Watt, Edison, Bell, et al., fulfilled their dreams that the rest of mankind benefited. If the great creators surrendered, betrayed or sacrificed the goals so dear to them, then their life-giving work would not have been brought to fruition. They would have suffered because of abandoning their values, and the lives of millions of others would not have been enriched.

Since egoism is the striving by a man for the ends that factually promote his life as a human being, a secondary but important consequence is that other human beings are benefited by his attainment of his values, not by his sacrifice of them

The Code of Self-Sacrifice

It has been tragically rare that the nature of egoism has been recognized in human history. The most influential moral codes taught mankind have abjured egoism or selfishness in favor of self-sacrifice in some form.

Any version of the code of self-sacrifice undercuts morality at its base.

"Life requires that man gain values, not lose them. It requires assertive action, achievement, success, not abnegation, renunciation, surrender. It requires self-tending – in other words, the exact opposite of sacrifice."[19]

Ayn Rand defines "sacrifice" as the surrender of a higher value for a lesser value or a non-value. For example, if a man values a new car more than anything else—if its purchase would give him more joy than any other use of his money—but he spends it instead to provide for his sick brother out of a sense of guilt, an action that brings him little or no joy, but only a drab sense of a duty discharged, then this is a sacrifice. On the other hand, if parents value their child's education more than a new car —as most do—then the expenditures on his/her schooling is not a sacrifice. Sacrifice is the betrayal of values – and the higher the value, the worse the betrayal. It is not a sacrifice to surrender what one does not value. Nor is it a sacrifice to pursue an exhausting course of action in support of another human being who is an enormous value, e.g., one's husband, wife, child or dearest friend.

The lives of the great men of the Scottish Enlightenment and British Industrial Revolution provide vivid examples. Thomas Telford, John Rennie, George Stephenson, et al., came from families vastly more deprived than what would currently be described in America as "disadvantaged." Each one endured unimaginable hardships to achieve his education and his success. Men such as these, to navigate the distance between the depths where they started and the heights they attained, necessarily scrimped and scrounged, went without, shivered with cold in unheated attics because their pennies were devoted to books, not to fuel. Conventionally, such heroic deeds are described as "sacrifices," because they chose to do without food or winter clothing.

Ayn Rand's analysis is much more accurate. These men were uncompromising valuers, egoists in the truest sense. Their education, their career, and their long-term success were far more important to them than the lesser values they temporarily denied themselves. It was only because they fixated on the shining goals before them that they were able to overcome every obstacle in their path. It was these grand-scale shining goals that they refused to surrender. These were men who would not compromise with themselves nor sacrifice what was dearest. Their unbreached commitment to values gave them the strength to wage and win their personal struggles.

Values come into existence only to sustain man's life—and because of this, it is exactly values that must not be sacrificed. In principle, man cannot live by the abandonment of his values; by this policy, he can only die. To attain values is the code of life. To sacrifice them is the code of death.

For example, human beings must strive to achieve an education, a productive career, a comfortable home, a fulfilling love relationship and/or family, a circle of intimate friends, etc. It is these values that enable a man to lead an active, flourishing, happy life. But in myriad forms the code of sacrifice dictates the surrender of these things— whether of your money to the poor—or of the man or woman you love to your disapproving family—or of your mind to a Nazi, Communist or Islamist dictator, etc. Without his values, a man's life loses all meaning; indeed, without his values, he cannot survive at all.

The nature of reality, of life, of morality demand that a man be egoistic. This is the only code of healthy, flourishing, joyous life.

Cynical Exploitativeness

But in the history of moral philosophy, egoism has often been interpreted as a code of callous victimization. It is generally believed that to be selfish means to victimize other human beings, to ignore their goals and their rights, to violate and abuse them. Is this the actual nature of egoism? Is this the code endorsed by Ayn Rand?

Egoism must be distinguished from the code that can best be described as cynical exploitativeness, the theory that human life is indistinguishable from a jungle struggle, that others are a man's natural prey, and that they exist solely for him to use and victimize. This is the code of the liar, the cheat, the criminal, of any man who seeks gain by duplicitous, dishonest and/or coercive means. The exploiter is not interested in working for what he wants; he doesn't seek to earn values, merely to get them.

To a significant degree, the *ancien regime* embodied the exploitative code. Lines of hereditary aristocrats were generally founded by conquest.

The serfs were forced into labor, virtually enslaved, and conscripted into the nobles' armies to fight and die in their interminable wars seeking power and plunder. The commoners more broadly were subjugated and forced into obedience. Economic restrictions were imposed. Taxes were levied. Freethinking was proscribed. Dissenters were imprisoned. The aristocrats, whose trade was warfare, did not work, but grew rich by impoverishing the commoners, who did. It was a system of institutionalized oppression: the lords claimed innate superiority by virtue of bloodlines and thereby rightful dominion over the "inferior" masses. In a word, the commoners had no rights, but existed to serve their masters, who ruled by force.

The egoist, on the other hand, recognizes that egoism is a principle, that it applies universally, that all human beings must unobstructedly pursue their values and happiness – and that this same principle that protects him from others, protects others from him. Men must work hard and earn their values and their happiness, not seek them by victimizing innocent others. On the egoistic code of Ayn Rand, none may be granted the license to impede the quest for values undertaken by another.

Egoism is a requirement of human life; consequently, every individual needs to act in accordance with his own thinking in pursuit of his own values. The clearest expression of this aspect of the Objectivist ethics is the oath taken by the hero of *Atlas Shrugged*: "I swear – by my life and my love of it – that I will never live for the sake of another man, nor ask another man to live for mine." The theme emphasized by this oath is the evil of human sacrifice – in all of its forms, regardless of who is the victim and who the beneficiary. Every human being is an end in himself. Ayn Rand advocated a non-sacrificial way of life – a mode of conduct that eschews both altruism and cynical exploitativeness, both the sacrifice of self to others and the sacrifice of others to self.[20]

Although, historically, altruism and exploitativeness have postured as opposites, Ayn Rand pointed out that they differ only as variations on a theme. Neither have outgrown the primitive call for human sacrifice. They differ merely regarding the question of who is to be sacrificed to whom. The altruist claims that self should be sacrificed to others; the cynical exploiter claims that others should be sacrificed to self. But they agree that a non-sacrificial mode of life is neither possible nor desirable. This is why Ayn Rand categorized the two together, calling the combination: the cannibal morality.

If a man rejects the principle of egoism, it makes no moral difference which school of oppression he advocates. Whether he holds that others should be sacrificed to self – or self to others – he claims that martyrdom and victimization are inherent, ineradicable features of human life. The only question then is: a man's life for the sake of others – or theirs for his? "This question does not represent a dispute about a moral principle. It is nothing but haggling over victims by two camps who share the same principle."[21]

Philosopher Leonard Peikoff points out that Ayn Rand emphatically rejected this viewpoint. Objectivism holds that the requirements of human life are not consonant with sacrifice in any of its forms, regardless of who is sacrificed to whom. In *The Fountainhead*, Ayn Rand argued that a moral individual repudiates sadism and masochism, domination and submission, the receiving of sacrifices or the making of them. What such a man stands for is "a self-sufficient ego," i.e., an individual who thinks and lives by his own mind and effort in pursuit of his own happiness.[22]

To some degree, the ethics of egoism was embraced during the Enlightenment. Thomas Jefferson wrote, after all, that men had the right to "life, liberty and the pursuit of happiness." At least implicitly, the doctrine of the Rights of Man upheld the moral principle that men had the right to their own lives. The political expression of this theme was explicit: men must be liberated from the tyrannical grip of the *ancien regime*, freed to pursue their own goals, to seek their own profit and happiness.

Though the code of egoism was neither grounded in an objective basis nor fully articulated until the work of Ayn Rand, even in its mitigated 18th century form it promoted the dramatic results described above.

Just as there is no such thing as too much health, too much intelligence or too much justice, so there is no such thing as too much egoism – for that would mean: too much pursuit of values. Properly conceived and fully implemented, it is a moral force that will transfigure the world to an even greater degree than was achieved by its causal role in the original Industrial and American Revolutions.

The Third Fundamental Moral Question

Ethics deals with three fundamental, interrelated questions. These are: What is the source of values – or the good? Who should be the beneficiary of values? By what means do human beings gain values? The answers to these questions identify the ultimate value, the specific beneficiary and the principal virtue supported by a moral system. So far answers have been provided for the first two questions. The objective requirements of life form the source of values. Each individual should strive to earn the values his own life requires. The answer to the third question remains to be discussed.

But the great creators of the Inventive Period already taught men the answer. By what means did George Washington Carver revolutionize agricultural science? How did John Roebling improve the design of suspension bridges and create his masterpiece, the Brooklyn Bridge? What instrument did George Eastman employ to utterly transform the field of photography? In all of these cases and in many others, the answer is: the reasoning mind. The great achievements of science, technology, industry, as well as those of philosophy, literature and the arts, that uplift men and carry them from the caves to the skyscrapers, are the province of genius, of superlative thinking, of rationality.

Man's mind—his rational faculty—as the primary means by which he promotes his life is the subject of the next chapter.

The Nature of the Good

Summary

The leading philosophers and thinkers of modern culture have generally held a moral code of self-sacrifice bitterly antithetical to capitalism's essence.

Ayn Rand identified and validated the fundamental principles of a rational ethics that establish capitalism's rectitude and explain its life-promoting successes. The requirements of human life form the standard by which good and evil are judged. That which promotes the life of a rational being is the good; that which harms or destroys it is the evil. It follows from this that an individual should pursue a course of action that furthers his own life, i.e., that he should be egoistic.

The next logical question is: By what means will men gain the values their lives depend on?

7: The Mind as Man's Instrument of Survival

All living beings are endowed by nature with specific attributes by which they seek survival.

For example, "plants survive by means of purely physical functions." Automatically, with no faculty of awareness and consequently no power of choice, they dig their roots into the soil to gain chemical nutrients and grow their leaves toward the sun to gain light.

The higher animals possess perceptual consciousness – the ability to perceive entities – and based on this the capacity of locomotion. They possess footspeed to catch prey (or outrun predators), claws and fangs with which to rend and devour their kill, superior size and strength to protect them, etc. "They have to learn a set of vital skills, such as hunting, storing food, hiding, or nest-building." These species survive by "instinct," i.e., by inherent, automatic, unchosen, non-reasoning responses to environmental conditions.

Given such limited awareness as afforded by instincts, animals survive by physicalistic means. They devour each other; they use twigs or sticks to build nests or dams; they discover caves, find or burrow holes, eat berries or nuts; etc. If the vegetative or animal life they require dies off, from drought, for example, then they migrate to more fruitful climes or they die. The primitive nature of their consciousness requires them to adjust to their background.

But human beings do not live by adjusting themselves to their environment. They do not possess the physicalistic attributes of strength or speed necessary to survive in the manner of animals – and the values on which their lives depend are not pre-prepared in nature. As philosopher Leonard Peikoff states: "bread, shirts, apartments, hammers, matches, light bulbs, and penicillin do not grow like weeds or wild berries, waiting for men to seize them." The goods and services required for human life must be produced.[1]

The Role of the Mind

The goods and services that men must produce to sustain their lives are myriad. From pens and pads, to rich agricultural harvests, to skyscrapers and cities, to a multitude of others, man's productive activities are fundamentally reliant on one human faculty: his reasoning mind.

Human beings come on earth unarmed. Whereas animals survive by means of such physicalistic characteristics as size, strength, footspeed, wings, etc., man has no similar abilities. His brain is his only weapon. To build shelter, he must know at least the rudimentary principles of architecture. To cure diseases, he must study medicine. To grow crops and to domesticate livestock, he must understand the basics of agricultural science. All of this, indeed, every advance and creation on which human survival depends, requires rational thought.[2]

This central truth of human life was illustrated by the glorious achievements of the Scientific, Technological and Industrial Revolutions described above. The accomplishments of Isaac Newton, Benjamin Franklin, Thomas Jefferson, James Watt, Thomas Edison, the Wright brothers, et. al., were not actuated by brute force, emotionalist whims or manual labor – but by the creative genius of man's mind. The abundance of food enjoyed in the capitalist nations is the result of advances in agricultural science and technology. Similarly, the medications and innovative surgical procedures by means of which the human life expectancy has been vastly increased are the consequence of progress in medical research and biological science. From breakthroughs in computer science to telecommunications to jet travel to a thousand others, all progress is brought about by the accomplishments of man's mind.

As Ayn Rand states in *Atlas Shrugged*, man's mind is his basic tool of survival.

Man's life, as required by his nature, is not the life of a mindless brute, of a looting thug or a mooching mystic, but the life of a thinking being – not life by means of force or fraud, but life by means of achievement – not survival at any price, since there's only one price that pays for man's survival: reason.[3]

The Errors of the Dominant Current School of Thought

But the dominant contemporary school of philosophy on this issue – Marxism – disagrees. Marx, claiming to be a "scientific" socialist, was a philosophical materialist, holding that man's mind and its thinking are but epiphenomena, i.e., incidental by-products of physical objects and processes – specifically, of the material "forces" that drive economic production. As materialists, Marx and his heirs argue that manual labor – the work of the body – is responsible for economic production and for all value creation. Man's mind is a secondary contributor at best, possessing little or no causal efficacy to promote material prosperity.

Frederick Copleston, one of the leading historians of philosophy, was correct when he stated that for Marx: "The fundamental form of human work is not thought but manual labor…" For the forces of material production are the dominant element of man's life. It is these economic, social factors that condition man's intellectual and moral existence. "The mode of production in material life determines the general character of the social, political and spiritual processes of life. It is not the consciousness of men that determine their existence, but, on the contrary, their social existence determines their consciousness."

Put simply: the means by which men produce and distribute material goods determines their thinking. Is a society one of hunters-gathers? Is
it essentially agrarian? Is it industrialized? Is it feudal or capitalist or
socialist? The philosophy, the education, the science, the culture of a society follow from, and vary in accordance with, such economic factors. The
means of material production determine men's ideas, not vice-versa.[4]

There are no rational grounds upon which to deride manual labor,
which is a necessary and important component of any constructive activity. But Ayn Rand correctly denies all materialistic claims, including the
relevant one in this regard – that thinking is at most an auxiliary factor
in the process of material production. The truth is that the intellectual
work inherent in value creation is more fundamental than physical labor
– i.e., it is logically antecedent to it. For example, before men could perform the tasks of carpentry, shingling, etc., necessary to build a house,
someone with knowledge of the principles of architecture and engineering had to design it. Similarly, electricians are skilled workers performing
valuable tasks, but their profession is predicated on a great mind like
Thomas Edison creating the electric lighting system.

Inventors and innovators, such as James Watt, Joseph Priestley,
George and Robert Stephenson, John Roebling, Alexander Graham Bell,
et al., were not glorified tinkerers, i.e., men of exclusively mechanical
ability who by means of dextrous manual labor put together inventions
and new technologies that revolutionized men's material lives. They were
geniuses. In some cases, they studied engineering or applied science; in
some, not. But in all instances, it was by means of superlative thinking
that they solved the problems involved in the creation of new technologies.

Related to this, men who perform skilled manual labor – carpenters,
construction workers, automotive mechanics, et. al. – do not engage in
exclusively physical labor as if they were so many oxen. They understand

their work; they learn their skills; they teach them to younger workers. Thinking is a vital part of their competence. Though many animals possess far greater physical strength than do men – bears, horses, elephants, for example – such brutes could not be taught the tasks of skilled human labor. Even if genetic science discovered a method by which to graft an opposable thumb onto the hands of gorillas, so they could clutch tools, they would still not be able to perform such skilled labor, for they could not understand it.

Further, if intellectual work was at most a subsidiary aspect of material production, a mere supplement to the more important physical effort, then horses and oxen – creatures who have long engaged in bodily labor – would be able to construct heated barns to shelter them from the elements, cure the ailments that afflict them, cultivate vast fields of oats, and irrigate arid regions to grow grass for consumption. But obviously they cannot.

Additionally, the more demanding the intellectual work, the fewer the number of men competent to expertly perform it. Many human beings have sufficient ability to become skilled and productive electricians (including perhaps the author) – but there are only a handful who can perform the intellectual work of an Edison (definitely excluding the author). Competent manual labor is valuable and, fortunately, in relatively abundant supply. Genius is far more valuable and, unfortunately, in short supply. Its very rarity supports the conclusion that superlative thinking – not the physical act of hammering nails into wood – is the most difficult aspect of improving men's material conditions.

For men's failure to yet cure cancer, invent a flying car or create a plane able to comfortably transport passengers from New York to Tokyo in an hour is not from a dearth of either skilled or unskilled manual labor. It is due, in part, to the infrequency with which the minds capable of such achievements arise (and, in part, to the absence of the political conditions the unfettered functioning of such minds requires).

The Capitalist Manifesto

In *Atlas Shrugged*, Ayn Rand, in effect, queries Marx: How much manual labor did it take to invent the steam engine – or the lighting system – or the airplane – or, to update her point, the personal computer and the Internet? How many physical workers toiling how many hours with how many pickaxes and shovels to discover a cure for polio – identify the laws of thermodynamics – formulate the theory of evolution – compose Beethoven's symphonies – write *Hamlet* or *The Brothers Karamazov*? Her answer, of course, is that the question is not applicable. No amount of manual labor will suffice to reach such distinctively intellectual achievements – and no reduction of intellectual to bodily work is possible. Fundamentally, these and many others, are accomplishments of the mind.

It should be obvious if one examines an electric generator, the research labs of medical science, the international network of telecommunications or one of a thousand other advances that they were not brought into existence by sheer muscle power. Ayn Rand pointed out the impossibility of growing food or creating any other value by means of nothing but physical motions.[5]

To explicate this further: reason is man's survival instrument mainly because it is the fundamental means by which he produces the goods necessary to sustain his life, i.e., it is the means by which he deals effectively with nature. But it is also the tool of discussion and negotiation with other men, the instrument by which he non-violently resolves disputes with them, whether interpersonal or international, i.e., it is the means by which he deals effectively with society.

To avoid the endless violence and senseless warfare that fills man's history – to make his future brighter than his past – man must learn to reason out his disputes, not fight them out, i.e., resolve them by intellectual, not physical means. (This does not imply that innocent men do not possess the right to self-defense against the brutes who physically assault them. On the contrary, it means that the brutes need to eschew physical

facts.

Ayn Rand describes such a self-destructive policy as "placing the 'I wish' above the 'it is.'" Its essence is treating one's desires, rather than facts, as the unquestioned primaries of cognition. Since reason is man's survival instrument, any policy of unreason – of denigrating facts, of demoting them, of subordinating them to any consideration whatever – undercuts the use and functioning of man's tool of survival. By what means then are men to survive? Men who choose not to think, to reason, or to honor facts will die, just as birds would if they could choose not to fly. Men, in fact, often choose to be irrational, but they cannot choose irrationality *and* fulfilled, flourishing life; the first negates the second. "Man has the power to act as his own destroyer – and that is the way he has acted through most of his history." In any circumstances, and under all conditions, the denial of facts is hazardous to a man's physical and mental life.

Irrationality is not ignorance – an honest error or innocent lack of knowledge. It is evasion, the deliberate, willful denial of facts. Whether it's a cocaine user, who pushes aside the knowledge of the damage the drug does to his health – or the Nazis, who ignored every known fact of biology to assert moral superiority based on their blood – or an "economist," who refuses to consider the long-term bankruptcy that will inevitably result from his policies of persistent deficit spending, and who flippantly replies to objections by stating "in the long run we're all dead" – or any other similar act of denying disagreeable truths, irrationality is, always and everywhere, a policy of trying to defraud reality.

Irrationality is "the act of blanking out, the willful suspension of one's consciousness, the refusal to think – *not blindness, but the refusal to see; not ignorance, but the refusal to know.*" Ayn Rand eloquently summarizes the consequences: "Irrationality is the rejection of man's means of survival and, therefore, a commitment to a course of blind destruction; that which is anti-mind, is anti-life."[8]

Virtues are the means, the character states, by which men achieve values. Because rationality is the fundamental tool of human survival, it is man's basic virtue, the source of all his other virtues.

As Ayn Rand identified: "The virtue of rationality means the recognition and acceptance of reason as one's only source of knowledge, one's only judge of values and one's only guide to action." This means that in every aspect of one's life – in education, in career, in love, in finances and in friendships – one must conduct oneself in accordance with as rigorous a process of logical thought as one can conscientiously muster.

Such a scrupulous devotion to one's own mind means an inviolable dedication to one's own life.[9]

The Virtue of Productiveness

Rationality, as a broad principle, has numerous derivatives and applications. The one most relevant in the present context is the virtue of productivity. "Productiveness is the process of creating material values, whether goods or services," the process by which men adjust nature to satisfy their needs of survival. It involves the recognition that man's life requires the attainment of values—and that values must be created by human effort.

Such productivity is a process that integrates man's mind and body. By means of productive work, man's consciousness improves his existence on earth. Human beings continuously gain knowledge, equipping them to fulfill their goals. They transform their thoughts into material form— and transfigure the earth in accordance with their purposes and values.

A point that bears endless repetition is that the goods and services upon which human life depends—from macaroni to MRI machines, from shoes to suspension bridges—do not exist ready-made in nature. They are produced, i.e., built, grown, created—and more: they are produced primarily by mind power.

The creation of even the most primitive human values -- the weapons and tools of the Iron Age, for example -- require a level of knowledge and thought unattainable by even the higher animals. But when analysis shifts to the advanced science and technology enjoyed currently in the capitalist nations, Ayn Rand's point becomes unmistakably obvious.[10]

After the Scientific, Technological and Industrial Revolutions—and after the 18th century development of the principle of individual rights that liberated man's creative consciousness—two interrelated conclusions must be drawn: man's life depends on productiveness—and rationality is the primary engine that drives the process. But the critical truth not recognized until the late-20th century was Ayn Rand's identification that the requirements of man's life constitute the standard of moral value. Because of this monumental insight, it can now be recognized that productiveness is a significant moral virtue.

The great producers of history, therefore, are not rapacious exploiters driven by mindless greed. They are men who preeminently live in accordance with the requirements of human survival; their activities make possible man's life on earth—and at an exceedingly high standard of living. Indeed, this profound virtue is sufficient to establish them as major heroes.[11]

The abuse characteristically rained on the heads of many of history's greatest producers constitutes a terrible injustice. Indeed, it is more than Bill Gates or John D. Rockefeller, et al., who are besmirched. For insofar as their creative activities represent a principled commitment to productiveness, they are exemplars of a rational code of ethics. It is the virtue of productiveness that is attacked in the lives and persons of these men; it is egoism, the mind as man's tool of survival, human life as the standard of moral value— all of the moral principles on which life depends—that are attacked. To glorify the great producers is to celebrate the virtues that make possible life on earth; to demonize them is to revile all of the requirements of that life, and to celebrate death. (See the Appendix.)

The Erroneous Theory of Emotionalism

Tragically, the dominant theory of cognition in the contemporary Western world repudiates the unbreached rationality necessary for man's survival. That theory, emotionalism, argues that emotions or feelings or "intuition" or some other ineffable, non-sensory, non-rational mode of cognition supersedes man's mind. Emotionalists treat their feelings as a fundamental source of truth. To them, desires are unquestioned absolutes to which reality is subordinated. In any issue in which his desires clash with the facts, the emotionalist chooses his desires and repudiates the facts that contradict them.[12]

Based on such a cognitive methodology, emotionalists can justify any belief or action whatever. On this view, X is a value not because it objectively, in the long term, promotes man's life, but because it subjectively, in the short term, makes the emotionalist feel good. But individuals (or groups of them) can and sometimes do desire things at wildest variance with the factual requirements of man's life. For example, the drug addict seeks the titillation of physical stimulation; the murderer seeks to get away with his crime; the Communists seek the eradication of capitalism and capitalists. These, and countless others, in a multitude of forms, stand for destruction, whether of self, others or both. When the standard of moral value is subjective gratification – whether of a single individual or an entire society – the requirements of man's survival have been abrogated, and men – many of them – will not survive.

Historically, the distilled essence of this view was embodied by the Nazis. In their doctrines, the triumph of anti-mind irrationalism, and the glorification of passion and instinct – "blood and bowels," in their terms– reached their fullest expression. "We must distrust the intelligence," stated Adolf Hitler, "and must place our trust in our instincts." "Trust your instincts, your feelings, or whatever you like to call them," proclaimed the Fuhrer. Hitler openly stated that "at a mass meeting thought is eliminated," replaced by the raw emotionalism of a crowd mentality – and that this was precisely the reason he required full attendance.

The Nazis believed that "the more inconsistent and irrational...their doctrine, the better." Herman Goering, a prominent figure in the Nazi hierarchy, stated the essence of this belief succinctly: "I tell you, if the Fuhrer wishes it then two times two are five." Summing up the inevitable consequence of the Nazi's war against the mind, one party functionary stated: "When I hear the word 'culture,' I slip back the safety catch of my revolver."

A contemporary philosopher eloquently sums up the meaning of the Nazi ideology: "The politics of Naziism...is unprecedented in the West, not for its collectivism but for its undisguised irrationality...Its distinctive feature is self-proclaimed barbarianism, i.e., undisguised boastfully trumpeted defiance of reason."[13]

Though the Nazis repudiated logic, there was a grim logic in the development of their totalitarianism out of their emotionalism. For having repudiated facts and reason, what constraint existed on their willingness to act on their feelings? If they felt in their viscera their moral superiority over "inferior" peoples, and their anointed status as rightful rulers, then no rational argumentation supporting individual rights, limited Constitutional government and political-economic freedom could give them the slightest pause. By making themselves impervious to reason, they necessarily made themselves implacably hostile to liberty. All the free men of the West could do was defend themselves against the inevitable physical assaults that followed—and in decisively vanquishing the aggressor demonstrate the superiority of rationalism and capitalism to irrationalism and anti-capitalism.

In various forms, emotionalism (or anti-rationalism) in epistemology leads to anti-capitalism in politics. For example, socialists and welfare statists consider "compassion" of central importance and, based on sympathy for the suffering, implement political programs that re-distribute wealth, i.e., that rob the rich and give to the poor. Motivated by their feelings, they ignore or deny rational ethical and economic principles that contradict their policies. So: that the government now employs its coercive power to steal does not matter to them. That forcibly removing capital from the hands of the productive both hampers production and diminishes incentive to produce is immaterial. That providing money to individuals who do not work undercuts their work ethic and self-reliance is unimportant. That the overall consequence is to make people less productive and consequently poorer is not to be considered. That the programs are, therefore, both unethical and uneconomic is not an issue. What matters is that society acts on "compassion." Anti-capitalism is inherently anti-rational.

Man's Fundamental Right

What is the inevitable result of man's abandonment of reason as the source of knowledge, especially in the area of ethics? Regarding the realm of human relationships, the question can be re-formulated: If you refuse to deal with men by reason, then you will deal with them by – what method? Ayn Rand's answer is: force.

To understand the evil of the initiation of force – of starting its use, not of defending oneself from those who start it – it is necessary to keep in mind the entire essence of a rational ethics. The good is that which furthers man's life on earth; the evil that which harms it. Further, man's mind is the fundamental method by which he, in fact, succeeds in promoting his life. Since the mind is man's tool of survival, it follows that the mind is each man's survival tool – and that his life and well-being depend on his full, unrestrained exercise of it. His capacity to do so must be protected; he must have the unequivocal right to act on his own most conscientious rational judgment, i.e., to live in accordance with the faculty that enables him to live.

The fundamental right is the right to life – and therefore, the right to act on one's own thinking. In Ayn Rand's eloquent formulation: "The source of man's rights is not divine law or congressional law, but the law of identity. A is A – and man is man."

An individual cannot live unless he has an unqualified right to his own life, which means: an unqualified right to use his own mind, to live in accordance with his own judgment, to pursue his own values, and to retain the product of his own effort. "If life on earth is his purpose, he has a right to live as a rational being; nature forbids him the irrational."

The questions must be asked: Who or what can violate a man's right to act on his thinking – and by what means? "To violate man's rights means to compel him to act against his own judgment, or to expropriate his values. Basically, there is only one way to do it: by the use of physical force. There are two potential violators of man's rights: the criminals and the government." In brief, only other men can violate a man's rights, i.e., prevent him from acting on his own rational judgment – and only by initiating force or fraud against him.[14]

The rational mind accedes before only one authority: the facts of reality as perceived by its own rigorous, scrupulously honest functioning. To think means to focus unrestrictedly on reality. If the force wielder intends the victim to change his mind, he cannot achieve it by means of brutality. The introduction of instruments of torture does not alter the fact that the earth revolves around the sun and does not constitute evidence for a contradictory conclusion. The force wielder may get his victim to mouth untruths, but he cannot force him to think differently.[15]

But the men of brute force often intend not to change their victims' minds – but to change their actions, i.e., to dominate, to control, to enslave, to rob or to murder them. "A simple example would be a gunman who says: 'I don't care what my prey thinks. I just want him to hand over his wallet.'"

In this regard, the initiation of force compels an individual to act against his own mind. The victim still understands that the money is rightfully his, but the imminent threat to his life renders this understanding impotent. If he desires to remain alive, he must hand over his wallet to the gunman.[16]

If it is appropriate to use the term "sin" in regard to a rational ethics, then the only sins, i.e., deadly moral transgressions – are those involving the denial or abrogation of man's mind. Irrationality, i.e., the refusal to think, and its ultimate consequence, the initiation of force—the preventing of others from acting on their thinking—are of the code of death, opposed to everything required by man's life. That which is anti-mind is anti-life.

As Ayn Rand makes the point: "Reality demands of man that he act for his own rational interest; [a thug's] gun demands of him that he act against it. Reality threatens man with death if he does not act on his rational judgment; [initiators of force] threaten him with death if he does." Initiators of force push men into a nightmare world where their lives depend on surrendering the virtues that life requires.[17]

It is of the first importance that the initiation of force be banned from human life. Since the fundamental right is the right to life, and since the mind is the means by which man's life is furthered, the initiation of force – the mind's antithesis, its abrogation – represents the distilled essence of an anti-life philosophy.

Man's fundamental right is to be protected from the initiation of force against him.

Human beings need to be guarded against both potential violators of their rights—criminals and the government. "The great achievement of the United States was to draw a distinction between these two – by forbidding to the second the legalized version of the activities of the first."

In the *Declaration of Independence*, Jefferson formulated the maxim that "to secure these rights, governments are instituted among men." This claim identified government's proper moral base and its single legitimate function: to safeguard the rights of human beings by protecting them against the initiation of physical coercion.

"Thus the government's function was changed from the role of ruler to the role of servant." The government was established to safeguard human beings from criminals and the Constitution was created to protect them from their protector. "The Bill of Rights was not directed against private citizens, but against the government – as an explicit declaration that individual rights supersede any public or social power."[18]

The right of each human being to live by his most conscientious rational judgment free of the initiation of force against him is the essence of individual rights. Further, the logical result of an individual's right to life is his right to defend himself. "In a civilized society, force may be used only in retaliation and only against those who initiate its use. All the reasons which make the initiation of physical force an evil, make the retaliatory use of physical force a moral imperative."[19]

But in order to establish a civilized society, human beings cannot allow the use of force to be left to whim, desire or caprice. Its use, even as retaliation against those who initiate it, cannot be a matter of individual discretion.

Even if an individual's neighbors are fully rational and eminently just, the use of force against him cannot be left to the arbitrary decision of others. To ensure that force is limited to retaliation against those who initiate it, men must formulate "objective rules of evidence to establish that a crime has been committed." They must be able to prove who perpetrated it, and define objective principles governing punishment and procedures of law enforcement. "If a society left the retaliatory use of force in the hands of individual citizens, it would degenerate into mob rule, lynch law and an endless series of bloody private feuds or vendettas."[20]

To establish civilization, to protect the rights of every individual, men must found an institution that subordinates the use of force to rational moral principles and to the rule of objective law. "A government is the means of placing the retaliatory use of physical force under objective control – i.e., under objectively defined laws."[21]

What is the basic nature of government? "A government is an institution that holds the exclusive power to enforce certain rules of social conduct in a given geographical area." It holds a legal monopoly on the use of force in that area. Its specific function – the one great benefit it can perform – is to legally restrict the use of force to self-defense, to retaliation against those who initiate it.[22]

In a proper society, individuals "agree to delegate their right of self-defense." They surrender the discretionary use of physical force "even in self-protection" (except in emergency situations when the police cannot be summoned in time).[23]

Protecting men from the initiation of force or fraud is an issue wider than restraining or punishing criminals. A further function is absolutely essential to a proper government: the protection and enforcement of contracts, "including the resolution of disputes that arise therefrom, their impartial resolution in accordance with objectively–defined laws." Such a system simultaneously protects an individual's rights and restricts him from taking physical action against any supposed victimizer(s). By defending men's rights, the government prevents any arbitrary initiation of physical force. Civil courts are a key component of any advanced society – for though criminals are a small minority, "contractual protection for honest undertakings...is a daily necessity of civilized life."

The government's ban on physical coercion is implemented in two ways: by safeguarding citizens against force-initiators both at home and abroad, and by "settling impartially disputes that involve men's rights."

A government properly dedicated to this purpose must fulfill three and only three functions: a police force to protect innocent men from criminals; a volunteer military to defend a free society from foreign invaders; and a court system to arbitrate legitimate disputes among honest men in accordance with objective laws. "Any additional function would have to involve the government initiating force against innocent citizens. Such a government acts not as man's protector, but as a criminal."

Government's power is negative. Force can destroy, it cannot create—and such power must be wielded only to destroy the destroyers among men.

An institution which has nothing to offer but the use of force must refrain from intervening in artistic, intellectual or moral matters. It must issue no laws and hold no views regarding literature, art, education, philosophy, science or sex (if adult and voluntary). "Its function is to protect freedom, not truth or virtue."

Since the mind is the faculty responsible for human survival and prosperity, a proper government provides an all-important service to man's life by protecting the free-thinking mind. "If the agency with a monopoly on coercion undertakes to enforce ideas, any ideas, whether true or false, it becomes the enemy, not the protector, of the free mind and thus loses its moral basis for existing."[24]

Through most of mankind's history and continuing in the current era, the agency with a monopoly on coercion has been man's oppressor, not his protector. Prior to the capitalist revolution of the 18th century, and abiding today in the non-capitalist nations, the governments under which mankind suffered embodied varying degrees of statism. (In a less virulent form, this includes the predominantly capitalist nations of the world, which to differing degrees were always, and remain, mixtures of free and statist elements.) A principled commitment to rationality, individual rights and a ban on the initiation of force has never existed in a consistent, non-contradictory form prior to Ayn Rand's intellectual achievement – not in theory, and certainly not in political practice. This is why, despite the accurate observation of numerous commentators that mankind's moral development is appallingly low, there is reason for hope. For if one remembers the brutal tyrannies under which mankind has so often suffered and continues to suffer, it becomes a wonder that men have created even a modicum of civilization. Indeed, one must offer a tribute to the indestructible human spirit that has refused to be broken though generally existing under crushing dictatorships and the abysmal destitution engendered by such regimes.[25]

Mankind's future may be far brighter than its past, because at least now – after both the political-economic revolution wrought by the best thinkers of the Enlightenment, and the intellectual revolution created by Ayn Rand – there exists some understanding, in the minds of some human beings, of the ideal political-economic system.

Capitalism, it can now be shown, embodies all of the essential principles of a rational philosophy.

Summary

The rational mind is responsible for creating the values on which human life depends; as such, it is mankind's survival instrument. Such theories as materialism and emotionalism that reject the mind are profoundly mistaken and, in practice, undercut the application of man's survival instrument, leading to countless unnecessary deaths.

Man's fundamental right is to his own life. From this it follows that he must be left free to live in accordance with his own rational judgment, i.e., in accordance with that faculty which enables him to live. The sole means of violating this right, the initiation of force, must be banned by the government. Men must be protected from the initiation of force by both private criminals and, of special urgency, the government itself. To achieve this requires the establishment of a government limited by Constitutional law to the protection of individual rights.

8: Capitalism as the Embodiment of Rational Philosophical Principles

The four principles of a rational ethics relevant to the validation of capitalism as the only proper social system are egoism, the mind as man's tool of survival, productiveness as a moral virtue, and life as the standard of value. These are the principles that must be consistently enacted in social practice if human beings are to survive and flourish on earth. Capitalism has brought men to previously undreamed-of heights of freedom and prosperity because its distilled essence embodies every one of these principles.

Capitalism as Egoistic:

This is a charge levelled against capitalism by its enemies. The claim is factually correct, although the enemies' negative assessment of egoism (and of capitalism) is mistaken without qualification.

The essence of egoism is man's rational quest for the values that sustain his life. Egoism is a moral code exhorting a man to be the beneficiary of his own actions, i.e., to pursue his interest, his fulfillment, his happiness. It emphasizes the importance of the individual, of a personal life, of privately held values, of a man's own aspirations, goals, dreams and hopes. Egoism urges men to achieve the values their lives require, not to sacrifice them. Consequently, egoism, in contrast to its antithesis – the code of human sacrifice in any of its incarnations – is a requirement of man's life on earth.

In every possible way, capitalism is the logical political-economic consequence of a consistently egoistic approach to ethics.

This does not mean that all of the institutions of the United States or of other generally capitalist nations, past or present, are egoistic. All the societies generally referred to as "capitalist," were and are, in fact, mixed economies. The claim is not that these societies fully embodied egoism. They did not and do not. The claim is that capitalism's nature fully embodies egoism. The philosophical essence of capitalism must be carefully distinguished from all flawed historical attempts to implement it. Again, the Empiricist Fallacy must be scrupulously avoided.

Individualism is a political theory holding that each human being is an end in himself, that men have inalienable rights, and that the sole purpose of civilized society and of government is to protect those rights. Its antithesis, collectivism, holds that society as a whole – the state – not the individual, is the unit of moral value, and that an individual's rights and values must be subordinated to its needs and dictates.

Egoism exhorts the pursuit of values – and is based on the nature of living beings, on their need to achieve values. The principle of individual rights that forms the essence of capitalism is simply the application of an egoistic ethics to politics. If a man must achieve values in order to sustain his life — e.g., earn money with which to purchase food, shelter and clothing — then it follows that he must possess the legally-protected right to engage in such pursuit of values. Bell and Edison, for instance, as all individuals, had the moral right to pursue the values that brought them both meaning and income; but without the legal protection afforded by the basically individualistic principles of the U.S. Constitution (or a similar document) they would not have been left free to do so.

Protection against the initiation of force or fraud by other men is the indispensable social requirement of an individual in his quest for values. If he receives such protection, then his efforts to attain the values his life requires may continue unrestricted. But if he does not, then those efforts will be impeded, even thwarted. The principle of individual rights is the political-economic requirement of value achievement and of man's life on earth.

This is just as true of wisdom, love, friendship and other non-monetary values. A perfect example from the Inventive Period was the life of George Washington Carver, who cared little for money or material goods but who needed the moral and legal protection afforded by the principle of individual rights to pursue the scientific achievements so dear to him.

The individualistic nature of capitalism follows directly from man's need to reach the ends upon which his life depends. Individual rights and capitalism form the necessary social condition of man's life-giving quest for values.

The value-promoting, egoistic foundation of capitalism can be identified regarding many issues. Among these are: the institution of private property, the profit motive, the rule of law, and a laissez-faire economics.

To take these one at a time: the moral principle of private property means that men own the product of their intellectual and/or bodily effort. The justice of this should be manifest. If an individual, for example, designs and constructs his own tables and chairs, then the result is a product of his thought and effort. Similarly, if by productive work he earns sufficient money to buy furniture, he is the proper owner by virtue of having created the monetary value-equivalent of the commodity and then trading for it. If a man has a right to his own life, his own body, his own mind, then it follows that he has a right to the product of his own intellectual and bodily effort.

For at least two reasons the right to private property furthers a man's ability to acquire the values upon which his life depends. First, when he realizes that what he earns or keeps stands in direct proportion to how much he produces, he has increased incentive to produce. Second, when the right of private property is protected by law, then neither criminals nor the government can legally expropriate a man's earnings.

This is an especially urgent point relative to the government, for the 20th century lessons of Communism must be learned and never forgotten: when the government holds the legal right to strip men of their property, it will do so at its whim – whether its purpose is to farm the jungle or force peasants onto collective lands or one of a thousand others – and leave countless millions to literally starve to death.

Under such conditions, there is no moral principle protecting men from arbitrary governmental confiscation and brutality; they are morally and legally at the mercy of the state. If men must exist for the collective, then it is logical to expropriate their private property and compel them to live on collectives. Those "counter-revolutionary traitors" who resist can be easily dealt with: withhold food and permit them to starve, a lesson brutally taught the peasants by Joseph Stalin, among others. Put negatively, if a man has no right to his earnings, then he has no right to his life – and shortly will possess no means to it.

The profit motive is the incentive to work productively in order to increase one's economic gain. Such a motive is logically dependent on private property, because it presupposes that men can retain both their earnings and the goods they purchase with them. Morally, if men have a right to their own lives, then they have a right to keep the values they have gained by their own effort, the values that their lives depend on. Under a properly capitalistic system, men possess the unimpeachable right to pursue their own interest, i.e., to create and keep the goods and services upon which their lives depend. Capitalism places economic rewards in service of men's need to create values.

It is no historical accident that so many of the intellectual pioneers of the Inventive Period earned significant fortunes, among them George Eastman, George Westinghouse, John Roebling, as well as Bell, Edison and others. The love of the ground-breaking work was the fundamental motivation of such creative minds, it is true, and some, like George Washington Carver, held little interest in material gain. Nevertheless, by nature, men have to live on earth; they have to earn their livings; they require material prosperity in order to live well.

Because the world human beings inhabit is not a Garden of Eden, because it is not a "paradise" of effortless existence, human beings are required by nature to be productive. Therefore, the political-economic system that most consistently rewards productive effort is the one that will achieve the highest degree of advance and prosperity. Since men must own the values they create in order to live, the profit motive provides – properly – an extraordinarily powerful incentive to productive effort. Since capitalism is the only system that consistently upholds the pursuit of profit, it is the system in full accordance with men's need to create values.

Capitalism is thereby the sole system consonant with human survival requirements. Consequently, many more men survive for many more years under capitalism than under any other system of history. Put simply, when it is judged morally proper that human beings keep what they produce — what their survival and prosperity require — and when they have the legally-protected right to do so, they will produce more and live better and longer.

The institutions of private property and the profit motive are obviously egoistic, for they involve an individual's moral right to assert his own prerogatives against the demands of others — against their claims on his values, and on the time and effort by means of which he created them. In the case of the rule of law, the point might not be so obvious.

The rule of law means that government officials – including the head(s) of state – are bound by moral principles embodied in the legal system, and that they cannot violate those principles. The alternative is the rule of men, which means: the rule of whim. The rule of men means that government officials are above the law, that they need not adhere to it, that they can use their power against private citizens at any random moment based on any random caprice. The rule of whim is an essential feature of any statist or dictatorial regime.

The rule of law in the capitalist nations is a direct application of the broader principle of individual rights. A written Constitution legally circumscribes the power of the state by guaranteeing to all citizens specific inalienable rights, including freedom of speech, freedom of religion, the right to own property, etc. The rule of Constitutional law subordinates all men and, crucially, government officials and agents to the principle of individual rights. It means that they cannot legally employ their power to violate the rights of private citizens. In performing such a function, the rule of law ensures that each individual remains legally protected in his quest for personal values and happiness. For men to be able to successfully pursue their own values, the rule of law is a necessary social condition.

As but one illustration: under capitalism, an individual's right to pursue any career he chooses is protected by law; unlike in a totalitarian state, where the government can decide, for any reason, that it needs more farmers or soldiers or engineers, and then force men deemed qualified into those professions. Capitalism's nature is that the laws protecting individual rights are not abrogated or altered for any consideration, including the whims of the heads of state.

The policy of laissez-faire – of "leave it be," of "hands off" – is simply the application of the moral principle of individual rights to economics. The principle of individual rights means that consenting adults are free to perform any actions they choose, so long as they do not initiate force or fraud against others. *This means that men are legally restricted from criminally interfering with the quest for values undertaken by other men.* Economic activity is the production and exchange of goods and services – the goods and services upon which man's life depends. If men produce and exchange voluntarily, then their mutual pursuit of values is reciprocally enhanced by the productive work of each other.

Capitalism as the Embodiment of Rational Philosophical Principles

The government's proper role in economics is a straightforward application of its broader moral role as the protector of individual rights: by providing a rule of law – by protecting private property and safeguarding contracts – it establishes a legal context conducive to the creation of values. By punishing criminals – and only criminals – by limiting government involvement in the marketplace to its proper function in all areas of human life – to the prevention of the initiation of force or fraud – the government of a properly capitalistic society provides an incalculable benefit to men's lives: *it protects those who create values and restrains those who destroy values or physically interfere with the creators.* Since value achievement is the essence of life's requirements, any governmental policy that promotes it is a boon to man's life.

Earlier, it was noted that in *Atlas Shrugged* one of the characters proposes an amendment to the U.S. Constitution that would prohibit Congress from making any laws abridging the freedom of production and trade. By eliminating all regulations and regulatory agencies, the government of a capitalist society would thereby lift all arbitrary restrictions on productiveness and commerce, i.e., it would repeal all laws not directed against those who initiate force or fraud. Such freedom for productive men would significantly liberate their creative abilities and result in a vast increase in the supply of values necessary for human life.[1]

Statists deride the laissez-faire system as "do-nothing government." Two points must be made to refute this claim. First is that such a government protects individual rights, including property rights, an enormous task and achievement in service of men's lives – and one possible only to the government. This is hardly a "do-nothing" policy. Second, such governmental protection liberates the entire population of a society to engage in the creation and exchange of life-giving values, including material ones. The so-called "do-nothing" government is actually a political-economic system of "free-to-do" individuals – of "do-much" productive citizens – who, protected by the principle of individual rights, create the

[213]

enormous abundance so characteristic of all capitalist societies.

A policy of laissez-faire frees each honest man to pursue his own economic interest.

In principle, the sole alternative to a laissez-faire system is some variant of collectivism or statism. By subordinating men's rights and minds to the state, this system hampers – and in its extreme, most consistent form abrogates – men's quest for values. When men cannot achieve values, they cannot live. Where they have no right to their creations, they have no right to their lives. This is the deepest moral reason that tens of millions of innocent human beings die untimely deaths under collectivism.

Capitalism as the System of the Mind

The antithesis to reason is brute force. The only important political-economic question regarding men's ability to use their minds is: Are they protected from the initiation of force against them? The only moral principle and the only political-economic system that can unequivocally answer "yes" are: individual rights and capitalism.

Any political-economic system rests logically on specific philosophical principles that underlie it. The deepest philosophical question regarding a political-economic system is: By what means are men to survive on earth? The historical (and current) answers have generally been virulently anti-mind.

A theocracy, for example, is the political rule of the clergy. Some leading illustrations were medieval Europe under the Catholic Church, and in recent times Iran under the Ayatollahs and Afghanistan under the Taliban. According to this system, men gain the important truths of human life by means of faith. Therefore, to the degree that survival and prosperity on earth are important, faith – men's means of knowledge – must be their guide to action.

Legally, reason is and must be proscribed. It is the method of science and secular philosophy. It raises questions, criticizes beliefs of revealed texts and challenges pronouncements of the clergy. Thinkers do not uncritically accept beliefs that lack supporting evidence or contradict the laws of nature. Thinkers are the gravest danger to a theocratic regime.

This is why questioners of doctrine were branded as heretics and burned at the stake. This is the reason that scientists were forced to recant their theories under threat of torture — and that, as late as the 18th century, the French *philosophes* were censored and imprisoned at various points in the writing of the *Encyclopedie*. Such societies necessarily unleashed brute force against their best minds. Man's survival instrument was abrogated – and men could not survive. The miserable living conditions of Dark Age Europe and Dark Age Afghanistan (under the Taliban) were and are necessary results of such a system.[2]

Communism was and remains the rule of the people (in theory) and of its "agent," the government, in practice. Most important is that according to Marxist doctrine, human beings survive by means of manual labor. Men are fundamentally physicalistic beings in whose lives mind plays a secondary role (at best). With men roughly indistinguishable from barnyard beasts, with the mind and its requirements shoved off of the political scene, there is no moral constraint to be placed on the initiation of governmental force. If animals can be forced to work productively, so can men. There is every reason to believe that cattle prods will be as effective against humans as against beasts.

The virulent collectivism of Communism augments its anti-mind nature. For the mind is an attribute of the individual — and if individuals are merely interchangeable parts of a larger whole, subordinate to its needs, then the individual's own judgment and thinking is likewise subordinate and of value only insofar as it submits to the state; if and when it seeks truths unacceptable to the state, it is a danger that must be silenced. The suppression and extermination of the intellectuals, as well as the banning (and even burning) of books under Stalin, Mao and Pol

Pot are events as well-documented as they are predictable. The Dark Ages of Communism produced the same repression of the mind, and the same resultant misery, as the Dark Ages of theocracy.[3]

Capitalism alone, the system of the Enlightenment, provides the life-giving answer to the most important question underlying a political system: men survive by reason. This principle was not explicitly formulated during the Enlightenment, but was implicit in the era's commitment to theoretical and applied science, to the Industrial Revolution and, above all, to the liberation of the freethinking mind from the grip of the *ancien regime*. A man who perfectly illustrated such Enlightenment commitment was Joseph Priestley, an unsurpassed chemist, a superb technical consultant to the industrialists of the Lunar Society, an outspoken champion of the free mind against all forms of tyranny — monarchical or clerical — and, logically, a staunch republican in politics, who eventually left the Old World to end his days in revolutionary America.

The concept of individual rights is more than a moral-political principle. It is the necessary social condition of an intellectual revolution, for *it is the guarantor of freedom and physical safety for the men of the mind against the brutes who would initiate force.* The best among men, those who choose to think, had found the social system that provided their haven. By protecting the lives and the freedom of the individuals most scrupulously devoted to the employment of man's survival instrument, capitalism is thereby the system of man's survival. If men seek to understand the deepest reason that the system of individual rights alone creates undreamed of abundance, this is the point they must grasp. *Men's lives require a social system whose essence embodies unbreached protection of their ability to unrestrictedly employ their minds.*

Capitalism as Embodying the Virtue of Productiveness

By this point in the argument, it should be clear that capitalism is the system of productiveness. The events of history and current affairs show this. One of many such instances from capitalism's Inventive Period was John Roebling — inventor, designer, millionaire manufacturer of wire. But the best examples from that or any other period are the so-called "Robber Barons" — Andrew Carnegie, John D. Rockefeller, James J. Hill, et al. — who, in justice, must be recognized and honored as history's most prodigious producers. (See the Appendix.) Further, the writings of the great economists partially explain capitalism's unparalleled productivity. The sole remaining task is to philosophically explain it.

Keep in mind that logically and historically freedom is based on egoism and reason. A principled commitment to liberty arises only when men recognize two related truths: that human beings have the inalienable right to their own lives — and that the mind is the means by which they gain knowledge and promote their lives. Therefore, men must be free to further their lives and to employ the instrument allowing them to do so. This forms the basis of the principle of individual rights that is the essence of capitalism.

In brief, capitalism is the system of reason, egoism, freedom. This means that it liberates the instrument by which men create values (reason); acknowledges their need, and rewards their attempts, to achieve their own values (egoism); and protects their legal right to pursue their own values (freedom). That men therefore produce values under capitalism is no mystery. The mystery is only that today, with all this knowledge available, some men still repudiate capitalism for various forms of statism.

For example, Marx and his more astute contemporary heirs argue(d) in support of global capitalism as a necessary condition of industrializing the world's impoverished regions. But Marx, in the Hegelian school of thought, saw capitalism as no more than a necessary stage in an inexorable historical march toward socialism. When capitalism "exhausted its capacity for development," it would be supplanted by the next and higher stage in the evolution of the modes of production.

But capitalism, as the liberation of the human mind, will never exhaust its capacity for development. As long as man's mind remains free, the possibility of advance, including in the technological and industrial fields, is literally—without hyperbole—limitless. This constitutes the fatal flaw in Marx's analysis. As a philosophical materialist, he was intellectually unequipped to identify the fundamental cause and nature of the revolution that transfigured the Western world during his lifetime. Hence the tragic result: no thinker of history studied capitalism more assiduously than did Marx and no thinker understood it less.[4]

Capitalism as Upholding Man's Life as the Standard of Value

Every aspect of capitalism's essence without exception is a means of promoting man's life. Do men need to be egoistic, i.e., to achieve values in order to sustain their lives? Capitalism is egoistic. Do men need to employ their minds in order to survive? Capitalism protects their right to do so without qualification. Do men need to ban the initiation of force? Capitalism is the sole system to do so. Do men need to produce the goods and services on which their lives depend? Capitalism rewards their productive activities. Capitalism, in its distilled essence, embodies every requirement of man's life on earth.

If the good is that which promotes man's life, then few breakthroughs of history have been as good as the Capitalist Revolution of the 18th century. Certainly, no other social system has led to even a pale approximation of the advances and wealth achieved under capitalism. It is long past time for justice to be done and for all honest men to acknowledge the unprecedented boon to humanity wrought by capitalism.

But the main point is not that judged by the standard of man's life capitalism is an unparalleled good. Rather, it is that the nature of capitalism embodies and promotes a rational standard of value, not an arbitrary or whim-based one. The essence of capitalist institutions proceeds logically from a rational standard of good and evil.

Capitalism as the Embodiment of Rational Philosophical Principles

A contrast with specific versions of statism is illuminating. One important question of ethics is: what is the nature and source of the good? The answer that gives rise to theocracy — Iran under the Ayatollah, Afghanistan under the Taliban, or any other — is: God's will. What God commands is the good and what He prohibits is the evil. Compliance with His will, and that of His initiated interpreters, the clergy — whatever His will may be — necessarily forms the standard of value.

Man is good to the extent he obeys, sinful to the extent he does not. For example, if the clergy rule that women are not to be educated, the virtuous course is to follow their will despite the virulently anti-life nature of such a prohibition on the mind. Adherence to the factual requirements of man's life is not, and cannot be, the ruling moral principle.

But when any other principle usurps the place of man's life as the rightful standard of value, then human life necessarily becomes a secondary concern. Man's life will then be sacrificed to the principle under which it is subordinated. Regardless of how in keeping with human survival requirements a man's work is — for example, the breakthroughs of a great scientist — if it clashes in any manner with clerical teaching, then the "culprit" and his supporters stand in danger of their lives. The brutal existential results are a matter of historical (and current) record.

Similarly, the answer regarding the proper moral standard that gives rise to modern collectivism—whether National Socialism or Communism—is the will of the people. What the people—and its "agent," an absolutist government—command is the good, and what it prohibits is evil. *Vox populi, vox dei.* In this secularized version of theocracy, man is again good to the extent he obeys the state's commandments, evil if he does not. If the state commands the extermination of the Jews (Hitler's Germany) or of the kulaks (Stalin's Russia) or the persecution and elimination of the intellectuals (Mao's China and Pol Pot's Cambodia), then such policies are morally right despite their unspeakable cruelty and

the impossibility of man's survival under conditions of bloodthirsty brutality. Collectivism forms the most vivid historical illustration of Ayn
Rand's identification that the supplanting of man's life as the proper standard of moral value leads necessarily to the most hideous atrocities and the
impossibility of human life.

By contrast, the standard of moral value giving rise to the system of
individual rights is the requirements of man's life. The supporters of capitalism did not explicitly formulate such a moral code until the philosophic work of Ayn Rand, but implicitly theirs was always the code of
life.[5]

The question is: what is the source of right and wrong? Although
Ayn Rand's seminal identification was not formally articulated until the
second half of the 20th century, some thinkers of earlier periods understood, at least implicitly, that the good is that which benefits man's life,
the evil that which harms it. Such intellectuals have further understood
that only individuals live and breathe and seek values. These were the
thinkers — of whom Thomas Jefferson was one prominent example —
who grasped that individuals must be left free to pursue their own happiness, i.e., to pursue the values that would enable them to survive and
flourish. The principles of rational egoism, individual rights and limited
Constitutional government followed logically from this implicit understanding.

As with the two forms of statism, the logic is clear-cut: if that which
furthers man's life is the standard by which good is judged, then the good
is for individuals to further their lives. It follows necessarily that they
require a political system protecting their right to do so. Indeed, individual rights can be morally validated only as a necessity of man's life on
earth. Simply put, if that which promotes man's life is the good, then
men promoting their lives, and possessing the legal right to do so, are
good.

If this is understood, then the manner in which so many men of genius pushed to the forefront during America's Inventive Period, though it remains impressive, is not astonishing. When a society recognizes, in some form, that the betterment of human life on earth is the ultimate moral goal, it protects the right of all individuals to pursue those values that will better their lives. Such protection of everyman's rights includes the protection of extraordinary-man's rights; so that the Eastmans, the Edisons, the Carvers, the Wrights, et al., legally assured the freedom to pursue their passions and their goals, devised means of bettering human life undreamed-of by men a scant few generations prior.

The right of an individual to his own life and his own mind clashes head-on with the theories that the good is determined by either the will of a theocratic or a collectivist state. It has been observed that men cannot serve two masters. If they adhere to the factual requirements of man's life, they cannot blindly obey the arbitrary and anti-life commandments of a theocratic or a collectivist dictatorship.

For example, what would have happened to women who did pursue education under the Taliban? What would have happened to Germans who opposed Hitler's commandments to build weapons of destruction and wanted the nation's factories to instead produce trucks, stoves and refrigerators? Those who held the standard of man's life in such repressive societies, and who tried to assert the judgment of their independent minds, were (and are) executed summarily or condemned to slave labor in a concentration camp.

Egoism, individual rights and limited government, the essence of capitalist institutions, are indispensable means of promoting man's life. They follow logically from life as the standard of value — and cannot be supported on the grounds of any other.

The philosophical and moral principles embodied in capitalism's nature form a consistent, non-contradictory commitment to the advancement of human life. By contrast, statist systems inevitably lead (and have led) to mass destruction because their social institutions pro-

[221]

ceed logically from a fundamental premise that subordinates the requirements of human life to opposing considerations, thereby causing those
requirements to be sacrificed. *Men cannot live when the basic rules of society mandate something else as more important than their lives.*

Historically, many of mankind's best have always sensed that the
requirements of human life took precedence over all other considerations, and were to be sacrificed to none. (They were called "Humanists.")
They simply failed to codify their not-fully-formed thoughts into an
explicitly-articulated moral theory. But based on their implicit grasp of
this rational standard, some of these thinkers (such as America's
Founders) revolutionized politics by inching mankind toward the principle of individual rights and the practice of limited government; not fully,
and by no means consistently, but they took the first pioneering steps forward. It is because of them that those of us living today in the capitalist
nations enjoy the historically-unprecedented freedom and prosperity that
we do.

Conclusions

For human beings to flourish on earth, their moral code must recognize and uphold man's life as its ultimate value, rationality as its primary
virtue, productiveness as a key subsidiary virtue, and an individual himself as the proper beneficiary of his own actions. Having identified this,
men must establish a political-economic system that consistently embodies these moral ideals.

The principle of individual rights is the political-economic embodiment of the fundamental components of a rational, life-based-and-pro-
moting ethics. This principle renders illegal all attempts to coercively
restrict the full deployment of man's mind. It provides the comprehensive
protection of the legal system to man's selfish attempt to achieve values.
Finally, it supports men's right to their own lives because it is the logical
political consequence of the deeper realization that the good is that which

promotes life, and the evil that which harms it.

The political system that provided flourishing life for countless millions in practice is, quite logically, the system that is the culmination of the moral code that consistently upholds human life in theory.

Summary

There are several moral principles consistent with man's nature and survival that must be embodied in a political-economic system if it is to promote man's life rather than his death. These are: egoism, the mind as man's tool of survival, productiveness as a virtue, and life as the standard of value. Capitalism succeeds spectacularly because it is the only social system that embodies these principles fully.

Part Three: Polemics

9: War and Imperialism

Today the Great Disconnect remains widely operative. Despite capitalism's protection of individual rights and its unprecedented success in promoting prosperity, it is the repeated target of moral accusations. Socialist intellectuals claim it is responsible for, among other evils, war, imperialism, and slavery.

Is it possible that freedom – the shining value for which men have struggled, bled and often died for millennia – is actually the cause of vast harm? To common-sense understanding, this does not seem possible – and in this case, common-sense is right. Individual rights and freedom, in fact, bring only benefits to human life. The causes of these horrors are not capitalism, but its antithesis – statism. To understand this point, war and imperialism will be examined in this chapter; slavery in the next.

The Charge That Capitalism is Responsible for War

The foundation of the charge is the Marxist claim that capitalism is inherently an aggressive, exploitative system that conquers and victimizes the weak. But in fact, capitalism, by its nature, bans the initiation of force — and to the extent that it has been implemented, is the system that respects the rights of all individuals, thereby protecting all men, including the weak. So this general accusation is untenable. Some other type of system is physically aggressive and responsible for conquering and victimizing the weak. To understand which system this is, it is helpful to

look at the facts of several modern wars and then extract the principles that explain their causation.

World War II was the most devastating conflict of human history. What were the facts regarding this war and its genesis? National Socialist (Nazi) Germany and Soviet Russia, as allies, invaded Poland in September 1939, precipitating global conflict. Germany invaded and conquered the Netherlands, Belgium, Denmark, Norway and France. The Nazis assaulted England in the famed Battle of Britain. The Nazis' ally, Imperial Japan – a military dictatorship – invaded China, conquered Singapore and attacked the United States. Germany's other ally, Fascist Italy, invaded Ethiopia and Greece. Adolf Hitler, of course, was the German dictator. Joseph Stalin was his counterpart in the Soviet Union, and Benito Mussolini in Italy. *It is important to recognize that the dictatorships were all on the same side, and were the aggressors.*

The freer, capitalistic countries of the mid-20th century – England, France, the United States – were, without exception, the innocent victims of the statists' aggression, and went to war in defense of their own freedom. The simple truth is: the socialist countries – those in which the state controlled the economic system and all aspects of the individual's life – invaded or attacked the capitalist countries – those in which individual rights and private ownership were still very much preeminent.

A first, provisional conclusion that can be drawn is: dictatorships, i.e., statist regimes are aggressors. The freer, capitalistic countries are not. To further support this, observe that National Socialist Germany and Communist Russia "seized and dismantled entire factories in conquered countries, to ship them home, while the freest of the mixed economies, the semi-capitalistic United States, sent billions worth of lend-lease equipment, including entire factories, to its allies." After achieving victory in the war, the United States and its allies packed up and went home; they did not enslave the countries they defeated. But Soviet Russia, on the other hand, kept in slavery all of Eastern Europe for more than forty

years, ruthlessly suppressing pro-freedom movements in Poland, Hungary and Czechoslavakia.[1]

Additionally, while the Communists looted relentlessly the conquered countries, the capitalist Americans spent billions to rebuild defeated enemies who had attacked them. Never in all of human history has so much (misguided) generosity been accorded defeated enemies, and never has it gone so ignored, unappreciated and/or reviled. This incident even inspired a comic film, *The Mouse That Roared*, in which a tiny, destitute country declares war on the U.S., confident that, after its inevitable defeat, the United States will lavish billions upon it, rebuilding its economy and creating wealth.

World War II was the most vivid, but by no means the only, example of the principle that dictatorships, not the freer, capitalistic nations, are responsible for war. There are many others. The Communist North initiated the Korean War by invading the freer South in June 1950, seeking to conquer it. That exact pattern was repeated in Vietnam, where Communist aggression took the form of guerilla, not conventional, assault.

The United States made the mistake of supporting the corrupt South Vietnamese regime of Nguyen Van Thieu, but the harsh policies of the South paled in contrast to the murderous pogroms of the Communists, who typically exterminated thousands of their own members in purges. It is not fashionable in the West even today to acknowledge the atrocities of Ho Chi Minh and his followers, because the truth would tend to morally vindicate America's opposition to Communism in that war.

Nevertheless, the Communists executed 50,000 Vietnamese in a paranoid witch hunt in the mid-1950s. "The exact number of losses is hard to gauge, but they were certainly catastrophic." In the few, brief weeks they occupied Hue during the 1968 Tet Offensive, they massacred at least 3,000 civilians, including priests and doctors. Dozens of Party members and sympathizers of the Revolution, imprisoned in stinking,

unhygienic hellholes in Ho Chi Minh City, smuggled out a note plead-
ing with the International Red Cross to deliver cyanide to them, that they
might end their sufferings. One recent author, writing of "land reform"
in North Vietnam and other Communist countries, stated: "Communist
agriculture could not produce good harvests—but it repeatedly produced
bumper crops of the dead." As always, the list of horrific crimes under
Communism is endless.

Nor should this truth be surprising. Ho Chi Minh, who had studied
in the Soviet Union, stated that the North Vietnamese Communists had
"the most clear-sighted and worthy elder brothers and friends of·
mankind — comrade Stalin and comrade Mao Tse-tung." But Stalin's
and Mao's "friends" did not appreciate their particular brand of "brother love": they fled for their lives. After the 1954 demarcation of the country, nearly ten times as many Vietnamese moved to the South as moved
to the North.

They had reason to flee. "The systematic execution, in village after
village of North Vietnam, of at least ten or fifteen thousand individuals
who had committed no crime or act of political resistance but had been
assigned to economic categories borrowed from Stalin's Soviet Union and
Mao's China constituted genocide on the basis of class identity..."

Representative of the differences between the South Vietnamese government and the Communists was the case of Doan Van Toai, a
Vietnamese student activist who protested the abuses of Thieu's regime
and was sympathetic to the Communists' goals. He found himself
imprisoned first by the military dictator, and later by the Communists.
Though Thieu's regime was undoubtedly corrupt and dictatorial, Toai
was immediately charged, brought to a speedy trial and acquitted. The
case was covered by the opposition press, criticized by members of the
National Assembly, and protested by anti-war activists in the United
States. It is not inconsequential to note that he had in fact aroused the
government's suspicion by his outspoken criticism of its policies, and by

working with men known to them as Communists. He later led an illegal takeover and month-long occupation of the Cambodian embassy in Saigon.

But he had never criticized the Communists nor worked with men committed to overthrowing their rule nor committed a crime under their jurisdiction. Nevertheless, shortly after coming to power, they arrested him without provocation, brought no charges, refused to offer trial, and for years held him imprisoned under unspeakable conditions that caused the deaths of fellow prisoners through dehydration, starvation, medical neglect, lack of waste disposal and torture. It goes without saying that there was no press coverage, and not even his family – much less the outside world – knew where he was held.

The conclusion must be that South Vietnam, despite the abuses of the military dictatorship, was vastly freer than the north under the Communists. As author Michael Lind noted: "The ultimate success of the Communists had less to do with their success in winning 'the hearts and minds' of the Vietnamese people than with...their more ruthless and efficient use of coercion." It was the totalitarian state that sought to conquer the freer south; not the south and its American allies who attempted to conquer the Communist north.[2]

The cause of the Persian Gulf War of the early 1990s was similar: the armies of the brutal dictator, Saddam Hussein of Iraq (armed, unfortunately, to some degree by the United States, but principally by the Soviet Union) invaded and conquered freer Kuwait. The freer countries of the West, led by the United States, did not initiate that conflict; they went to war — rightly or wrongly — to prevent Kuwait (and, eventually, Saudi Arabia and the entire Middle East) from being conquered by Saddam Hussein.[3]

The current "war on terror" was initiated by the brutal Islamist tyrannies of the Middle East, pre-eminently Iran, who sponsored terrorist organizations whose specific purpose was to attack the freer West, espe-

cially America. It is a proxy war in which murderous dictatorships, too weak to assault America and the other free nations directly, fund, train and support terrorists to do their dirty work. America did not initiate the conflict; it fought only after decades of repeated terrorist attacks culminated in the atrocities of September 11, 2001; and even then, unfortunately, used only a miniscule fraction of its military might to defend itself and only against a part, not the totality, of the despotic alliance assaulting it.[4]

Observe that every prominent dictatorship of the 20th century — the Fascists, the Communists, the Islamists — hated their antipode, the world's freest nation, America, and initiated war against her in some form. Hitler's ally attacked the United States at Pearl Harbor. The Soviets enslaved Eastern Europe and then threatened America's allies — the free nations of Western Europe — with conquest, and America herself with nuclear annihilation. It was with Stalin's approval that North Korea launched its murderous invasion of America's ally, freer South Korea. Today, and in recent decades, the world's blood-drenched Islamic dictatorships — Iran, Iraq, Syria, Afghanistan — sponsor(ed) terrorist attacks against Americans and America.[5]

That statism, not freedom, is responsible for war should be clear. The question is: why? So far, only the external relations of a dictatorship have been examined — but the answer lies in its internal nature. Again, it is good to examine the facts. The Nazis enslaved their own citizens, forcing all to serve the state. They murdered a whole segment of their own population – the Jews – and terrorized the rest by means of their secret police, the Gestapo. The Communists have done the same. In Soviet Russia, Stalin murdered untold millions of Soviet peasants in the attempt to force the rest onto the collective farms. In China, among other atrocities, Mao turned loose the Red Guards to intimidate and murder all "enemies of the revolution," the overwhelming majority of whom were native Chinese. In Cambodia, Pol Pot and the Khmer Rouge slaughtered virtu-

ally twenty-five per cent of the country's population in less than four years.[6]

Nor does a dictator have to be a Nazi or Communist to murder his own citizens. Saddam Hussein murdered any number of Kurds within Iraq, and silenced (often fatally) any Iraqi citizen who questioned his regime. In Uganda, Idi Amin murdered an estimated 300,000 people in his eight year reign of terror – one in every forty of the country's population. "Bodies floated down the Nile and turned up by the hundreds in Mabira and Namanve forests. The prisons filled up and prisoners were forced to stand in line and beat each other to death with ten-pound sledgehammers; the last man was shot." In Afghanistan, the recent Islamic dictators, the Taliban, brutally oppressed the country's entire female population.[7]

The principle is: statist regimes are at chronic war with their own citizens.

Statism — in fact and in principle — is nothing more than gang rule. A dictatorship is a gang devoted to looting the productive citizens of its own country. When a statist ruler exhausts his own country's economy, he attacks his neighbors. It is his only means of postponing internal collapse and prolonging his rule. *A country that violates the rights of its own citizens, will not respect the rights of its neighbors. Those who do not recognize individual rights, will not recognize the rights of nations:* a nation is only a number of individuals. Statism *needs* war; a free country does not. Statism survives by looting; a free country survives by production.[8]

The cause of war is that men still accept the primitive notion that they can properly achieve their goals by initiating the use of force against their fellow men. To abolish war it is first necessary to outlaw the initiation of force. Any so-called "peace" movement which endorses socialism

is bound to fail. To the extent that it succeeds in promoting socialism, to that same extent it will cause war. This is so, because a socialist regime, by its very nature, stands for the initiation of force against its own citizens, and therefore, no moral principle constrains it from following an aggressive policy toward the citizens of neighboring countries. The central point must be reiterated until mankind finally learns the lesson: No government which violates the rights of its own citizens can be expected to respect the rights of foreigners. Statism is the system of war.[9]

The principle that a government exists to protect the rights of its citizens is the direct application to politics of the broader Enlightenment creed of the Rights of Man, the conviction that every individual – domestic or foreign – has inalienable rights that include those to life, liberty, property and the pursuit of personal happiness. It follows that a government based on the principle of individual rights must both protect the rights of its own citizens and refuse to violate those of foreigners. There is a fundamental similarity in regard to its treatment of both domestic and foreign residents: *it must refrain from the initiation of force or fraud against any and all of them.* Capitalism, as the only system based on the preservation of individual rights and the consequent banning of the initiation of force, must be understood as the system of peace.

"Laissez-faire capitalism is the only social system based on the recognition of individual rights and, therefore, the only system that bans force from social relationships. By the nature of its basic principles and interests, it is the only system fundamentally opposed to war."[10]

World peace, therefore, requires the establishment of global capitalism. If there is ever to exist an enduring peace among men, then statism — the root cause of war — must be finally and fully extirpated from their political systems.

The essence of capitalist foreign relations is international free trade. Free trade simply means that individuals and companies in one country can trade with individuals and companies in other countries without bar-

riers and taxes imposed by their respective governments. The moral right of peaceful, non-criminal individuals to trade and interact across national boundaries is protected. International free trade is simply the principle of individual rights applied to economic and cultural relationships across national borders. Practically, such a policy of abolishing tariffs and trade barriers opens nations to various forms of peaceful intercourse, including mutually-beneficial commerce, emigration and immigration, and cultural exchange. Free trade removes the economic incentive to war, by making it possible for citizens of one country to gain by trade the goods produced by citizens of other countries.

Capitalism renders unnecessary the murderous practice of plunder, and replaces it with the cordial and mutually-beneficial relation of trade. The institution of such a policy is a major step toward the diminishment of suspicion and hostility between nations that have often developed over centuries. It is no accident "that capitalism gave mankind the longest period of peace in history – a period during which there were no wars involving the entire civilized world – from the end of the Napoleonic Wars in 1815 to the outbreak of World War I in 1914." It is also no accident that, with the 20th century emergence of the most virulent form of statism in history – the socialist regimes of Germany and Russia – the world was plunged into its most destructive war ever.[11]

Even Marx and Engels introduced a semi-admiring note into their pervasive hostility toward capitalism when they described the universal benefits of free trade.

> In place of the old wants, satisfied by the productions of the country, we find new wants, requiring for their satisfaction the products of distant lands and climates. In place of the old local and national seclusion and self-sufficiency, we have intercourse in every direction, universal inter-dependence of nations. And as in material, so also in intellectual production. The intellectual creations of individual nations

become common property. National one-sidedness and narrow-mindedness become more and more impossible, and from the numerous national and local literatures, there emerges a world literature.[12]

Insofar as national policy makers are concerned with the rational self-interest of their countries, they would do well to realize that individual rights and free trade — not war, conquest, plunder and imperialism — will promote wealth and power; the only rational, life-giving power: that to produce.

The Charge That Capitalism is Responsible for Imperialism

Imperialism is the policy of establishing and maintaining an empire. Webster's dictionary defines "empire" as: "a major political unit having a territory of great extent or a number of territories or peoples under a single sovereign authority." Logically and historically, the "single sovereign authority" who governed such "major political units" established his power by means of military conquest and/or physical intimidation. If peoples of other nations or foreign territories voluntarily align themselves with a powerful nation, the result is a commonwealth of freely-associated peoples, not an empire. For example, Puerto Rico has long been such a commonwealth of the United States. But the ancient Romans, the Ottoman Turks and the mercantilist Spaniards, among many others (including the British), established empires. Imperialism entails war and conquest, i.e., the governmental initiation of force on a wide, sometimes global, scale.

In the late-19th century, many European countries – including Britain, France, Germany, Belgium and others – conquered vast areas of land in Africa and Asia, and often brutally subjugated the local populations. "Between 1870 and 1898, Britain added 4 million square miles and 88 million people to its empire; France gained nearly the same area of territory with 40 million souls attached; Germany won a million

[square] miles and 16 million colonials; Belgium took 900,000 [square] miles and 30 million people..." The Scramble for Africa was underway.[13]

For almost a century, Marxist intellectuals and Communist dictators have blamed this empire building on capitalism. The main points of their arguments can be traced back to a turn-of-the-20th-century British writer named J.A. Hobson. An eccentric economist and teacher, Hobson became friends with freethinking British businessman and daring mountaineer, A.F. Mummery. The two of them sought to overturn classical economic wisdom by arguing that the previously discredited theory of underconsumptionism was, in fact, true. They held that British working class wages were inadequate to enable workers to buy back the product; that British manufacturers, therefore, produced an excess of goods and services. The rich could afford to buy this enormous supply, but their personal consumption did not require such plenitude. Hence they saved instead of bought. Since the poor couldn't afford to buy and the rich didn't need to, the result was the inability of the capitalist system to sell its plethora of goods on the domestic market.

Mummery died on the slopes of Nanga Parbat in 1895, but Hobson, after a trip to Africa, published his book, *Imperialism*, in 1902. He used his theory of underconsumptionism to explain the aggressive policies of colonialism pursued by so many European powers during the late-19th century. With an already-existing overproduction of goods for which there was no domestic market, he argued, investment opportunities shrank dramatically at home. Consequently, investors needed to move into overseas enterprises in order to maximize their returns. Given that the political climate of many of these countries made the investments risky, wealthy investors pressed their governments to intercede on their behalfs. "Investors who have put their money in foreign lands upon terms which take full account of risks connected with the political conditions of the country, desire to use the resources of their Government to minimize these risks, and so to enhance the capital value and the interest of

their private investments." The military adventurism of European colonial powers of this era was ultimately a consequence of pressure from wealthy capitalist investors.[14]

Hobson's theory exerted a significant influence on Lenin, who articulated what became the major Marxist treatment of the subject. "The necessity for exporting capital arises from the fact that in a few countries capitalism has become 'over-ripe' and...capital cannot find 'profitable' investment." Since it is difficult for bankers to find profitable domestic investments under such conditions, they invest overseas, generally in backwards countries where they can exploit cheap labor, land and natural resources. From the "enormous super-profits" thereby gained, the capitalists are able to bribe the leaders of the working class to accept capitalism. Millions of Western workers are able to gain a "bourgeois" standard of living only by means of capitalism's brutal exploitation of starving overseas workers.[15]

There are so many things wrong with the Hobson-Lenin theory of imperialism, it is difficult to know where to begin. But it is possible to start with the economic errors and then proceed to the historic and moral ones.

First: Hobson's theory of underconsumptionism on which Lenin's theories were based is utterly mistaken. If capitalist economies produce a general abundance of goods (as they do) then the result of such a great supply is diminishing prices, i.e., rising real wages. This is exactly what happened historically. The real wages of workers rose steadily, virtually from the first days of the Industrial Revolution, as seen above. Exactly because of the abundance of consumer goods and consequent lower prices, workers were able to buy sufficient food, new cotton clothing, and later, telephones, automobiles, radios and televisions.

In principle, in a free market there can be no such thing as too great a supply and too small a demand. The ruling principle is Say's Law of Markets, which can be formulated simply: Supply constitutes demand. It

is only by producing that an individual acquires the means to obtain the values produced by others. In economic terms, demand for a good means more than need or desire for it; it means need or desire backed by purchasing power. For example, it is only the shoes produced by the shoe maker that constitutes his demand for the eggs produced by the farmer — or the values created by any other producer. In order to consume the goods created by others, a man must first produce and then trade. Hence Jean-Baptiste Say's famous exhortation: "Produce, produce, that is the whole thing!"

The vast general supply of goods and services produced under capitalism necessarily means that a vast number of producers have the means to buy the products created by others; that is, such abundance is the result of the productive work of many individuals, who now possess the means to obtain the other goods and services they seek. Therefore, demand, properly understood, is premised on successfully supplying. A man's demand is nothing other than his supply used to gain the other values he desires from the men who produced them. The final conclusion must be that it is profoundly mistaken to hold, a lá Hobson and Lenin, that there can be an excess of supply or a deficiency of demand across an entire economy. Rather, an enormous demand for goods and services requires an enormous supply of them; indeed, is that supply looked at from the perspective of trade.[16]

Second: Evidently, it never occurred to Lenin and his ilk that capitalists ceaselessly innovate, creating new products and methods. Despite publishing his work on imperialism in 1916, after the epoch-making success of America's Inventive Period – and roughly a century after the Industrial Revolution had indeed revolutionized the life of the common man in Great Britain – he apparently still did not realize the enormous opportunities for investment in such then new technologies as the electric lighting system, the telephone, the automobile, the airplane, the radio, etc.; just as his intellectual heirs fail to recognize the opportunities

in such later developments as the nuclear power, computer and bio-tech industries of the current day.

J.P. Morgan, as one prominent example, in 1878 was one of the first to invest in Edison's electric light, and, in 1909, to support the Wright brothers' manufacture of airplanes. (See Chapter Five and the Appendix.)

Overwhelmingly, investors in capitalist nations invest in companies in other capitalist nations – for it is there that the profitable opportunities exist. Nineteenth century British capitalists, for example, invested heavily in the developing U.S. railroads. By 1899, "something like $3 billion in American securities were owned abroad [by Europeans], for the greater part in American rails. British investors held $2.5 billion of this amount..." No similar investment opportunities existed in destitute Africa.[17]

The Hobson-Lenin vision of "an over-ripe" capitalism whose domestic market was saturated with unpurchased consumer goods would, in fact, constitute an enormously wealthy society where items were not selling even at the low prices such vast supplies would generate. That would be a society in which all human desires were already satisfied. But, in fact, since it will always be possible to discover new ways to fulfill human desires more fully, more rapidly or both, there will never be a dearth of investment opportunities in a capitalist society. Capitalism, as the liberator of the individual mind, as a consequent on-going revolution that continually originates new life-promoting technologies and methods, is a system that creates an inexhaustible series of opportunities.

Third: Related to the preceding point, Lenin's claim that Western capitalists were investing heavily in non-industrialized countries was and remains empirically false. Lenin gave an enormous amount of statistics to show that Western foreign investments were growing, and then asked the question: where does the money go? But his answer was disastrously imprecise. The three categories he used were: Europe, North America (the entire Western hemisphere), and, as one class, the rest of the world — Asia, Africa and Australia. He used entire continents, even multiple

continents joined together as classifications, despite the mixture of industrialized and non-industrialized nations contained within each.

"Statistical data on a country-by-country basis show very nearly the opposite of what Lenin claimed. Industrial nations tend to send their foreign investments to other industrialized nations, rather than to industrially undeveloped nations...Even Lenin's own table in *Imperialism* showed that France and Germany each had more than twice as much invested in 'Europe' as in all of 'Asia, Africa, and Australia' put together."

This fact remains true today. "The United States...has more invested in Canada than in Asia and Africa put together — and it has more invested in Europe than in Canada." Investments in impoverished countries were not and are not some kind of "safety valve" for "over-ripe" capitalist economies.[18]

Fourth: Insofar as Hobson — the Marxist writer, Rosa Luxemburg — and others believed that imperialism was caused by a desire for new markets, it must be pointed out that a market for goods involves demand for those goods, i.e, it requires more than persons who need or desire them. A market requires people who possess purchasing power. "Countries...constitute markets...to the extent that they produce and supply goods. Only to this extent are they in a position to earn the wherewithal to purchase goods and thus to constitute markets." But virtually all of late-19th century European imperialism involved conquest of destitute regions of Asia and Africa. To be blunt, hundreds of millions of half-starved individuals in the world's poorest regions did not constitute a market for European manufactured goods. With what would the natives purchase such goods? "Contrary to consumptionism...hordes of impoverished beggars do not constitute markets." Historically, the belief that markets require conquest did indeed motivate some economically-ignorant politicians to embark upon imperialist ventures. But this is insufficient to make imperialism profitable and thereby in a capitalist nation's rational self-interest. The solution is for politicians to learn eco-

nomics, not to cast unjustified aspersions on capitalism.[19]

Fifth: Foreign investments and markets can certainly be in a capitalist nation's self-interest, but not when gained by military conquest. When examined from a purely economic standpoint, it is seen that the maintenance of large armies and navies is expensive, as is the administration of colonial empires. Further, wars kill industrious human beings and destroy valuable property, thereby undercutting production. "Great fleets and armies...acquire nothing which can compensate the expense of maintaining them." Empires often face widespread rebellions, as peoples rise up in quest of freedom, and the chronic wars of suppression are costly in both blood and dollars.

What is in a free society's economic interest was understood and identified by Adam Smith long ago: production and international free trade. Raw materials can be purchased in trade without the enormous cost in blood and wealth required by conquest; overseas workers can be similarly hired without violence for market wages in those countries; domestic goods can be sold in foreign markets to mutual advantage if all countries involved lower trade barriers. The leading theoreticians and practitioners of capitalism have known for over 200 years that the most effective means of gaining and retaining wealth is not plunder but production and peaceful trade. But to this day, even scholarly historians still subscribe to the crude economic fallacies of Hobson and Lenin.[20]

Sixth: In a free market, trade with and investments in foreign nations benefit all parties. If, for example, a Western oil company discovers oil in an impoverished country, the most effective means of developing the deposits is not for the government of the company's country to conquer the destitute nation. Rather, it is to buy the land, pay royalties on the oil and hire and train local workers. The peaceful trade of value for value avoids the horrors and waste of war and the problems of ruling a conquered empire; it is a voluntary, contractual agreement on both sides, and is in everybody's rational self-interest. The only circumstances in which it

is morally appropriate and economically gainful for a capitalist nation to invoke force is if the host country is ruled by a dictator who nationalizes, i.e., steals the investor's property and/or threatens his life. But then the goal is not to conquer the country and subjugate its population; it is simply to protect the lives and property of productive men.

Central to understanding the causes of imperialism is to recognize how rarely and incompletely nations, including Western ones, have adopted capitalism throughout the ages. Historically, statism in some form has been the status quo. Most societies have not legally delimited the power of the state in an attempt to safeguard individual rights; rather, they have generally been ruled by monarchies, feudal aristocrats, theological dictators or military despots. Even the Western nations of the 19th century, that embraced capitalism to a greater or lesser degree, were always mixed systems which combined individual rights and limited government with elements of statism. In capitalism's early days its supporters fought against the feudal-mercantile system of government controls; later, against the controls imposed by the socialists and welfare statists. Even the United States of the Inventive Period suffered from government-franchised monopolies, regulation of the railroads and germinating trust-busting.

Examine the historical record: statism, not freedom, was always responsible for imperialism. It was the military power of the state, employed often to coerce its own citizens, as well as to conquer foreigners, that made possible the Assyrian, Persian, Roman and Ottoman Empires. These were political/economic systems ruled by the decree of kings and/or emperors, established and backed by force.

In the centuries before Christ, for example, the Assyrian kings brutally carved out an empire in the Middle East. Sennacherib and his armies, for instance, "sacked 89 cities, 820 villages, captured 7,200 horses, 11,000 asses, 80,000 oxen, 800,000 sheep, and 208,000 prisoners..." A captured city "was usually plundered and burnt to the ground..."

Prisoners of war were often enslaved or slain; captive nobles and their children "were beheaded, or flayed alive, or roasted over a slow fire." To maintain their vast conquered empire, the Assyrian monarchs had to be perpetually prepared to militarily suppress the inevitable revolts against their rule. "The army was therefore the most vital part of the government." Taxes were levied and tribute imposed. The reign of conqueror Tiglath-Pileser "was a symbol and summary of all Assyrian history: death and taxes, first for Assyria's neighbors, then for herself."

The story of the mighty Persian Empire was much the same. The conqueror, Cyrus, for example, subdued the Near East, then died in battle with the Massageta, a tribe peopling the southern shore of the Caspian Sea. The Emperor Darius ruthlessly put down widespread revolt against his rule. In Babylon, for instance, "he crucified three thousand of its leading citizens as an inducement to obedience in the rest..."

Roman history is one of endless battles and conquests. At the height of their power, the Romans had conquered most of Europe, excluding modern Germany, much of the Middle East and the northern coast of Africa. They battled for two centuries to subdue Spain, and Spanish women often killed their children rather than permit them to be taken by the Romans. After they conquered Britain, the Romans put down a revolt led by Queen Boadicea and put 80,000 Britons "to the sword."

The Ottoman Empire was even more aggressive, engaging in virtually ceaseless warfare from its founding around 1300 until its demise following World War I. Its history reads like a single bloody saga of conquest, desecration, massacre, rapine and enslavement. In one horrific 14th century example, the Sultan ordered "10,000 captives to be put to death...several thousand Christians were slaughtered in a bloody ritual that went on from sunrise to late afternoon." At the Empire's height under Suleiman I in the 16th century, the Ottoman Turks had militarily conquered North Africa, Egypt, Syria, the Balkans, Hungary, and had twice laid siege to Vienna.

Nor were conditions much different in sub-Sahara Africa. For example, Shaka, the tribal chief who founded the mighty Zulu Nation, carved out a sizable empire on Africa's southeast coast in the early 19th century by a series of bloody conquests. "He waged war for the sake of war," grew rich on vast supplies of pilfered cattle, and in one typical battle "slaughtered most of the women and children" of his vanquished foe. His power over his subjects was so complete that his bodyguards "a dozen times daily, bashed in skulls or twisted necks at a flick of Shaka's hand." Such executions were inflicted for the slightest offense, and "the people he killed meant no more to him than so many ants."

The only rational conclusion is that historical empires have not been instigated by private investors or businessmen seeking the initiation of governmental force to protect their foreign investments or to conquer new markets. It cannot be doubted that some domestic merchants profited from the various conquests (although more often they were victimized by taxation, military conscription and battlefield death), but one would have to torture the facts to yield the conclusion that business interests led to the interminable warfare. Rather, the primary cause has been the insatiable lust of kings, emperors and tribal chiefs to gain power and plunder by means of military conquest. "In interpreting world affairs most people have a tendency to overestimate the part played by...the lust for wealth, and to underestimate the lust for power."[21]

The Spanish and Portuguese colonial empires originated in the 16th century; the British in the 17th. These were established more than a century before the advent of capitalism, and were largely driven by the feudal-mercantile belief that the wealth of nations lay in the acquisition of bullion and conquered territory by the aristocrats who ruled the state, and not in the production of consumer goods to enrich the lives of the common man. It was consequently "Gold, Glory and God" that drove the Spanish Conquistadors to plunder the civilizations of the New World.

The Capitalist Manifesto

An important preliminary conclusion is that imperialism existed extensively long before capitalism appeared on the historical scene; therefore, appeals to uniquely-capitalist principles and institutions are, at best, inadequate to formulate a comprehensive theory of imperialism as such. At worst, such appeals are not merely utterly false; they are polar opposite to the truth.

The Scramble for Africa did occur after capitalism was widespread in Western Europe. But all of the imperialist nations were mixed economies, combining elements of freedom and statism. Which element of the mixture was responsible for the brutal military conquests? Take representative examples one at a time.

When the Scramble for Africa commenced in the 1870s, Germany was a recently united land still ruled by a hereditary monarch, the Hohenzollern dynasty of Prussia. But earlier in the 19th century, the ideals of liberalism, i.e., the Enlightenment principles of individual rights and capitalism, had penetrated Germany from the West. As a result, Prussia legally freed its peasantry in 1807, and serfdom collapsed fully following the revolutions of 1848. Under the influence of Enlightenment ideas, Germany by the 1860s had undergone the beginnings of an Industrial Revolution, creating a rising middle class hungry for greater freedom and weakening the power of the aristocracy. Though many liberals had been imprisoned or exiled by 1850, liberalism in the two decades leading up to German unification in 1871 was not yet defunct.

Tragically, the Constitutional Conflict that dragged on for years in the 1860s resulted in triumph for the autocratic Prussian monarch and defeat for the Parliamentary liberals and their supporters. Germany was therefore unified not under the principles of individual rights and constitutional republicanism but under their antithesis – militarist Prussian authoritarianism. The king appointed as chancellor the Prussian aristocrat, Otto von Bismarck, a fervent supporter of the Hohenzollern dynasty. The executive leader of the government, Bismarck reported only

to the Prussian king (and German emperor), who held sole power to dictate all foreign policy. Germany's "Iron Chancellor," after a brief initial period of supporting free trade, commenced his statist program, leading Germany relentlessly away from liberal ideals. He nationalized the railroads, abandoned free trade for protectionism, instituted the world's first modern welfare state, and considered it of the highest importance that Prussia's powerful army be unquestioningly loyal to the king. Though skillful at diplomacy, Bismarck was steadfastly true to his earlier pronouncement that "the great questions of the day will not be settled by speeches and majority decisions…but by blood and iron."

To his credit, Bismarck suspected the unprofitability of German African colonies. But an empire might be useful as a weapon against European rivals, as well as a boost to national prestige, so Bismarck permitted himself to be convinced by "the leading colonial enthusiast in the Foreign Office…Heinrich von Kusserow, the Privy Councillor in the legal-commercial department…" that colonies would not be a drain on the Reich. German merchants who had established trading posts on Africa's west coast lobbied for the establishment of German "protectorates," and significant segments of the country's domestic populace, caught up in a jingoistic fervor, clamored for empire. In July of 1884, on the orders of the Iron Chancellor, German forces took control of Cameroon, Togo and Angra Pequena (southwest Africa).

Although von Kusserow had convinced Bismarck that the colonies did not have to be administered by the state, that private companies could be granted charters for their operation, the event proved otherwise. Though German merchants in Africa had been part of the broader yelping for imperial protection, German businessmen refused to accept the state-franchised monopoly. Put simply, there was insufficient profit to justify colonial administration. "The cost of accepting a charter would be too high for any German firm, however patriotic. After all, this was not India or the East. It was poverty-stricken Africa." The Reich would have

to assume the expense of governance. Because of the debacle in west Africa, Bismarck demoted von Kusserow to a minor post in the Foreign Office. "Bismarck did not easily forget Kusserow. He had achieved more than most: he had fooled Bismarck."

Bismarck's establishment of the east African portion of Germany's empire in March, 1885 was primarily the work of that extraordinary character, Dr. Carl Peters, simultaneously a brilliant academic and swaggering, freebooting explorer. Undoubtedly, Peters possessed generous helpings of audacity, courage and leadership qualities, but he was a ruthless gunslinger who "openly confessed to the 'intoxication' of killing Africans." With high-powered rifles and a handful of men, he fought his way through the territory of the savage Masai tribe, leaving a swath of devastation in his wake, claiming present-day Uganda, among other territory, in the name of the Kaiser. "I got tired of being accounted among the pariahs," Peters wrote later, "and wished to belong to the master race." Though Bismarck scorned him as more buccaneer than patriot, he (and later the Kaiser) accepted and made use of his conquests. He first granted Peters a state-approved charter for his East African Company, and then later, when Peters and his men proved to be neither businessmen nor administrators, he revoked it and made German East Africa an official appendage of the German state. In truth, Germany's colonial holdings in East Africa were established by pirates and military men, not investors or businessmen, and were eventually sanctioned and taken over by the Reich. Men of force, not of productive achievement, were responsible for these land grabs.

Germany's expropriated lands and new colonies had "value" only for "German prestige," and were not economically profitable: at the outset of the First World War, the mother country's trade with its colonies constituted less than .5% of Germany's total foreign trade. In the same period, Germany's exports to tiny Belgium alone were more than five times greater than to its entire colonial empire. "Out of Germany's total exports

to the world, less than one percent went to its colonies in Africa." Such amounts hardly constituted a sufficient sum to offset the military and administrative expenses of conquering and maintaining an empire, and of constructing, staffing and maintaining a mighty navy to protect it. During the pre-World War I era, Germany's colonies were a significant financial drain on her working taxpayers.

Germany of this period was primarily a militaristic state of "disguised absolutism with a phantom constitution and a powerless parliament," largely lacking the principles of individual rights and limited government. Under the principles of capitalism, the Germans would have eliminated protectionism, embraced free trade and competed for foreign markets based on the superiority of their products — not sought conquest based on the power of their arms. (This is a policy that recent history shows the Germans quite capable of implementing.)

But, unfortunately, the liberal principles that had been alive in Germany at mid-19th century were all but dead by the turn of the 20th. The statist regime was the first cause and prime mover of German imperialism, for authoritarianism, militaristic power and nationalism, not individual rights and international free trade, were its defining principles. Because of the financial drain, the Kaiser seriously considered in 1891 abandoning Southwest Africa to the British. But he did not. Overwhelmingly, it was power and national prestige, not profit, that the militarists sought.[22]

During the Scramble for Africa, Belgian imperialism, seeking to pillage the natural resources of the Congo, was another example of virulent statism. It was initiated by King Leopold II, who had for decades dreamed of establishing a Belgian colonial empire. In the early 1860s, as Duke of Brabant, he had incessantly urged Senate liberals (who were consistently opposed to the expense of colonies) to extend Belgium's overseas possessions. As king, in 1876, he acted upon these desires: he hired the famed explorer, Sir Henry Stanley, to acquire as much land in the Congo

Basin as he could. Leopold set up a personal fiefdom in the Congo with himself as emperor. To plunder the area's rich supply of rubber and ivory, he employed a personal army who enslaved the local population, often torturing and/or murdering recalcitrant villagers. The European governments meeting at Berlin under the auspices of Chancellor Otto von Bismarck in 1884-85 upheld Leopold's claim to his "Congo Free State," believing that the king intended to carry on philanthropic work there.

Largely through the efforts of journalist E.D. Morel and his Congo Reform Association, the civilized world in the early years of the 20th century became aware of Leopold's atrocities, and public opinion, especially in Britain and the United States eventually forced the king out. Incredibly, the Belgian government compensated the king for his "loss" in relinquishing his feudal demesne. The great Austrian economist, Ludwig von Mises, quite accurately described Leopold II as a "belated conquistador."[23]

British imperialism of this era, though manifesting important differences, also held an essential similarity. Unlike in Germany, British liberals had gained enormous influence by the middle of the 19th century. Richard Cobden, for example, a successful Manchester textile manufacturer and young member of Parliament, led the intellectual and political attack on the Corn Laws. In the late 1830s, Cobden and his important associate, John Bright, were instrumental in founding the Manchester Anti-Corn Law League, which after years of struggle succeeded in gaining repeal in 1846. The results were the elimination of the tariff on imported grain, and consequent lower bread prices for English consumers. During the same decade, William Gladstone, a rising liberal star in the British political firmament, as Chancellor of the Exchequer, removed or reduced taxes and duties on hundreds of items, including many foodstuffs, soap and tea. "A 70-year era of British free trade began; in the popular mind, free trade now signified cheap bread."[24]

The growing Liberal Party of Bright, Cobden and Gladstone gener-

ally supported limited government, individual rights and free trade, opposing protectionism, military expenditures and conquests, and imperialism. Cobden and Bright, for example, as leaders of the "Manchester School" of essentially laissez-faire principles, opposed the Crimean War, holding that "free trade was inseparable from a pacific foreign policy. Trade [they held] is based on mutual cooperation and evokes goodwill among nations." (Presumably, they also recognized the inevitable destruction, for the Crimean War cost England thousands of lives and some 80,000,000 pounds sterling, with no possible offsetting gain.)

Gladstone believed that Britain's self-interest lay in permitting her long-held colonies self-determination and self-government, then engaging with them in free trade. He "disclaimed the policy of holding the colonies by force or by the exercise of power over their internal arrangements." The Liberals generally favored greater freedom for the colonies, the gradual atrophy of the Empire, and great mutual advantage from international free trade.[25]

Cobden fully understood the role of free trade in promoting world peace. In 1860, acting as England's unofficial envoy to the French court of Napoleon III, he argued indefatigably for the lowering of trade barriers between these two centuries-old enemies. Recognizing Britain's growing prosperity and loathing war, he wrote to Gladstone: "I would not step across the street just now to increase our trade, for the mere sake of commercial gain...But to improve the moral and political relations of France and England, by bringing them into greater intercourse and increased commercial dependence, I would walk barefoot from Calais to Paris." Gladstone feared the choice was Cobden's treaty or war with France. Again, Cobden writing to Gladstone: "The scheme begun in the name of commerce must be pursued in the interest of European peace." Cobden's efforts were largely responsible for the epochal Anglo-French Commercial Treaty of 1860 that was an early step in the long period of peaceful relations between these two nations that continues to the present day.[26]

While Gladstone and the Liberals generally supported free trade, reduced naval expenditures and the gradual extension of self-government to England's colonies, Benjamin Disraeli and the Tories "seized upon the idea of Imperialism as a positive theme." Disraeli, who disliked and despised the rising middle class of manufacturers and merchants, was the champion of the Conservatives, the party essentially of the country landowners and hereditary aristocrats. An eloquent illustration of the parties' differences was that, in the 1860s, Gladstone and Bright advocated the extension of the vote to the working class, provoking a horrified Disraeli to the accusation that the Liberals had "revived the doctrines of Tom Paine."

After 1867, Disraeli's "main interest was the extension of British power in the world." He had been consumed with dreams "of Empire so wide that some of his critics have suspected them of being altogether removed from actuality." It was in his years as Prime Minister in the late 1870s that Britain expanded its policy of imperialism, annexing the Transvaal, invading Afghanistan and declaring Queen Victoria "Empress of India." "For a fortnight [Gladstone] stumped Midlothian in an ecstasy of moral indignation at the iniquities of Imperialism. He poured invective on a ministry that had annexed Cyprus and the Transvaal, made war on the Zulus, interfered in Turkey-in-Asia, and was now engaged in war against the Afghans."

After his re-election, Gladstone did what he could to mitigate the new imperialism. In 1881, he restored independence to the Transvaal; he made no attempt to re-conquer Sudan, despite the feverish sentiments of jingoism in England after the Mahdi's forces killed General Gordon at Khartoum in 1885; and was able to avert war with Russia by negotiating a peaceful settlement of their differences over Afghanistan.[27]

The party of capitalism and free trade generally opposed the second wave of British imperialism. The aristocrats, with their glorification of war and conquest, and their traditional disdain for business and com-

merce, had been responsible for Britain's initial empire building centuries earlier; and in the late-19th century, in the last gasp of their historical influence, their views were unchanged. Neo-mercantilists to the core, they conceived England's self-interest not in the liberation of her colonies and the practice of international free trade, but in further conquest and the establishment/administration of a vast overseas empire.

Further, it must be remembered that Britain's empire under the influence of liberal Enlightenment ideals was essentially one of free trade. "Committed, as they were, to the principles of free trade, they had no desire to exclude other people." But as significant portions of the globe became dominated by their protectionist competitors the "English felt that they had to take over large blocks of territory if only to prevent them falling into the hands of exclusive rivals." Again, statist policies, not the capitalist principle of free trade, spurred imperialism.[28]

Fairness to the historical record shows that it was government officials, often aristocrats and their political supporters – the German Kaiser, Bismarck, King Leopold II, the British Tories, et al. – who were the prime movers of late-19th century European imperialism. Capitalists, private investors and businessmen played a minor role. "It is a Marxian invention that the nineteenth-century colonial expansion of the European powers was engendered by the economic interests of the pressure groups of finance and business." It was the militarist-statist philosophy of conquest and plunder that was responsible, not the capitalist philosophy – so clearly enunciated by Adam Smith – of production and international free trade.[29]

Commentators can properly refer to many late-19th century Western countries as "capitalist," because the element of freedom was generally uppermost, especially in Great Britain – but they were, without exception, mixed economies, and it was the statist element of the mixture that led to imperialism.

As one final objection, since there are no private bankers, investors or

capitalists under Communism, one wonders how supporters of the Hobson-Lenin thesis explain the establishment of a widespread Soviet Empire in Eastern Europe following World War II or the brutal conquest and continuing occupation of Tibet by Communist China. The Hobson-Lenin claim that the exportation of private capital is responsible for imperialism is utterly false. An altogether different theory is required to explain the known facts.[30]

It is important to note that the United States, the rising capitalist power – who in this period took the world lead in industrial production – established no vast overseas empire. But the U.S. was not unaffected by the imperialist mania of the era. Again, it was politicians and naval personnel who took the lead, not businessmen.

The American naval officer, Alfred Thayer Mahan, published in 1890 a book entitled *The Influence of Sea Power upon History, 1660-1783*. In it, he argued for the construction of a mighty American navy to make possible the establishment and protection of a far flung empire. Mahan opposed free trade, and glorified protectionism, conquest and empire. Mahan's arguments greatly impressed Kaiser William II, who made his book the official textbook of the German Navy and who "had the complete sea-power series supplied to public institutions, libraries, and schools at government expense." English naval officers and imperialists used Mahan's teachings to wring from Parliament greater appropriations for the fleet. At home, Theodore Roosevelt unfortunately "made Mahan's work his Bible of politics for the United States."

Sounding more like a European aristocrat than a citizen of the American Republic, Mahan criticized business and glorified war. "He considered peace the false idol of a civilization grown fat and soft on the sterile pursuit of material pleasures and the senseless amassing of wealth...Away with them! True salvation lies in cultivating the masculine, combative instincts." Roosevelt, who had "no occupation at all except politics," similarly derided the comfortable middle-class existence

afforded by capitalism, opting instead for the "strenuous life" of "hunting, hard riding and fighting." As with Mahan, "war held no horrors for Roosevelt."

Though other imperialists did not necessarily embrace the same pugnacious admiration for warfare, they often shared the hostility toward profit seeking. Congressman and then Senator Henry Cabot Lodge was scornful of his commercial family, possessing "a contempt quite aristocratic for the raucous hustle and bustle of the market place." Lodge's colleague, Senator Albert Beveridge of Indiana was an anti-business Progressive and supporter of Roosevelt. Beveridge articulated the same false view of markets held by Hobson and Rosa Luxemburg. "American factories are making more than the American people can use; American soil is producing more than they can consume...the trade of the world must and shall be ours." In Congress, Lodge and Beveridge championed the imperialist cause.[31]

But American capitalists generally did not. The great builder of railroads, James J. Hill, was a strong free trader who "did not agree with the...drift toward imperialism and war with Spain." Andrew Carnegie vehemently opposed the Spanish War and annexation of the Philippines, warning against the "mistake which dragged [the American Republic] into the vortex of International militarism and a great navy." Carnegie, a tireless activist for world peace who donated millions of his own money to the cause, recognized that the one insurmountable obstacle to pacific European relations was not Britain but the Kaiser's unswerving commitment to German militarism.

Several years later, Henry Ford, a pacifist who opposed U.S. military preparedness and involvement in wars, stated: "If I had my way, I'd throw every ounce of gunpowder into the sea and strip soldiers of their insignias." Roosevelt, complaining of the reluctance to carve out an empire manifested by President McKinley – a man generally sympathetic to the achievements and goals of American businessmen – stated that

the president had the "backbone of a chocolate éclair."

Additionally, "the principal weight of 'Wall Street' was against the war on Spain in 1898." Nor were U.S. bankers interested in investing in China during President Taft's administration; rather, "it is truer to say that they were 'dragooned' into it by the politicians." American businessmen – sometimes supporting free trade, generally viewing profit in terms of production and construction, and recognizing the economic destructiveness of wars and conquests – did not frequently support the Mahan-Roosevelt imperialist crusade. Not insignificantly, Mahan, whose book was already successful in Europe, for three years could find no publisher at home, and failed in an attempt to solicit from financier J.P. Morgan advance money for its publication. (Although Morgan did contribute a modest sum toward defraying Mahan's costs.)

Even the distinguished American historian, Charles Beard, generally no friend to capitalism, stated: "Loyalty to the facts of historical record must ascribe the idea of imperialist expansion mainly to naval officers and politicians rather than to businessmen…beyond question, naval officers and politicians were the principal initiators of imperialist expansion…"

Another accomplished student of American foreign policy reached essentially the same conclusion: "According to a popular assumption in the years following the [Spanish] war, America was drawn into the war by businessmen in search of new markets and investment opportunities. But actually, businessmen…were…generally more reluctant than most citizens to disturb the ordinary patterns of peace and commerce…"

As Ayn Rand eloquently explained: "The trader and the warrior have been fundamental antagonists throughout history. Trade does not flourish on battlefields, factories do not produce under bombardments, profits do not grow on rubble. Capitalism is a society of traders — for which it has been denounced by every would-be gunman who regards trade as 'selfish' and conquest as 'noble.'"[32]

War and Imperialism

Imperialism is a specific type of warfare — it is military aggression for the purpose of conquest of territory and the subjugation of its populace. An empire, in its literal meaning, is a political union established by military conquest or intimidation. It is no surprise then that historical research reveals the same causation for varying forms of war: imperialism is an effect of statism.

The most consistently capitalistic power in the world of that era, the one closest to laissez-faire, possessing the most attenuated statist institutions, and consequently, the wealthiest and most powerful nation — the United States of America — established the scantiest empire. (If possession of the Philippines for four decades may be considered an "empire.")

It is an important but secondary issue that capitalists generally opposed imperialism. For the fundamental point is not historical, but philosophical. As discussed above, capitalists do not necessarily support capitalism; they certainly do not consistently practice or advocate capitalistic policies. There is not necessarily a full (or even partial) congruence between the nature of capitalism and the practice of capitalists. It would, therefore, make no difference if most, or even all, businessmen in a nation advocated the establishment of military empire for the imagined purpose of maximizing investment opportunities, gaining markets, or pursuing any other faddish economic fallacy.

Imperialism remains a statist policy incompatible with the capitalist principles of individual rights, a ban on the initiation of force, and international free trade. Those who advocate imperialism *ipso facto* advocate statism regardless of their profession. Capitalism is not rationally defined as "that which capitalists do" — or as "those policies or that system advocated by businessmen." Rather, it is the system of individual rights. The Empiricist Fallacy must be conscientiously avoided.

A related distinction is drawn by the American historian, Burton Folsom. He differentiates between two classes of businessmen: "market entrepreneurs" and "political entrepreneurs." Market entrepreneurs seek

profit on a competitive marketplace without aid or intervention from the government. Political entrepreneurs, on the other hand, seek profit by means of government favors, whether in the form of subsidies, land grants, legal monopolies, tariffs or others. Market entrepreneurs favor and thrive under capitalism; political entrepreneurs favor and "thrive" under a mixed economy. Market entrepreneurs generally support free trade and oppose protectionism and imperialism; political entrepreneurs often fear free trade, favoring protective tariffs and sometimes even imperialism. The critical distinction is that market entrepreneurs seek profit by production; political entrepreneurs by the introduction of governmental force to legally suppress competitors or to gain other advantages.

Earlier, Ayn Rand had made essentially the same point: "The Money-Appropriator may become that...destructive product of a 'mixed economy': the businessman who grows rich by means of government favors, such as special privileges, subsidies, franchises; that is, grows rich by means of legalized force."

It is no surprise that a superb market entrepreneur like Hill generally favored free trade and repudiated imperialism — because he (at least implicitly) understood that both his rational self-interest and the nation's lay in individual rights, political-economic liberty, productiveness and peaceful trade. On the other hand, businessmen of any nationality who embrace protectionism and, especially, conquest, do so because they perceive their self-interest and their country's to lie in the philosophy and practice of statism rather than in the philosophy and practice of capitalism.[33]

If all businessmen were political entrepreneurs seeking wealth through statist measures, it would not change the nature of capitalism. It would simply mean that the men responsible for creating wealth had repudiated the principles of individual rights and limited government—and thereby driven another nail into capitalism's coffin.

Summary

War and Imperialism

Capitalism, the system of individual rights, requires the government to protect the rights of its citizens and refrain from violating the rights of foreigners. Under statism, on the other hand, the rulers are at chronic war with their own population. A government that recognizes no rights of its own citizens exists under no moral constraints regarding foreigners. Individuals of any nationality are its victims or its potential victims.

Statism is responsible for war.

Imperialism is warfare for the express purpose of conquering a territory and, in establishing political hegemony, abrogating the rights of the local population. Again, statism, not capitalism, is responsible.

10: Slavery

The charge that capitalism was responsible for slavery in the American South, for the brutal subjugation of blacks, is as historically and philosophically fallacious as the anti-capitalist claims regarding war. Before refuting that accusation, it is helpful to acquire historical perspective.

The Historical Truth Regarding Slavery

The heartbreaking truth is that history is filled with the hideous practice of human slavery. The Greeks, the Romans and many other conquerors, for example, often enslaved captives of war. Nor was the primitive practice confined to Europe. "Slavery was...common on every inhabited continent for thousands of years." The institution of slavery pre-dated Buddhism, Christianity and Islam. In Asia "the Manchus raided China, Korea and Mongolia for slaves." Slavers from what is now the Philippines swept extensive areas of Southeast Asia on large-scale raiding missions. Indeed, the practice of slavery was not stamped out in the Philippines until American occupation in the early 20th century. Among some of the Indian tribes of the Western Hemisphere, slavery existed "before Columbus' ships appeared on the horizon."

The very word "slave" is a derivative of the name "Slav," because Slavic peoples were enslaved on such a massive scale by both other Europeans and by the Ottoman Empire. In the late-18th century, Adam

Smith could accurately write of the slavery that still existed in Poland, Russia and Hungary.

Nor were conditions appreciably different in Africa. The current idealization of Africa has it that slavery existed only in a more benign fashion on that continent. The harsh truth, however, is that "paternalistic arrangements were at one end of a spectrum that included brutal subjugation and even using slaves as human sacrifices." Africans were used as plantation slaves in parts of Egypt, Sudan and Zanzibar, and "the numbers of people enslaved within Africa itself exceeded the numbers exported." Powerful tribes, such as the Bantu and the Yao, enslaved members of weaker tribes. The Ashanti and the Fanti tribes were inland suppliers for European slave traders who dared not venture into the interior largely because of their susceptibility to then-incurable tropical diseases.

Based on the indigenous institution of slavery, some African chiefs found it easy and lucrative to cooperate with Islamic and European slave traders. Indeed, when first the British and later the French engaged in a global struggle against the slave trade, "tribal leaders in Gambia, Congo, Dahomey and other African nations that had prospered under the slave trade sent delegations to London and Paris to vigorously protest the abolition of slavery." Further, late-18th century British attempts to establish a safe African haven for freed slaves at Sierra Leone were often defeated by hostile indigenous tribes who attacked, slaughtered and enslaved the settlers. The later American attempt in Liberia met with the same hazards. "Slavery and slave trading had prevailed among African peoples since prehistoric times."[1]

It should be obvious that slavery, like imperialism and war, is an institution founded on the initiation of force, generally by the state. It is hardly surprising that over the centuries and across the globe, two of the most prevalent forms of original enslavement have been captivity in warfare and kidnapping. Researchers have generally understood the role played by the initiation of force. For example, the black Caribbean scholar of

slavery, Orlando Patterson, is quoted accurately on this point: "For Patterson slavery is preeminently a relationship of power and dominion originating in and sustained by violence."

Unfortunately, the recurrent statist element is rarely identified. But, in fact, a population's political rulers – whether king, emperor, tribal chief, Parliament, Congress or President – initiate, approve, sanction or fail to repeal the legal empowerment granted to the men of force to enslave their victims. For slavery to "flourish" on a wide social basis, it requires legal sanction; the institution cannot survive its legal repeal within a geographical area. The antidote to slavery, both philosophically and historically, was and remains the principles of individual rights and limited government with their underlying moral base of a ban on the legal initiation of force.[2]

This is why it is appalling but not surprising that nowhere in the world was there a persistent intellectual questioning of the moral rectitude of slavery leading to a concerted abolitionist movement until the Western Enlightenment of the 18th century. Only in Europe and North America of that era did advanced thinkers finally begin to assail the horrors of slavery's theory and its practice with the express intent of putting an end to them.

The Roman Stoics had abhored slavery, but their commitment to serene acceptance of painful events in a divinely-ordained world – to "bear" and "forbear" as Epictetus put it – led to a cultivated apathy rather than a moral crusade for abolition. Later, Christianity, by means of its belief in the sacredness of the personal soul, introduced the notion of the value of each individual human being; and, based on this belief, some Christians through the ages opposed the practice of slavery.

But this religious principle, by itself, was not sufficient to convince Christian societies to oppose slavery or to cease using the Bible as a source of pro-slavery arguments. Catholics and Protestants, as well as Muslims and Jews, were perfectly content to own slaves, and for centuries to live

in societies that legally sanctioned the practice; indeed, often believed that enslavement under their faith was noble, because it contributed toward the righteousness and salvation of the heathens. Something more was needed to create the abolitionist movement of the 19th century.[3]

The Role of the Enlightenment in Creating the Abolitionist Movement

That something more was the Enlightenment. The 18th century's confidence in rationality meant a commitment to man the rational individual, to the inalienable rights of commoners in contrast to aristocratic privilege, to the Rights of Man. The logical consequences were the *philosophes'* battles for political/economic liberty, freedom of speech and of the press, religious toleration, and abolition of slavery and the slave trade.

The Enlightenment's leading thinkers were virtually unanimous in their repudiation of slavery. The *philosophes* opposed the practice on both moral and practical grounds; they argued that it was unprofitable as well as inhuman. Early in the 18th century, for example, Montesquieu was among the first in France to voice opposition to human bondage. In his *The Spirit of Laws*, Montesquieu argued that slavery was "evil by its very nature," and "corrupting for the master quite as much as for the slave." Both Voltaire and the *Encyclopedie* of Diderot supported Montesquieu's arguments. Said the Sage of Ferney: "If anyone has ever battled to restore liberty, the right of nature, to slaves of all kinds, surely it was Montesquieu. He pitted reason and humanity against all kinds of slavery..."

In Great Britain, Jeremy Bentham pointedly questioned whether coffee, sugar and other delicacies were worth the brutal subjugation of hundreds of thousands of human beings. "Are there any considerations of luxury or enjoyment that can counterbalance such evils?" he asked. Samuel Johnson, though he "detested the *philosophes* as unprincipled infi-

dels," nevertheless "accepted much of their program"; he insisted that "no man is by nature the property of another," and was a firm abolitionist.

Regarding practical matters, Adam Smith argued convincingly to many that slavery was uneconomic in contrast to liberty and free labor, a view with which Bentham agreed. In a famous passage of *The Wealth of Nations*, the great economist claimed that man's psychological drive to dominate others often outweighed his rational quest to earn wealth, and led to the generally unprofitable institution of slavery. Although Smith's claim has been widely criticized, it is nonetheless true, as will be shown below.

Across the Atlantic, all the leading minds of the American Enlightenment challenged the primitive practices of slave trading and holding, even those who themselves still owned slaves. The immortal Franklin, president of the Pennsylvania Abolition Society, just months before his death in 1790 petitioned the First United States Congress to promote "the abolition of slavery, and [to discourage] every species of traffic in slaves." Thomas Paine condemned slavery as no less vicious than "murder, robbery...and barbarity," and formulated a practical plan for the abolition of American slavery. In 1780, Paine wrote the preamble to the Pennsylvania act that abolished slavery in the state, one of the first acts of emancipation in the soon-to-be United States. John Adams was an "outspoken enemy of slavery," and Alexander Hamilton helped found the New York Manumission Society and was another "staunch anti-slavery advocate."

Even influential members of the Virginia aristocracy favored emancipation. George Washington, who swore to never "purchase another slave," made it clear that he favored abolition "by slow, sure, and imperceptible degrees." In the *Declaration of Independence*, Thomas Jefferson wrote a denunciation of the slave trade that was edited out by Congress. In 1784, he brought a bill before Congress, seeking to prohibit slavery in all the western territories, but it was repudiated by a single vote. In his

book, *Notes on the State of Virginia,* Jefferson worked out a plan "whereby all slaves born after 1800 would eventually become free." Indeed, as early as 1769 he had attempted in the Virginia Legislature to emancipate slaves by law.[4]

The intellectual and moral revolution of the Enlightenment caused the American Revolution. The 18th century principles embodied in America's founding doomed slavery in the U.S., even though a mere century earlier human bondage was an institution that had been universally practiced and unquestioned for millennia. Rational men can judge the American Revolution's consequences for themselves.

> Before 1776, slavery was legal in every state in America. Yet by 1804, every state north of Maryland had abolished slavery...Southern and border states prohibited further slave importations from abroad; and Congress outlawed the slave trade as soon as it was allowed to, in 1808 [a bill signed into law by President Thomas Jefferson]. Slavery was no longer a national but a sectional institution, and one under moral and political siege. 'Before the revolution, Americans like every other people took slavery for granted...But slavery came under indictment as a result of the same principles that produced the American Founding. In this sense, the prospect of the Civil War is implicitly contained in the Declaration of Independence.'

Slavery was referred to in the United States as "the peculiar institution," but historically it was an ancient and exceedingly widespread one. "Slavery was 'peculiar' in the United States only because human bondage was inconsistent with the principles on which this nation was founded. Historically, however, it was those principles which were peculiar, not slavery." Supporting this claim, Orlando Patterson pointed out: "There was no word for 'freedom' in most non-Western languages before contact

with Western peoples." Slavery could not long survive the creation of individualistic codes and laissez-faire systems in Great Britain and the United States during the Enlightenment era and its immediate aftermath. Its essentially feudal, aristocratic, anti-individualistic character doomed it. Nor did its demise take long.[5]

In Great Britain of the late-18th century, the abolitionist movement was growing into what would, in the 19th century, become a crusade. Many of its political leaders, like William Wilberforce, were devoted Christians. The Quakers in particular were active in the movement, and had been far ahead of their time in requiring church members to emancipate their slaves. The English preacher, John Wesley, was only one of many Christian ministers of the era who were uncompromising in their opposition to slavery. One recent supporter of religion's role in the growing abolition movement made his claim powerfully: "New World slavery provided Protestant Christianity with an epic stage for vindicating itself as the most liberal and progressive force in human history."[6]

But, for all the undeniable intellectual and political support that sincere Christians poured into the abolitionist movement, fundamentally, it was the Enlightenment, not religion, that liberated the slaves, just as, and for the same reason, it was the Enlightenment that brought down the *ancien regime*. The *philosophe's* confidence in the cognitive efficacy of reason, their conviction that by means of education and science the critical faculty of each individual could be cultivated, led logically to the view of man as a rationally self-governing and independent being. It was not right to keep such a being in bondage – not to the aristocrats, not to the plantation owners, not to the state.

Further, the egoistic ethics implicit in the era's philosophy, coming to the surface in the revolutionary conception that individuals possessed the right to pursue their own happiness, also militated against slavery. How could it be morally justifiable to impose slavery on a being with a right to independent life? Obviously, it could not. Only when such theories of

man's nature and of morality were widespread in Western society, was it logically possible to assail serfdom, slavery and the *ancien regime*.

It was the Enlightenment philosophy of man's rational nature, individual rights and political/economic liberty that liberated the slaves, the serfs, the common man. Religion was lacking in neither the Christian world of the Middle Ages nor the Islamic lands of the 18th and 19th centuries, but serfdom, slavery and despotism flourished. It was the same 18th century Western principles of secular rationalism, individualism and limited government responsible for capitalism that created the abolitionist movement. *Capitalism and abolitionism proceeded from the same intellectual/moral base: the principles of inalienable individual rights and political/economic liberty.* As Indian-American scholar, Dinesh D'Souza, stated: "The reason for the acceptability of slavery prior to the 18th century is that the idea of freedom simply did not exist in an applied and comprehensive sense anywhere in the world." During and because of the Enlightenment period, the ideals of individual rights and political-economic liberty became deeply embedded in Western culture.[7]

All societies were and are intellectual mixtures; but in the 18th century and its aftermath, those societies in which Enlightenment principles flourished – Britain, France, America – took steps, however halting and at times tortured, to eradicate despotism, serfdom and slavery. These were the progressive societies moving toward liberalism, freedom, capitalism.

The countries in which Enlightenment principles only slowly (if ever) took hold – e.g., Prussia, Austria-Hungary, Russia – moved much more slowly, if at all, to overthrow the aristocracy, free the serfs and crusade for global abolition. Observe that in Russia, where Enlightenment rationalism and liberalism barely penetrated, all of the culture's faith was inadequate to protect it from monarchical despotism and prolonged serfdom; indeed, was deeply interwoven with those traditional institutions.

It was only within the philosophical/cultural context of the

Slavery

Enlightenment that the best, the most humane members of Western society were intellectually and politically free to effectively wage a campaign to emancipate the slaves. Only after Washington, Franklin, Jefferson, Paine, et al., forged a revolution and a republic did it become intellectually and morally plausible to petition Congress to abolish slavery. Only when the principles of Locke, Montesquieu and Adam Smith – and supporting them the enormous respect for reason generated by the achievements of Newton – swept parts of Europe could an abolitionist movement gain ascendancy in Britain.

Christian Humanitarianism was awakened by and first became a viable political force during the period in which the Enlightenment credo of the Rights of Man was at the zenith of its influence. Even Bishop Wilberforce, for all his conservative opposition to the ideals of the French Revolution, studied Voltaire and Gibbon. "William Wilberforce, a British politician [was] already well aware of Enlightenment thinking." One historian, properly praising the important role played in abolitionism by Christian Humanitarians, still pointed out that such "Anglo-American reformers succeeded in appropriating many of the principles and arguments of the 'modern paganism,'" i.e., of the Enlightenment.[8]

The capitalist countries, under the self-same liberal principles that had given rise to their systems of political/economic freedom, led the global campaign against slavery. Britain, one of the world leaders in implementing laissez-faire principles during the early 19th century, conducted a global campaign to first stamp out the vile trafficking in human flesh and then to wipe out the institution of slavery itself. "The impetus for the destruction of slavery came...from a moral revulsion against slavery which began in the late eighteenth century..." Religion was not unique to the 18th century. The Enlightenment culture was.

The Worldwide Struggle Against Slavery

Such humanitarian reformers as Parliament member, William

Wilberforce, wealthy banker and innovative monetary economist, Henry Thornton, and other members of the "Clapham sect," were "repeatedly and resoundingly defeated in Parliament" in their attempts to abolish the slave trade. Finally, however, in 1807, after twenty years of indefatigable effort, victory came when the House of Commons passed such a bill. The bill was passed to a significant degree because of the will of the British public: Parliament had been besieged by letters and petitions demanding the abolition of slave trafficking. At one point, Parliament received more than 800 petitions within a month, containing a total of 700,000 signatures. In effect, the British slave trade was abolished by popular demand. Not coincidentally, it is believed that Thomas Paine's *The Rights of Man* sold over a million-and-a-half copies in Britain at the turn of the 19th century.

Slavery had previously been declared illegal in Great Britain by the joint results of the celebrated Somerset and Knight legal cases of 1772 and 1778, actions that made Britain probably the first country in history to abolish slavery. Subsequently, in 1833 the abolitionist movement succeeded in convincing Parliament to ban slavery throughout the British Empire. Then proceeded the struggle to eradicate slavery around the world.

British warships boarded first British, then foreign merchant vessels on the seas, searching for slaves. "Even while fighting a major war against Napoleon, Britain kept some of its navy on patrol off the African coast to intercept slave ships." The British exerted remorseless pressure on the Ottoman Empire to ban the extensive slave trade within its boundaries, which finally occurred in 1847. The British Navy patrolled the Indian Ocean and the Persian Gulf to enforce the Sultan's ban. "In 1873, British warships anchored off Zanzibar and threatened to blockade the island unless the slave market there closed down. It closed." The British Navy, in utter disregard of Brazilian territorial waters, pursued slavers right into Brazilian harbors in 1849 and 1850, seizing and destroying the vessels of

the offenders. In July of 1850, Brazil's government acceded to British demands to outlaw the slave trade.

The British took the lead and other Western countries followed. "[Britain's] example inspired abolitionists in the United States, and the French government later abolished slavery in its own empire and then sent its navy on patrol in the Atlantic to help intercept slave-trading ships." Spurred on by the successes of the British in the first half of the 19th century, the abolitionist movement gradually grew in the northern states of the United States.[9]

In the tragic and blood-drenched American Civil War, the armies of the North prevented the South from seceding and establishing a sovereign slave-based society. The obvious truth is that the South, like all slave systems, had not integrated the liberal principles of individual rights and limited government throughout its society; it was an agrarian, essentially feudal system in which the lords of the manors were legally empowered by the government to enslave the black population. Slavery and the plantation system involved the legally-sanctioned initiation of force against millions of innocent individuals. The industrial, capitalist North neither practiced nor permitted slavery, but wiped it out at great cost on the battlefield in the Civil War. Again, statism was responsible for this evil. The liberal principles of individual rights and political/economic freedom were and remain the cure.

Indeed, subsequent to the British crusade, the 20th century resurgence of statism in its new, most virulent form ever – socialism – led to a massive revival of the primitive institution. Soviet Russia, National Socialist Germany, Communist China and Castro's Cuba are only four of the 20th and 21st century dictatorships that have used and/or continue to use slave labor, including that of political prisoners.[10]

Further, slavery continues to be an ongoing atrocity in parts of the Islamic world. The Muslims had long been among the most egregious perpetrators of slavery, including the subjugation of black Africans. "In

the middle of the 9th century A.D., six hundred years before Portuguese voyages initiated an oceanic slave trade from West Africa to the Iberian Peninsula...many thousands of black slaves worked in regimented gangs on the tidal flats of southern Iraq." Islamic trafficking in African slaves began centuries before the Atlantic trade of the Europeans, continued in full force during those centuries and survived decades longer, being largely extinguished only by British intervention. But it was never eradicated, and today is back in all of its fiendish character.

Over the centuries, the trans-Sahara Islamic traffic delivered an estimated 14 million black Africans into bondage in comparison to roughly 11.5 million transported to the Western Hemisphere by the European slave trade. Additionally, it is estimated that ten percent of the slaves shipped across the Atlantic died in crossing; but that the in-transit death rate of the Islamic trade was double that. "Thousands of human skeletons were strewn along one Saharan slave route alone – mostly the skeletons of young women and girls...Slaves who could not keep up with the caravans...were abandoned in the desert to die a lingering death from heat, thirst and hunger. In 1849, a letter from an Ottoman official referred to 1,600 black slaves dying of thirst on their way to Libya." One scholar of the Islamic slave trade estimates that for every slave to reach Cairo alive, ten died in transit. It is believed that no slave, no matter how youthful or robust, survived more than five years in the Sahara salt mines of the Ottoman Empire.[11]

Slavery survived in Yemen until the 1960s, and at least two decades longer in Saudi Arabia. Today, early in the 21st century, tens of thousands of black Africans are enslaved in Sudan and Mauritania. Despite repeated claims of abolition by the Islamic regime governing Mauritania, the Anti-Slavery Society of London estimated in 1981 that the country "probably holds a minimum of 100,000 total slaves..." Conditions have changed little, if at all, over the past twenty years.

In Sudan, the Islamic government of Khartoum has conducted

relentless persecution of its black (Christian or animist) population centered in the country's south. A *New York Times* reporter, witnessing a Sudanese slave auction in 1999, observed: "The train pulls in and refugees are herded out. They are sold to waiting merchants, into slavery. Slavery, not forced labor or some such euphemism...They were captured and sold in Sudan by government soldiers and militias...The number in Sudan can roughly be estimated – tens of thousands. Only owners take precise slave-counts." Francis Bok, a member of the Dinka tribe who escaped from ten years of Sudanese slavery, writes that for his Arab captors, the term "abd...was a very useful word: it meant both 'black person' and 'slave.'"[12]

The Boston-based American Anti-Slavery Group is one of several private Western organizations that raises money to purchase these slaves for purposes of emancipation. Such early 21st century abolitionists continue the battle begun by the British roughly two centuries ago to stamp out the worldwide scourge of human slavery. Though the author contributes regularly to their efforts, he recognizes that the ultimate solution is intellectual, not financial. The liberal Enlightenment principles of individualism and political/economic freedom that wiped out slavery throughout the Western world are still largely unknown in the non-Western lands. Until these cultures go through a similar Enlightenment period, there will be no philosophical movement promoting freedom, individual rights and capitalism, and consequently no end there to slavery. Statism, warfare, conquest and enslavement will continue to accelerate in those regions, and on-going human misery will be the result.[13]

The principles that underlie abolitionism — individualism and individual rights — are a rare, minority viewpoint all over the world, even in the West, where they were culturally dominant principles only during the 18th and 19th centuries. Therefore, abolitionism has been and continues to be a minority viewpoint in the world.

On the other hand, the principles that underlie slavery — collec-

tivism, tribalism, statism, the denial of individual rights — historically have been and remain the status quo. Therefore, slavery has been and remains the status quo throughout wide portions of the globe.

All instances of abolitionism involve Western, Enlightenment-based, freer, capitalist nations or sections – most often Britain or the United States – struggling against statist regimes that reject individual rights and liberties for the rule of brute force. It must be recognized that "abolition constitutes one of the greatest moral achievements of Western civilization."[14]

The Astonishing Birth of "the Dismal Science"

Today it is unfortunately not widely remembered that the free market economists of the mid-19th century waged an intellectual battle in favor of abolition against some of England's leading literary figures (and blatant racists). Agreeing with Adam Smith, such economists as James Mill, John Stuart Mill and John Elliott Cairnes opposed slavery. They held that no racial group of men is better than any other; that belief in the "uplifting" quality of servitude to one's "betters" is fantasy; and men should be left free to make rational choices and act on them. In brief, they upheld freedom in contrast to authoritarian, hierarchical slave systems, including those racially based.

These ideas were anathema to the leading English essayist, Thomas Carlyle, and the influential critic, John Ruskin. They argued that whites were naturally superior to blacks; that slavery to their "betters" improved "inferior peoples"; and that true liberty for the "lower races" consisted of bondage – security within a hierarchy – to the paternalistic care of superior men. They excoriated the economists for disturbing the natural order of things and for proclaiming inferior men the equal of their betters.

In his 1849 essay, "Occasional Discourse on the Negro Question," Carlyle coined and applied the now-famous epithet "dismal science" to economics because its leading representatives opposed racial slavery and

the joys of service to one's betters, standing instead for the freedom of all men regardless of race. In a later piece, Carlyle advocated the extermination of recalcitrant slaves. "…shirk the heavy labor, disobey the rules – I will admonish and endeavor to incite you; if in vain, I will flog you; if still in vain, I will at last shoot you – and make God's Earth…free of you."

But ideas have consequences. When, in 1865, Governor Eyre of Jamaica slaughtered hundreds of blacks because of a minor disturbance, the battlelines were clear. The free market economists and abolitionists, led by John Stuart Mill – and including the influential advocate of free-trade, John Bright – demanded "colorblind justice" and punishment of Eyre. Opposing them were the leading literary racists – John Ruskin, Charles Dickens, Alfred Tennyson – who joined with Carlyle "in making the case that it could not be murder to kill Jamaicans of color because one could only murder people."[15]

The point is not to conduct an *ad hominem* attack on Carlyle and his allies – that would avail nothing. Nor is it simply to provide a further illustration that liberalism's principles were in the vanguard of the abolitionist movement. It is to point out that the pro-slavery convictions of Carlyle, Ruskin, Dickens, et al., were logically consistent with their virulent anti-capitalism and with their support of statist economics. Why did they think slavery a more benign social institution than free markets? They opposed abolition and capitalism for the same reason: freedom cut loose "underqualified" peoples – black slaves, European serfs, Irishmen, low-born workers – from the paternalistic relationship with their betters that alone would improve their lot.

Despite the fact that by the mid-19th century, capitalism had already significantly improved the life of English workers, as discussed above, they held, in effect, that the lower class worker could no more be expected to advance without benign governmental oversight than a black slave could prosper without the benevolent white master to direct his life.

Their brutally-succinct claim was that many individuals are not fit for freedom, but must be ruled.

The opposition of Carlyle and his colleagues to emancipation proceeded from the same belief in an authoritarian, hierarchical political structure that instigated their opposition to capitalism. "Carlyle makes a point of vital importance: the economics of his contemporaries in its idealization of market relationships among equals stands in opposition to his dream of slavery's hierarchical obedience."

In their view, slavery and government economic intervention were both paternalistic policies in which ruling elites could uplift the lives of the "lower" type of men. Today, it is generally forgotten that the major moral-economic battle of the mid-19th century was not capitalism vs. socialism, but capitalism vs. an economy of race-based slavery. In the early 21st century, in a politically correct cultural atmosphere, socialist intellectuals simply ignore the racism and pro-slavery arguments and extol Carlyle, Ruskin and Dickens for their "crusading" antipathy to capitalism.

It is true that these 19th century writers, endorsing serfdom and essentially feudal in outlook, offered a different variant of paternalistic statism than do their modern socialist counterparts – but government paternalism in both cases, in contrast to free minds, free men and free markets, it remains. It is of one logical piece that both Engels and the Nazis admired Carlyle; that Dickens dedicated his scathing anti-capitalist novel, *Hard Times*, to Carlyle; and that contemporary socialist intellectuals continue to esteem Dickens, Carlyle and Ruskin.

Capitalism and abolitionism proceed logically from the same fundamental commitment to individual rights and liberty. Similarly, socialism and slavery proceed logically from the same fundamental commitment to the paternalistic rule of a government of intellectual-moral elites.[16]

Slavery and the Industrial Revolution

A few last points remain regarding the relationship between capitalism and slavery. Some anti-capitalists claim that the profits made from slavery by British merchants and plantation owners provided the necessary capital to fund Britain's Industrial Revolution — so that, in effect, capitalism was (at least in part) a product of slavery.

In fact, however, "even if all of the profits of slavery had been invested in British industry, this would have come to less than 2 percent of Britain's domestic investments during that era." One economic historian estimates that on the unlikely hypothesis that all slave trade profits were invested, the total would reach merely 1.59 percent of British national investment. He adds that profits from the plantation economy also constituted a "contribution [to national investment that] cannot have been considerable. Indeed, on certain premises, the plantation economy brought actual loss to the nation." Further, the historical evidence indicates that slaveowners did not tend to be frugal investors, but were more commonly ostentatious spendthrifts often in debt.

It is also not to be overlooked that Britain's total costs of waging a decades-long naval campaign against the slave trade added to her related expenses of compensating former owners of emancipated slaves with an 1833 payment of 20 million pounds sterling — and bribing foreign governments and African tribal leaders to curtail the slave trade — at the very least ate up any profit accruing to her citizens from slavery. Additionally, what were the British costs in establishing African resettlement colonies for freed slaves, first at Sierra Leone and in 1816 at Bathurst? Such expenses, of course, diminished the funds which might otherwise have been invested in her burgeoning industries. Slavery neither funded the Industrial Revolution nor benefited the British economy.[17]

But a far more important point must be made. Since slavery existed universally, it can be asked why its "profits" did not fund an industrial revolution in a different time or place. Why Great Britain and why in the 18th century? The answer, after the earlier discussion of this point, is evi-

dent: the Industrial Revolution was not based on slavery or its proceeds, whatever those might be. It was based on the scientific advances of the post-Renaissance period, and the glorification of reason and freedom these contributed to in the ensuing Enlightenment era. James Watt, studying the powers inherent in steam with Professors Black and Robison at the University of Glasgow, required neither slaves nor profit from slavery. He required only confidence in the human mind and sufficient freedom to demonstrate that confidence justified. An earlier point can be reprised in a new form: slavery was not unique to the 18th century era; the Enlightenment culture was.

On a related point, Marxist professor and former Prime Minister of Trinidad and Tobago, Eric Williams, in his controversial book, *Capitalism and Slavery*, claimed that capitalist Britain scourged the international slave trade and sought a worldwide ban on slavery not primarily due to moral principles but because of economic self-interest.

The present author hopes the British gained prodigiously from their moral accomplishment – and if they did, it wasn't enough. Just as an individual patient cured of an otherwise terminal ailment by a great physician could not sufficiently reimburse his benefactor – so the human race could never adequately repay Britain for the enormity of its contributions to mankind's prosperity. It was its Lockean philosophy of liberalism giving rise to capitalism and the Industrial Revolution that was its fundamental achievement and contribution. The rest, including abolition, were important practical applications.

What greater compliment could be paid to capitalism than that its nature, interest and profitability stood in diametric opposition to the immediate financial interests of the slavers? It is true: the rational self-interest of free men clash irrevocably with the supposed interest of statists and despots of every variety, including slave drivers. Britain and her cultural progeny, America, taught that particular lesson to Hitler and later the Soviet Union.

The error inherent in this "criticism" (made also by some of capitalist Britain's "supporters") is the conviction of a dichotomy between humanitarianism and self-interest, between virtue and profit, between morality and practicality. In fact, virtue and rational self-interest are allied principles; they do not oppose each other. For example, when a competent physician performs his medical tasks to the conscientious best of his ability, he receives the pride of work well done, the joy of bringing health where previously there was illness, and a well-deserved fee; he is honest, productive, responsible and diligent – hence moral; and other human beings, his patients, benefit. There is no split for rational men between a moral life and the requirements of practical success.

Nor is financial gain the only or even the greatest reward a man or nation can earn. Wealth well-earned is a significant value. But perhaps wisdom, freedom, mental and/or bodily health, romantic love, are even more so. That Britain provided mankind an incalculable moral benefit is not to be doubted. Even better, it was not a selfless or altruistic action on its part, for the British above all benefited. Abolitionism was a direct result of Britain's liberal, capitalist ideals – the selfsame ideals that generated the country's growing freedom and soaring prosperity of that era.

The best, the most rational and the most virtuous men on earth, will always be the ones to create freedom, wealth and flourishing life. This should be a joyous recognition – for do men of justice desire to see the most virtuous among them suffer or gain because of their lofty character?

Is Slavery Profitable?

A final point is the long-standing dispute regarding slavery's relative profitability. Adam Smith argued that slavery is economically inefficient, because the slave has no profit-based motive to work productively. "A person who can acquire no property, can have no other interest but to eat as much, and to labor as little as possible. Whatever work he does beyond what is sufficient to purchase his own maintenance, can be squeezed out

of him by violence only, and not by any interest of his own." One free market economist who studied the slave economy concluded that its "economical defects...are very serious. They may be summed up under the three following heads – [labor] is given reluctantly; it is unskillful; it is wanting in versatility." As under Communism, when an individual's output is sundered from his profitability, the only logical consequence is diminished productivity.[18]

Smith's argument is attractive to common sense. After all, whereas an employer has merely to pay a free laborer's wages, a plantation owner must first purchase a slave, then feed, clothe, shelter and medically care for him. A slave, in economic terms, is a capital investment – a commercially valuable one – and must be treated accordingly. This is why, in the Old South, plantation owners refused to risk their slaves on hazardous tasks, but preferred to hire free Irishmen instead. "A northern visitor in the antebellum South was surprised to find slaves throwing 500-pound bales of cotton down a ramp to Irish workmen on a riverboat who had the hazardous job of catching the heavy bales. He was told: 'The niggers are worth too much to be risked here; if the Paddies are knocked overboard, or get their backs broke, nobody loses anything.'"[19]

Nevertheless, historical research establishes that slavery was often profitable for plantation owners and slave traders. Some students of the subject go so far as to claim that slave plantations in the American south were significantly more efficient than free northern farms. Slaves may be less productive per hour of output than free men, but slaves can be worked for longer hours over more days and years than hired laborers. They cannot demand greater leisure or quit after receiving training or form unions or go on strike. They may be valuable and require care – but only in the same way as horses or oxen. As long as they receive the care necessary to sustain them, they can be worked relentlessly. Among free people, some are unemployed and some supported by others; but among slaves, all worked. During the height of the cotton season, for example,

most slaves – whether field hands or not – men, women and children, labored in the fields from sunrise to sundown.[20]

But that slavery may have profited some of the slave traders and owners does not make it an economically viable system. Many policies may profit some in the short term but because they violate individual rights be egregiously unproductive. An armed robber, for example, may "profit" in the short run from his loot, but his crimes lead to diminished productivity; in part because he's not working, in larger part because his "successes" undermine the incentive of his hard-working victims, perhaps even maim or kill them — and finally, because by compelling honest men to build more prisons, hire more police officers and security guards, etc., it diverts money and manpower from the creation of consumer goods and services. Men are poorer, not wealthier, because of the robbers' "profits."

Similarly, slavery is a system that undermines the levels of productivity that could otherwise be reached.

Numerous writers point out the "hidden" costs of slavery that do not exist for free labor. For example, since slaves are held involuntarily, the system must be enforced. There must be armed guards, fences, slave patrols, etc. These not only cost money, but take men away from productive activities in which they might otherwise be employed. Part of the plantation owners' profits were made possible by their ability to legislatively foist their enforcement costs on to other non-slave owning whites. The legal system of the antebellum South drafted white men, many of whom owned no slaves, to form slave patrols and sweep the countryside, their purposes to maintain firm control over blacks and search for runaways. The slave patrols were established in every slave state, and "patrol duty was compulsory for most able-bodied white males."

Similarly, for decades the Fugitive Slave Law in the north legally required local law enforcement officers to help southern slaveowners recover runaways. Such laws lifted enforcement burdens off of plantation

owners, thereby diminishing their costs and enhancing their profits – and dragged other whites from productive work, thereby undercutting their incomes.[21]

Further, there exists the possibility of alternative allocation of resources. Slavers, like armed robbers, have the capacity to make other choices. If robbers chose to work, rather than steal, for example, crime would drop, productivity would rise, living standards would climb. Similarly, what would happen if slavers traded in their whips and guns for hammers, saws or plowshares? If slave hunters, traders, guards and owners actually worked, rather than initiated force, productivity again would rise. If slaves were emancipated and their rights protected, they could work for their own profit. Some would then seek an education, some would upgrade their skills in other ways, and their productivity would rise. Merchant vessels could ship consumer goods rather than human victims. The British government would not require as many warships to suppress the slave trade, taxes could consequently be lowered, and that money invested in productive enterprises.

The explanatory principle is not difficult to apprehend: If men worked rather than initiated force — or were free to work without force initiated against them — productivity and living standards would rise. It is hardly an accident, after all, that the freest countries of history were and are the wealthiest.

By far the most significant harm slavery does to an economy is in terms of foregone benefits, i.e., the values not created because of the system. For example, since ignorance is one means by which to keep a population suppressed, the Southern states legally prohibited education to slaves, and did not even permit free blacks to attend schools at their own expense. *Blacks were not allowed to use their minds.* The skills they were permitted to acquire were limited, and output in most cases was restricted to manual labor. With the brain power of millions left unutilized, their lives were immeasurably impoverished; and similarly, the economic

system was deprived of the inventors, entrepreneurs, physicians, educators, scientists, lawyers, etc., who under freedom would have emerged, and whose productive activities would have helped raise general living standards. It is impossible to calculate how many potential George Washington Carvers were denied the opportunity to cultivate their genius by the slave system.

The general incomes of "the white population of the United States has been lowest in the region in which slavery has existed." Southern whites were generally poorer than Northern whites. Further, "within the South, those parts in which slavery has been particularly concentrated (Mississippi, Alabama, and other deep South states) have long had the very lowest incomes among white Southerners." Part of the reason has been that slavery and its legacy of racism has driven or kept away from the area some of the most rational, talented whites whose productivity would have enhanced the region's prosperity.[22]

But the most important reason is deeper than this and bears a fundamental similarity to the conclusions reached here regarding imperialism and war.

General Conclusions Regarding Capitalism and Statism

In 1933, the British writer, Norman Angell, won the Nobel Peace Prize, largely for his seminal 1910 book, *The Great Illusion*. Angell, recognizing the heightening political tensions and nationalistic rivalries of early 20th century Europe, argued for the economic futility of war. He pointed out that in pre-industrial mercantile systems, when wealth consisted of bullion or jewels, "prize horses...princesses and the like..." then war and conquest, despite its manifest expense in blood and money, might be viewed as in the victor's self-interest. Sufficient plunder might possibly make it economically feasible (although even this is doubtful.)

But in the modern era of capitalism and free trade, he argued, war was economically senseless. For example, German bankers and investors

owned significant shares of Britain's productive ventures – and vice-versa. Similarly, German citizens gained much in trade with British producers (again, the reverse was also true); so that the destruction of British industries in war would only impoverish many Germans, and that of German industries, many Britons. Bank credit, office buildings, skyscrapers, steel mills,' textile plants, etc., which formed the bulk of the stupendous wealth created by the capitalist world, were not so easily plundered. What would happen to the value of these industries on the world market when their creators and owners were expropriated and possibly killed? What would plummeting stock prices and terrified would-be investors do to the value of the properties owned by citizens of the "victorious" country? Obviously, nothing good.

Repudiating Marx's theory of the primacy of economic motives, and echoing Adam Smith, Angell recognized that wars were often fought for irrational reasons unrelated and opposed to a country's rational self-interest – such primitive motives as jingoism, nationalist and/or ethnic hatreds and the lust to dominate others; but insofar as policy makers considered such rational considerations as economic gain a value, they needed to appreciate how drastically war undermined that goal. Put in simple terms, Angell's thesis was that war does not pay.[23]

Angell is not merely correct, his conclusion is more broadly applicable. Imperialism, slavery *and* war do not pay. The broadest truth is that statism as such, in all of its brutal manifestations, does not pay. It is not a coincidence that the capitalist system of individual rights and limited government – standing opposed to the centuries-long policies of imperialism, slavery and endless, internecine warfare – has created by far the wealthiest societies of human history; has created wealth unimaginable to the blood-drenched plunderers, conquerors and slave drivers of the past.

There is a life-and-death lesson here that mankind has not yet fully understood – but must. As discussed above, the capitalist, industrial and technological revolutions of the late-18th century period were based

in their inherited scientific advances of the Age of Reason. The Enlightenment thinkers, recognizing the minds and rights of individual human beings – of commoners – advocated and, in America, created a political system embodying the principle of individual liberty and limiting the power of the state. With the mind glorified, and the individual liberated, there followed the outpouring of technological advances of America's Inventive Period and of the capitalist age more broadly. It cannot be sufficiently stressed that capitalism is the system of the mind.

Statism, on the other hand, is the system of brute force. It abrogates the mind and rights of its victims as a matter of principle. Observe the variations of this truth, the countless ways in which statism undercuts and discourages the mind's full functioning.

Slavery, as merely one example, obviously grossly underutilized the slave's mindpower. But, additionally, what did it do to the master? Historically, some slaveowners were educated, refined men, able to appreciate Homer, Virgil, Shakespeare; fluent in English, French and Latin; delighting in Bach and Mozart. But were their minds generally applied to improving their means of production? Not often. Why should they be? Unlike industrial capitalists who were integral members of a system grounded in scientific, technological and industrial advance, and consequently driven by the competition in applied mind power to incessantly improve, invent, and innovate, slaveowners profited by means of legally-enforced, whip-driven physical labor. Thinking was irrelevant to their survival and prosperity. What they relied on instead was brute force.

Not surprisingly, there were no innovative advances in the application of muscle power. It functioned in the 19th century exactly as it had in the 9th. Not coincidentally, on the eve of the Civil War in the antebellum South, the plantations produced cotton just as they had in the 19th century's opening decades, fifty years earlier. This in an era when industrial capitalism was revolutionizing the lives of the common man in England, and was on the verge of doing so in the American North.

Slavery, and statism more broadly, in stifling and discouraging the independent mind, result in economic stagnation.

The brilliant educator, Booker T. Washington, grew up a slave, and made the following observations. "The hurtful influences of [slavery] were not by any means confined to the Negro." Because "the whole machinery of slavery was so constructed as to cause labor, as a rule, to be looked upon as a badge of degradation, of inferiority..." the white man's incentive to work and produce was undercut. Washington points out that his former master had many children, but that none of them ever learned a productive trade. "The slave owner and his sons had mastered no special industry." It is true that Washington referred to manual labor, but his point can be applied more broadly. Since rational intelligence applied to the problems of creating goods and services is the fundamental source of production, any factor that undercuts the necessity to produce necessarily undermines the application of the mind to those problems.[24]

More fundamentally than economics, capitalism was based in and perpetuated a culture of free thinking, respect for the mind, individual rights, inventiveness and technological advance. As the political/economic system of the Enlightenment, its revolutionary philosophy upheld the primacy and unimpeachable right of man's mind. But slavery, on the other hand, was an integral component of the *ancien regime* – of feudal privilege, monarchy, bondage of the serfs, endless warfare, bloody conquest, plunder. Its philosophy celebrated brute force, emphatically not the mind and rights of the individual.

. This is the deepest reason that America's magnificent Inventive Period was almost exclusively a northern, not a southern phenomenon. Thomas Edison, for example, was born and raised in Ohio, and worked largely in New Jersey. Westinghouse came from New York and worked in Pennsylvania. Eastman was centered in New York. The Wright brothers were from Ohio; Ford from Michigan; Rockefeller from Ohio; James J. Hill a Canadian who settled in Minnesota; Carnegie a Scottish immi-

grant who located in Pennsylvania; Bell, also a Scottish immigrant who settled and worked in the Northeast. Vanderbilt of New Jersey and then New York revolutionized northern transportation while the south slumbered. Even Eli Whitney, whose cotton gin was instrumental in making southern cotton profitable, was a Yankee inventor from Massachusetts who worked his way through Yale as an engineer. The list goes on.

Even the "exceptions" prove the rule. Obed Hussey, "a one-eyed sailor from Maine," who settled in Ohio, preceded Cyrus McCormick by six months in obtaining a patent for his reaper. But McCormick's machines won the competitive battle. The point, however, is that McCormick, a Virginian, sold few reapers in the South. He moved to Illinois, opened a factory in Chicago, and sold many in the Midwest, where both terrain and local culture favored his innovations.[25]

Regarding the untapped mental power of the enslaved black population, remember that the brilliant educator, Booker T. Washington, was fortunately freed from slavery at age nine, and later struggled to get an education at Hampton Institute. He founded Tuskeegee Institute in 1881, and headed the school until his death in 1915. In 1896, he hired the brilliant scientist, George Washington Carver, as director of the Department of Agricultural Research at Tuskeegee, where Carver performed his pioneering work. It goes without saying that Washington, born in 1856, and Carver, in 1864, would have received no education or opportunities if slavery had persisted. Carver's achievement of vastly improving southern agriculture is the economic superiority of freedom over slavery in a microcosm. The mind, not brute physical labor, is the source of productivity.

It is the anti-mind philosophy of force underlying and giving rise to statism that fundamentally makes it impossible for it to generate the universal prosperity of capitalism. For example, it is not just that conquest and imperialism require expensive militaries and wars, and that they destroy human life and property – but fundamentally, that they are

implementations of the primitive code of brute force. These phenomena do not proceed from, and are in direct contradiction to, the philosophy upholding the power, the rights and the freedom of the mind.

Even the short-term gain from plunder is based on more rational men – the brutes' victims – using their own minds to create wealth. What would result for everybody's standard of living if the conquerors renounced the initiation of force, embraced the mind and proceeded to live productively? Or, conversely, if the rational men repudiated productivity and beat their plowshares into swords and their tractors into tanks?

A study of history, economics and rational philosophy combine to show that mankind's legitimate self-interest lies in the principles of individual rights, limited government, political/economic freedom, capitalism, an industrial revolution and international free trade. Men need to understand and embrace Enlightenment principles universally, glorify and liberate the creative mind, produce abundance and trade freely around the globe. This is the path to world freedom, prosperity and peace.

Angell provides a vivid picture of the abundance and mutually-beneficial trade created under the system of free minds, free men and free markets.

> Here is the ironmaster in Essen [Germany] making locomotives for a light railway in an Argentine province (the capital for which has [come from] Paris) – which has become necessary because of the export of wool to Bradford [England], where the trade has developed owing to sales in the United States. But for the money found in Paris (due, perhaps, to good crops in wine and olives sold mainly to London and New York), and the wool needed by the Bradford manufacturer (who has found a market for blankets amongst miners in Montana, who are smelting copper for a cable to China, which is needed because the encouragement

given to education by the Chinese Republic has caused Chinese newspapers to print cable news in English) – but for such factors as these...the ironmaster in Essen would not have been able to sell his locomotives.[26]

The outstanding American economist, Julian Simon, accurately referred to the human mind as "the ultimate resource," the one upon which creation of all others — food, oil, computers, etc. — depended. One day, when the human race has learned that lesson, the mind will be glorified, the initiation of force revoked, laissez-faire capitalism will prevail, and global prosperity will abound. But until that day, men will suffer from war, imperialism and slavery.

Summary

Slavery existed all over the world for thousands of years. A concerted moral drive to enact abolition was born during the 18th century Enlightenment based on the same principles of individual rights and limited government that created capitalism. Today, slavery is still widespread in the non-capitalist (and only the non-capitalist) world.

Slavery is a non-productive economic system, because it relies on brute force, thereby undercutting the role of the mind in man's life.

Part Four: Economics

11: The Great Laboratory

To demonstrate the economic superiority of capitalism to statism, it is best to start with the facts and then proceed to the theory explaining them.

The world today and of the recent past provides a series of countries with contrasting political/economic systems – capitalism and socialism, freedom and statism side-by-side. Relatively-free South Korea sits on the border of brutally-controlled North Korea. Two capitalist Asian countries, Hong Kong and Taiwan, exist in close geographic proximity to Communist China. China itself is divided – on the one hand, are the Special Economic Zones (SEZs), which include a higher degree of economic freedom, and on the other hand, the rest of the country, whose economy is still controlled by the government.

The Cuban dictatorship is a scant 100 miles from the free Cuban-American community of Miami. In recent years, the freer societies of Western Europe and the totalitarian states of Eastern Europe shared a lengthy border. Indeed, West Berlin's liberty and East Berlin's totalitarianism were showcased side-by-side in what was called the "Great Laboratory," as if an experiment testing the nature and consequences of capitalism and communism were underway.

A different form of the experiment can be examined in Scandinavia: Sweden, for example, was a capitalist system at the beginning of the 20th

century and a mixed economy welfare state at the end. What were and are the results in practice of the two systems in the same country? Finally, the capitalist U.S. and the communist U.S.S.R. conducted a global struggle that tested the political/economic viability of the two systems. If these neighboring contrasting systems are viewed as a test, what were the results?

The cases will be examined one at a time, starting with the conflict between the United States and the Soviet Union.

America vs. Soviet Russia

There are degrees of freedom and dictatorship. A government can control men's lives to a greater or lesser extent. For example, U.S. society was much freer in the late-19th century than it is at the turn of the 21st. But Russia, even prior to the advent of Communism in 1917, was never a free society. The Czars tended to be particularly authoritarian rulers even relative to many of Europe's other monarchs. With a few exceptions, they stifled intellectual dissent, repressed political opposition and taxed their subjects heavily. They maintained serfdom until the 1860s. In general, Russia under the Romanov dynasty was less free and more backward than the other European monarchies. Certainly, the liberal Enlightenment philosophy of respect for the mind, individual rights, limited constitutional government and political/economic freedom that was born (and to some extent spread) in Western Europe never took hold in Russia.

But, though brutally repressive, Czarist Russia, by the turn of the 20th century, was not a Nazi/Communist-type totalitarian state. Borders were open – for emigrants who sought to depart, for immigrants who looked to settle, even for those who wished to import Western books and ideas. To a significant degree, private property was permitted to exist, and many individuals owned their own farms or businesses. The government did not typically rail against "the evil Western capitalists," and generally

sought investment from foreign private companies. Several of the Czars earnestly sought to Westernize their country – to import Western innovations and industrial advances.

Indeed, in the late 19th and early 20th centuries, Russia was, with enormous help from the freer countries of the West, rapidly beginning to industrialize. The Swedish Nobel brothers helped develop the Baku oilfields, European (especially French) capital and engineering was largely responsible for the construction of the Trans-Siberian railroad, and U.S. farm machinery was widely used in agriculture. By 1900, a good 300 foreign joint stock companies functioned in Russia – mostly Belgian, but also French, German and English. From 1885 to 1889 and again from 1907 to 1913, the "average annual rate of growth of industrial output in Russia" exceeded that of the U.S., England or Germany. Russia, less free than the capitalist nations of the West, was not as industrialized or as advanced as they. But Czarist Russia – not a full dictatorship, permitting some elements of individual liberty and welcoming widespread help from freer nations – was making significant economic advances prior to World War I.[1]

This ended in 1917. The Communist takeover in Russia was a moral, political and economic calamity for the people. The slaughters and persecutions, especially during (but not limited to) the Stalin era are well documented. It is becoming widely known that the Communists created a crushing dictatorship, murdered 20 million of their own citizens, and eventually constructed an "iron curtain" around their territories, shooting those who sought to leave. One brief comparison highlights the relative difference in repression between the monarchy and the Communists. For the entire period of 1825-1917, the total number of political prisoners sentenced to death in Czarist Russia was some 6,300, of whom 3,932 were executed. Under Lenin, by contrast, 10,000-15,000 political prisoners were executed in two months of 1918 alone. "In the space of a few weeks the Cheka [the Soviet secret police] had executed two to three

times the total number of people condemned to death by the tsarist regime over ninety-two years."[2]

Today, a full decade after the collapse of the Soviet Union, some of its archives are available to Western researchers and the moral abominations of Communism are openly revealed and thoroughly documented. The terror unleashed by the Soviets, including the Party purges, the phony trials, the deliberate, murderous famines, the persecution of the intellectuals and the clergy, the vast gulag system, the alliance with the Nazis, the invasion of Poland, the post-War conquest of Eastern Europe, etc., can no longer be denied. Awareness of the moral nature of the Soviet Union and of Communism generally is becoming increasingly widespread.[3]

But the economic truth regarding the Soviet period is not as widely known. Many Americans believed during the Cold War – and still believe – that Soviet Russia was a prosperous land similar to those of the capitalist nations. Their attitude was, in effect, that Communist methods were brutal but achieved salutary economic results; that Communism and capitalism were merely divergent paths toward a similar goal. Indeed, many educated people believed – as late as the 1980s – that the Soviets would eventually exceed the Americans in productivity and prosperity. The economic conditions resulting from totalitarianism need to be known and understood.

The first point is to remember that, in terms of natural resources, Russia is exceptionally wealthy. The country is blessed with extensive amounts of oil, coal, iron, manganese, copper, gold, asbestos, timber and some of the world's most fertile agricultural lands. It has mighty rivers to potentially generate hydro-electric power, and deep-water harbors on three oceans. It possesses a large population of talented, hard-working people. The country has all the natural resources conventionally associated with economic development and wealth.

Nevertheless, in 1920, after three years of Communist rule, the

The Great Laboratory

Soviet economic conditions were desperate. H.G. Wells, a socialist and a sympathetic observer, traveled the Russian countryside, and reported "an unparalleled example of civilization in a state of complete collapse; the railway tracks were rusting and becoming gradually unusable, the cities were falling into ruins." Industrial production had dropped to one-seventh of the pre-war level. Many factories stood abandoned and the mineshafts were flooded. The state of the metal industry was disastrous, with the output of pig iron down to a mere 3 per cent of the pre-war total. One example of industrial collapse was the gigantic Russo-Baltic plant at Taganrog – its furnaces, hammers, hydraulic presses, and power station, as well as 2,000 machine tools all physically intact – but, in 1926, idle since the revolution's inception in 1917.

In Moscow and St. Petersburg, "the economy had nearly stopped, and the transport system had ground to a halt. Most of the factories were closed or working at half speed because of lack of fuel, and food supplies to the cities were in danger of ceasing altogether." There was a severe shortage of consumer goods, as well as of heating fuel and food. Indeed, in the years between 1917 and 1921 five million Russians starved to death.[4]

No doubt, some small part of the decay was a result of the Civil War following the Communist seizure of power. But the Russian industrial facilities were only slightly affected by the Revolution and Civil War; except in the Don Basin in southwestern Russia, there was little physical destruction. The problem was Communism.

The truth is that between 1918 and 1922, Lenin attempted to run the country on the basis of "socialist self-sufficiency," extirpating all vestiges of private ownership and private enterprise. The Communist victory caused many of Russia's foreign engineers and technicians to leave the country – and resulted in a similar brain drain of educated Russians, either abroad or to the countryside where food was easier to find. These men of technical ability were replaced by men of unquestioning Party

loyalty. Managers of industries were selected by reference to their ideology, not their knowledge or ability in the relevant field. Across a broad range of industries, men ignorant of their respective businesses were elevated to the heights of authority. For example, in the electrical equipment industry, "Communists possessing little or no technical ability served as technical directors, and [non-Communist] skilled engineers were serving in minor posts."[5]

Adhering to Marx's belief that money is a capitalistic tool of exploitation to be shunned in a socialist system, Lenin deliberately inflated the ruble in order to obliterate its value. The inflation instigated a collapse toward a primitive barter economy – for, understandably, individuals would not exchange goods for paper money that steadily diminished in value.

Further, socialist theory undercut industry in other ways. An example was the Soviet steel mill built with contempt for all details of expense. When engineers complained that raw materials had to be conveyed a distance of 1,250 miles, the Party responded that transportation costs were not a determining factor in a socialist economy. Concern for costs, stated the Communists, was a capitalistic idea. The collapse resulting from such policies was so complete that even Lenin was forced to do an economic about face.[6]

Lenin instituted his New Economic Policy (NEP) in 1921. This involved a temporary repeal of certain controls, permitting once again private, profit-seeking ownership of small manufacturing, retailing and wholesaling companies. (The Communists did, however, retain control of what Lenin called "the commanding heights" of the economy, including heavy industry, mining, transportation and foreign trade.) Regarding the failed socialist methods, Lenin remarked, "Our program was right in theory, but impractible."

So he turned to Western capitalism for salvation. He offered Western firms generous "concessions" in return for the rapid industrialization of

the Russian economy. English, German, Italian, Swedish, Danish and American companies accepted, and hurried to provide the USSR with airfields and railroads, with gold, copper and iron mines, with oil refineries and much more.

But before Western industry could rebuild the shattered Soviet economy, massive famine again swept the country, impelling the West to organize famine relief on a grand scale. Future U.S. President, Herbert Hoover, set up an international organization. The Quakers collected money, and the great Norwegian Arctic explorer, Fridtjof Nansen, also organized relief. The figures for the full Western aid are lost, but it is known that the United States alone sent 700,000 tons of foodstuffs.

While food from the capitalist nations arrived, scores of concessionary agreements were signed between the Soviet government and private companies from the West. A concession was a contract in which the Soviet Union hired a foreign company to open and operate a specific enterprise. The company gained no rights of ownership, but, in theory, was permitted to earn a profit for an allotted number of years, at the end of which all assets were to become Soviet property. Naïve Western businessmen trusted the Communists and flocked to seize the concessionary "opportunities."

Many German firms were involved. The great manufacturing firm of Krupp, the "Steel King" Otto Wolff of Cologne, the Linke-Hofmann Works (the leading manufacturer of railroad equipment) and other private companies exported industrial plant and supplies to the Soviet Union. German engineers, technicians and contractors went to the USSR. Krupp's technicians taught the Soviets how to produce certain types of steel, and, in the Salsk area north of the Caucasus, developed a vast mechanized agricultural estate, complete with the latest machinery for ploughing, harrowing, manuring, sowing and harvesting. The great German aeronautical expert, Hugo Junkers, went to Soviet Russia with many of his top technicians in 1922. He gave the Soviets the blueprints

of his designs, and, at Fili in the Moscow area, built for them a factory manufacturing aircraft. Junkers opened the first Russian airline from Moscow to current-day Gorki in 1922. Additionally, diesel engines were manufactured in Russia under German supervision.

American companies were also actively involved. The Standard Oil Company gained an oil-boring concession, U.S. firms won gold-prospecting rights on the Amur and General Electric sold the Soviets some twenty million dollars of electrical equipment. From 1921 to 1925 alone, U.S. businesses poured thirty-seven million dollars worth of machinery and equipment into Soviet Russia.

U.S. companies were instrumental in bailing out the Soviets from the disastrous consequences of their economic policies. The Communists all but ruined the thriving Russian oil fields in the Caucasus that, in 1900, had been the world's largest producer of crude oil. Antony Sutton, one of the world's leading experts on the Soviet economy, states that, as a consequence of Soviet ineptitude, "water percolated into the wells, and the flow of crude oil became first a mixture of oil and water and finally a flow of oily water."

It was the International Barnsdall Corporation, a U.S. firm operating on concession, that restored the Soviet fields, giving Russia the benefit of its experts and the most modern equipment. The situation was similar regarding Soviet coal production. The Russian mines in the Donetz Basin had, in 1910, produced three-fourths of the country's total coal output. Under the Soviets, the situation deteriorated so rapidly that, in 1921-23, coal was imported into the region from the U.S. and England. Again, an American company, Stuart, James and Cooke, Inc., rescued the Communists, restructuring Soviet coal mines by use of the most modern methods of American mining.[7]

The English, too, contributed to Soviet development. Lena Goldfields Ltd. invested millions of rubles in the task of creating then state-of-the-art gold-mining installations in the area around Vitimsk on

the Lena River. The company sent a staff of geologists, chemists and engineers, employing the latest English machinery – dredges, sifters and conveyor belts – and succeeded in making the mines productive.[8]

But the real Western contributions came during the first Five Year Plan. On October 1st 1928, Stalin's plan for the massive industrialization of the Soviet Union began. At this time, 125,188,800 out of a total Soviet population of 153,955,600 worked on or near the land. Stalin's goal was to catch up to the industrialization achieved by the capitalist West. The method was essentially the same as that employed by Lenin's New Economic Policy: to rely on the knowledge and ability of the capitalists. And the capitalists helped.

Henry Ford, for example, despite years as a favorite Communist target for attack, agreed to do business with them. On May 1st 1930, Soviet representatives signed contracts with the Ford Motor Company for patents, licenses, technical assistance and spare parts. Ford supplied the Communists with designs and blueprints of its own models – and, below market price, 74,000 complete sets of automobile parts ready for assembly. Ford sent its engineers to the Soviet Union to supervise the Russians, and permitted the Soviets to send their own people to the Ford plant at Dearborn, Michigan for training. The Austin Company of New York and Ohio built the enormous factories and buildings that were needed for the Ford project at Gorki.[9]

The Cleveland firm of Arthur G. Mackee supplied the equipment and expertise to build huge steel plants at Magnitogorsk. During the course of this work, the Americans dammed the Ural River for the Soviets, constructed eight blast furnaces, ran training courses for Russian personnel and sent to America for advanced technical training the best of the Soviet workers.[10]

The superb American engineer, John K. Calder of Detroit, helped build and equip tractor plants for the Soviets, first at Stalingrad, then at Chelyabinsk. Stocked with American machinery and staffed by American

engineers, Calder and his associates built a modern factory at Stalingrad capable of manufacturing 50,000 tractors per year, seeking to transfigure a country blessed with superb farmlands but afflicted with backward agriculture.[11]

But the crowning achievement of American capitalism during the first Soviet Five Year Plan was the construction of the giant hydroelectric facility at Dnieprostroi. The dam and power station at Dnieprostroi – the largest in the world – became the showpiece of Soviet propaganda, designed to establish the superiority of Communism. Its capacity was vast, its construction time record-breaking, its size colossal. All of these facts the Soviets broadcasted. There was only one they neglected to mention. It was built by the Americans.

Colonel Hugh Cooper, creator of the mighty Wilson Dam at Muscle Shoals, Tennessee, designed a dam over a mile in length and two hundred feet in height to block the Dniepr. The giant facility contained nine turbines, each of 85,000 horse power, to be imported from the U.S. Cooper's plant generated 2,500,000 kilowatts of power, dwarfing his own Wilson Dam which put out 456,320 kilowatts. Dnieprostroi increased fivefold the electrical power output of the Soviet Union, elevating the Communist state to third place among power-producing countries, trailing only the U.S. and Germany. Cooper and his staff were on the spot from the start of construction in May 1927. His colleagues were all Americans – Milton Thompson from Montclair, Frank Fifer from Baltimore, Louis Puls from New York, James Johnson from North Carolina and Henry Wilkinson from Washington. These engineers lived on the huge construction site, surrounded by the most advanced machinery. Thirty forty-ton locomotive cranes, ten steam shovels, fifty locomotives, eighty dump cars – all American made – were employed in the building. With America's best engineers and equipment, it is no surprise that the dam was completed in record time.[12]

These are merely some of the achievements of American capitalism

during the first Soviet Five Year Plan. There were many more. Additionally, numerous European firms aided the Soviet process of industrialization. German, English, Italian, Swedish and Norwegian companies among others lent the Communists their expertise in countless productive fields — from agriculture to the manufacture of machine tools to the construction of whaling vessels.[13]

How did the Soviet Union pay for all of this? One method was with grain. In the Ukrainian "black earth" country, the Soviets possessed the world's most fertile grain-producing soil. The Communists under both Lenin and Stalin followed a policy of "Starve, but export," shipping grain abroad to finance industrialization while millions of Russians starved to death. It was only Western aid that prevented a worse catastrophe. Professor Sutton writes of one case in which the Soviets loaded a boat with Ukrainian wheat bound for German markets, while alongside was an American relief ship unloading wheat for the starving areas north of the Ukraine. "Despite the massive international relief effort, at least 5 million...Russians...died of hunger in 1921 and 1922."[14]

But the Soviets also employed other methods. Gold was one. First came the British company, Lena Goldfields. Then, in 1926, American firms received gold-prospecting rights on the Amur. In the late 1920s, the gold era dawned in Russia. Gold mines were constructed by Professor Serebrovsky, who had been sent to both the U.S. and South Africa to study the most modern methods of mining gold. Two hundred American mining engineers came to work on the Soviet gold projects. In the 1930s, the most effective U.S. mining equipment was introduced, worth millions of dollars. The Communists sent hundreds of thousands of slave laborers to work in the mines – and, equipped with the latest U.S. mining technology, the Soviet gold operation began to produce. Each country contributed to the productive process in accordance with its own distinctive system and underlying philosophy: state-of-the-art technology, courtesy of American capitalism; slave labor, courtesy of Soviet commu-

nism.[15]

The Communists had other means of raising hard currency. They looted and sold great art works to foreign museums and stripped the Orthodox churches of their historic treasures. In a letter addressed to the Politburo on March 19, 1922, Lenin pointed out that because of the millions who were currently starving, the moment was propitious to loot all church property; the masses, he argued, though religious, would support the Communists if they believed the money would be used to purchase food. This massive plundering peaked during the spring of 1922, leading to protests from church officials and massive arrests. "According to church records, 2,691 priests, 1,962 monks, and 3,447 nuns were killed that year." According to Lenin's same letter: "The more representatives of the reactionary clergy...we shoot, the better it will be for us."[16]

While Russians starved, the Communists set up special shops, Torgsin, in all major cities, and sold food that could be purchased only for gold, silver, jewelry and foreign currency. In effect, they sought to buy and sell human beings: they encouraged friends and relatives of Soviet citizens living abroad to ransom their loved ones from Stalin's prison state by paying large amounts in foreign currency. Worse, the Soviet secret police, the GPU, set up torture chambers across the country to which were brought any Russians suspected of owning valuables. The GPU proceeded to torture these unfortunates until they yielded their gold pieces, dollars, silver spoons or pieces of jewelry. People with relatives in the U.S. were forced to write letters begging for dollars, which were seized by the state when they arrived.[17]

Further, as part of their unremitting class struggle, they executed thousands of individuals in the period of 1919-1921 alone for the "crime" of being bourgeois. But first they levied and collected taxes totaling hundreds of millions of rubles; they required their victims to fill out questionnaires detailing their most mundane possessions, including shoes, bedding, sheets and bicycles, as well as more valuable goods, all of

which were expropriated; and they confiscated their apartments and living quarters. For good measure, they enslaved the women, forcing them to clean the toilets of the Red Army barracks, and indulged in the obligatory "brutal reality of rape"on a scale of "gigantic proportions."[18]

Often, the Communists paid nothing for the goods and services they received, for they commonly broke contracts, expropriated private property and expelled the foreigners on various trumped-up charges. The Soviets had a number of methods by which they rid themselves of Western businessmen after the foreigners had completed the desired task. One example was in their 1925 expulsion of the Junkers company. The German aeronautics experts had built Soviet aviation, and were no longer needed. The Soviets simply broke their contract, revoking the concession, which had been guaranteed to last thirty years. Further, the Communists encouraged crippling labor strikes; they falsely accused foreign companies of bribing Soviet officials; they trumped up charges of industrial espionage. One of their favorite policies was to raise taxes to prohibitive levels, then nationalize a company's assets when it was forced to close.[19]

Professor Sutton cites one particularly striking example of Soviet dishonesty. This involved the concession rights to mine manganese. Russia in 1913 had mined greater than 50% of the world's supply of this metal, but by 1920 production fell to zero and in 1924 reached merely 25% of its capacity. The Soviets granted concessions to several German companies, and then unilaterally changed the terms of the agreement. When the German firms protested, the Soviets expropriated their assets and negotiated a contract with American businessman, W. Averill Harriman. The Soviets' fundamental motive in the new concession was political: to establish that a major U.S. businessman had taken the assets of foreign firms, thereby legitimizing the Soviets' right to seize private property. Harriman, too, became a Soviet victim. After only a year in operation, he brought Soviet manganese production back to half of the pre-war total. A year later, the Soviets expropriated his multi-million dollar investment

– and employed a rare offer of compensation to cajole Harriman into using his influence to arrange a commercial loan for them.[20]

Nor was Western capitalism's role in building Soviet industry limited to Lenin's NEP or to Stalin's first Five Year Plan. There was enormously more. The German historian, Werner Keller, in *East Minus West Equals Zero*, shows how the World War II U.S. policy of Lend-Lease led to Soviet development. Under Lend-Lease, writes Dr. Keller, "the immense industrial potential of the United States was put freely at the disposal of the Soviet Union." During World War II, a staggering amount of goods was shipped or flown to Soviet Russia: raw materials, manufacturing plants, tools, machinery, spare parts, clothing, textiles, canned food, flour, in addition to a vast supply of armaments.[21]

Lend-Lease was arranged as an interest free loan. Not a penny was repaid. It ended up a gift from capitalism to communism – a gift worth $10,800,000,000 (which represents an even vaster sum when the dollar's greater value in the 1940s is remembered.) FDR, who once stated he was certain that "Stalin is not an imperialist," openly believed in giving to the Soviet dictator everything he could while asking for nothing in return. He consequently made these enormous shipments at a time when the U.S. armed forces were themselves confronted with "inevitable, unavoidable shortages," and thereby made America more vulnerable to Nazi Germany at the time and Soviet Russia in the future.[22]

Dr. Keller also describes the systematic looting carried out by the Soviet Union during the 1940s and 1950s. During World War II and the years following, the U.S. was a haven for Soviet spies. The Roosevelt Administration trusted its Soviet allies, and permitted Russian Lend-Lease agents virtually unlimited access to witness and/or study U.S. inventions and industrial secrets. Soviet spies memorized, copied and/or stole plans of American products and industrial methods. The Soviets pilfered materials in enormous quantities: blueprints, inventions, machinery, and such classified materials as uranium and heavy water. The

Communist agents packed them into huge crates marked "diplomatic mail," and shipped them from the U.S. airbase at Great Falls, Montana, a principal link in the American airlift to Russia. The U.S. military provided the planes in which their Soviet "allies" shipped the stolen goods to Russia.[23]

Examination of recently-opened Soviet archives and the 1995 declassification of the top secret Venona Project — the World War II undertaking by means of which American spies and cryptographers cracked the Soviet code — validated with full certainty the shocking truth: the Roosevelt and Truman administrations were rife with Stalin's agents. Harry Dexter White, Assistant Secretary of the Treasury Department, was a Soviet agent. Alger Hiss, a top ranking official at the State Department and a trusted advisor to President Roosevelt at Yalta, was a Soviet agent. Lauchlin Currie, senior administrative assistant to President Roosevelt, was a Soviet agent. There were hundreds of others, including many not working directly for the U.S. government.

The espionage against the United States engaged in by American Communists resulted in the pilferage of vital American military and industrial secrets, leading to the immense strengthening of the Soviet Union. This included, of course, the infamous theft of information by Julius and Ethel Rosenberg that led to a Soviet atomic bomb. The Soviets, though not very good at science, technology or industry, were expert at spying and stealing.[24]

Bad as this is, the full truth regarding Soviet industrial development is even worse. After the war, still protected by President Roosevelt's earlier sanction, the Soviets proceeded to loot the conquered nations on a massive scale. From Manchuria, the Russians stole almost all of the Japanese heavy industry, worth $858,000,000. From the enslaved nations of Eastern Europe, they seized minerals, machinery, petroleum and food supplies in sufficient amounts to leave those countries destitute. From Germany, the Communists looted iron and steel plants, chemical works, automobile fac-

tories, electric power stations, railroad supplies, shipyards, munitions plants and the entirety of the Germans' rocket research and manufacturing facilities. Forty-one percent of Germany's industrial machinery was dismantled and shipped to the Soviet Union. Officially, Russia was awarded reparations for war damages totaling $10,000,000,000, which Germany paid. Dr. Keller points out that the additional property stolen was worth four times that sum.

But the worst crime was the enslavement of the human mind. On October 22nd, 1946, the Soviet military seized six thousand German scientists and forcibly deported them to the Soviet Union to work in the stolen German aircraft and rocket factories. Additionally, millions of Europeans were enslaved – 380,000 Germans, one million Poles, hundreds of thousands of Eastern Europeans (including about 15% of the population of the Baltic States) – and sent to slave labor camps in Russia to work for Soviet economic development.[25]

The economic result of Soviet Russia's policies? Throughout the Soviet Union's history and continuing to its final days, chronic shortages existed of the most elementary consumer items. At various times it was impossible to find dish soap, kitchen spoons, toothpaste, towels, axes, locks, vacuum cleaners, kitchen china, hand irons, rugs, spare parts for devices from toasters to automobiles, and myriad other commodities. Decent shoes, for example, were notoriously difficult to get at all times. Shortages of consumer goods were so chronic that Soviet shoppers raced to get in line on hearing of the availability of the most mundane items, from pineapples to rugs. Further, Russian housewives, on average, spent two hours in line, seven days a week — and often found that supplies had run out by the time they reached the front.

Despite the massive aid from the capitalist countries, by the 1960s, after 50 years of communism, the country's gross domestic product was less than 50 percent of America's. In the 1970s, "the level of living...was merely one-third of that in the United States." In the 1980s, the Russian

people suffered from "an inefficient, top-heavy economy convulsed in crisis," and saw working class families still often living four "in one room... sharing a bathroom and kitchen with other families." In the 1990s, communism collapsed.

A contemporary philosopher describes the Communist debacle vividly: "In the final decade of the Soviet Union, only a third of households had hot running water. As late as 1989, meat and sugar were still rationed—in peacetime. After sixty years of socialism, an average welfare mother in the United States received more income in a month than the average Soviet worker earned in a year."[26]

Nor were conditions appreciably better in the Communist nations of the Soviet bloc. There, too, economic dependency on the West was insufficient to avert collapse. For example, in the 1970s Poland struggled to feed its own population and found it necessary to import enormous amounts of food. Additionally, the government borrowed billions of dollars from the West. But even this massive aid was unable to prop up the tottering totalitarian state. As political scientists Aaron Wildavsky and John Clark wrote: "Economic growth declined; by 1981 per capita GNP was more than a fourth less than its level in 1978. Pause for a moment. The loss of a quarter of GNP is no ordinary setback. It is a catastrophe." By the end of the 1980s, of course, Communism collapsed in Poland and across Eastern Europe.[27]

That Communism is as evil a system as Nazism should be clear – but is not the main point in this context. The fundamental issue here is: Communist economic development relied to a staggering degree on the achievements of Western capitalism. It was the private companies of the United States and the other capitalist countries that built Soviet Russia into an industrialized power, to the extent that it was at all. That the relationship between capitalist America and communist Russia was adversarial is not to be doubted; but what is revealing (though not surprising) is the degree to which it was a dependency relationship, a parasitical inter-

action. Stalin himself acknowledged to Eric Johnston, an American visitor in 1944, that "about two-thirds of all the large industrial enterprises in the USSR had been built with U.S. material or technical assistance."[28]

A totalitarian state, which repudiated the Enlightenment glorification of the mind, individual rights and political/economic liberty in favor of brute force and systematic terror, was powerless to achieve the advances that depend on the mind's free functioning – and so, inevitably, relied on the nation of the Enlightenment for an enormous proportion of whatever progress it attained.

A Philosophical Clash

The fundamental source of the horrors perpetrated by Communism is its philosophy. Marxist-Leninist ideology, upon which Communist practice is based, provides a comprehensive — albeit systematically mistaken — view of the world and of man's life. It holds that reality is composed essentially of matter and that mind is a mere incidental, inconsequential by-product. Knowledge is gained by obedience to the Party leaders who are attuned to the evolution of historical forces that drive history; independent thinking is impermissible. Man is matter. Production is by means of manual labor. Virtue is selfless toil for the masses. The ideal society is a collectivist dictatorship. Communism renounces the mind for materialism; egoism for altruism; individualism for collectivism; freedom for dictatorship. Man's life as the standard of moral value is repudiated, replaced by the will of the people. Communism abjures every central principle of a rational philosophy upon which human life depends.

To discuss only a few: egoism — the individual's need and right to pursue the values his life requires — is unequivocally condemned and treated as a capital offense. Private ownership and profit-making are abolished. Men are executed for such "crimes" as speculating, black marketeering and possessing wealth. Peasants are forced off of their own land and compelled to work the collective farms. The government, not an

[310]

individual, "plans" his education, his career, his life. The state determines what he does, where he lives, what he reads, what he writes, what he says, what he thinks. Individuals cannot be permitted to have minds of their own because they do not possess lives of their own. When men's ownership of values is theoretically and practically severed from their creation of values — when they possess neither moral nor legal right to utilize values in the furthering of their lives — then they cannot live. To separate values from life is to end life. Where the state owns all values, it is to be expected that only those who run the state will possess and utilize values. The rulers can live; the ruled cannot.

A related point: Communism, like National Socialism, is a collectivist system; it requires the subordination of the independent mind to the people, to the proletariat, to the state. Men who do not obsequiously mouth every aspect of the Party line, but who dare to think, to speak and to act on their own judgment are summarily shot or condemned to slave labor in the massive gulag system. But the great minds responsible for human progress honor truth above and before political authority, and do not surrender their minds to grovel before a Lenin or a Stalin. It is impossible to calculate how many potential Watts, Edisons, Wright brothers, et al., the Communists executed or, at minimum silenced and stifled, but the result of their massive war against the mind was manifest in the country's inability to rise above the poverty – and, in many cases, the starvation – level. Lenin had infamously promised that the capitalists would provide the wealth and the goods with which Soviet Russia should destroy them. In the event, the capitalists provided; but the communists, unable to produce even life's basic necessities, collapsed, victims of their own oppression.

A recent economist pointed out ironically that "the Soviet Union had gained a respectable audience as an industrialized power which had somehow accomplished in twenty years what had taken a hundred in capitalist countries." Lamentably, many Third World countries in the post-

World War II era built their economies on the Soviet rather than the American model. It is long past time that such tragic delusions are dispelled.[29]

The Infamous Case of Lysenko

A perfect illustration of the crippling impact of totalitarianism on the ability of rational intelligence to promote progress can also be found in the history of the Soviet Union – in the case of the infamous scientific imposter, Trofim Lysenko. He ruled Soviet agriculture for almost thirty years, from the early 1930s to the mid-1960s, with one brief eclipse between 1955 and 1958. Lysenko denied the existence of genes. He maintained that acquired characteristics could be passed on to succeeding generations in both plants and animals. Lysenko argued that Mendel's laws of heredity were erroneous despite the extensive evidence amassed in their support by thousands of biologists.

Though Lysenko possessed a "green thumb," and had a way with plants, his "scientific" theories were utterly false. The American geneticist, H.J. Muller, a Nobel Prize winner in biology, on visiting Lysenko, found him woefully ignorant of scientific method, clinging to outmoded theories that were no better than superstitions. Virtually all Russian biologists were astounded that Lysenko's charlatan claims were taken seriously by the Communist Party, in the face of overwhelming experimental evidence to the contrary. Worst of all for Lysenko – but predictably – his theories proved utterly false in agricultural practice. How, then, did he become the darling of Soviet agronomy? The answer was simple: the greatest scientist of all, Comrade Stalin, liked him.

Lysenko's theories emphasized the role that environment played in the development and change of species. In this way it vaguely agreed with Marx's economic or social determinism – organisms (including and especially human beings) could be conditioned by their surrounding milieu to be what the Party desired them to be. If no fixed and unalterable biologi-

cal inheritance existed to affect the final outcome, then the Communists had carte-blanche to shape plants, animals and men in any way they chose. Essentially, genes and the laws of genetics were rejected because they were not "politically correct," i.e., did not correspond to Marxist political/economic doctrine. Further, Soviet agriculture was in such desperate condition that any agronomist who promised to work miracles – no matter the unscientific basis of his claims – could acquire enthusiastic political supporters.

Stalin's support of Lysenko led, predictably, to a reign of terror in the field of biology. With Party support, Lysenko accused his opponents of being capitalist flunkies, stooges for the West and counter-revolutionary enemies of Marxism. As a result, many accomplished Russian scientists lost their jobs, their liberty and even their lives. In 1932, two cystologists, G.A. Levitsky and N.P. Avdulov, were sent to concentration camps for the crime of thinking. In 1935, the geneticists, I.J. Agol and L.P. Ferry, were executed by the Soviet police. In 1937, Avdulov was shot, as was S.G. Levit, past head of the internationally-respected Moscow Institute for Medical Genetic Research. In 1940, one of Russia's greatest scientists, Nicholas Vavilov, was arrested. Two years later, a prisoner in Siberia, Vavilov died. This list of Lysenko's victims is merely the beginning. "Whole staffs of anti-Lysenko scientists died similarly, in prison or labor camps, of bullets or slow mistreatment."[30]

The Party's acceptance of Lysenko's mistaken doctrines had devastating results for Soviet biology and science in general. Genetics and the theory of evolution were not taught – driven first from the schools of agriculture, then from the secondary schools and, finally, from the universities and research laboratories in the years 1948-1953. The cost in ignorance, aborted research, lack of progress and diminished food production are incalculable.[31]

The point, in this context, is that science – and progress more broadly – cannot flourish in a state-controlled society. When the laws of genetics

are passed by the Politburo, it means that the whim of the dictator is supreme. Whole fields of research are then outlawed; scientists are shot; the creative mind bows before ignorance in authority – and progress ceases.

Contrast this with events in a free society and on a free market. The United States, for example, may well possess more cranks per capita than any nation on earth. The country is rife with those who promote astrology, numerology, tarot cards, UFOs and alien sightings, conspiracy theories, faith healing, speaking in tongues, bizarre cults, apocalyptic doomsayers and every type of spiritualism, witchcraft and the occult. In a sense, this is good. Political/economic freedom extends to charlatans, as well as to more rational men.

But in the U.S., in contrast to a state-controlled society, there is no dictator to legally mandate some crackpot's doctrine, outlawing dissenting thought by decree. Rational men are free to repudiate these bizarre notions, and even to publicly expose their practitioners, as the famed science writer and magician, James Randi, has done repeatedly. Rational men in the field of biology are free to create (or work for) bio-tech firms, creating new methods of using the body's own defenses to thwart disease and promote health. New ideas, theories and research findings are presented regularly, in science and in other fields. All honest men are then free to examine, analyze or critique the new products or ideas. Entrepreneurs are able to bring new products into the marketplace – such as in the computer field – for the judgment of the customers.

There exists a popular saying, "The truth will out." With innovative theories and inventions, it often takes a long time for the truth to come out. But when men are free to think and to act on their thinking, true ideas gradually gain recognition and fraudulence is eventually exposed and rejected. Not surprisingly, where men were free to think – in the West – they utterly repudiated Lysenko's doctrines, and moved ahead in genetic research. Freedom is a necessary condition of scientific, technological and economic advancement. Statism results in the kind of repres-

sion and institutionalized quackery exemplified by Lysenkoism.

What must be recognized in the contrast between Soviet Russia and the United States is not merely that the former was repressed and poor and the latter free and rich – but that the communist and capitalist systems embodied opposing philosophies. This was not merely a contest between capitalism and communism, but something vastly broader and deeper. It was commitment to the mind, egoism, individualism, freedom, and man's life as the standard of moral value versus commitment to materialism, altruism, collectivism, dictatorship and the people's will as the standard of moral value. This was much more than a political struggle: it was philosophical war. Given that the one creed was fundamentally true to man's nature and the requirements of his life — and that the other was utterly false and abrogated every principle on which human life depends — the final results could not have been other than they were. No amount of Western aid could alter the laws of reality; neither President Roosevelt nor any other Soviet supporter had that much power. The basic fact was and remains that man's survival requires devotion to reason, egoism and freedom — and Communism categorically repudiates every one of these principles.

Cuba vs. Cuban-Americans

The former Soviet Union was by no means the only example of the failure of state-controlled societies. All Communist countries subsist in misery, and the semi-socialist countries lag behind their capitalist neighbors in prosperity. The contrast between Castro's Cuba and the Cuban-American community of Miami is another example.

The brutal oppression so characteristic of Communism is as tragically prevalent in Cuba as elsewhere. Thousands of political prisoners, including women, are routinely subjected to both physical and psychological torture. Prison conditions are abominable: sanitation is often nonexistent, "the food is contaminated, and infectious diseases such as typhus

and leptospirosis are common." By conservative estimate, hundreds of prisoners have died just of exposure and lack of nutrition and medical care. Concentration camps in which political prisoners are used as slave labor still exist in Cuba. Over the years, tens of thousands of dissenters have been shot. Borders, of course, are closed and "Castro has tried to prevent people from leaving by sending helicopters to drop sandbags onto the [rafts] when they are at sea. In the summer of 1994, 7,000 people lost their lives while attempting to flee." Castro's list of criminal atrocities is long.[32]

The economic consequences of oppression are inevitable. The Communist regime still regards private business as legalized robbery. Small, family-owned restaurants are the only concessions to capitalism that Castro allows. Such restaurants are permitted no more than twelve seats, and only family members may be employed. Hundreds of stores along Avenida Bolivar, Havana's former shopping district, stand closed and empty, as they have been since they were nationalized in 1968. The city's streets are filled almost exclusively with bicycles and pedestrians, as there are few cars. There are buses – in theory. Fodor's guide warns tourists to be prepared to wait three days for the next available bus. The country roads are so deserted that cows graze on weeds growing through the pavement's cracks.

Food in Cuba is perpetually rationed. It is common for a family to get just one liter of cooking oil – for months; to get fourteen eggs per family for thirty days – when eggs are plentiful; to get two bars of soap a month – some months; and to get no meat. Although the country has a population of over 11 million, it has a total of just 229,000 telephones; indeed, Cuba possesses one of the world's least developed telephone systems.

Everybody, including Cuban government officials, agree that the island's economy has shrunk by at least one-third since the 1980s. Cuba lost "$5 billion to $6 billion in Soviet subsidies" after Communism col-

lapsed there in 1991. This means that America propped up Soviet Russia and the Soviets propped up Cuba. So much for the U.S. embargo. Cuba's average annual income per household was estimated at $4,330 in 1982. Its per capita GDP was claimed to be $2,902 (by the Cuban government) in 1995 and $1,200 by the National Bank of Cuba in 1998. The Communist regime issues no accurate figures regarding living standards, so nobody knows for certain. But by anybody's arithmetic, Cuba subsists in a desperate poverty that would be vastly worse were it not for a widespread black market that "is larger than its legal economy." A black market, it should be noted, is simply entrepreneurship under a political system that legally prohibits it.[33]

Cuba's medical system, vaunted by Castro and leftist ideologues worldwide, is a shambles. Though Cuba's physicians are generally proficient – a heritage stretching back to well before the Communist takeover – there exist chronic shortages of the most rudimentary medical supplies. Forget MRI machines, the system lacks basic medicines. "Much of what doctors are prescribing for their patients in Cuba today, if available at all, is being sent from Miami to those souls who are fortunate enough to have relatives in the U.S." The hospitals lack soap, clean linen and towels, in addition to medications, and patients must bring their own.

In the early 1990s, a mysterious ailment that stymied local treatment caused blindness among thousands of Cubans. Castro eventually swallowed his pride and permitted American physicians to examine the problem. "Dr. Maurice Victor, an eminent American neurologist, commented that there was nothing mysterious about the affliction. It was classic beriberi, caused by the nutritional deficiency of vitamin B1, thiamine...Since that time, Cubans have been treated with vitamins from the U.S. and the free world pharmaceutical industry."[34]

By sharp contrast, the Cuban-American community, centered in Miami, enjoys all the freedom of U.S. citizens and suffers no gulags, no political imprisonment, no torture, no slave labor and no murders when

attempting to emigrate. The economic result of America's freedom is significant prosperity for Cuban emigres.

The Cuban community in capitalist America had a per household income of $27,700 in the 1980s, at least triple (and probably significantly more) the wealth earned by their countrymen at home. That gap has only widened since. Further, a large number of Cuban immigrants came to America with little or no money (though with education and skills), having lost their possessions in the Communist takeover. "Between 1960 and 1980, at least a million Cubans emigrated – 10 percent of the island's population" – and most settled in Miami. Many of the early emigres had been well-educated and successful in Cuba; indeed, by 1961, just two years after Castro's takeover, approximately "three-fourths of the faculty of the University of Havana were living in South Florida." The Brain Drain from statist regimes to free countries was in full operation.

But in some cases, Cuban education and training were insufficient to gain entry into the U.S. economy, and many lacked the INS's green cards. "Cuban accountants, doctors and lawyers found themselves toiling in factories or pumping gas, driving taxis or shelving stock" – anything to earn a living. As with so many destitute immigrants before them, however, the modern Cubans benefited from the freedom which enabled the most enterprising and skilled to start their own businesses or to rise in other professions. "By the late 1970s, Cuban-Americans had become the wealthiest group of Hispanic origin in the United States." By the 1980s, "the combined purchasing power of Miami's Cubans exceeded the total purchasing power of Cubans still on the island," though representing a fraction of their number. By the 1990s, Cuba was so poor that Castro encouraged remittances from Cuban-Americans, and began referring to the refugees as "economic immigrants" rather than as "traitors."

Currently, Cuban-Americans with family members and friends on the island legally remit to Cuba the enormous sum of $400 million to $600 million annually – money that in many cases might suffice to raise

individuals and families above the bare subsistence level. Further, the millions spent in Cuba by the hundred thousand or so Cuban-American visitors per year (124,000 in 1999) "help keep the Cuban economy afloat." Socialism's parasitical survival off of capitalism takes many forms.[35]

A common apology for the disastrous conditions of existence in Cuba is to blame it on the United States, specifically on the American trade embargo. But this concedes a fundamental point. For socialist intellectuals have argued at least since Marx and Engels that socialism would out-produce capitalism, and would one day, in Krushchev's infamous term, "bury" the West in the overwhelming abundance and superiority of its consumer goods. But reality has shattered such delusions. Contemporary socialists acknowledge that without trade and/or aid from capitalist nations the socialist countries can only subsist in wretched poverty. The new mantra reduces to the plea that socialism must be permitted to be parasitical off of capitalism in yet another form.

By the early twenty-first century, it is becoming known that Communism represses the mind, murders millions and stifles economic development — and that such countries as Cuba suffer in abysmal poverty. Today, there are few educated people who believe that Communism is either a moral or a practical political/economic system. But many still believe that socialism is effective, and they point to the prosperity of such "socialist" countries as Sweden and Norway to support their claims. What is the truth of these beliefs?

The Truth Regarding "Socialist" Scandinavia

First, socialism is a system in which the principle of individual rights is denied. The state controls – at minimum – all aspects of the economic system, and individuals are permitted to neither own property nor seek profit. Cuba, for all practical purposes, is a socialist economy. The few, small family-owned restaurants are negligible elements of economic freedom.

The Capitalist Manifesto

The Scandinavian countries, legally permitting significant private ownership, are not examples of socialism. Technically, they are mixed economies with a preponderance – but by no means a totality – of state ownership. Numerous private businesses exist today in Sweden and Norway. In Norway, for example, there are many privately-owned shops and small businesses. In addition, there exist such larger capitalist companies as: Kloster (a shipping firm and cruise line), Braathen (an airline), Helly-Hansen (a sports clothing manufacturer), Mustad (a fishing equipment firm), Lowenskjold (a lumber company), Nycomed (a pharmaceutical producer) and others.

It is similar in Sweden, where such productive giants as Volvo, Saab and Ericcson, as well as many smaller shops and stores, are privately-owned and profit-driven. Sweden continues to maintain low tariffs and to engage in free trade, as does Norway. Because of such truths, the *World Factbook 1999* describes Sweden as "a capitalist system interlarded with substantial welfare elements" – and *The Index of Economic Freedom*, co-published by the *Wall Street Journal* and the Heritage Foundation, characterize the economies of both Sweden and Norway as "mostly free." Among the 155 nations evaluated in *The Index*, Sweden and Norway ranked in the top 25 percent of the world's freest nations.

Further, for one hundred years, from 1870 to 1970, Sweden had a higher rate of economic growth than almost any country in the world. By the 1950s, Sweden had a per-capita GDP that was twice the European average, 25 percent higher than Switzerland, its closest rival. This meant that "by the early 1950s Sweden was by far the richest country in Europe."

Several factors contributed to this development. One was land reform in the 19th century that enabled farmers to enclose common areas, creating greater private ownership and incentive, leading to increased agricultural productivity. A second was that medieval guilds, which gave monopolies to artisans, were abolished in 1846, and business

freedom was guaranteed by law in 1864. Finally, since Sweden had timber, iron and other minerals to export, a policy of free trade was established. "Thus, from 1870 to 1930 Sweden was characterized by limited government, free trade, free enterprise, and social mobility." In short, Sweden built its prosperity on the basis of capitalism.

The Social Democrats did not come to power until the 1930s, and though they might have believed in the nationalization of business in theory, they did not do it in practice. Refusing to kill the goose that laid the golden eggs, they left the preponderance of Swedish businesses in private hands. They did raise taxes, of course, but even in that they were moderate. As late as 1960, Sweden's tax levels were roughly equal to America's at the turn of the 21st century. Government spending was 31% of GDP.

It was only in the post-1960s period that Sweden began a pronounced move toward a social welfare state. Massive welfare programs were instituted, major industries were nationalized and taxes were raised significantly. The tax level is now the highest in the industrialized world, and income is thereby severely restricted. Holding a job became unnecessary to gain income, and hard work was rewarded with higher taxes, not higher profits. Not surprisingly, productivity began to decline. Swedish doctors, for example, in the 1990s worked an average of only 1600 hours per year, compared to 2800 hours worked by U.S. doctors. Sweden has an adult population of 7 million, of which 2.7 million are not working, most of whom live off of some kind of state-financed welfare program. For 25 years, Sweden's economic growth has been slower than that of the other industrialized countries, and in the early 1990s the economy shrunk by 5 per cent. With such a decline in productivity, even Sweden's massive income tax and 25% national sales tax are inadequate to cover government spending. "Sweden's experience demonstrates that over time a welfare state based on socialist-inspired ideas of income redistribution erodes wealth-creating forces."

How does Sweden pay for its welfare state? With a great deal of bor-

rowing. Sweden's national debt is nearly equal to its GDP, and just to pay the interest on it requires 7 per cent of everything produced in the country. The national debt is proportionally 40 per cent greater than that of the United States. At some point, Sweden – and any country similarly deep in debt – must pay its bills. Then the folly of its economic policies gets driven home.

Two conclusions must be drawn. First: Sweden rose to prosperity as a capitalist system, and the massive socialist elements of its post-1960s period is slowly lowering its standard of living. Certainly, as with all countries possessing a substantial degree of political/economic liberty, Sweden is prosperous – and is fabulously wealthy relative to the starving Third World dictatorships that never had a capitalist period. Still, "Sweden's rapid economic growth occurred before the imposition of the welfare state. As government control became more pervasive...previous gains were eroded and were insufficient to maintain Swedish prosperity." [36]

However, a second, more fundamental conclusion regards the nature of innovation. The Swedes and Norwegians, et al., are wealthy to a significant degree because they possess automobiles, airplanes, electric lights, telephones, televisions, modern medical and agricultural technology, personal computers, state of the art software, Internet access, etc. But these products were not invented in modern Sweden, Norway or in any other semi-socialist state. Overwhelmingly, they were created in capitalist America, many during the Inventive Period of America's greatest freedom.

Similarly, Norway is wealthy based largely on oil exports – but the innovative methods of extracting oil were and remain largely American achievements. For example, Phillips Petroleum (of Oklahoma), Shell and Exxon were primarily responsible for discovering and making possible the production of oil in the treacherous North Sea — not Stat Oil, the Norwegian state-controlled company.

The North Sea weather conditions could hardly have been worse.

"'There's nothing quite as vile as the North Sea when she's in a temper,' was the lament of one skipper." Phillips's rig, the Ocean Viking, struggled against storms so fierce that on one occasion capsize was likely and evacuation a necessity. At another point, "the rig broke off from its anchors and began to drift away from the bore hole." But the crew of the Ocean Viking accomplished their mission. "In November 1969, [they] made a major find on Block 2/4 in the Ekofisk field, on the Norwegian side of the median line." Only months before, American astronauts had landed on the moon. When the Ocean Viking's drilling superintendent examined the high quality of the oil brought up from 10,000 feet beneath the seabed, he said to the rig's geologist: "What the astronauts have done is great...but how about this?" As one historian of the oil industry summed it up: "The North Sea oil rush was on." Norway proceeded to benefit from both geographical locale and American technology.[37]

There is a principle involved here that mankind must learn: to the extent that any semi-socialist society is prosperous, it is so because of the diffusion of technology and wealth created in the predominantly capitalist countries. This includes themselves during their freer periods.

The most telling contrast regarding Sweden is not between it and another country – but between its capitalist past and its semi-socialist present. "Sweden's dismal economic performance from 1970 to 1990 was no less striking than its high growth from 1870 to 1930." The so-called "middle way" leads to decidedly middle ground: moderately statist regimes are not close to the rampant destitution of full dictatorships, but they undercut the prosperity they had achieved and could continue to achieve under capitalism. Were it statism, not freedom, that leads to wealth, then the Soviet Union and Cuba would have been rich and the United States poor. But the reverse was and remains true. Similarly, in such mixed economies as Sweden, it is the element of freedom that generates prosperity; the element of statism provides only the obstacles.[38]

South vs. North Korea

The outcome does not change when the analysis of laboratory findings shifts from Europe to Asia. In 1945, when Korea was divided, for example, the Communist North received the bulk of the Japanese-built industry; the freer South got very little. Further, South Korea was devastated by the Communist invasion of the early 1950s. The war ended in 1953, and it was not until 1963 that the South's per capita GNP reached $100.00. Nevertheless, long before the turn of the 21st century, South Korea was well on its way to becoming an economic power, while the North was engulfed in massive poverty and widespread starvation.

The political/economic causes are manifest. Communist North Korea is the most brutally repressive dictatorship on earth. Mass murder, torture, imprisonment and enslavement are the regime's commonplace policies. The magnitude of suppression and terror is unimaginable in the West – and, not to make light of such horror, makes the former Soviet Union seem like Disneyland by comparison. The result, of course, is the utter stifling, even execution, of the innovative minds and entrepreneurial spirits necessary for economic development. It must be noted that the globe's most oppressive tyranny is one of the most destitute, starvation-riddled hellholes to be found.

By contrast, the cause of the South's relative prosperity is the large element of private ownership and profit-driven business permitted in its economic system. South Korea is a mixed economy, combining large elements of economic freedom with government interventionism and political authoritarianism. But at its worst it is far freer than is the totalitarian North. In terms of economic freedom it is classified as "mostly free," and under the influence of Stanford-trained economist Kim Jae-Ik it moved towards privatization and diminished state intervention in the 1980s. Its economy is colloquially referred to as one of "the Asian tigers," because of its rapid and extensive rise from poverty to relative prosperity. Its growth is especially impressive when its current per capita GDP in excess of $11,000 is compared with the $100.00 figure of barely 40 years

ago. Today, early in the 21st century, South Korea is comparatively wealthy by Asian standards, despite the financial crisis of the late 1990s.

North Korea, on the other hand, is so primitive that satellite photographs at night reveal mostly darkness — because the country lacks electricity; and even massive aid from the United States and other capitalist nations was insufficient to prevent a minimum of tens of thousands of people from starving to death there in the late 1990s.[39]

Hong Kong and Taiwan vs. China

Similarly, Hong Kong and Taiwan sit in close geographic proximity to China. The freedom and consequent prosperity of Hong Kong in the decades leading up to the new millennium have become a matter of legend. Indeed, by the late 1990s, Hong Kong had a standard of living second only to the United States.

But it had not always been that way. Immediately following World War II, the British colony had a population of merely 600,000 – but after the Communist conquest of China "a flood of refugees" arrived. Many of the penniless Chinese who had fled the mainland subsisted in the mid-1950s in temporary quarters, in "one-room cells in a multistory building that was open in the front: one family, one room."

But in the post-war years, the British sent John Cowperthwaite – a Scot and a disciple of Adam Smith – to Hong Kong as its financial secretary. While Britain itself moved towards socialism, Cowperthwaite kept Hong Kong on a path of laissez-faire. When, in 1963, American economist, Milton Friedman, asked him regarding the dearth of official economic statistics, Cowperthwaite replied that if he permitted such statistics to be computed the British government would want to use them for central planning. He kept taxes low, he imposed no tariffs, he eliminated bureaucracy and made it easy to start a business. The Hong Kong government enforces laws against crime, provides a court system to adjudicate legitimate disputes among honest individuals and upholds contracts.

In short, the government provides a rule of law that protects honest individuals.

Imagine the horror of the anti-capitalist, socialist mentalities if it was said to them: what if there were a country in which the government stays out of the economy? One with no tariffs or other legal restrictions on international trade – with no regulatory agencies, no minimum wage laws, no price or wage controls. Imagine, it is said to them, that the government limits neither investment coming in nor profit going out. There's no capital gains tax, no interest tax, no sales tax and a pittance in corporate bailouts for companies that fail to compete on a free market. This imaginary country has a 15 percent flat tax, enabling its citizens to retain the preponderance of their earnings. Further, it extends no unemployment benefits, enacts no labor legislation and provides no Social Security, no national health insurance and scarcely any welfare. The welfare statist would recoil in horror from such a proposal; he would drown his interlocutor with dire warnings regarding the misery of the numberless poor and exploited who would be the inevitable victims of such a heartless, callous system. But, in fact, that country exists, it is real; it's Hong Kong, one of the wealthiest nations of history.

In mere decades, at a breakneck pace, the island colony rose. "In 1960...the average per capita income in Hong Kong was 28 percent of that in Great Britain; by 1996, it had risen to 137 percent of that in Britain." In fewer than 40 years, the overcrowded little colony's per capita income rose from roughly one quarter that of a great modern power to roughly one-third larger.

Hong Kong has virtually none of the factors that modern intellectuals view as a source of wealth. Hong Kong has no natural resources. It has no oil, no coal, no iron ore, no timber, no fertile agricultural lands. The former Soviet Union, for example, had vastly more such resources, as do many African countries, yet they were and are poor, even destitute, while Hong Kong is wealthy. Further, Hong Kong has an extraordinarily high

population density, which is a factor that modern thinkers often consider a cause of poverty. The Sham Shui Po district of Kowloon has a population density of greater than 425,000 people per square mile, which makes it 18 times as crowded as New York City. Hong Kong, per square mile, has 14 times as many people as Japan, 20 times as many as India and 185 times as many as the U.S.

While Hong Kong has, as do many places, a great harbor, its greatest natural resource is one that it shares with every country on earth: the intelligence of its inhabitants. What enables Hong Kong to employ that intelligence to create wealth more effectively than other places is a factor that is not natural, but man-made: political/economic freedom. Not coincidentally, the only countries that rival Hong Kong for economic freedom – Singapore, Bahrain, New Zealand, the United States, Switzerland, Great Britain and Taiwan – are among the world's most prosperous.[40]

Taiwan is also a "rags to riches" story. In 1949, after the Nationalists' military defeat on the mainland, the per capita income on the island was an abysmal $100.00. But Chiang Kai-shek, the political leader, sought to create an environment in which entrepreneurs would flourish. He appointed such economic advisers as K.Y. Yin and K.T. Li, both strong advocates of a free market system. Li realized that the best thing a government could do was provide a rational legal framework that would establish the rule of law. He proceeded to put himself in the shoes of investors and look at the situation from their perspective. Taiwan opened up to foreign investment and world trade, and phased out protectionism, strengthening domestic firms by subjecting them to foreign competition at home. The result of Taiwan's freedom has been a spectacular drive toward prosperity. Its per capita income in 1998 was roughly $14,000, meaning that *its wealth grew 140 times in just 50 years*. Or, to state the point in another form: its per capita income doubled seven times over that period.[41]

The situation in neighboring China, under the Communists, was just the opposite. Mao Tse-tung, one of the most brutal dictators in mankind's history, instituted oppressive policies that led to China's economic collapse. One example was his ill-named "Great Leap Forward," begun in 1958. Seeking to establish "self-reliant communes," each with its own industrial and agricultural capabilities, he herded 700 million people onto hundreds of huge sites, demanding that they become self-supporting. In particular, they were not merely to farm but also to produce their own steel. Mao wanted "true Communists," who could farm in the morning and produce steel in the afternoon. With a degree of insanity reminiscent of Lysenko, "Mao...had proclaimed his belief that 'in company grain grows fast; seeds are happiest when growing together' – attempting to impose class solidarity on nature. Accordingly, seeds were sown at five to ten times the normal density, with the result that millions of young plants died." Making matters worse, the intensive farming methods dried out the soil.

The devastation resulting from such state-imposed lunacy was predictable. With uneducated peasants running backyard steel mills, and with Soviet-trained steel engineers forced to scratch the soil, China's production of both steel and food plummeted. The Soviet dictator, Nikita Krushchev, was so incensed at the waste of Soviet resources that he withdrew all Russian support. In July of 1959, even Mao had to admit failure, and called it off. But the Chinese steel industry was wrecked and had to be entirely rebuilt. Agriculture was worse as crops failed and livestock were slaughtered. Tens of millions of human beings starved to death over the next few years – to this day, nobody knows how many. There are no exact figures, but estimates range from 20 to 43 million. On anybody's math, the Communists created the "most murderous famine of all time, anywhere in the world."[42]

The man-made famine was an inevitable consequence of statism, the deadly logic of which mankind must come to understand. Only an irra-

tional brute seeks life-and-death power over his fellow man. Entrenched in authority, the dictator – in this case Mao – commanded bizarre and grossly mistaken Marxist theories into political and agricultural practice, stifling or murdering the rational thinkers who voiced dissent. The fundamental atrocity was collectivization — the denial of an individual's right to his own life by denying him the right to private property.

Mao, having declared the state an omnipotent power to whom men's lives belonged, was unrestrained by moral principle from performing the most irrational political and agricultural experiments on his population. As in the Stalin-Lysenko catastrophe, scientific investigation – indeed, rational inquiry more broadly – was prohibited; the mind was stifled; consequently, the productive, life-giving achievements of the mind were lost, and devastation was the inescapable result. Statism, grounded in the related doctrines that individuals possess no right to their own lives, hence no right to their minds, chronically and inexorably entails massive loss of human life. Only the forms of the atrocities vary.

China's economy did not improve until Mao's successor, Deng Xiaoping, began to introduce capitalist elements into what remained a totalitarian political system. Deng, like Mao, wanted total political control, but was unconcerned regarding the economic means by which to raise living standards. Seeing that Communism was an economic disaster, and capitalism a rousing success, he began China's move toward capitalist elements in the late 1970s. It doesn't matter if the cat is black or white, he held pragmatically, as long as it catches mice. Deng was a dictator, but evidently sufficiently rational to understand that capitalism catches mice and socialism breeds them.

First, he permitted farmers to keep part of their output. They could consume or sell for profit whatever they produced above state quotas. The result was that agricultural production increased by more than 50% in just 16 years. One of Deng's economic advisers, Li Yining, studied the thought of free market economist Friedrich Hayek, and actually urged

the creation of property rights. Deng went so far as to establish Special Economic Zones (SEZs) These SEZs established elements of free enterprise in Guangdong province, across from Hong Kong, and in Fujian province, across from Taiwan. Elements of private property and profit making were allowed, foreign investment was encouraged and Chinese goods were exported to world markets.

The consequent prosperity of these freer provinces contrasted sharply with conditions in the rest of China. The state-owned industries continued to be wasteful and inefficient: they produced goods that were unmatched to demand, they lost money, they drained resources from the Chinese budget. By contrast, the semi-private enterprise zone of Guangdong showed an economic growth rate of 13.9%, significantly above the national average. Guangdong, possessing a mere fraction of China's total population, was responsible for 30% of the country's exports. Even China's limited amount of capitalist elements has produced dramatic results. When Deng came to power in 1978, the country was desperately poor; 60 percent of the population subsisted on less than a dollar a day. The new elements of free enterprise helped the country's per capita income to double between 1978 and 1987, and then to double again between 1987 and 1996. Politically, China remains a brutal dictatorship. But the creative ability of man's rational mind is such that even a fractional amount of freedom is sufficient for it to dramatically raise living standards in an otherwise destitute statist regime.

In 2001, Communist China had a per capita GDP of $727 – its living standard still desperately low, but gradually rising from the starvation level at which it was mired under Mao. Taiwan, by contrast, had a per capita GDP of $12,461 in 2001 – and Hong Kong of $21,726. No oppressive dictatorship denying the rights and suppressing the minds of individuals could ever match the living standards of semi-capitalist Taiwan, much less the wealth of capitalist Hong Kong.[43]

Conclusion

The Great Laboratory

In the United States, the poverty threshold is officially reached when a family of four subsists on an income of $16,000 per year, truly a pittance by the standards of capitalist America. But such a per capita figure of $4,000 per year represents an amount 10 or 12 or 15 times *the average* income in non-capitalist countries of both the past and the present.

The non-capitalist nations of the world today are more brutally repressed even than those of feudal Europe, which explains why, despite the global diffusion of American technology, their living standards are virtually identical to that earlier era. When the mind is suppressed, technological, industrial and agricultural development – the achievements of the mind – are stifled.

Capitalism protects the inalienable right of the individual to his own life, and is, therefore, the only moral system. Because it respects the rights and minds of all individuals, it thereby creates vast wealth, and is the only practical system. By contrast, statism systematically violates the right of an individual to his own life, and is, therefore, immoral. Because it abrogates men's rights and suppresses their minds, it thereby causes abysmal poverty and is utterly impractical. There are degrees of statism, to be sure, but the principle remains the same: To the extent a society is statist, to that extent it violates individual rights and consequently diminishes living standards.

Capitalism is freedom – and freedom leads to prosperity. The moral is the practical. On the other hand, statism is oppression – and oppression leads to destitution. The immoral is the impractical. Men's choice today is stark: freedom and prosperity – or statism and misery. Capitalism, and the Enlightenment principles upon which it rests, if and when chosen, will bring freedom and prosperity to the oppressed masses of the Third World exactly as they did to the oppressed masses of feudal Europe.

A final point: some statist intellectuals still claim that socialism failed, in Soviet Russia and elsewhere, because it was a system intended for

advanced industrial states imposed on essentially backward agrarian ones. One point against this is that in East Germany, a heavily-industrialized state, socialism also failed; as it did in North Korea, the more fully-industrialized portion of that country.

Further, the claim concedes the point that only capitalism can enable a country to rise out of agrarian, backward conditions into technological and industrial advance; socialism is incapable of it. Most important, the claim utterly avoids the main point: socialism fails because its abrogation of liberty restricts, curtails and, in its most consistent form, strangles the freethinking mind upon which economic progress unqualifiedly depends.[44]

Summary

The "controlled experiment" performed in the great laboratory yielded conclusive results. In every case, without exception, the freer societies provided significantly (if not vastly) more prosperity than the statist ones. This remained true despite the massive help given to the statist regimes by the freer nations.

12: Capitalism as the Economic System of the Mind

A comprehensive explanation of capitalism's economic superiority to statism would take several volumes (and has already been accomplished by the leading economists). Ludwig von Mises's *Human Action* and George Reisman's *Capitalism: A Treatise on Economics* do precisely that. But a brief, essentialized presentation can focus on one fundamental point: the specific economic forms in which capitalism alone liberates the creative human mind. This is true across every aspect of an economy, including individuals in their roles of producers and consumers, businessmen and workers, inventors of devices and users of them, etc. This chapter will present key economic points from a unique philosophical perspective.

The Liberation of the Producers

The first involves the essential role of production and producers. The previous chapters have described the innovators, inventors and entrepreneurs whose pioneering minds and work have created the widespread wealth enjoyed in the capitalist nations today. The new cotton clothes, the automobiles, the personal computers, etc., had to be originated, then mass produced in order to be the enormous boon they are. Human life requires the production of all the goods and services men use daily, from

the milk and eggs of their breakfast to the homes and office buildings in which they live and work. The values upon which human life depends do not grow readymade in nature, like berries on a bush, but must be grown, built and created by human effort. Production is fundamental to the economy because it is critical to men's lives. Productivity, it must be repeated, is a significant moral virtue.

The production of wealth – of the goods and services necessary for human survival and prosperity – is the central activity of men's economic lives. The desires of rational men, of those who seek to live productive and joyous lives on earth, are, for practical purposes, limitless. Even Americans, wealthy as they are, enjoying the highest standard of living of human history, desire more: greater incomes, finer homes, more profitable investments, the financial means to send their children to the best schools, etc. Such rational men, born into the tragically destitute nations of the Third World, seek to emigrate to the capitalist nations, or, in the past 50 years, to transform their lands into capitalist nations, e.g., the "Asian Tigers."

Production is logically and causally antecedent to consumption. This central fact must be recognized, and the requirements of production be granted priority in an economic system. One contemporary economist refers to what he calls "the Primacy of Production Principle." Logically and chronologically, production exists prior to and distinct from men's capacity to consume. Whether it is food, a home, effective medical treatment or one of a million other possibilities, the goods and services must be created before they can be distributed and used. The new knowledge such creation takes, the effort required to conceive and then mass produce these goods and services, is the most serious challenge confronted by human beings seeking survival and prosperity. It is imperative to human well-being that the needs of the producers be recognized as the first and highest priority in the economy.

Say's Law of Markets was just such a recognition by a leading

Capitalism as the Economic System of the Mind

Classical economist. It will be remembered that Say's Law stated that all demand comes from supply — or, phrased differently, "supply of x creates demand for y." Say himself said it perfectly: "Produce, produce, that is the whole thing!" The individual who doesn't produce has nothing with which to trade for the values his life depends on. But if, for example, he grows apples, he can trade part of his yield for the other goods and services he requires. Since supply constitutes demand, it is fair to claim that producers create and make possible the market.[1]

The main economic reason that capitalism is superior to statism is that it liberates the producers. Capitalism – the political/economic system of the Enlightenment – is based on a recognition that the creative mind is the source of all values and that the mind must be left free to invent, manufacture and advance. Under feudalism and socialism, it is hereditary aristocrats and collectivist dictators – the Romanovs and the Bourbons, the Hitlers and the Mussolinis, the Stalins and the Castros – who hold economic authority. Power hungry rulers, not creative thinkers or productive geniuses, ultimately determine the goods and services that are permitted and produced. For monarchs and dictators, the standard of value invariably is that which furthers their power, not that which advances man's life on earth.

But under capitalism, it is the great inventive/creative minds – the Watts and the Telfords, the Edisons and the Bells, the Carnegies and the Rockefellers – who determine what gets created and produced. Generally (perhaps always), they are ahead of their time, and must educate the customers regarding the superiority of their inventions and new products/methods; but they do not require the permission of a tyrant to think or act; nor do they require the consent of their prospective customers. All that they require is political/economic freedom and the willingness to take entrepreneurial risks.

Under capitalism, it is the producers that set the economic terms. In a free society, markets are made by the producers. Rational men are free, in

time, to recognize the benefits of the innovative products and methods, and to choose to buy and use them, thereby rewarding the creators; but these new goods and services exist because of the producers' original thinking. They, the prime movers of technological and industrial progress, are liberated to act as the great progenitors of human prosperity.

The evidence of ages has now sufficiently accumulated for all honest men to understand and acknowledge this fundamental truth: it is capitalism – the system of Enlightenment principles, the system based on recognition of the efficacy and sovereignty of man's mind, the system of individual rights and limited Constitutional government – that has finally liberated the great creative thinkers who have always existed.

Historically, there has been no "problem" of production; there has been a problem of liberation. Men's minds have always been able to make the advances in philosophy, science, technology and industry necessary to promote human life; but the repressive regimes under which they have suffered for millennia made it impossible.

For example, for more than a thousand years human knowledge and living standards stagnated under the *ancien regime*; but the Enlightenment, building on its inheritance from the Renaissance and the Age of Reason, shattered those intellectual and political constraints. The consequence was the outpouring of technological and industrial advances during the late-18th and 19th centuries. Capitalism, by unleashing mankind's most creative individuals, has led to an unparalleled increase in material production, a degree of progress utterly lacking in all non-capitalist societies, both historically and currently.

(This does not mean if the feudal monarchies had magically been transformed into laissez-faire systems that men would have been immediately able to create jet travel, electric light and personal computers. It means that given the proper philosophy of reason, egoism and individual rights, and the capitalist system proceeding from it, man's mind would have initiated the research that would gradually lead from ignorance to

these advances and more.)

At the same time, it must be understood that the Primacy of Production Principle does not entail an exclusivity of production theory. It is production that makes consumption possible, it is true. But men do not produce in order to produce; production is not an end in itself. Production is a means to an end, it is the pre-condition of consumption. Ultimately, the meaning and the glory of production is that it makes possible the consumption of wealth. Consumption is the using of wealth in the enjoyment of life, and it is this alone – living joyously – that is an end in itself.

Under capitalism, there is a sense in which the phrase "The Customer is King," is true. Since businessmen profit insofar as they satisfy customer demand, and since in a free market they have competitors, they strive to maintain customer service and ensure customer satisfaction. This is an important truth. But the more fundamental truth is that very often it is the innovative producer – such as the pioneering minds of America's Inventive Period – who, by creating new time-energy-and-life-saving products/methods, teaches the customer what to desire.

For example, few men originally saw value in the creations of Fulton, Morse, Bell, the Wright Brothers, et al. Samuel Morse, after the demonstrated success of his telegraph, was willing to sell the rights to it to the federal government for a mere $100,000. The government, however, saw little value in the invention and spurned Morse's offer. But despite this and many similar rejections, the creative minds went ahead, often started their own companies – and eventually, millions of customers recognized the worth of the new products. Western Union, the telegraph company eventually founded on Morse's invention, went on to create enormous value and reap tens of millions of dollars in profit. Given sufficient time, rational men saw – and will see – the value of such an invention(s). In capitalist countries, the customers are satisfied precisely because of the original thinking and the freedom of the creators.[2]

A more recent example is the personal computer. Such innovators as Steve Jobs and Steven Wozniak started in Jobs's garage in the 1970s when few thought that personal computers would ever be more than entertainment for enthusiastic hobbyists. Though they struggled to convince the market of the serious possibilities and commercial value of personal computers, they nevertheless moved ahead, founded Apple Computer and, in time, convinced many customers that their vision was accurate.

The Liberation of the Customers

An important philosophical point regarding the mutually-beneficial relationship between innovative entrepreneurs and customers under capitalism is the role played by human nature. Because human beings have a definite identity – they are what they are, and are not what they are not – certain things will, in fact, benefit their lives whether society yet recognizes it or not. Among these are: the steam boat, the steam-generated power loom, the telegraph, the air brake for trains, the telephone, the alternating current motor, the automobile, the airplane, the personal computer, the Internet, nuclear power, stem cell research, etc. Though society has often been slow to identify the significance or worth of innovations, what makes the creative minds special is that they, in some terms, whether explicit or implicit, understand such value early on and commit themselves to its full development. Often, these brilliant thinkers carry mankind forward. Under capitalism, society always benefits and the innovators – in the long term – generally profit. Innovators and entrepreneurs often must, in effect, educate their prospective customers – but where men are free to think and act, their rational faculty enables them to recognize, in the long run, the advances that are in their actual self-interest.[3]

The intellectual and political/economic liberation of the producers is the fundamental, but by no means only reason for the matchlessly progressive nature of capitalism. The equivalent liberation of the customers

is also a decisive factor. The prospective customers are left free to evaluate the worth of a new creation to them. For example, a lighting system generated by the incalculable power of electricity will be frightening to people who have never previously encountered it. It necessarily takes time to convince them that electric light is safer, cheaper and cleaner than gas lamps. But the most advanced, far-seeing, rational minds in society are open to the facts, including those new to them. In a free country, they are unrestricted from examining and assessing the functioning and value of the new creations. They are not restrained from speaking or writing about their findings. Nobody can prevent them from purchasing the revolutionary product and deploying it in their practical lives. Eventually, though the process might take years, the most forward-thinking customers identify the virtues of the innovative product and form a vanguard promoting its widespread acceptance. An innovative thinker relies on the rational vision of prospective customers that will enable them to apprehend the value of previously untried products. The triumph of technological advances is based on the prescience and freedom of society's most rational members — the eventual users of a new device, as well as its inventor, manufacturer and investors.

Today, this phenomenon has a name: such early adopters form the first market for high-tech products. Those with the greatest economic need or who are technology buffs are willing to pay the higher price for a product newly released. For example, doctors and stockbrokers formed an early market for cell phones. Companies depend on the early adopters for their first market, for the profits they can use to expand their research and development, improve the product, lower the manufacturing costs and decrease the price to one affordable by the masses.

In a mixed economy, and certainly under socialism, the early adopters are restrained by the government. They are not allowed to use a new product because it might be "unsafe" or because it is considered "unfair" for the vanguard to have the new device when many people do

not yet have the old, etc. In such a way, the minds of both the innovative producers and the visionary customers are curtailed by the state.

The Vital Issue of Planning

It has been claimed in this chapter that capitalism's economic superiority to statism is founded in its liberation of the producers. A related and more technical point can be introduced. Given the mind's central role in man's life, and given the mind's need of political-economic freedom, it should be no surprise that one important source of capitalism's superiority to statism is its ability to maximize the utilization of human brain power.

By way of explanation, it is possible to start with a story that is fictitious but bears similarities to the stories of numerous real-life individuals. Oscar and Jorge Velez are brothers living in Cuba. Oscar and his family escape to America but Jorge and his family remain in the totalitarian state. The brothers had a strong interest in fashion design, but at first Oscar must work long hours at two jobs to support his family; he pumps gas at a service station and stocks shelves at a grocery store. His wife also works. Oscar plans to eventually attend design school and initiate a career in the field he loves. He and his wife work out a budget, enabling them to live frugally and save money. They take a small apartment in an old building. It is crowded and the neighborhood is not the best, but it is inexpensive and their capital slowly grows. Oscar keeps most of his savings in the bank, but elects to invest 10 percent of it in the stock market. He is conservative and does not get rich, but he does make modest profits.

He researches the schools of design in the Miami area, and when he possesses sufficient funds he enrolls in the one best suited to his interests. His workload is heavy, but this is the field he loves; he works hard and excels. After graduation, he gains employment with a company specializing in men's fashions; his talent and work ethic stand out. He saves

money, and within five years starts his own company. His designs are original, soon gain popularity and, in time, he competes with the heavyweights in his field. After years of frugality and apartment living, he and his wife have the means to buy their own home. Though now relatively wealthy, their tastes are modest; they reject opulence and select a middle-class home in a quiet residential suburb. Oscar lives his dream, and because of his originality and output, the customers of men's clothing are now that much wealthier.

But in Cuba, Jorge and his family live out a different story. It is a socialist economy and the sole employer is the state. The country consequently subsists in terrible poverty and the government has no resources to devote to fashion design. There are no private firms to hire him, nor is he legally permitted to start his own. Jorge works in a factory for fifteen dollars a week, and considers himself lucky to have a job. But when his brother and family defect to America, he loses many privileges, including his employment. After months of hardship, he finally finds a job as an orderly at a psychiatric hospital for twenty dollars a month. He and his family are forced to share a single large room with another family. Often he thinks about his brother and the life he could have had as a fashion designer in America.

In capitalist America, Oscar is able to run his life by his own thinking. He plans his budget, his investments, his career, his housing. His mind is the dominant factor determining the course of his life. But in socialist Cuba, Jorge's thinking is irrelevant in determining the course of his life. There is no possibility to plan investments, career or housing; he must take what the state gives him. A relative handful of government officials — not each individual for himself — plans the entire economy. Multiply these stories by the examples of millions of human beings, and what becomes clear is an essential difference between capitalism and socialism that greatly favors freedom: *under capitalism, vastly greater brain power is devoted to planning economic, as well as all other creative, activities.*

The Capitalist Manifesto

This was the great economic debate between capitalism and socialism that raged for most of the 20th century. The disagreement focused on the question: which system better utilizes human mind power in planning an economy? Socialist theorists have long claimed that socialism alone is "the planned economy," because a central governmental authority maps out every aspect of production and distribution and is, therefore, able to achieve an "integrated" allocation of resources.

Capitalism, these theorists claim, lacks such a central planning board, resulting in random and disintegrated economic activity. Each capitalist plans only his own output, solely in pursuit of his own gain, and is unconcerned about the greater needs of society as a whole. Capitalism thereby generates "a chaos of production." Related, the greed-driven nature of for-profit enterprise means that capitalism is essentially a system dominated by impulses and irrational whims, not by careful rational thought. Overall, socialists have created "the impression that what individuals do under capitalism is run about like chickens without heads in an 'anarchy of production,' and that rational action — planned action — is a prerogative of the government."

In fact, the exact opposite is true. Capitalism is the only system of rational planning, which is impossible under socialism. This is a critical point in understanding the specifically economic cause of capitalism's prosperity and socialism's penury.

Planning takes place every day under capitalism on the part of millions of thinking individuals. The economist, George Reisman, states:

> An individual is engaged in economic planning when he plans how much of his wealth and income to save and how much of it to consume; when he plans where to invest it and what ways to consume it. He is engaged in economic planning, for example, when he plans to put his money in a bank or in the stock market; when he plans to buy more clothes or a new stereo; even when he plans to drive to work or take the

train, instead.

Every businessman is engaged in economic planning when he plans to expand or contract the production of any item; when he plans to introduce a new product or discontinue an old product; when he plans to change his methods of production or retain his existing methods; when he plans to build a new factory or not to replace an existing one; when he plans to change the location of his business or let it remain where it is; when he plans to buy new machinery or not; to add to his inventories or not; to hire additional workers or let some of his present workers go.

Every wage earner under capitalism is engaged in economic planning when he plans to seek new employment or to retain his present employment; when he plans to improve his skills or rest content with the ones he has; when he plans to do his job in one particular area of the country, or in one particular industry, rather than in another.[4]

So, for example, in a capitalist society, Thomas Edison can independently work on an electric lighting system; his backers and supporters can start a company, invest funds, and promote the new product; prospective customers can choose between the innovative lighting method and the older one(s). Alexander Graham Bell, his supporters, backers and customers are free to do the same regarding telephone technology. The same is true of the Wright brothers, their supporters, backers and future customers. In the fields of heavy industry, Andrew Carnegie can employ his expertise in the creation of steel; John D. Rockefeller in the refining of oil, James J. Hill in the construction of railroads, etc. Prospective investors and customers can choose to fund or patronize these firms and their products — or not. Potential workers can decide to leave their native lands or domestic farms to seek the higher wages of industrial employment in American factories. Millions of individuals, deploying

their own minds and pursuing their own values, plan their own careers, their investments, their purchases.

"In short, every one of us under capitalism is engaged in economic planning every time he plans any aspect of his personal finances or business affairs. We are engaged in economic planning every time we think about a course of action that would benefit us in our capacity as a buyer or seller."[5]

Such multiplicity of thinking, this torrent of released brainpower does not and cannot function under socialism. Under true socialism, there is no private ownership of property — not of homes, not of farms, not of businesses. The government owns all property and operates all productive undertakings. The ruling principle is: it is the thinking of those who own property and operate businesses that controls those enterprises. This means that millions of human beings, the vast preponderance of a country's population, with all of their intelligence, their knowledge, their specialized expertise, are excluded from the planning of an economy. Several thousand bureaucrats plan for tens of millions of human beings; the tens of millions of men and women — including doctors, researchers, entrepreneurs, lawyers, farmers, workers, et al. — are excluded from the planning process, their minds forced to lie dormant and inoperative regarding the economic realm.

> *The essential problem of socialism is that it requires economic planning to take place without benefit of an intellectual division of labor.* It requires that one man (the Supreme Director) or each of several men (the Supreme Board of Directors), hold in his head and utilize the knowledge that can be held and utilized only by millions of separate individuals freely cooperating with one another on the basis of private ownership of the means of production.

A tiny fraction of the population would have to gain the knowledge,

the expertise, the specialization possessed by tens, in some cases hundreds of millions of human beings. For all practical intents, socialism requires its central planners to gain economic omniscience, i.e., the knowledge and specialized mastery possible only to vastly greater numbers of thinkers.

The overwhelming majority of people have not realized that all the thinking and planning about their economic activities that they perform in their capacity as individuals actually is economic planning. By the same token, the term "planning" has been reserved for the feeble efforts of a comparative handful of government officials, who, having prohibited the planning of everyone else, presume to substitute their knowledge and intelligence for the knowledge and intelligence of tens of millions, and to call that planning.[6]

Socialism has insuperable difficulties regarding the quality, as well as the quantity of the minds planning. For example, it has already been discussed how Lenin wrecked the Soviet economy by appointing industrial managers based on Party loyalty rather than on technical expertise. Further, a charlatan like Lysenko can have an entire agricultural system delivered into his incapable hands by virtue of convincing the ignoramus-in-chief, Joseph Stalin, that his crackpot theories are viable.

Men who seek and gain the power to plan other people's lives, who desire to render irrelevant men's minds and then dictate to them the course of their existences, are not after maximum production but maximum power. The men they appoint are ones who honor their power, not those who honor the requirements of production. No producer of the caliber of Thomas Edison, George Westinghouse or Andrew Carnegie was ever one of the "planners" of a socialist regime, and no such individual ever will be. For one thing, no independent-minded genius would be appointed by such a regime; for another, the first act of such a man upon

appointment would be abdication—for he would never be able to fulfill his vision within the strict restraints of a statist regime.

The bitter truth is that under socialism planning is conducted by statist politicians and bureaucrats, i.e, by power seekers and their flunkies, not by inventors and entrepreneurs, i.e., by men of productive ability. Economically, socialism vs. capitalism reduces to the Stalins and Castros vs. the Edisons and Carnegies. Regarding planning and production, this is no contest.

But the full truth is even more to the advantage of capitalism — and to the disadvantage of socialism. It is not merely that capitalism devotes vastly more intelligence to solving the problems of economic planning than can socialism. It is also the case that the minds planning under capitalism do so with vastly more information at their disposal.

Economic Calculation

The price system generated by the twin institutions of private property and the profit motive provides indispensable data upon which to make economic calculations.

Professor Reisman points out:

> Prices have a twofold function in the planning of capitalism. First, they enable the individual planner of capitalism to perform economic calculations. That is, they enable him to compute the money cost and/or money revenue of various modes of conduct. If the planner is a businessman, he weighs a money cost against a money revenue. If he is a consumer, he weighs a money cost against a personal satisfaction. If he is a wage earner, he weighs a money revenue against his personal efforts. These economic calculations provide a standard of action for the planner under capitalism. They tell businessmen to produce the products and use the methods of production that are anticipated to be the most profitable.

They tell consumers to consume in ways that, other things being equal, occasion the lowest cost. And they tell wage earners to work at the jobs that, other things being equal, pay the highest wages. Thus, prices are an indispensable guide both to the planning of production and to the living of one's personal life under capitalism.[7]

But prices also do more than this. They serve to coordinate the plans of each individual with the plans of untold millions of others.

> The consideration of prices is what integrates and harmonizes the plans of each individual with the plans of all other individuals and produces a fully and rationally planned economic system under capitalism.
>
> For example, a student changes his career plan from actor to accountant when he contemplates the vast difference in income he can expect to earn. A prospective home buyer changes his plan concerning which neighborhood to live in when he compares house prices in the different neighborhoods. And businesses change their plans concerning product lines, methods and locations of production, and every other aspect of their activities, in response to profit-and-loss calculations.
>
> All of these changes represent the adjustment of the plans of particular individuals and businesses to the plans of others in the economic system. For it is the plans of others to purchase accounting services rather than acting services that cause the higher income our student can expect to earn as an accountant rather than as an actor. It is the plans of others willing and able to pay more to live in certain neighborhoods, and less to live in certain others, that determine the relative house prices confronting our home buyer. It is the

plans of its prospective customers, of all competing sellers of its goods, and of all other buyers of the means of production it uses or otherwise depends on, that enter into the formation of the prices determining the revenues and costs of any business firm and thus what it finds profitable or unprofitable to produce.[8]

In a free or relatively-free society, the price system is a result of millions of rationally egoistic individuals, who, seeking their own gain, produce and voluntarily exchange privately-owned values. Prices for goods and services result from the thinking and valuing of millions of individuals who decide what and how much a given exchange means to each of them. In short, prices are a sum of the thinking and valuing performed, and the choices made by millions of human beings. That gasoline may sell for $1.89 a gallon, for example, indicates not merely the relative value-preference of millions of customers, but also of the oil companies, their shareholders and employees, the producers of the capital equipment deployed by the oil companies, and of other firms that use the same capital goods and/or the raw materials that are employed in the construction of those goods, etc.

But the price system does much more than provide information to the final consumer of a value, enabling him to engage in economic computation. It provides similar information to businessmen regarding the costs of such factors of production as raw materials, machinery and labor, enabling them to calculate the most efficient, inexpensive means of producing goods and services.

The price system depends on the twin institutions of private property and the profit motive; for prices are exchange ratios, and a voluntary exchange is a relationship in which each party to it trades what is his to mutual advantage. But it is exactly these institutions that socialism eradicates. Property is owned by the state and operated for the "public good," not for private gain. Under true socialism, the state alone plans produc-

tion of values and determines their allocation to consumers. The market-place — that polling place, the scene of daily elections — where millions of private individuals, based on their own thinking, voluntarily exchange goods and services in accordance with their selfish values, is abolished. The prices generated by men's preference for specific values is lost with the prohibited market.

This raises an insuperable difficulty. How will a socialist government identify the values its people want? Further, how could it ascertain the most efficient means of producing those values?

They know, for example, that people want shoes. But how many pairs per year? What size? What color? What style? Made from what material(s)? Manufactured by which methods, employing what machinery, how many workers and in what geographical locations?

Under capitalism, all of this information is available, and "these choices are determined on the basis of economic calculations." The quantities and styles are those that the customers are able and willing to pay for. Generally, "the methods of production, the materials used, the geographic locations are all the lowest cost." Ultimately, economic calculation based on prices ensures that the shoes manufactured are those the customers are willing to pay for and generally at the lowest cost at which manufacturers can create a competitive product.

George Reisman states: "Under socialism, the lack of economic calculation makes it impossible to make any of these choices on a rational basis. The extent of attempted shoe production is determined arbitrarily — most likely on the basis of some official's judgment about how many pairs of shoes are "necessary" per thousand inhabitants...Style is determined arbitrarily — according to what suits the tastes of those in charge. The methods, materials, and locations planned must be selected arbitrarily." Further, this is equally true of all other consumer goods and of the factors of production employed to create them.[9]

Even if the socialist leaders were benevolent men who sincerely cared

about satisfying the wants of their populace, the information necessary to do so could not exist under their regime. In the absence of a price system, the rulers have means of ascertaining neither the values of their citizens nor the most efficient means by which to create those values. The necessary result is the exact chaos that socialist theorists mistakenly ascribe to capitalism, i.e., the endless shortages, the waiting lists, the notoriously shoddy quality, the miserably low living standards, and the dreary, gray, depressing sense of hopelessness that pervades such societies.

The paltry quantity and, especially, quality of minds engaged in "planning" coupled with the dearth of information available to the "planners" guarantees that the economy's ultimate performance will be a pathetic failure compared to what is daily accomplished under capitalism. If an honest inquirer seeks the fundamental economic cause of capitalism's vast productive superiority to socialism, he need look no further than this issue. If, by analogy, a capitalist economy is a sparkling new Ferrari, a socialist economy is a horse-and-buggy — one created by human mindpower, the other depending on the muscle power of a poor, brute animal.

Philosophical Conclusions

The price system provides a calculus of men's economic values, an up-to-the-moment accounting of the goods and services men act to gain and/or keep. Philosophically, the price system is a key economic implementation of rational egoism, both reflecting men's value choices and, by providing indispensable data, furthering their ability to rationally plan the means to achieve them.

The price system, as a logical outcome of private property and the profit motive, is a necessary economic tool of men's value achievement. With it and the foundation upon which it rests, men can attain the values of their choice. Without it and the foundation upon which it rests, men get the values the government deems necessary in the quantity the

[350]

government deems appropriate — and fortunate if they receive that.

The alternative is: individuals decide what they want or the government renders their wants irrelevant. Millions of individuals are free to pursue their own values — or they receive only those values the government sees fit to grant them. Related, a government that imposes its standards on millions, that stifles their freedom to pursue their own value preferences, is a repressive dictatorship and hardly benevolent.

Capitalism, through its price system, maximizes the available knowledge upon which to perform an economic value calculus. Additionally, capitalism's protection of the right of individuals to buy and sell as they wish is an example of the benevolence of the system. On the other hand, socialism, by abrogating the price system, minimizes the available data upon which to perform economic calculation. Further, by denying the right to freely buy and sell values, socialism curtails benevolence in a society.

The choice between capitalism and socialism is: knowledge and benevolence versus ignorance and malevolence.

The price system is not merely an economic feature of capitalism. It is not even just a moral instrument expediting value achievement. It is an epistemological aid, providing invaluable information that enables men to achieve a higher level of economic understanding. The price system, therefore, is simultaneously an economic institution of capitalism, a moral instrument of egoism and an epistemological tool of human economic cognition.

An important philosophical conclusion can be drawn from the above discussion: capitalism is superior to socialism on both sides of the subject-object, knower-known, mind-matter relationship.

From the perspective of the subject or knower, capitalism applies vastly greater intelligence to solving the problems of production and distribution. From the perspective of the object or the things known, it enables those intelligent minds to gain vastly greater factual information

about the economic world. Greater brain power operating with greater information equals superior planning. Lesser brain power operating with lesser information equals inferior planning. Capitalism is the system that maximizes human economic cognition. Once again, from a new perspective, it is seen to be the system of the mind. Conversely, socialism's fundamental and insurmountable problem can be stated simply: too few minds — above all, too few outstanding minds — and too little data are permitted into the planning process. *Under socialism, the attempt to plan necessarily takes place in the absence of the fullest knowledge and most high powered intellectual ability available in a society.* Socialists are entirely correct in claiming that planning is vital to an economy. Unfortunately for them, planning is possible only under capitalism.

Part One of this book showed the great minds — the Watts, the Edisons, the Wright brothers, et. al. — who, shackled for centuries under the *ancien regime*, were then liberated by the Enlightenment philosophy of rationality and individual rights to attain magnificent and historic technological advances. Part Two showed that the mind is man's instrument of survival, and that capitalism — the system of intellectual freedom — is thereby the system empowering men to the full employment of their survival instrument. The current section shows the specific economic consequences of this philosophical principle: because the laissez-faire system leaves men unrestricted in the productive application of their intelligence, it necessarily holds a vast advantage over socialism regarding rational planning and economic calculation.

Earlier, it was also seen that socialism — Communism and National Socialism combined — murdered well over 100 million innocent victims in the 20th century. In its most widespread form, socialism was founded on Marx's materialist philosophy, which, despite paying lip service to science, necessarily glorified manual labor and brute force, and anathematized the independent reasoning mind. In economics, socialism prohibited the overwhelming preponderance of society's members from engaging

in planning.

Historically, philosophically and economically: capitalism is the system that liberates and empowers man's mind.

Historically, philosophically and economically: socialism is a system that shackles and stifles man's mind.

These differences are inherent in the nature of capitalism and socialism and are ineradicable. In practice, these form the deepest reasons that the United States has a per capita income in the range of $30,000 and the statist-socialist regimes, despite the diffusion of American technological advance, have per capita incomes scarcely one-tenth that; indeed, as discussed above, suffer from chronic shortages of every conceivable consumer good and are regularly swept by horrifyingly-destructive famines.

Many people, including some professional philosophers, believe that intellectual theories are merely so much "ivory-towered hot air," with no impact in "the real world." The contrasting theories upon which capitalism and socialism are based show, for better and for worse, such a claim to be rubbish.

Summary

In every possible way, capitalism liberates the human mind — the producers and the consumers, the inventive geniuses and the everyday planners, the entrepreneurs and the workers, the spenders and the savers. This liberated human brainpower is the fundamental epistemological cause of capitalism's great success.

The Austrian economist, Ludwig von Mises and his supporters, are correct: planning is possible only under capitalism. Related, the price system, which does not exist under state-dominated economies, provides necessary data for the minds engaged in planning.

13: Refuting the Economic Charges Against Capitalism

Just as capitalism is accused of such moral crimes as war, imperialism and slavery, though, in fact, statism is responsible, the same pattern holds true regarding economic failings. The truth is that statism is responsible for monopolies, unemployment, inflation and depressions. The travesty is that statism, the cause of the problems, escapes condemnation — while capitalism, the solution, takes the blame.

Capitalism's enemies project onto freedom the results of dictatorship. By arguing that under capitalism individuals are helpless victims of coercion (monopolies), that their money is devalued and, in effect, stolen (inflation), that they are cast into grinding poverty (depressions), etc., anti-capitalists can then plausibly claim that extreme capitalism leads to the same destructive results as extreme statism; that, therefore, a middle-of-the-road mixed economy, a "social democracy," is the preferred system.

But, in truth, there are degrees of statism. A full system of governmental initiation of force — e.g., National Socialism or Communism — results in starvation slavery, gulags, extermination camps, genocide. A partial system of governmental force — a mixed economy — does not lead to such atrocities but does result in the lesser evils that are the topic of this chapter.

The Capitalist Manifesto

Monopolies

It is possible to start with the issue of monopolies. Critics claim that on a free market, unregulated by the government, ruthless entrepreneurs will carve out huge business empires, use their wealth and influence to suppress competition, and charge customers arbitrarily high prices. The truth, however, is that this claim is both historically inaccurate and economically invalid.

There are and have been such coercive monopolies in American history. One notorious example was the Central Pacific Railroad, which virtually controlled California for nearly 30 years. This railroad, built and operated by the "Big Four" of Leland Stanford, Collis Huntington, Charles Crocker and Mark Hopkins, was guilty of all the abusive practices of which monopolies are popularly accused. Its leaders bribed and controlled the state legislature, legally suppressed competition and charged rates ruinous to its shippers. From the mid-1870s until the turn of the 20th century, its insatiable appetite gobbled virtually all the profits of California's farmers and other commercial shippers.

How was the railroad able to acquire such power and perpetrate such unscrupulous practices? By the power of government backing.

The most important point is that the California state legislature granted the railroad a legal monopoly in the state, legally debarring competitors from entering the field. For example, the legislature granted to the railroad control of the coastal areas surrounding San Francisco Bay, prohibiting any other railroad from gaining access to the harbor. During the thirty year period of the Central Pacific's power, legislative action defeated many attempts by private businessmen to open competing lines.[1]

It is important to note that none of the abuses could have occurred without the status of legal monopoly granted by the state. The state's intervention in, and control of the railroad industry was the decisive factor responsible for the injustices. "Efforts to remedy the situation were

uniformly unsuccessful because of the railroad's control of the legislature, of state regulatory bodies, of city and county governments, and in many cases, of the courts."

If all governmental bodies are constitutionally debarred from economic intervention, if they are relegated by law solely to the protection of individual rights, then corrupt businessmen could not buy their political favors. It has been pointed out by both critics and supporters of capitalism that government regulatory bodies often come under the control of the businesses they're designed to regulate — to the detriment of competition. The solution is a constitutional restriction prohibiting the government from regulation of business.

The logic of a mixed economy favors the already successful, entrenched companies at the expense of start-up firms. Theoretically, regulatory agencies are established to serve the "public good." But for many reasons, a successful company can plausibly claim that its business serves the "public good." For, the company executives will point out, the firm contributes to many worthy causes (including campaign contributions to the elected officials who appoint the regulators), and it employs thousands of workers, satisfies millions of customers, etc., and has performed such productive functions for many years. Therefore, to hurt the company's business is to undermine the very "public good" the bureaucrats seek to preserve. Can the entrepreneurial firms, just starting up, say the same? Obviously not. In the nature of things they have not yet established a track record or accumulated sufficient capital to contribute to campaign coffers or hire expensive lobbyists. They are inherently at a disadvantage in negotiating with regulators and influencing policy.

Under laissez-faire, innovative entrepreneurs only have to convince the customers that they have a superior product — and though that often takes time, they have succeeded in doing so in innumerable cases. But if the economy is controlled, the entrenched canal interests, for example, can convince the bureaucrats to grant them monopoly status in the ship-

ping industry, legally banning the germinating railroads. The gas light interests can do the same, resulting in a legal prohibition on the nascent electric light. The carriage makers and blacksmiths can promote the same effort regarding the automobile, etc. The logic of regulation militates against innovation and entrepreneurship in favor of preferential legal status for already-entrenched companies who seek to avoid the necessity of competing.

If the government had not granted the railroad the status of legal monopoly, then other entrepreneurs could have entered the field. The resulting competition would have prevented the Central Pacific from charging arbitrarily high rates. The open competition of a free marketplace would have avoided the harm done farmers and shippers. Government regulation was not the solution to the abuses of the Big Four; it was the problem. Capitalism was not the problem; it was the solution.

Cornelius Vanderbilt and his backers demonstrated the nature of the laissez-faire system when they took on the Fulton monopoly in the field of steamship transportation in 1817 and the years following. It was the New York State government's legal ban on competition that granted the Fulton company monopoly status and the ability to charge prices much higher than would be possible on an open marketplace. The liberty of capitalism, expressed perfectly by Vanderbilt's masthead flag reading "New Jersey must be free!" led directly to the extensive price cutting that so benefited the customers.

The same point was illustrated when Edward H. Harriman took over the Union Pacific, the Central Pacific's "Siamese twin," which, built with federal subsidies and land grants, had been poorly constructed and corruptly managed, ultimately collapsing into bankruptcy. Harriman, a brilliant capitalist, renovated the line, engineered "grades, curves and roadbeds for maximum, heavy-tonnage efficiency," introduced modern equipment, and built it into "a highly competitive carrier."

In the absence of legal monopoly status, Harriman had to compete. He could not arbitrarily charge high prices. He profited at competitive rates by means of his extraordinary efficiency. As but one example: when Harriman purchased the Union Pacific in 1898, the railroad averaged 476,000 tons of freight shipped per mile of its track; by 1909, it averaged over one million. To further corroborate the point: "During the period of Mr. Harriman's administration freight rates on the Union Pacific decreased by from fifteen to seventeen percent."[2]

A coercive monopoly is one that can charge virtually any price it pleases without concern for the interest or evaluation of its customers. Business economist, Alan Greenspan, in the years before he became Federal Reserve Chairman, defined such a monopoly as "a business concern that can set its prices and production policies independent of the market, with immunity from competition, from the law of supply and demand." No company on a free market can do this. Under capitalism, every company, no matter its wealth or its popularity, must compete everyday in the marketplace with countless rivals.[3]

A company must compete not only with competitors in its own field, but with companies in related fields whose products or services can be used as substitutes for its own. The Coca-Cola Company, for example, is hugely successful with an enormous share of the international market, and has been so for decades. Despite its wealth and popularity, however, Coca-Cola is limited in the prices it can charge, for it has many competitors. Pepsi and RC are merely two of the colas with which it competes; there are others. Additionally, there are other types of soda, as well. Coke must compete with Seven-Up, with Canada Dry ginger ale, with A&W root beer, with various companies manufacturing orange, black cherry, cream and other soda flavors. Further, Coke is in competition with other types of soft drinks. There are major producers of iced tea, iced coffee, lemonade, fruit drinks and punch, etc. There are many companies today selling spring water, whether carbonated or uncarbonated. The thirsty

customer, looking for a non-alcoholic beverage to drink, has a plethora of choices. The result is that Coca-Cola must constantly win new customers and win anew its old ones. The only way it can do this, of course, is by providing customers with the best product it can at the best price. Open competition on a free market precludes the possibility of coercive monopolies like the Central Pacific Railroad.

The only monopolies that can be formed on a free market are productive monopolies, i.e., those that gain exclusive market dominance (or even enormous market share) by means of prodigious productivity. An excellent example of such a productive monopoly was the Aluminum Company of America (ALCOA) prior to World War II. ALCOA kept the price of aluminum at a level conducive to the largest growth of its market. It did not seek the highest price it could procure, but rather, the highest price that was sufficiently low to discourage prospective customers from choosing any of the available aluminum substitutes. With prices consequently lower than they otherwise could have been, profits were made only by the most strenuous efforts at increasing efficiency and cutting costs.

In 1886, Charles Martin Hall discovered a method to economically produce metallic aluminum. Prior to this, aluminum had been considered a semi-precious metal, "despite the fact that it is the most abundant element in the earth's crust." Indeed, in 1884, the total production of aluminum in the United States had been 125 pounds. Hall formed the Pittsburgh Reduction Company in 1888, but at first nobody knew what to do with the manufactured aluminum. Eventually, it was realized that the metal could be used for "cooking utensils, foil, electric wire and cable, auto bodies" and in construction and aviation, as well. Aluminum, which in 1885 had cost $11.33 per pound, in 1892 cost a mere 57 cents for the same amount. In 1907, the company Hall founded changed its name to the Aluminum Company of America. Its struggle to rise included not merely successful competition against such substitutes as cast iron, cop-

per and tin — but the need to convince prospective customers that the new metal was a potential substitute for the older, established ones. An aluminum manufacturer, as all producers on a free market, faces competition from products that can be employed as substitutes for his own.

ALCOA became a monopoly, having no competitors in the production of aluminum. But it certainly was not a coercive monopoly. It could not set its prices without regard to the market, for it had no way to restrict competitors from entering the field. "In fact, only because the company stressed cost-cutting and efficiency, rather than raising prices, was it able to maintain its position as sole producer of primary aluminum for so long. Had ALCOA attempted to increase its profit by raising prices, it soon would have found itself competing with new entrants in the primary aluminum business."[4]

This is the only type of monopoly possible on a free market. But such a productive monopoly is an enormous boon to the customers, because it keeps competitors out only by achieving such efficiency of production that it makes a profit at prices lower than those at which any would-be rival could prosper. As a matter of deliberate policy, it permanently undersells any prospective competitor.

A coercive monopoly requires governmental intervention. "The necessary precondition of a coercive monopoly is closed entry – the barring of all competing producers from a given field. This can be accomplished only by an act of government intervention, in the form of special regulations, subsidies or franchises." Under capitalism, as soon as a monopolist or conglomerate of monopolists set prices at a level high enough for other companies to profit, the monopolist(s) are inviting competition.[5]

This last point is illustrated by the story of the Dow Chemical Company. In the late 1890s and early 20th century, the young Herbert Dow engaged in a famous "bleach war" with the English monopolists, the United Alkali Company. It was a conglomerate of about forty companies, and controlled the huge potash deposits in Britain from which it

made bleach. United Alkali believed it could set high prices because it was a near global monopolist. But Dow improved the efficiency of the manufacturing process, and was able to undersell them. What engaged was a protracted price war, with prices falling from $3.50 a hundredweight to 86 cents for the same quantity. Although Dow lost large quantities of money for several years, eventually the British conglomerate gave up trying to oust him from the chlorine business. The continuing competition kept the price of bleach steady at $1.25 a hundredweight, a price at which Dow profited and the customers saved.[6]

At about the same time, Dow engaged in a struggle with another global monopoly, the German manufacturers of bromine, Die Deutsche Bromkonvention. Again, by developing more efficient manufacturing methods and cutting costs, Dow was able to undersell the less efficient monopolists. The price war lasted for four years (1904-1908) until the Germans finally relented. Competition resulted for most of the global market, and "low-priced bromine was now a fact of life." Under capitalism, would-be monopolists cannot keep out competition. By charging high prices, they make themselves vulnerable to hungry, up-and-coming, efficiency-conscious entrepreneurs like Dow.[7]

Unfortunately, many capitalists seek government intervention in various forms as a means of suppressing competition — thereby undercutting capitalism. It is a manifestation of a mixed economy — and it would properly be obviated by a policy of laissez-faire. But monopolies formed by such a method — by coercion, by legally closed entry — must be sharply differentiated from those formed by superior productiveness. One is an evil to be eliminated; the other is a magnificent value to be celebrated.

Unionism and Unemployment

But there is a form of coercive monopoly that anti-capitalists generally support: labor unions.

Refuting the Economic Charges Against Capitalism

Unions seek, and through government intervention gain, monopolistic control over an industry's labor supply. This situation can best be understood by contrasting it with the functioning of a labor market under capitalism.

Under the laissez-faire system, an employer is free to hire any workers, unionized or not, willing to work at the wage levels and terms he offers. Where freedom prevails, monetary wage rates are set by the market, i.e., by the competition among employers for workers and among workers for jobs.

But in the American mixed economy, such governmental policies as the National Labor Relations Act (1935) and others, and a succession of Supreme Court rulings, often compelled employers to recognize and bargain with unions — and forced non-union workers to accept the union as their sole bargaining agent.

As if this was not sufficient violation of the rights of both employers and workers, the government also required companies to bargain with such coercive unions "in good faith." No matter how outrageous a union's demand, the company was legally obligated to respond with a counter-offer the National Labor Relations Board (NLRB) considered serious, i.e., that made some concessions — or else suffer penalties. Such legislation as the Taft-Hartley Act (1947) undercut the political power of the unions only slightly.

Perhaps most important, law enforcement agencies and the court system often "tolerate behavior in the course of labor disputes that they would never tolerate under other circumstances." In American history, there is an endless number of cases in which union members initiated hideous violence against workers independent enough to cross picket lines during strikes ("scabs" in the unions' non-objective nomenclature) and suffered little or no legal punishment for their crimes. In one typical example, the Kohler Strike in Wisconsin in 1954, "employees attempting to enter the plant were slugged, kneed in the groin, kicked, pushed and

threatened." In general, it "is almost impossible to obtain legal protection against so-called mass picketing, which is inherently intimidating." Nor is it uncommon during strikes for independent workers to be murdered by union violence. In one such case, dozens of "scabs" were murdered by members of the striking United Mine Workers in Herrin, Illinois in 1922.

> Now a strike is not...merely the act of a worker in "withholding his labor," or even merely a collusion of a large group of workers simultaneously to "withhold their labor" or give up their jobs. The whole point of a strike is the insistence by the strikers that they have not given up their jobs at all. They contend that they are still employees — in fact, the only legitimate employees. They claim an ownership of the jobs at which they refuse to work; they claim the "right" to prevent anybody else from taking the jobs that they have abandoned. That is the purpose of their mass picket lines, and of the vandalism and violence that they either resort to or threaten. They insist that the employer has no right to replace them with other workers, temporary or permanent, and they mean to see to it that he doesn't. Their demands are enforced always by intimidation and coercion, and in the last resort by actual violence.

Unions' violence against independent workers is eminently logical given the basic premise of coercive unionization, because such workers threaten their monopolization of the labor supply. If companies were free to bargain with any and all workers, as they should be, unions would lose their coercive advantage in negotiations.[8]

It should go without saying that, in a free country, workers have the right to unionize and present a united front to management during labor negotiations. But the owners also have rights. They have the right to

refuse to negotiate with unions, if they choose; to hire non-union workers — or to negotiate separately and independently with non-union workers. Further, just as workers have a right to organize, so they have a right to refuse to join a union and to negotiate independently with employers. Everybody's rights must be protected, not just those of unions and their memberships.

Legislation supported by such coercive unions is responsible for significant amounts of unemployment.

Statists argue that high rates of unemployment occur inevitably under capitalism and that government spending is necessary to stimulate the economy and maximize employment levels.

But the truth is that unemployment for those who seek to work is caused by government intervention in the labor market. When the government imposes minimum wage laws, for example, or when it compels employers to bargain exclusively with labor unions, two results logically follow: higher pay for those who can get jobs — and an increase in the number of those who cannot.

Consider the effects of minimum wage laws. To choose an arbitrary figure, imagine the government sets the minimum wage at $6 per hour or $240 for a forty-hour week. One immediate consequence is that no one whose labor is worth less than $6 per hour will be employed. "You cannot make a man worth a given amount by making it illegal to offer him anything less." The minimum wage merely deprives him of the opportunity to work at a level that his talent and current skills permit — and it deprives the firm and, ultimately, the customers of the modest output of his labor. The essence of the situation is that, for a low wage, the government has substituted unemployment.[9]

Indeed, the situation is even worse than this. For now without a job, the would-be worker is deprived not merely of an income but also of an opportunity to enhance his work skills with which to earn a higher wage in the future. Employers often find it in their rational self-interest to train

employees and help them upgrade their skills. Such a phenomenon occurs so frequently under capitalism that the phrase "on-the-job training" becomes a commonplace expression.

In the name of helping the poor worker, minimum wage laws have the following impact on the poor worker: they deprive him of income, work experience, an opportunity to build a résumé showing his work ethic and personal responsibility, possible on-the-job training, and the pride of supporting himself by honest effort.

The minimum wage laws require employers to discriminate against persons with low skills. Nobel Laureate Milton Friedman points out that very often it is teenagers who are the victims, because they have not yet had the opportunity to develop marketable skills.

> The high rate of unemployment among teenagers, and especially black teenagers is...a scandal...Yet it is largely a result of minimum wage laws. [After World War II] the minimum wage was...raised sharply to 75 cents in 1950, to $1.00 in 1956...After minimum wage rates were raised sharply, the unemployment rates shot up for both white and black teenagers. Currently [1980, when the minimum wage was $2.90], the unemployment rate runs around 15 to 20 percent for white teenagers; 35 to 45 percent for black teenagers.[10]

The effect is similar when the government caves in to the political demands of the unions. By means of a government-enforced monopoly on an industry's labor supply, and/or by the initiation of coercion against independent workers during strikes, or the threat of such initiation, unions are often able to raise wages above the levels they would attain if labor negotiations remained fully voluntary. Such gains come principally at the expense of other workers.

"The key to understanding the situation is the most elementary prin-

ciple of economics: the law of demand — the higher the price of anything, the less of it people will be willing to buy. Make labor of any kind more expensive and the number of jobs of that kind will be fewer." For example, the more construction workers are paid, the more the cost of building rises. Buying a home becomes correspondingly more expensive, and fewer people will buy. Consequently, fewer houses will be built than otherwise, and fewer workers will be hired.[11]

A union that coercively raises wage rates reduces the number of jobs in the field it controls. The workers unhireable at the higher wage, who would be employed at a lower one, must look elsewhere for employment. But the increased supply of workers in other fields necessarily drives down the price of labor in those fields. Wages forced above market levels for one group inevitably reduce the wages paid to others. By 1980, extensive research indicated that, on average, about 10 to 15 percent of the workers in the U.S. had been able, through union power, to raise their wages roughly 10 to 15 percent above market levels. Their gain had reduced the wages of the other 85 to 90 percent of the workers by some 4 percent below what they otherwise would have been.[12]

Moreover, all individuals, including the workers whose salaries are raised by governmentally-backed unions, suffer in their roles as customers. The point again is simple: if the teamsters' union, for example, is able to raise wage levels above market prices, then everybody will pay higher prices for goods delivered by truck, including the teamsters.

The solution is not, as some union leaders propose, to unionize all workers and proceed to force wages above free market levels universally. The necessary result of such a policy is widespread unemployment.

The economist, Henry Hazlitt, pointed out the steps that must be taken. "If employers were not legally compelled to 'bargain' with (in practice, to make concessions to) a specified union, no matter how unreasonable its demands; if employers were free to discharge strikers and peaceably to hire replacements, and if mass picketing and violence were really

prohibited, the natural competitive checks on excessive wage demands would once more come into play."[13]

All that is necessary to attain a productive full employment is the operation of an unrestricted labor market in which employers and employees are free to pursue their own self-interest. If wages are free to fall to levels at which even the most unskilled worker can be productively employed, then unemployment will be eliminated. This is certainly in the self-interest of the employee, just as it is the employer's interest, for it is far superior to be employed at a lower wage than to be unemployed at a higher one. As George Reisman states: "Unemployment is caused by an improper relationship between money wage rates and the demand for labor in the economic system...If wage rates are too high relative to the demand for labor, unemployment is the result."[14]

Nor does such a reduction in monetary wages necessitate a diminished standard of living for workers. Indeed, an elimination of the monopolistic status of labor unions, and a progression toward a free labor market, will eradicate the numerous anti-productivity policies of the coercive unions.

The unions blatantly attack productivity in numerous ways: they support "feather-bedding" practices, in which more men than necessary must be hired for a job. They promote "rigid subdivisions of labor," in which workers qualified for a specific task will nevertheless be prevented from performing it because it falls outside their narrow job description. They often oppose the implementation of "more efficient or more labor-saving machinery." They have "opposed payment on the basis of output...and insisted on the same hourly rates...regardless of differences in productivity." They have demanded "promotion for seniority rather than for merit." They discourage competitions among workers that seek to increase productivity. "They impose make-work schemes, such as requiring that pipe delivered to construction sites with screw thread already on it, have its ends cut off and new screw thread cut on the site." When an

organization's goal is not to maximize productivity, but to keep as many men employed for as long as possible, such depredations, and countless others, are inevitable.

Statist intellectuals, politicians and union leaders ignore the critical truth that only increases in productivity can raise real wages; and related—any factor(s) that generate increases in productivity will lead to rises in real wages.

With an end to minimum wage laws and government-backed unions, two important boosts to productivity will occur: full employment will be attained; and the unions' perverse war against productiveness will cease. Additionally, the achievement of full employment would eliminate the burden of providing for the unemployed that always falls to working men and women. The result will be climbing output, increasing supply, and rising real wages. The purchasing power of workers will be consistently higher, even though monetary wages will often be lower. Workers will consequently be wealthier, not poorer.[15]

Observe an important parallel. On a free market, a private company cannot gain a coercive monopoly. If the government does not deny entry, a powerful company has no legal means to exclude rivals. The possibility and the reality of competition keeps companies from imposing arbitrary prices and terms on their customers.

Similarly, on a free market, a labor union cannot gain a coercive monopoly. If the government does not deny employers and non-union workers the right to negotiate independently — and if it protects their physical safety in doing so — then a powerful union has no legal means to exclude rivals. The possibility and the reality of competition keeps unions from imposing arbitrary wage rates and terms on their employers.

Coercive monopolies are possible only under a system of government interventionism, and are not possible under capitalism. The supporters of capitalism, upholding the principle of individual rights, universally condemn all coercive monopolies. But the enemies of capitalism, essentially

influenced by Marx, are still fighting the "class struggle," and claim to side with the poor. In their view, the rights of individuals can be mercilessly trampled, including those of countless workers, as long as the powerful labor unions benefit. The only coercive monopolies they morally oppose are those that supposedly provide advantages to corporate "fat cats." Those that theoretically benefit union members are morally praiseworthy.

Inflation

In addition to causing coercive monopolies and unemployment, a mixed economic system that only partially permits governmental initiation of force leads to other economic and moral ills. Inflation is one.

There is pervasive confusion regarding this issue that is often perpetuated by famous economists and influential politicians, i.e., by the very people whose job it is to provide clarification. This widespread confusion needs to be remedied.

Many people mistakenly believe that inflation is an increase in the prices of goods and services. The truth is that rising prices is a consequence of inflation. The phenomenon of inflation itself is simply the government's expansion of the money supply. "Inflation, always and everywhere, is caused by an increase in the supply of money and credit. In fact, inflation *is* the increase in the supply of money and credit."[16]

Henry Hazlitt, a brilliantly clear writer on economics, offers the following story as a first step toward understanding inflation. Imagine, he says, that by some miracle, every family in the United States were to wake up one morning with four times as much money as it possessed the day before. People would then proceed to buy many of the things they wanted but had previously been unable to afford. The people who arrived first would be able to get the goods at the original price. But the increased demand would begin to bid prices higher, and the latecomers would find they could no longer get what they wanted at the lower price. Merchants

would find their inventories dwindling and consequently re-order, thereby raising wholesale prices. The manufacturers, now doing a larger volume of business, would increase production and seek to hire more workers. This, of course, would raise wage rates. In time, the result would be higher prices and wages across the board.[17]

This story is a fantasy, and people do not acquire increased money and purchasing power in this magical way. Nevertheless, this is exactly what happens to a country in an inflationary period. This is what happened in the U.S. during much of the 20th century. For instance, at the end of 1939, the quantity of money that was in people's hands, outside of banks, equaled $6.4 billion. The bank deposits available to withdrawal by check was 29.8 billion. Therefore, the total active money supply in the country equaled slightly more than $36 billion. By 1959, this supply had increased to $145 billion -- four times what it had been just twenty years earlier.[18]

"With this hugely increased size of money bidding for goods, wholesale prices at the end of 1959 had increased 136 per cent above those at the end of 1939. In the same period the cost of living, as measured by the retail prices paid by consumers, had increased 113 percent. In other words, the purchasing power of the dollar fell to less than half of what it was in 1939."[19] This is not just an American phenomenon. Between 1950 and 1959, the money supply in Chile increased nineteen times, and the cost of living increased in that country twenty times. Similarly, in Bolivia during the same time period, the money supply increased seventy times, and the cost of living a hundred times. The correlation between an expanded money supply and higher prices is similar in other countries.[20]

The more money there is relative to the supply of goods and services, the more that can then be bid for those goods and services, necessarily driving up prices. What this means is that the value of the monetary unit declines with the increase of money. Each dollar now buys less than

it did previously. Whenever "the quantity of anything whatever increases, the value of any single unit of it falls. If this year's wheat crop is twice as great as last year's, the price of a bushel of wheat drops violently compared with last year. Similarly, the more the money supply increases relative to the supply of goods, the more the purchasing power of a single unit declines." The proof is in the facts: the money supply of Great Britain increased some 226 per cent between 1937 and 1957 and the cost of living increased by 166 per cent over that time. In France, the money supply increased about 36 times over those same years; as a consequence, the cost of living rose about 26 times.[21]

What is the cause of such increases in the supply of money? Governments engage in deficit financing, seeking to eliminate all restraints on their spending. "All of the great inflations of earlier and modern times have been primarily the result of reckless deficit financing on the part of governments, which wanted to spend far more than they had the courage or ability to collect in taxes. They paid for the difference by printing paper money."[22]

The modern inflationary method is slightly more sophisticated than to simply require the treasury to print more money – though it leads to the same consequence. Generally what occurs is governments "'sell' their interest-bearing securities to the central bank. The central bank then creates a 'deposit' for the face value of the government securities, and the government draws checks against the 'deposit.'" Credit has thereby been created and increased buying can occur. How does the government pay the debts it thereby incurs? By printing more money. So the net result is the same. The government ultimately puts more money into circulation by the simple expedient of printing more. This is what is meant by inflating or expanding the money supply.[23]

George Reisman makes the important point that the government's cost in its creation of paper or checkbook money is virtually nil. "The cost of printing any piece of paper money, whether a dollar bill or a hun-

dred dollar bill, is only a fraction of a cent. The cost of crediting the Treasury's checking account with a billion dollars is not much greater. As a result, there is nothing intrinsic to paper or checkbook money that operates to preserve its value."[24]

When the government expands the money supply at whim, the inevitable result is a debasement of the monetary standard and the theft of honest people's wealth. With immensely more money in circulation, and a consequent steady rise in prices, each dollar, each monetary unit, now buys less. Over a period of years, people's life savings are vastly diminished in value. For example, in the United States in 1998 the purchasing power of $100 was less than that of $20 a mere 30 years earlier. "Among other things, this means that people who saved money in the 1960s had four-fifths of its value silently stolen from them over the next three decades."[25]

The harm caused by governments' continued commitment to inflation is extensive. In causing the depreciation of the monetary unit, it raises everybody's cost of living. (In this regard, it particularly harms the working poor, who are less able to afford the resulting price hikes than are their middle-class and wealthy fellows.) It wipes out the value of the life savings of honest, hard-working men and women; and, in doing so, discourages future savings. Any policy which discourages saving diminishes not only an individual's ability to rise from poverty to comfort or wealth — but also limits the investments that can be made in productive enterprises. In this way, inflation causes declining productivity and living standards.

Worst of all is the way it undermines confidence in capitalism. When people believe that capitalism, not statism, is responsible for their declining purchasing power, they are more inclined to tolerate steadily increasing doses of oppressive government policies as supposed countermeasures. For example, governments often impose wage-price controls as an alleged anti-inflationary policy.

But restricting prices from rising merely tinkers with one effect; it does not address the underlying cause. The growing supply of money increases demand for goods relative to their supply. (In fact, it ensures that supply will not increase, because prices cannot rise to a level at which profits grow, spurring greater production.) Now, not everybody able and willing to buy at the fixed prices can procure the items they seek, i.e., shortages occur. To combat the state-created shortages, the government imposes rationing, with the consequence that virtually everybody now makes do with less than they otherwise could have — a policy of poverty. The country moves toward statism at an accelerated pace. Economic freedom is openly attacked; production and living standards decline.

The cure for monetary inflation is for politicians to get out of the way and let human beings freely choose their money, i.e., what they will accept as a medium of exchange. They will choose the metal that, historically, they have generally chosen when left free: gold.

An international gold standard is mankind's primary protection against arbitrary expansion of the money supply by the politicians. Because gold is relatively rare in nature, and its mining generally involves laborious and expensive work, the money supply grows only gradually. The technological progress of free men leads to an increase in the supply of goods that generally exceeds the increase in the supply of gold. "The result would be that prices would show a tendency to fall from year to year...this is actually what happened in the nineteenth century, in the generation preceding the discovery of the California gold fields, and again, in the generation from 1873 to 1896," that is, during the Inventive Period.[26]

Further, whenever credit inflation occurred under a gold standard, a specific chain of events quickly followed. Prices in that country rose. Since prices then tended to be lower abroad, imports were encouraged and exports discouraged. Gold started to flow out of the country. "This caused a contraction of the bank credit based on the gold, and brought

the inflation to a halt." What this meant was that "domestic currency tampering and anything more than a relatively moderate inflation were impossible."[27]

But most contemporary politicians want to inflate the money supply. There are various goals they think they can reach by inflationary means. Some believe that by putting into effect an "easy money" policy, thereby making it easier for businessmen to borrow, they can create a perpetual economic boom. Some inflate because it is the only means to finance the social welfare programs that they advocate. Some inflate because the increased credit enables them to build their military and prepare for war. But whatever their specific intentions, the vast majority of current politicians do not want to be restrained from inflating whenever they desire to. They want to be free to manipulate the money supply at will (and then lie regarding the causes of inflation.) They seek the license to inflate on caprice. Because of this, they are opposed to the gold standard, which stands as an implacable obstacle to their inflationary schemes.

> The gold standard is not important as an isolated gadget but only as an integral part of a whole economic system. Just as 'managed' paper money goes with a statist and collectivist philosophy, with government 'planning,' with a coercive economy in which the citizen is always at the mercy of bureaucratic caprice, so the gold standard is an integral part of a free-enterprise economy under which governments respect private property, economize in spending, balance their budgets, keep their promises, and refuse to connive in overexpansion of money or credit.

Only when men are ready to move to a system consistently upholding individual rights, private property and the rule of law can the gold standard be effectively restored. Until mankind establishes a capitalist system, it is senseless to try to force the government to adhere to a gold

standard, because it would be only a matter of months before it found some pretext to again inflate and dispense with gold.[28]

But the worst economic calamity wrought by mitigated statism is: depression. Fully statist regimes, such as the former Soviet Union or present day North Korea, subsist(ed) in chronic depression. Partially statist systems, such as the Western mixed economies, suffer only periodic depressions. Unrelieved statism engenders unrelieved poverty. Statism mixed with freedom yields a mixture of prosperity and poverty.

The Great Depression

The worst depression of American history occurred between 1929 and 1946. What were the political/economic conditions of the years immediately preceding it? What were the cause(s) of the Great Depression?

Though the United States of the 1920s was a mixed economy, and decidedly less free than it had been 40 years earlier, it was vastly freer than it would be after the imposition of the New Deal. For example, after World War I, the government had significantly reduced tax rates. President Calvin Coolidge had the good sense to understand that "the business of America is business," and generally held to principles of limited government. He retained the famed Pittsburgh banker, Andrew Mellon, as Secretary of the Treasury, and by 1925 the top U.S. tax rate was 25%, down from the 77% high reached during the war. Mellon also successfully campaigned for slashing taxes across the economic board. Between 1921 and 1929, Mellon's tax revolution chopped rates on America's poor from 4 to 1/2%; and on the middle-class from 8 to 2%.[29]

Additionally, relative to the New Deal years, governmental regulation of business was less extensive; legislation and court rulings empowering coercive labor unions less pervasive; and a welfare state virtually non-existent.

Contrary to common belief, including that of many economists, the

prosperity of the 1920s was genuine, not a chimera built on air. The decade was a period of extraordinary economic growth. Invention in the nation flourished; the number of patents issued during these years exceeded prior records. New industries in automobiles, chemicals, appliances, telephones, radios, aircraft and other fields grew rapidly. Real wages rose significantly, as did the general standard of living. From spring 1921 to summer 1929, industrial production in America more than doubled (+109%). In all of American history before or since, the only eight-year period of comparable growth was during the industrial revolution of the 1870s — the Inventive Period.

The spectacular stock market rise accurately reflected this productivity. From the summer of 1921 to the summer of 1929, stock prices of U.S.-traded firms increased by 385%. It must be pointed out that for the same time frame profits for these very companies rose by 387%. Profits expanded so dramatically in part because of the increases in output and in part because business was reducing costs through the introduction of new technology and the assembly line.

Further, it must be remembered that for all its faults, the Federal Reserve remained on the gold standard in the 1920s. The dollar held the same, fixed amount of gold as it had for decades — and it was freely convertible to any bank or dollar-holder. There was no debasement of the U.S. monetary standard. "It is true that the money supply in the U.S. — the sum of currency and checkable bank deposits — grew in the 1920s. But it grew at a rate that was less than one-third as fast (29%) as the growth in money demand — as reflected in the growth rate of industrial output (109%).

"No wonder, then, that general indexes of wholesale and retail prices in the U.S. actually fell in the eight years ending in 1929. Prices each year were slowly declining." The great increase in stock prices during these years were real gains, based on the immense productivity and profitability of American business. These were not "allegedly false gains due to the

Fed 'pumping in money.'"

What factor(s) then caused the shattering crash of 1929? In a phrase: growing statism. For one thing, President Hoover supported a tariff proposal that by the summer of 1929 had grown ominously into the Smoot-Hawley Tariff Act: duties would be imposed on thousands of imported items of all kinds. The American economic growth rate peaked in July; stock prices in September. On October 21st, an amendment to limit tariffs to agricultural products was defeated in the Senate. On October 24th, the stock market suffered its first one-day crash. On October 29th, amid rumors that Hoover would not veto the Smoot-Hawley Bill, stock prices crashed even further.

The new tariffs imposed an effective tax rate of 60% on more than 3200 products imported into the United States. Predictably, in response to this quadrupling of import duties, other nations retaliated with tariffs. Spain, for example, increased tariffs on American cars by 150%, and Italy doubled its tariff on the same commodity. Over the next three years (1930-1933), U.S. exports plunged 64% and farm exports by 60%. The monetary value of farm exports dropped from $1.8 billion in 1929 to $590 million in 1933. Total world trade sunk 61% in those years. Further, the tariff war raised U.S. business costs, thereby depressing profits. "That's what the stock market was anticipating in 1929." Profits had grown by more than 25% that year, compared to 1928. But in 1930 profits dropped 34%, compared to the previous year — and they kept going down.

Additionally, for several years leading up to 1929, Congressmen, Federal Reserve officials and Hoover openly criticized what they saw as the exorbitantly over-priced heights reached by the stock market. In February of 1929, the Fed made a rare public announcement: it would pressure banks to restrict loans to investors buying stock on margin (although this was a small fraction of investors.)

Starting in February of 1928 and continuing throughout 1929, the

Fed continued to raise the interest rate it charged for the borrowings of member banks, increasing it from 3.5% to 4% to 5% and, in August of 1929, to 6%. "This was a punitive policy." For, it sought to limit the funds available for investment, despite the booming productivity of the American economy. Throughout 1929, "the Fed became increasingly obsessed with the stock market and its so-called 'speculative excesses.' The Fed fixated on ways to curb otherwise perfectly legitimate stock gains." Such policies and pronouncements showed that the government held the belief that the stock market can go "too high," that the stocks of superbly productive and profitable companies could be over-valued. In short, the Fed conducted a relentless campaign against the market's properly bullish attitudes that, tragically, contributed to the crash. "Precisely because the gains were extraordinary, rather-ordinary observers could not fully comprehend (or believe) them. Instead they resorted to doubting the gains — or ridiculing them…"

Business economist Richard Salsman points out: "Central banking…is a feature of statism — not capitalism." The Federal Reserve System is America's version of it; but through much of the 1920s it exerted relatively little influence. By the end of the decade, however, the Fed was seeking to curb the stock market boom, to intercede aggressively and arbitrarily "in matters that previously had been left to market professionals." Now the central bankers would control the stock market as they thought best. "No fully private, capitalist banking system could ever wield such power — or ever become so arbitrary. Capitalism has no 'official' credit policy to which all must conform — or else suffer."30

Today, it is certain that the growing preponderance of professional economists agree on two broad points: it was government intervention in some form — not the free market — that initiated the crash and, similarly, it was statism that exacerbated the depression, causing it to last for an agonizing decade, even into the 1940s. As contemporary economist, Gene Smiley, stated: "The 1930s economic crisis is tragic testimony to

government interference in market economies."[31]

An important part of the statist catastrophe was the extensive string of bank failures that caused individuals to lose their savings and wrecked the local economy in many parts of the country. "Between 1929 and 1933 there were 9,765 bank failures in the United States," 90% of which were in small towns. The cause of the problem was that too often small town bankers believed that "competition and big-city bankers were their enemies." They successfully lobbied in many states for unit banking laws, which prohibited a bank from opening branches. Many small-town banks then found it difficult to "diversify their loan portfolios and their sources of deposit." Often their clients were farmers. When hard times for agriculture struck, and farmers withdrew their deposits or struggled to repay their loans, many one-unit banks could not survive. Not surprisingly, "almost all the failed banks were in states with unit banking laws that suppressed competition." By contrast, during the same depression years, not a single Canadian bank failed. In Canada, where there were no unit banking laws and branch banking was legally permitted, the banks were better able to diversify their investments and sources of deposit, and therefore able to survive when a specific industry or region experienced hard times.[32]

Further, the Hoover administration proceeded to impose massive government intervention on the economy, i.e., more of the problem's cause. The president applied pressure on business leaders to keep prices and wages high – at exactly the time when they needed to fall – and to keep increasing capital outlay – at a time when capital needed to be accumulated. Hoover, with the creation of the Farm Board, put the U.S. government into the wheat business, again attempting to artificially hold up prices at a time when they most needed to fall.

But worst of all, the Smoot-Hawley Tariff Act ushered in a worldwide trend toward protectionism at exactly the moment when international free trade was most urgently needed. Virtually all of the nation's

leading economists urged Hoover to veto the tariff, but he left their advice unheeded. The result of these and other interventionist follies was that business activity continued to decline until it reached the Depression's lowest ebb in 1932.

Hoover pushed burdensome tax increases on the country in 1932, one resulting in a doubling of federal personal income tax rates. Such a policy, of course, left that much less money available for investment in productive enterprises. Hoover significantly increased government spending for social welfare programs, so that between 1930 and 1931 "the federal government's share of GNP soared from 16.4 percent to 21.5 percent." Revealingly, Rexford Tugwell, one of FDR's top advisers, stated decades later: "We didn't admit it at the time, but practically the whole New Deal was extrapolated from programs that Hoover started."[33]

In one of the tragic ironies of economic history, Hoover – an unremitting interventionist, and original architect of policies that, later, under Roosevelt, became known as the New Deal – is known historically as an advocate of laissez-faire. Indeed, for several years, Hoover served in Calvin Coolidge's administration, lobbying ceaselessly for greater government intervention in the marketplace. Coolidge, in general an advocate of capitalism, remarked: "For six years that man has given me unsolicited advice – all of it bad."[34]

Though FDR generally blasted the free market system in his 1932 campaign, he occasionally uttered pro-capitalist statements, promising to reduce government intervention and spending, thereby permitting the private sector the unhampered opportunity to recover. "During the campaign, Roosevelt blasted Hoover for spending and taxing too much, boosting the national debt, choking off trade, and putting millions on the dole. He accused the president of 'reckless and extravagant' spending, of thinking 'that we ought to center control of everything in Washington as rapidly as possible,' and of presiding over 'the greatest spending administration in peacetime in all of history.'"

John Nance Garner, FDR's running mate, accused Hoover of "leading the country down the path of socialism." Roosevelt and Garner were right, and some of their campaign promises contained sound economic reasoning. However, Roosevelt was a notorious liar, whose behavior in a 1919 Naval Training Station scandal was described by an investigating Senate subcommittee as "immoral." Further, he was "always, by family tradition, training, instinct, and conviction, anti-business..." so it is not surprising that, in office, Roosevelt did a 180-degree about face, repudiated his semi-free market mouthings, and continued and heightened Hoover's interventionist programs.[35]

The interventionist schemes of the Roosevelt administration were an unmitigated economic disaster. Suffice it to say that by 1937, after more than four years of Roosevelt's policies (and after eight years of the combined Hoover-Roosevelt New Deal) – after the National Industrial Recovery Act, the abandonment of the gold standard, the tripling of taxes, more labor legislation and many similar acts of governmental interference – unemployment rose to more than ten million, and business activity fell virtually to the same low reached in 1932.

As one accomplished American economist described it: "Governmental economic planning is back seat driving by a man who doesn't know how to drive and who...doesn't know where he wants to go." The result is that one gets hopelessly lost – and that is certainly what happened to the United States under the interventionist policies of Hoover and Roosevelt.[36]

One leading example of the Roosevelt economic debacle was the National Recovery Administration (NRA). It was enacted into law by the National Industrial Recovery Act (NIRA) in June, 1933, and forced most manufacturing industries into government-controlled cartels. "Codes that regulated prices and terms of sale briefly transformed much of the American economy into a fascist-style arrangement..." a system perfect for Roosevelt's hand-picked director, General Hugh "Iron Pants"

Johnson, a bullying, self-professed admirer of Mussolini, who personally threatened to sock in the nose anyone failing to comply with NRA dictates.

There were regulatory codes and price controls for hundreds of industries, "covering more than 2 million employers and 22 million workers." Jack Magid, a New Jersey tailor was jailed for pressing clothes for 35 cents, 5 cents cheaper than permitted by the NRA. Many Americans violated these dictatorial laws, and a black market formed. To combat it, the NRA cracked down. Its police "roamed through the garment district like storm troopers. They could enter a man's factory...line up his employees, subject them to minute interrogation, take over his books on the instant. Night work was forbidden." Squadrons of officers battered down doors with axes, searching "for men who were committing the crime of sewing together a pair of pants at night." Understandably, the United States Supreme Court outlawed the NRA as unconstitutional in 1935 (as the High Court did with other of FDR's programs.)

But despite the Court's protection of individual rights, Roosevelt's policies wreaked terrible harm on the economy. The prohibitively high tax rates, the endless regulations, the wasteful spending of the Works Progress Administration (WPA), etc., severely damaged the business climate and undercut any significant recovery. In 1938, for example, unemployment climbed back up to 20 percent: 11,800,000 Americans were out of work, more than the 11,385,000 that were unemployed when Roosevelt was first elected in 1932.

"The stock market crashed nearly 50 percent between August 1937 and March 1938." Further, "from 1934 to 1940, the median annual unemployment rate was 17.2 percent. At no point during the 1930s did unemployment go below 14 percent." Indeed, on the eve of America's entry into World War II in 1941, twelve years after the 1929 stock market crash, and more than eight years after Roosevelt's assumption of office, ten million Americans were still unemployed.

FDR's policies were, for years, aggressively anti-business. "The Roosevelt administration proposed and Congress enacted an unparalleled outpouring of laws that significantly attenuated private property rights." Further, the endless anti-business, anti-private-property legislation was accompanied by a similarly-virulent rhetoric. In 1936, FDR railed against "economic royalists," who, he claimed, sought to establish a "new industrial dictatorship." Speaking before a roaring crowd at Madison Square Garden, he ripped the masters of "organized money...[who were] united in their hate for me." He promised: "I should like to have it said of my second Administration that in it these forces met their master."

The Supreme Court's opposition to some of FDR's most flagrant violations of economic liberty led to his infamous "court-packing" scheme. To dilute the power of his opponents on the High Court, the president proposed legislation that, in effect, would have permitted him to appoint an additional six justices who, presumably, would have sided with New Deal policies. To their credit, many Democratic members of Congress, though favoring New Deal legislation, recognized the blatant attempt to bend the judiciary to the power of the chief executive, and balked, voting to preserve the Constitution's system of checks and balances.

Though his court-packing scheme was defeated, FDR did in the years following manage to gain greater influence over the Supreme Court. Perhaps just as important regarding economic recovery, he understandably convinced many Americans that he sought unconstitutional semi-autocratic powers.[37]

Businessmen and investors were justifiably scared by the combination of interventionist action and anti-capitalist talk. A 1939 public opinion poll showed that 54 percent of Americans believed that the administration's attitude toward business was delaying economic recovery – while only 26 percent thought not. In the same year, almost 65 percent of businessmen polled held that FDR's policies had severely undermined business confidence and held back recovery.

Refuting the Economic Charges Against Capitalism

Many Americans found Roosevelt so unremitting a statist that they feared an end to or massive undermining of the free enterprise system. "Many businesspeople, among others, had feared that FDR harbored dictatorial ambition." It was an understandable conclusion, for, in effect, the New Deal was America's (less virulent) version of the statism that was sweeping so many countries of Europe. In short, the government's policies created an economic atmosphere in which potential investors were not willing to risk their money. The "Roosevelt recession" of 1938, sometimes referred to as "a depression within a depression," was accompanied by a sharp drop in private investment. Because of this, the economy was deprived of the funds it needed for growth.

Full recovery from the Depression, i.e., a return to prosperity, was not achieved until after World War II. To be blunt, President Truman was not on a crusade against "economic royalists," i.e., the wealthy. Though much of the New Deal legislation remained on the books, the Truman administration's rhetoric and policies did not exude the overtones of class warfare. To some degree, the increasing Congressional power of the Conservative Coalition, made up of Republicans and Southern Democrats, stymied "most efforts to extend the New Deal domestically." But additionally, Truman himself fired or accepted the resignation of "a host of New Dealers," often replacing them with Missouri cronies less ideologically opposed to business.

It is unfortunately easy to underestimate the importance of the psychological atmosphere created by a government's programs and attitudes. Private investment is the fuel that drives economic progress. It is of the first importance that investors are confident the government will protect, rather than undermine or expropriate their property rights. In an atmosphere of fear that property rights will be increasingly abrogated, they will not invest.

Post-war polls showed that businessmen overwhelmingly believed Truman was more favorable to the private property system than

[385]

Roosevelt. "'For most business leaders, the mood during the first couple of years after V-J Day was one of cautious confidence and optimism,' a far different mood from that of business leaders between 1935 and 1941." With Republicans again influential in Congress, and with a moderately, rather than a rabidly statist president, times were once again propitious for investment.

The economic facts bear out this assessment. In 1929, for example, gross private investment reached almost 16% of GDP; it fell to less than 2% in 1932; recovered somewhat during the later years of the decade; but never again reached 16% until 1946. During the 1930s, net private investment declined by $3.1 billion. "The data leave little doubt. During the 1930s, private investment remained at depths never plumbed in any other decade for which data exist...Only in 1946 and the following years did private investment reach and remain at levels consistent with a prosperous and growing economy." The economist, Lester Chandler, makes the point succinctly: "The failure of the New Deal to bring about an adequate revival of private investment is the key to its failure to achieve a complete and self-sustaining recovery of output and employment."

But there is a perhaps more important factor. Capitalism's greatest advances are based on inventions and innovations, on technological and industrial progress. Are these compatible with the unremitting statism of the New Deal? How, for example, would Thomas Edison fare under the NRA or some similar coercive policy? Edison often worked 18 hours per day. Would "Iron Pants" Johnson have him arrested for working nights?

Under programs of government intervention, the productive process is governed by the judgment of such statist politicians and bureaucrats as FDR and General Johnson, not by that of thinkers like the Inventive Period's pioneering geniuses. To the degree that men of physical force control a political-economic system, to that degree the men of creative mind power are shackled. To that same degree, then, men should expect the process of wealth creation to be curtailed. If governmental policy dis-

allows the cause of wealth, then it *ipso facto* eliminates the effect. The increasingly statist policies of the Hoover-Roosevelt era did more than curb investment; they curbed creativity.

The factors responsible for initiating, aggravating, and extending the worst depression of American history should be noted. Such policies as central banking in the form of the Federal Reserve System, the Smoot-Hawley Tariff Act, state laws prohibiting branch banking, the cartelization of American business by the NRA, the abrogation of the gold standard, the seizure of American gold, heavier taxes, etc., were far-reaching policies of the state. They were universally applicable, as programs responsible for wrecking a nation's entire economy would have to be. In the words of a contemporary economist, the Great Depression "was prolonged and exacerbated by a litany of political missteps: trade-crushing tariffs, incentive-sapping taxes, mind-numbing controls on production and competition...It was not the free market which produced 12 years of agony; rather, it was political bungling on a scale as grand as there ever was."38

Private business(es) have neither the coercive power nor the extensive influence to reach their tentacles into every area of the economy, causing widespread bank failures, pervasive monetary mismanagement, production-strangling regulations, erosion of investor confidence and a shattering stock market crash. Mismanaged private companies can fail, harming their shareholders, suppliers, customers and employees, but they lack the legal authority and the nationwide jurisdiction necessary to profoundly damage the financial status of virtually every citizen of the country. Only the government possesses sufficient power to wreak such havoc.

The Failure of Government Intervention

A mixed economy, in contrast to a laissez-faire system, suffers from coercive monopolies, the abrogation of the gold standard, inflation, tariffs, regulation and cartelization of industry, unemployment, depressions

and a host of other economic ailments. Notice the essence of various governmental interventions in the marketplace.

Entrepreneurs are legally restricted from entering a given field because of an exclusive franchise granted to a rival. The central bank can expand the money supply, debase the monetary standard and erode the value of men's savings. Customers must pay higher prices for imported goods — and the cost of domestic producers doing business overseas will increase as other nations impose retaliatory tariffs. Significant numbers of individuals able and willing to work will not be able to find employment. Taxes of all kinds are levied and are always subject to increase. Economic readjustments that, on a free market, would be brief recessions are transformed by governmental mismanagement into severe and extended depressions. The litany is endless.

The common thread uniting these examples and others is: a war on producers and production. To legally ban entrepreneurs from a field, to undermine the value of men's savings, to price productive men and women out of the labor market, etc., is, ultimately, to "accomplish" one goal: the curtailment of productivity.

The essence of the government is a legal monopoly on the use of force. The government renders an invaluable boon to productivity by protecting the rights of the men and women of the mind responsible for creating abundance. But the government itself cannot create abundance. *Force can be protective but it is not productive.* By its nature, it cannot contribute to the creative process. The retaliatory use of force against those who initiate it will protect producers — but its initiation will only undermine them; the more extensive such initiation, the more widespread the undermining. Mixed economies, therefore, are vastly more productive than totalitarian states; but vastly less so than those closest to a laissez-faire policy. For example, given the low-level technological and industrial baseline from which America of the Inventive Period started, the creativity and productivity of that society — the freest of history — was

prodigious.

An examination of the economic hardships generally ascribed to capitalism reveal two related conclusions: these problems occur under mixed economies, not under laissez-faire; and as a result of the statist component of the mixture, not the free one.

Summary

All of the economic ills commonly ascribed to capitalism are caused by its antipode — by statism.

Coercive monopolies are formed by governments legally debarring entry into a field. Unemployment is caused by minimum wage laws and laws granting coercive power to unions. Inflation is government expansion of the money supply leading to the debasement of the monetary standard. Finally, depressions are caused by a series of regulations and interventions that strangle an economy, e.g., the tariffs, taxes, restrictions on banks, etc., of the combined Hoover-Roosevelt New Deal that caused, exacerbated and extended the Great Depression.

Afterword:
The Great Disconnect Revisited

Given the disastrous consequences of FDR's programs, why the pervasive myths regarding his heroism? Even today, it is still proclaimed that "his policies got us out of the Depression" or that "he saved capitalism." For example, the historian, Eric Hobsbawm, recently stated that the Great Depression "had been due to the failure of the unrestricted free market" - and that the post-War success of capitalism was a result of governmental "economic management," or, put "in American terms [of] Rooseveltian New Deal policy, with substantial borrowings from the USSR[!]" The carefully-researched conclusions of the economists demonstrate such claims to be diametrically opposed to the truth. Why their popularity among historians and writers who continue to lionize Roosevelt?

The answer is that Roosevelt, many of his advisors and assistants, and their admiring biographers and historians share(d) the same altruist-collectivist-statist philosophy. As merely one important example, Rexford Tugwell, an influential member of FDR's "Brain Trust," was a socialist who visited and admired the Soviet Union, and who advocated such policies of central planning as the NRA.

To contemporary collectivist intellectuals, the New Deal represented a noble attempt to restrain the "greed" of the capitalist system and to pro-

mote policies of "social justice and equality." These programs may have been an abject economic failure but — to their supporters — they were a resounding moral triumph. Today's committed collectivist intellectuals so admire New Deal principles that they are blind to New Deal consequences. Faced with the stark alternative between their theory and practice, they choose their theory. A zealous allegiance to their moral code trumps facts. Their philosophical premises make it impossible for them to either understand or appreciate capitalism. In short, the Great Disconnect is responsible for the continued hagiographies regarding Roosevelt.

This principle has vastly broader applications and can be re-examined now in light of the material in this book.

It has been shown that capitalism brought freedom to millions suffering under the remnants of feudalism, and that, from the Industrial Revolution's earliest days, brought the beginnings of relief from the ubiquitous and crushing poverty that was feudalism's economic legacy. The system of individual rights and political/economic liberty grew directly from the Enlightenment glorification of the mind and the individual; and that period, so influenced by its mind-and-life-affirming philosophy, saw the rise of the self-made man — the man of genius, of drive, and of low-born origin, who, during the Industrial Revolution and America's Inventive Period, began to remake the world.

It has been seen that both the moral and economic transgressions that capitalism has been charged with are, without exception, the product of its antithesis — statism. The capitalist nations are uniformly and simultaneously the freest and the wealthiest countries of history. Their antipodes, the statist regimes, are, to the degree of their statism, politically repressed and economically backward.

Above all, it has been shown that the political-economic system of capitalism rests logically on a deeper moral philosophy upholding egoism, rationality as the cardinal virtue, and man's life as the standard of

value; that when this philosophy is uppermost in human society, at least implicitly, and only when it is, society will flourish.

Fewer than three centuries ago, the Western world was brutally repressed and unspeakably poor. Today, these nations are the freest and wealthiest of history. The rarefied heights to which the Capitalist Revolution brought men, in an amount of time amounting to a historical blink of the eye, is a staggering achievement; one wrought by the minds and works of giants.

But today, an anti-hero mentality dominates, and giants are neither sought nor admired. Biographers of great men seek a "balanced account," as if the full truth regarding their subjects is necessarily mixed, a middle ground between achievements and flaws.

But the important truths of life are absolute and extreme, not middle-of-the-road amalgams of opposites. The earth, in fact, is spherical; not half flat and half round. It does not revolve around the sun on Monday, Wednesday and Friday, only to see the reverse transpire on Tuesday and Thursday. Nazis, Communists, Islamists, and all murderers are 100% evil, not mixtures of good and bad.

The thinkers who regard capitalism, or the individual heroes of capitalism, as mixed cases are profoundly mistaken. Freedom has no downside — and the mistakes made by the productive geniuses, whatever their nature, pale to inconsequential details relative to the enormity of their live-giving achievements.

The above combination of points makes an integrated and rationally-unanswerable case for capitalism. But will this change the minds of freedom's enemies?

Here is a challenge presented respectfully to the most honest and humanistic individuals among capitalism's critics. After 200 years of capitalism, 80 years of socialism and millennia of statism more broadly, there can no longer be any doubt that capitalism, and its philosophical antecedents, constitute the only moral-political-economic system that

promotes man's life on earth. Thousands of years of political history serving as a vast laboratory produce no facts showing otherwise.

The altruist-collectivist-statist philosophical axis is a thoroughly false, bankrupt ideology that reached its inevitable and gruesome climax in the 20th century doctrines and practices of National Socialism and Communism. Mixed systems simply mix in elements of such poison with better ones.

Socialist intellectuals still cling to socialism solely because of their commitment to this ideology. The evil of its theory has been exposed by Ayn Rand's analysis; of its practice, by history and current events. Early in the 21st century, commitment to it is exclusively an act of faith in its literal epistemological meaning: acceptance of an idea not merely in the absence of supporting evidence but in defiance of overwhelming evidence to the contrary.

It is time for such socialist thinkers to exercise the rational judgment and free will that is theirs by virtue of their humanity — and to change their minds.

There is still time to save the world. Indeed, there will always be time; for the human capacity to reason, and the yearning for freedom and prosperity, will survive as long as humanity itself; no degree of irrational philosophy or repressive government will suffice to stamp these out.

A necessary component of making mankind's future far brighter than its past or present is to identify and embrace the only political system consonant with the requirements of human life. It is time to finally repudiate the altruist-collectivist-statist code and thereby to eliminate the great historical disconnect between the facts of capitalism's performance and its moral evaluation by men. Better belatedly than never to celebrate the life-giving code of egoism-individualism-capitalism.

Appendix: Robber Barons or Productive Geniuses

The same historians who refer to late-19th century America as "The Gilded Age" term its leading industrialists and capitalists "Robber Barons."

That American inventors and designers of this era – many of whom became successful entrepreneurs and businessmen – helped revolutionize the country's material standard of living is not to be doubted. But what of the towering figures in heavy industry – in steel, oil and railroading – and the capitalists who financed them? It is often claimed that Andrew Carnegie, John D. Rockefeller, Cornelius Vanderbilt, James J. Hill, Edward H. Harriman and J.P. Morgan used immoral, fraudulent, even violent methods to accumulate great wealth. To understand the history and the nature of capitalism, it is important to identify the truth of such claims.

Above all, the questions to be answered are: When judged by the standard of man's life, were the business activities of these men good or evil? Did their dealings advance or retard man's quest for values? Put simply: were they productive giants or exploitative leeches?

Anti-capitalist intellectuals are vivid in their portrayal of fraud and peculation among the leading business figures of the era.

> Analyze the most talked-of men of the age and one is likely to find a splendid audacity coupled with an immense

wastefulness. A note of tough-mindedness marks them. They had stout nippers. They fought their way encased in rhinoceros hides. There was the Wall Street crowd – Daniel Drew, Commodore Vanderbilt, Jim Fisk, Jay Gould, Russell Sage – blackguards for the most part, railway wreckers, cheaters and swindlers, but picturesque in their rascality.

The distinguished historian, Charles Beard, stated that "beyond all question an enormous proportion of the capital amassed between 1860 and the end of the century represented profits from protective tariffs, from natural resources fraudulently or surreptitiously acquired, and from water [i.e. dilution of value] injected into industrial and railway corporations." The barons of capitalism would "sometimes hire strong-arm men to help them seize the property of a coveted company; and occasionally they planned real battles among workingmen in an effort to appropriate a railway or pipe line."

Regarding Rockefeller's rise, he wrote: "All through this drama, from the start, dishonesty, chicane, lying, vulgarity, and a fierce passion for lucre" were evident, though admittedly combined with better elements.[1]

Such accusations need to be examined in the broader context of the Inventive Period. In the torrent of forward motion in this era, pathbreaking innovations were not limited to the inventors. There were other advances in addition to the creation of new devices and the improvement of earlier designs. Inventions become widely valuable only to the extent that they are successfully introduced to the marketplace – and it is not always the case that inventors themselves have the necessary business acumen to accomplish that. Edison, for one, did; many do not.

It was more common for changes in technology to be introduced by men who were not themselves inventors, but who, nonetheless, had sufficient knowledge of the economic potential of critical changes to introduce those changes suc-

cessfully...The 'innovators' who built the foundations of many of the nation's industries were primarily men who bridged the gap between the technological advances of the inventors and effective economic change.

In this regard, American entrepreneurs made breakthroughs in the field of heavy industry that revolutionized the way people lived.[2]

For example, Andrew Carnegie's life was everything the legends about him claim. The son of a poor Scottish weaver, he emigrated with his family to America at age 12. On board ship, while the other passengers suffered from seasickness, young Carnegie delighted the sailors with his boundless energy – and by learning many details of seamanship and assisting the undermanned crew. Shortly after, in Pittsburgh, he got a job as a factory boy for $1.20 per week, and within three years earned more money than either of his parents – though both worked – and became "the main support of the family."

When 13 years old, determined to rise, he traveled into Pittsburgh two or three nights a week to study double-entry bookkeeping with an accountant. Later, when a messenger boy, he was required to be at work an hour early to sweep out the office. He raced through his chores and then dashed into the telegraph operating room to study the instruments. "In a twinkling the boy had learned the Morse alphabet." When no operators were present, he had the temerity to take an emergency message himself. Shortly after, when a seasoned operator who resented his young colleague's new importance, refused to transcribe dots and dashes, Andrew astonished the office staff by calmly taking the message by ear. "According to authentic history, Andrew Carnegie was the third operator in the United States to take messages 'by sound.'"

He had little formal schooling, but became a voracious reader of serious literature – Shakespeare and Robert Burns were his favorites – a lover and patron of the arts, and the author of a dozen books and countless articles. When still a youth, his extraordinary talents and ambition

enabled him to rise as an employee of the Pennsylvania Railroad. Early in the Civil War, Carnegie – a devout abolitionist – worked hard to keep in repair the telegraph lines for Union forces. In 1862 at age 26, weak from sunstroke and overwork, he took the first vacation of his life *after 14 years of continuous effort.*

Carnegie was already wealthy by the time he went into steel. Though later famous for the saying, "Pioneering don't pay," large parts of his career belie that claim. He innovated at every level of his working life, starting with a pooling method he devised as a messenger boy to dole out "bonus" money in an equitable way that avoided quarrels among the boys. When he was employed by the railroad, Theodore Woodruff approached him with an original idea for railway sleeping cars in which he instantly saw value. He successfully pressed his superiors to adopt the innovation – and his investment in Woodruff's firm was the beginning of Carnegie's fortune.

Later, he convinced George Pullman – a late arriving but inventive and industrious force in the sleeping car business – to merge the two companies, to the betterment of all parties. In 1859, after Colonel E.L. Drake's famous drilling of oil in Western Pennsylvania, Carnegie recognized the opportunities and – despite the bumps and knocks of the rough journey – rushed to the region. The Storey farm that he purchased for $40,000 was soon worth $5,000,000 – and "he had made a comfortable fortune in oil when the name of Rockefeller was unknown."

But his great work was coming. Recognizing that railroads would soon sweep the vast American West, and that they would require enormous quantities of iron, he organized the Keystone Bridge Company of Pittsburgh to construct iron railroad bridges to replace the outmoded wooden ones. Carnegie was justly proud that, in contrast to those of wood, not one of his iron bridges ever collapsed. In the 1860s, he organized another company to manufacture iron rails and two years later established the Pittsburgh Locomotive Works. In 1866, as soon as patent liti-

gation permitted it, he began converting his Freedom Iron Company into plants capable of producing the new Bessemer steel. In 1872, after visiting an English Bessemer plant, he realized he needed "an entirely new mill with the most up-to-date equipment available" to produce steel in vast quantities. This was the future – and Carnegie early on recognized it. Despite his partners' lack of confidence, Carnegie insisted that "we must start the manufacture of steel rails, and start at once." He founded a new company, the Edgar Thomson Steel Company – named after his friend, the president of the Pennsylvania Railroad – to do exactly that.

His genius manifested itself in a hundred ways. He boldly expanded business operations during depressions when others merely sought to ride out the storm. He kept careful watch over a diverse array of companies, "any one of which could have provided him with a full-time career." He possessed an extraordinary grasp of human beings and an unsurpassed eye for talent and initiative: "one of his innovations was a system of 'promotion within the ranks,'" whereby he sought, cultivated and rewarded one critical human trait: productive ability. He was a fiend for cutting cost, delighting in "tearing down antiquated structures and replacing them with new" and was willing to spend great sums of money "to improve the productive efficiency of his enterprises and thereby reduce his operating costs."

He was first to employ a chemist at the mills to improve the quality of cheaper ore. He took the lead in introducing open hearth furnaces in America. He purchased the American rights to a new steelmaking process devised by an English experimenter, Sidney Gilchrist-Thomas, though the prestigious Iron and Steel Institute of London rejected it, and successfully employed it in his open hearth furnaces. "No one was...more willing to embrace each new business or technological opportunity than Carnegie."

The adoption of the Bessemer process was a major innovation. Henry Bessemer (1813-1898), though born in rural England and pos-

sessing only a grammar school education, was a successful inventor who created a new method of making steel. Previously, the steel manufacturing process required days of effort by skilled workers and large amounts of fuel. The result was a brittle steel costing $300.00 per ton. The Bessemer method, which involved the injection of cold air into the blast furnaces, resulted in a tougher steel of uniform quality made in twenty minutes. This enormous reduction in labor and fuel meant that steel could sell for merely $50.00 per ton. Bessemer's advance made him the "Father of the Steel Age." Though many metallurgists deemed the new process impossible when they heard of it, Carnegie saw its merits. He and his partners bought out other steel producers and converted their plants to Bessemer's process. Simultaneously, they developed new methods of making "the process simpler, quicker and cheaper."

Carnegie produced steel for the Brooklyn Bridge, for the New York subways, for railroads, for the Washington Monument and for the U.S. Navy. His furnaces produced "nearly one-third of America's output and they set the standards of quality and price." In the three decades from 1870 to 1900 the American production of steel rose from 69 thousand tons to more than 10 million tons per year. Prices, of course, dropped accordingly – steel rails, for example, which were $160 per ton in 1875 cost only $17 a ton in 1898.

Carnegie himself described the "eighth wonder of the world": iron ore, coal, limestone and manganese mined in diverse geographic locations, then shipped to Pittsburgh and manufactured into "one pound of solid steel...sold for one cent." Such savings spurred construction of every kind in America – including of office buildings, apartment houses, automobiles and later trucks, railroads, farm equipment, etc. – to the immense material betterment of virtually every man, woman and child in the country. A student of history might look far to find another single individual who so contributed to the economic prosperity of his fellow man.[3]

Robber Barons or Productive Geniuses

Unless, that is, he turned his gaze from Pittsburgh to Cleveland of that same era – and to the life and work of John D. Rockefeller. Rockefeller matched Carnegie barrel of oil for ton of steel, and between the two of them they created the indispensable necessities of modern industrial civilization – building material and fuel. Their lifespans largely paralleled each other's – Carnegie's 1835-1919, Rockefeller's 1839-1937, so that for 80 years they were peers. They were the greatest productive geniuses the world has seen, but as men they couldn't have been more different: Carnegie the secular humanist and agnostic, Rockefeller the devout Baptist – Carnegie the lover of literature, the arts, philosophy and high culture, Rockefeller's interests confined to business, family and religion – Carnegie the ebullient friend of princes and presidents, an accomplished raconteur and a quenchless fountain of bonhomie, Rockefeller at home mostly with his family and in church. Harvey Firestone, the tire manufacturer, said it; Carnegie and Rockefeller proved it: "Thought, not money, is the real business capital." Together, they made the United States the greatest industrial power and wealthiest nation of history.

The oil magnate's career, like the steel baron's, began inauspiciously. His father was an itinerant peddler and scamp in western New York State, although able to support his family; young John D. was not poor in childhood. Nevertheless, the father was mysteriously absent for long periods of time, and John D. had to begin full-time work in 1855 as an assistant bookkeeper at age 16 for roughly $4 per week. Rockefeller was fanatical about honest business dealings – even his worst enemies acknowledged that his word was always good. His first partner claimed: "If there was a cent due us he wanted it. If there was a cent due a customer he wanted the customer to have it."

In the late 1850s, such innovative Americans as George Bissell and Benjamin Silliman – Professor of Chemistry at Yale – pioneered the understanding that, if refined, the oil that had oozed to the surface and troubled farmers for decades in Western Pennsylvania made a superb illu-

minant, besides yielding useful by-products. When E.L. Drake became the first to successfully drill for oil in 1859, the oil rush and age dawned. But the early period of the oil industry in the 1860s was rough-hewn chaos. Adventurers and fortune seekers of all kinds descended on the Oil Regions, much as they did during a gold rush. Waste was rampant. Fortunes were made and lost virtually overnight. By contrast, the foundation of Rockefeller's extraordinary later success was his painstaking devotion to detail, to efficiency, to the arduous task of extirpating waste.

Rockefeller chose the refining end of the business and his home town of Cleveland – with its advantages of Lake port and multiple railroads – as his base. He then declared war on waste. He and his partner, Samuel Andrews, sought ways to get more kerosene per barrel of crude oil. They "searched for uses for the by-products: they used the gasoline for fuel, some of the tars for paving, and shipped the naptha to gas plants. They also sold lubricating oil, vaseline and paraffin for making candles." By contrast, some of his competitors let their gasoline, "for which the market was not yet developed," run into the Cuyahoga River, supplying sport for tugboat men who would throw overboard a shovelful of hot coals to set the water ablaze.

Like Carnegie, Rockefeller was a stickler for cutting costs. He built his refineries efficiently and saved on insurance. He employed his own plumbers and "almost halved the cost on labor, pipes, and plumbing material." Barrels for oil cost $2.50 a piece; but by buying his own timber, kilns and wagons for transportation, Rockefeller reduced the cost per unit to 96 cents. He plowed his profits back into the business, buying bigger and better equipment, generating significant economies of scale. He hired chemists to develop hundreds of new by-products from each barrel of oil, including paint, varnish and lubricants.

One, a brilliant German immigrant named Herman Frasch, worked out a process that enabled Standard Oil to profitably market millions of barrels of Lima-Ohio oil that, because of high sulphur content, was orig-

inally "foul-smelling crude" and therefore unusable. Rockefeller and his partners "manufactured their own sulphuric acid, and devised means for recovering it after use." Further, they were "among the first to ship by tank cars," an economical means of transportation; by 1869, they already owned 78 such cars. They built tanks for storing both crude and refined oil, and no longer had to rely on barrels like the small firms.

By these methods he became the most successful refiner, and was able to buy out many smaller competitors when hard economic times caused them to struggle in the early 1870s. The enormous quantities he could then ship enabled him to demand and receive the largest rebates, i.e., the lowest transportation costs from railroads. Rebates were a common feature of American business at that time, brought on by the intense competition between railroads for heavy freight traffic. Nobody had the goods to turn the practice to his advantage like Rockefeller. And nobody was as remorseless – his enemies said ruthless – in using every advantage to dominate and then absorb weaker competitors.

But the most telling truth is that nobody knew the oil industry like he did either – from the big picture to the last detail. Over the years, Rockefeller brought together a dazzling array of brilliant men whose talents he harmonized into a single cooperative effort. These executives "all recognized that Rockefeller was an expert in management, that he knew the refineries down to the last pipe and vat, that he had full information upon cooperage, shipping, purchasing, buying, and the manufacture of by-products." They knew also that when emergencies struck, Rockefeller left his desk, rolled up his sleeves and went to work in the plants, yards and in the freight cars.

The great brainpower of Rockefeller and his associates was recognized by other leading businessmen. William Vanderbilt said: "I never came into contact with any class of men as smart and able as they are in business, and I think a great deal is to be attributed to that." John Archbold, a president of Standard Oil, stated: "In business we all try to

look ahead as much as possible. Some of us think we are pretty able. But Rockefeller always sees a little further ahead than any of us – and then he sees around the corner."

Such foresight served Rockefeller well in Standard's struggle for European markets against Russian oil fields operated in large part by the Nobel brothers. Believing that Standard could dominate in Europe despite the Russians' geographical advantage, Rockefeller made his company even more productive. He spurred his research team to perfect large steamship tankers and to devise new processes by which to get even more useful products from a barrel of oil. He re-intensified his quest for efficiency: "In a classic move, he used the waste (culm) from coal heaps to fuel his refineries." Such tactics enabled Rockefeller to sell oil for mere pennies a gallon and and often capture "two-thirds of the world's oil trade from 1882 to 1891..."

The final result of Rockefeller's genius was inexpensive oil for the common man. By the mid-1880s, Standard Oil controlled 90 percent of America's refining industry and "had pushed the price down from 58 cents to eight cents a gallon." Rockefeller wrote one of his partners: "We must...remember we are refining oil for the poor man and he must have it cheap and good."

Millions were now illuminating their homes for "one cent an hour" with the inexpensive kerosene made available by Standard Oil – and for many Americans "working and reading became after-dark activities" for the first time. By the 1880s oil stoves were widely used in the United States, particularly in rural regions, and also depended largely on Rockefeller's company for affordable fuel. Later, Standard's supply of cheap gasoline played a significant part in Henry Ford's ability to dramatically upgrade America's system of personal transportation. Rockefeller, like Carnegie, was more than a self-made man; he was a creative genius of the material, not the spiritual, realm – but a creative genius in his own field each was, every bit as much as were Michelangelo and Leonardo in

theirs. These were producers on a grand scale whose achievements made millions of human beings immeasurably wealthier.[4]

The railroads, at their best, were key players in this drama of American development. For example, in his old age, when most men are retired, Cornelius Vanderbilt shifted his focus from the steamboat to the railroad industry. In 1865, when he was 71, his net worth was approximately $10 million; at his death in 1877, after a decade of furious activity in the railroad business, it was $104 million.

Vanderbilt was as profane as any of his yard hands and possessed an ungovernable temper; at times he was a swaggering bully; he built statues of himself, printed his picture on bonds, and proposed to New York City a monument to commemorate his accomplishments equally with those of George Washington. But as a railroad man in the immediate post-bellum years he had no peer. In building up the New York Central and other roads he acquired, he reduced freight rates on the Central by 22 percent in two years. He "ripped up the old iron rails and re-laid them with steel, put down four tracks where formerly there had been two, replaced wooden bridges with steel, discarded the old locomotives for new and more powerful ones, built splendid new terminals, introduced economies in a hundred directions, cut down the hours required in a New York-Chicago trip from fifty to twenty-four, made his highway an expeditious line for transporting freight," and made reliable, convenient, long-distance rail service a reality.[5]

But the greatest achievements of railroad building belonged to James Jerome Hill (1838-1916), who constructed his Great Northern Railroad from St. Paul, Minnesota to Seattle, Washington – a line constructed entirely from private investment. The railroads built with government aid and land grants – the Union Pacific, the Northern Pacific and others – ended in bankruptcy. Generally, they received subsidies based on the miles of track laid, a policy that encouraged hurried, not careful, construction. One American historian characterizes the process by which a

government-backed businessman built his line: "he rushed into the wilderness to collect his subsidies." However, Hill, operating with private money, had to make a profit, and therefore had to concern himself with costs of operation. During the business depression of the 1890s, most of the subsidized lines went bankrupt, but Hill's line remained profitable.

Like Carnegie and Rockefeller, Hill stressed efficiency. "What we want," he said, "is the best possible line, shortest distance, lowest grades and least curvature that we can build." He built his line to compete and to endure, not to gain government subsidies. Because he used the latest steel rails, and relentlessly sought low grades and short, straightline routes, he saved on repairs and fuel. His knowledge of the railroading industry, from broad vision to tiniest detail, became legendary. He paired long hours at his desk with "frequent forays into the field" and knew each engine, its repair history and engineer on sight. "He traveled back and forth along the line in his business car, looking for dips and bumps and spying out curves that could be straightened and grades that could be lessened."

Further, he built slowly, developing the Northwest through which his line passed. Realizing that the sparsely populated states of Minnesota, North Dakota, Montana, Idaho and Washington had to be built up before his line could profit, Hill encouraged development of various kinds. He promoted dry farming to increase wheat yields, he advocated crop rotation, he distributed 7,000 English cattle without payment. "He even set up his own experimental farms to test new seed, livestock and equipment." Throughout the 1880s, as his Great Northern inched relentlessly toward the West Coast, Hill primed the pump of Northwestern economic development, even offering to transport immigrants for a mere $10 each if they farmed near his line.

Hill employed the stellar engineer, John Stevens, who became a legendary figure for his discovery of the almost mythical Marias Pass. Lewis and Clark had described a low pass through the Montana Rockies in

1805, but eight decades later nobody knew where it was or even if it existed. But Hill recognized that Stevens – who was part engineer and part explorer – was the man to find it. Stevens "represented the beau ideal of Victorian manhood. Ramrod-straight, ruggedly handsome, and self-confident," he headed into the mountains in the dead of December with a lone Indian companion. Trundling on snowshoes through heavy snows, they approached the headwaters of the Marias River. When the brutal conditions caused his guide to refuse to go further, Stevens – who in his life had survived "Mexican fevers, Indian attack...Canadian blizzards" and an episode in which he had been treed by wolves – intrepidly continued alone. On the night of December 11, 1889, stomping through the long pre-dawn hours in minus-forty-degree cold, Stevens found the pass he sought. Marias Pass, "along the southern border of today's Glacier National Park, lies at only 5,214 feet elevation, the lowest crossing of the northern Rockies." The resulting avoidance of grades and curvature "spelled out...the torah of [Hill's] credo: a highly efficient, low-cost line that could, better than any competitor, carry long-distance cargoes of heavy tonnages."

In the early 1890s, Hill's explorer-engineer also found a pass through the Cascade Mountains just east of Puget Sound. Standing at 4,061 feet above sea level, Stevens Pass is a "formidable passage but still less than half the elevation of some of the surrounding peaks." Eight years later in 1900, Stevens constructed the two-and-a-half mile Cascade Tunnel, but for now trains would have to employ a nightmarish series of switchbacks over the top of what became known as "Death Mountain." Though Hill was enraged when he first heard the proposal and cleared the tracks ahead to race westward, "Stevens coolly explained his decision" in the teeth of one of his boss's legendary explosions. The expensive switchbacks drained much of the "cost-efficiency from the tightly built Great Northern system," but Hill recognized the incontestable logic of his subordinate's case, and raised his salary by 50 percent on the spot.

Despite such obstacles, the Great Northern was able to cut the first-class fares "below prevailing Northern Pacific rates," from $60 to $35, and second-class rates from $35 to $25. In F. Scott Fitzgerald's *The Great Gatsby*, one of the characters says of the slain Gatsby that if he had lived he would have been "a great man. A man like James J. Hill. He'd of helped build up the country." Such a claim may or may not have been true of the fictional Gatsby – a bootlegger – but it was undoubtedly true of Hill, who played an enormous role in building up the American Northwest. The man who for decades ran the Great Northern as either its President or Chairman of the Board at no time accepted any salary for his work. He was compensated by the value his work added to the stock in the company that he owned and in which he so strongly believed.

Later in his career, John Stevens was the man who turned around the floundering Panama Canal project. Hill, who said of his by-then chief engineer that "he is always in the right place at the right time and does the right thing without asking about it," recommended him unreservedly to President Theodore Roosevelt despite his disgust for both the project and, especially, the trust-busting president. Working 12, sometimes 18 hours a day, expecting the same from others, Stevens backed the American doctors fully in their efforts to stamp out the dreaded yellow fever that had wreaked havoc on the canal project.

Most important from an engineering point of view, Stevens was first to recognize that construction of the canal was preeminently a railroad job. He replaced the toy-like French line with giant sized equipment built to Great Northern specifications. "Equipment on the Great Northern was four times the size of that used on the little jungle line. Hill had been the first railroad baron to equip his road with large-capacity freight cars and monster locomotives." The Americans have always recognized that bigger is better, and in that lies one reason for their historically unparalleled constructive achievements. Stevens immediately identified something the French had missed: the railroad was the key to suc-

cessful construction of the canal; it was responsible not merely for shipping men, food, supplies to the work site, but for carting away the enormous quantities of dirt that had to be moved.

Stevens, who considered Jim Hill "the finest man he had ever known," had much of his former boss's spirit in him. He had no tolerance for labor unions or government officials. When steam-shovel engineers came to his office threatening to strike, Stevens responded: "Get the hell out of this office and back to work." A rueful Roosevelt, who loved him, complained to William Howard Taft that Stevens seemed "incapable of understanding that he was no longer working for James J. Hill." As the president reminded his chief engineer, the Panama Canal was a government project – but in the end, its construction was "one of the greatest of all triumphs in American railroad engineering," and only fitting that its prime mover was the top man of the greatest railroad builder the world has known.[6]

Such daring entrepreneurs and others were able to revolutionize the fields of heavy industry on which general prosperity depended. Between 1860 and 1900, American output of bituminous coal increased by 2,260 percent, crude petroleum by 9,060 percent, steel by 10,190 percent, and other industries increased by similar amounts. Rockefeller was quite right in his assessment that he had created far more value in building Standard Oil than in all of his massive philanthropy, because he made inexpensive petroleum products available to millions of customers. American businessmen were creating vast amounts of inexpensive goods and services.[7]

But growing industries require capital – and the Wall Street capitalist who towered over his peers in late 19th century America was a man who has since virtually passed into legend: John Pierpont Morgan (1837-1913). In studying his life, one is struck even by the titles of his biographies: Frederick Lewis Allen's, *The Great Pierpont Morgan* – John Winkler's *Morgan the Magnificent* – and Cass Canfield's *The Incredible Pierpont Morgan*. Are such titles ironic, adorning texts that demonstrate

the unworthiness of the subject to such exalted claims? Or are they manifestations of sincere admiration for a lifetime of extraordinary achievement? A careful reading shows the authors seeking a "balanced" account. They expose what they consider the man's flaws – his overwhelming self-confidence, for example, which is generally portrayed as intolerable arrogance. But they often marvel at his financial accomplishments.

Morgan "was one of Thomas A. Edison's earliest backers." In 1878, when an electric lighting system was still merely a dream, Morgan already put money into the Edison Electric Light Company. In September 1882, when Edison completed his famous Pearl Street power station in lower Manhattan, Morgan's Wall Street office, the Drexel Building, was one of the first to be electrified. Morgan was also among the earliest to install the new electric lights in his home at 219 Madison Avenue – and he stayed the course after a short circuit and resulting fire "ruined the rug and the desk and filled the house with the odor of charred wood."

Shortly after, Morgan permitted his partners to traffic in Edison stock only on the condition that for every share they bought for the customer, "they buy one for me." Still later, "when a million dollars was needed to build an uptown power station, he subscribed half of the amount himself." As Jean Strouse, a recent biographer of Morgan, with access to the latest research, put it, "Morgan stayed with this experiment at considerable personal inconvenience and cost," because he understood that innovations succeeded only with difficulty and time.

But it was the vital railroad industry that perhaps saw Morgan's most productive accomplishments. In the depression years of the 1890s, many of the nation's leading lines – including the Baltimore & Ohio, the Erie, the Northern Pacific and the Union Pacific – sank into bankruptcy. Many of the railroads had received government subsidies and been plagued by consequent fraud, corruption, political opportunism, shoddy construction and poor management. One by one they crept to the door of the country's financial titan.

Robber Barons or Productive Geniuses

Painstakingly, over a period of four years, he and his associates reorganized on sound financial footing the Richmond Terminal, the Erie, the Reading, the Norfolk & Western. Morgan was no dry, plodding accountant hunched over his books, however; he was undoubtedly a lightning-quick mathematical genius, and a tall, powerful, physically-imposing man with a stare that was likened to the glare of an onrushing locomotive. The overwhelming force of his character and personality was not to be trifled with. Archibald McLeod, defiant president of the Reading line, remarked that "he would rather run a peanut stand than be dictated to by J.P. Morgan" – and very nearly became a prophet; he was sacked during Morgan's successful reorganization of his floundering line.

Recognizing the railroading genius of the rough-and-tumble Hill, Morgan reconstituted the Northern Pacific under the Minnesotan's aegis, who brought to its control the same credo of tight construction that had enabled the Great Northern to trailblaze the Northwest. "Under Hill's able management, the Northern Pacific soon showed profits almost comparable to the Great Northern. The Morgan-Hill group now controlled in the Northwest a system of some 11,000 miles."

This set the scene for perhaps the greatest Wall Street battle of history. For the brilliant capitalist, Edward H. Harriman – physically small, son of a penniless Episcopal curate, but of unsurpassed genius, unmatched energy and unquenchable ambition – acquired first the "rickety, old, bankrupt Union Pacific," then in rapid fire succession, the Central Pacific and Southern Pacific. His roads amounted to some 25,000 miles of tracks by 1906, a true empire; all of which, by means of the same philosophy and methods of Hill, he quickly built into lines to rival any in the nation.

Harriman, combative to a fault, of whom it was said "he feared neither God nor J.P. Morgan," came into Wall Street swinging after losing control of the valuable Chicago, Burlington and Quincy Railroad to the Morgan-Hill group. In alliance with Jacob Schiff of Kuhn and Loeb – the

powerful Jewish brokerage house to whom Morgan, an anti-Semitic upper crust WASP, was unfailingly condescending – he contrived the daring plan to purchase a controlling interest in the Northern Pacific and wrest it away from the Morgan-Hill empire. With Morgan away on one of his many trips to Europe, Hill, in Seattle, became suspicious of the NP's steadily rising price. Boarding a special train, he barreled across the continent and into the Wall Street offices of Kuhn and Loeb on the morning of May 3, 1901 to confront his old friend, Schiff. The resulting stock war shot the price of Northern Pacific to astronomical heights and threatened to ruin numerous brokers and speculators who had sought to sell NP stock "short." When the smoke of the high stakes shootout cleared, Morgan and Hill held a decisive advantage, but Harriman had clawed out a substantial position as a minority owner.

The result, on Hill's insistence, was Morgan's formation of the monumental Northern Securities Trust, a gigantic holding company that enabled Hill, its president, to consolidate under one "unified and cost efficient management" the three roads he owned. Several of Morgan's colleagues, as well as Harriman and Schiff sat on its board of directors.[8]

Northern Securities did not seek to bar other lines from entering the Northwest – nor, under the freedom of the American system, could it have prevented other entrepreneurs from doing so. (Indeed, several years later, while Hill still controlled his two transcontinentals, a company that included William Rockefeller successfully completed a line that paralleled the Great Northern and the Northern Pacific across the country, terminating in Seattle.) Further, Hill's relentless attention to maximizing the efficiency of his roads, to reducing curves and grades, caused freight rates on his line to continue to drop. In 1881, his line "charged an average rate of 2.88 cents per ton-mile," but by 1907 that rate was down to .77 cents.

None of this was important to President Theodore Roosevelt, who considered Northern Securities "in restraint of trade," and who launched the federal suit that led to the company's dissolution. The enormously

productive Hill was quite right in expressing his contempt for statist politicians (an attitude fully shared by Morgan): "It really seems hard when we look back at what we have done and how we have led all western companies in opening the country and carrying at the lowest rates, that we should be compelled to fight for our lives against the political adventurers who have never done anything but pose and draw a salary."

But Morgan accomplished far more than the reorganization on a sound financial basis of the country's railroads. Not once but twice he saved the country from financial disaster in response to the federal government's urgent pleas. In February, 1895 – the first time – the United States government had reached a crisis: for a complex of economic reasons it was unable to stem the flow of gold from its treasury. The country was in a depression and men sought to turn in their greenbacks for something of tangible value: gold. The treasury's supply of the precious metal had slipped far below the $100 million amount deemed the minimum necessary for safety; by January 28th, it was $56 million and shrinking daily. Because the influential Populists of the day opposed the gold standard and had support in Congress, President Grover Cleveland, a Democrat, could not get legislative support. The administration turned to a prominent Democratic banker on Wall Street, who informed the officials that there was "one man without whose aid no plan for restoring the government's gold reserve could succeed: Pierpont Morgan."

Though President Cleveland originally rebuffed Morgan's subsequent plan, the banker traveled to Washington where Daniel Lamont, Secretary of War, stated that the president would not meet him. Morgan, a bulwark of the Republican Party, replied, "I have come down to Washington to see the President, and I am going to stay here until I see him." On February 5th, Cleveland received Morgan at the White House where, confronted by both the financier's arguments and his commanding presence, the President reconsidered.

When Morgan stated that his firm would guarantee that the gold

bought by the government from Morgan's colleagues in America and Europe would not be shipped abroad for the duration of the agreement, the President was impressed. He understood the immense commitment Morgan had undertaken: he had pledged "himself to control what for years past had been uncontrollable – the course of international exchange and ...gold shipments." Morgan succeeded in this and his "operation was a thumping success."

But the following year a Congressional committee was concerned regarding his power and his profits. After all, how could a private individual be powerful enough to save the government? It asked Morgan why he had been unwilling to let others take the lead role in preventing the panic – and he answered with unshakable confidence in his own unique stature: *They could not do it.*

Similarly, in the Panic of 1907, when a run on the banks threatened the country's entire financial structure, the Secretary of the Treasury, George Cortelyou, placed at the disposal of the 70 year-old Morgan what funds the government had. Wall Street bankers, as well as the United States government, unreservedly rallied behind the leadership of the old warhorse, who held the ultimate judgment regarding which banks were solvent and to be supported and which were terminally ill and to be allowed to expire. In the process, Morgan raised $25 million dollars as a loan for the New York Stock Exchange, averting the calamitous consequences of a premature closure – and wrote out "a commitment to buy thirty million dollars' worth of six per cent New York City bonds," thereby saving the City of New York from bankruptcy.

One of his biographers entitled the two chapters relating these gripping events: "Saving The Country – First, 1895" and "Saving The Country Again – Panic of 1907." In 1912, near the end of his life, Morgan testified before another Congressional investigation, the Pujo Committee. He held that character, not money, ruled the financial world. The committee's lawyer, Samuel Untermeyer, asked: "Is not commercial

credit based primarily upon money or property?" Morgan replied, "No, sir, the first thing is character." "Before money or property?" Morgan's answer, astonishing many in the room, was: "Before money or anything else. Money cannot buy it...Because a man I do not trust could not get money from me on all the bonds in Christendom." The nobility of character that Morgan embodied in his business dealings was and remains inconceivable to anti-capitalist intellectuals. But as one historian put it: "he meant it, and it was true."9

The extraordinary accomplishments of Edward H. Harriman (1848-1909) are unfortunately no longer widely remembered. Determined, upon its acquisition in 1898, to rebuild the outmoded Union Pacific, Harriman put together a special train in Kansas City with an observation car in front and the engine in the rear pushing. He then rode, slowly, the thousands of miles to Portland, Oregon, and back to Omaha, "stopping frequently so he could ask questions and examine things. When he came back, Harriman knew, as no other mortal knew, what the Union Pacific was." He then laid down hundreds of miles of new track and millions of new ties. He scrapped 200 obsolete locomotives, replaced them with more powerful ones, added 4,760 new cars and laid down 42,000 miles of heavy-steel rails. By 1902, the reorganized line had spent $45 million on reconstruction, and from 1898 to 1909 $175 million.

Improvements were dramatic. "The average U.P. locomotive weighed 37 tons in 1898, 68 tons in 1909. In 1898 the average U.P. freight train hauled 277 tons; in 1909...548 tons. In 1898 there were 476,000 tons of freight carried for every mile of U.P. track. In 1909 for every mile of Union Pacific track more than 1,000,000 tons were carried...The estimated value of farm lands along the U.P. route nearly tripled in those years." The Union Pacific in 1897 may have been in better condition than its "rusted streak of iron" reputation led many to believe – but it was hardly a modern or efficient line. Twelve years later it was the "most efficient railroad for its size in the West and possibly the entire nation" and

earned a pre-dividend net profit of $42 million. Harriman's enormous productivity benefited all – shareholders, customers and himself.

He wrought the same modernization when he shortly after acquired the Central Pacific and Southern Pacific Railroads. Harriman's lines, like Hill's, were built to carry heavy tonnage efficiently and inexpensively, greatly helping to develop the western states. One accomplishment in rebuilding the Central Pacific that is especially worthy of note was the construction of the Lucin Cutoff across the Great Salt Lake in Utah. The bottom of the lake was treacherous, and many times "the fills and trestles seemed about to be wholly swallowed up in abysses of quicksand and mud." But state-of-the-art railroad technology coupled with enormous perseverance prevailed – and the embankment over the lake, though costing $9 million to complete, enabled the Central Pacific to shorten its distance by greater than 40 miles, eliminate 4,000 degrees of curvature, and reduce maximum grades from 90 feet to 21 feet per mile. In the end, the reconstruction of the Union Pacific, Central Pacific and Southern Pacific Railroads cost $400 million dollars, an extraordinary sum of money at the turn of the 20th century.

Additionally, Harriman used his lines to battle natural disasters. For example, on April 18th, 1906 the terrible San Francisco Earthquake struck the city, precipitating fires that raged out of control for three days and nights, leaving the "whole business part of the city and some of the residential part" – an area of more than five square miles – nothing but "heaps of smoking ruins." More than 200,000 people were left without shelter and bereft of the immediate necessities of survival. "Food, water, shelter, clothing, medicines, and sewerage were all lacking."

From the moment Harriman received word of the catastrophe, on the afternoon of the 18th, he put "all the resources" of the Union Pacific and Southern Pacific "at the service of the stricken city." He left his office in New York the following morning and sped to the Bay Area to take personal charge of rescue efforts. Within 24 hours of the disaster his railroad

bought, delivered and distributed $20,000 worth of food. "As a result…the burned-out inhabitants of the city were not compelled to go hungry, even for a single day."

Further, his lines carried scores of thousands of survivors to nearby towns or to their relatives in the East – where the necessities of life were plentiful. By Harriman's orders, relief trains and refugee trains were given right of way over all other traffic – and, all told, his railroads provided San Franciscans with roughly $1 million worth of emergency rail service. Harriman was utterly undaunted by the massive damage – after all, he was spending more on the reconstruction of his lines than the $325 million necessary to rebuild the city – and was relentless in his spirited and infectious optimism regarding the city's rebirth.

Several years later, *Railway World* made this point succinctly in an editorial: "When San Francisco was laid in ashes, it was Mr. Harriman who took personal charge of the situation; his railroads rushed supplies into the city and carried thousands of refugees away from the city, without charge for either service. It was primarily due to his organizing genius and energy that San Francisco rallied so quickly from its great disaster."

One might disagree with only one part of this assessment, for the great capitalist *was* paid – in future business, in good will and in the pride derived from a construction project – indeed, a Herculean labor – superbly performed and beneficial to all parties.

When his San Francisco triumph was barely completed, Harriman engaged in another struggle with the titanic forces of nature; he was instrumental in winning "the fight with a runaway river." By the spring of 1906, the wild, capricious floodings of the Colorado River threatened with destruction the fertile agricultural lands of southern California's Imperial Valley. The area at that time had only recently been converted from inhospitable desert by the completion of a gigantic irrigation project utilizing water from the Colorado – and now the river threatened to inundate it, to drown 60 miles of Southern Pacific track along with thou-

sands of acres of productive farms. In late April, one of Harriman's officers hurried to San Francisco to inform him of the magnitude of the impending disaster.

Harriman's biographer describes the dramatic scene. "Mr. Harriman was not a man to be daunted or 'rattled' by a sudden and menacing emergency. There, in the bustle and confusion of temporary offices, with the ruins of San Francisco still smoking, with the facilities of his roads taxed to the utmost in carrying people away from the stricken city," with his railroads facing unknown financial demands in meeting the northern disaster, the "Little Giant" turned to squarely confront the southern danger. He pledged hundreds of thousands of dollars to fight the runaway river.

By this time the Colorado discharged "more than seventy-five thousand cubic feet of water per second, or six billion cubic feet every twenty-four hours" – and the fresh water lake newly formed in the valley "rose at the rate of seven inches per day over an area of four hundred square miles." The main line of the Southern Pacific was swamped, and "five times in the course of the summer the company had to move its track to higher ground."

The runaway river sent 360,000,000 cubic feet of water per hour plunging 400 feet into the basin below. No men had ever controlled such a torrential flood before. Expert engineers argued that it could not be done. "Mr. Harriman, who believed and who once said that 'nothing is impossible,' never doubted that the control of the Colorado River was within human power and…resources." Harriman pointed out that building the Lucin Cutoff had also been considered impossible. Employing top-of-the-line railroad technology and innovative methods, working at enormous expense through months of round-the-clock effort, Harriman's engineers constructed a rock-fill dam that successfully stemmed the torrent.

But a month later, in December of 1906, a new flood breached other defenses of the Imperial Valley, and it became clear that it was necessary

to build a "massive levee along the west bank of the river for a distance of at least twenty miles." At President Theodore Roosevelt's insistent urging – though ultimately without a penny of government funding – Harriman's railroad undertook and successfully completed the enormous project in less than two months. The rich fertile lands of the Imperial Valley, and thousands of farming families, were saved from ruin.

Because Congress ultimately refused to repay a penny of the railroad's $3 million expense, the task turned out to be a primarily pro bono gift from Harriman to the men of the Imperial Valley and the nation, for the area contributed only a fractional amount of the Southern Pacific's over-all freight traffic. But before moralists rush to extol the glories of finan-cially non-remunerative work, it is well to remember who alone was able to accomplish it, and to whom the trust-busting president turned in the country's need – the profit-driven, "can-do" men of the Southern Pacific Railroad.

One of the project's primary engineers wrote: "the accomplishment of the work was due primarily...to the independent judgment and courage of Mr. Harriman, who persisted in his belief that the breaks could be closed...in the face of opposition" from eminent engineers who claimed that "the closure was a physical impossibility."

Late in his career, Harriman's vision centered on the establishment of an around-the-world, combined land-sea transportation system. The Little Giant's grand-scale plan was to buy, build and connect railroads into a vast trans-Asian line that extended into Europe and terminated in the Baltic seaports – and then to link his intercontinental railroads by means of the Pacific Mail Steamship Company, which he already owned. Tragically, death overtook him before he could bring such an enormous undertaking to fruition.[10]

These six men—Carnegie, Rockefeller, Vanderbilt, Hill, Morgan, Harriman—are by no means the only great creators of the era, but are representative of its best. In truth, they were neither "robbers" nor

"barons." They did not steal their wealth; nor did they conquer, plunder or inherit it. They created it. Hill built the Great Northern Railway, Carnegie organized and oversaw one productive company after another, Rockefeller generated a vast concern that produced previously undreamed-of quantities of inexpensive petroleum products. These men were the driving force behind companies that inundated the country with goods previously unavailable. In justice and in gratitude, they must be recognized, admired and named in accordance with their actual accomplishments: they were Productive Geniuses.

Although many people, including some historians and biographers, have admired such men and their accomplishments, it remained for Ayn Rand to explain and validate the deeper reasons for which they should be honored: these men, and many of their peers, embodied, to the greatest degree of history until that point, the life-giving moral virtue of productiveness. Any ethical creed proclaiming fealty to humanitarianism that morally condemns such productive giants must immediately check its basic premises or thereby lose all title to the claim of love for mankind. True humanitarians must recognize and celebrate the life-giving benefits conferred by all productive men — and especially those resulting from the prodigious output of the productive geniuses.

Pointed questions must be directed at those who hold the Robber Baron thesis. Is it possible that the leading industrialists of the years 1870-1910 were thieves when their work flooded the country with increasingly inexpensive steel, oil, rail transportation, etc., for use not merely by the wealthy but by the average man? Were the fortunes of these businessmen characteristically gained by fraud or graft, not production, at a time that national wealth showed "a fourfold increase," from $30 billion to roughly $127 billion – and per capita income grew by almost 3 percent per year? How could they be considered "exploiters" when real wages, i.e., wages measured in terms of what workers could buy with their money, rose 20 percent? Why did destitute workers by the millions

keep coming to this country from such non-capitalist areas as Ireland, Sicily and Eastern Europe, submitting to "slave-driving capitalists" who derived "ill-gotten gains" from the sweat of their bodies? And why, in overwhelming numbers, did they refuse to return?[11]

The great wealth of the Productive Geniuses was abundantly earned. Again, it was Ayn Rand who first fully understood the enormous benefaction represented by such wealth creation. "It is not the moochers or the looters who give value to money. Not an ocean of tears or all the guns in the world can transform those pieces of paper in your wallet into the bread you will need to survive tomorrow. Those pieces of paper, which should have been gold, are a token of honor – your claim upon the energy of the men who produce. Your wallet is your statement of hope that somewhere in the world around you there are men who will not default on the moral principle which is the root of money."[12]

But what of the specific charges made against these producers? There is an endless litany of accusations. Did Carnegie exploit his workers, leading to the bloody Homestead strike of 1892? After all, he was, according to one biographer, "the cruelest taskmaster in American industrial history." Was Rockefeller morally culpable for demanding and receiving the largest rebates from the railroads? Did he squeeze and financially intimidate smaller competitors until they sold out to him? Was J.P. Morgan's fortune founded in a Civil War deal in which he knowingly sold defective guns to the Union Army? Similarly, did Carnegie defraud the United States Navy (and put at risk the lives of American sailors) by selling defective steel armor for its warships? This brief list barely scratches the surface of the accusations made.[13]

Carnegie is a representative example. Matthew Josephson says that the steel magnate was a master of "the art of using men." He was "full of brass" and "intruded himself everywhere." He constantly "cajoled and flattered" men of influence, and "was never a hard worker." "He spent half his time in play and let other men pile up his millions for him."

What is the truth regarding such claims?[14]

The minor point is that often the charges made by the anti-capitalists are half-truths, distortions or outright falsehoods. For example, Josephson's claim regarding Carnegie's lack of a work ethic is a quote from p. 122 of volume 1 of Burton Hendrick's detailed biography of the steel-master. There are several problems with Josephson's account. The first is that Hendrick had established in the first 100 pages just how hard a "nose-to-the-grindstone" worker Carnegie was in rising out of poverty during his early years between ages 12 and 30.

The second is that Josephson overlooks the rest of the very passage he quotes from. "He [Carnegie] was the thinker, the one who supplied ideas, inspiration and driving power, who saw far into the future, not the one who lived laborious days and nights at an office desk. Only in the years occupied as a telegrapher and railroad executive was Carnegie cramped by office routine…"

The main response to Josephson's charge is not that it was only through 18 years of unrelenting toil that Carnegie was able to rise to his eminent position – but that his genius, his superb knowledge and thinking, was the first cause of his vast steel-producing empire. Mechanized production, deploying incessantly-innovative industrial processes, is not based primarily on manual labor but on the creative work of the mind. All of this, thoroughly documented in the Hendrick biography, Josephson ignores.[15]

Further, J.P. Morgan did not sell defective guns to the Union Army during the Civil War. The charge against Morgan was a pure invention on the part of socialist writer, Gustavus Myers, in his book *History of the Great American Fortunes*, which has been unfortunately accepted and repeated by other anti-capitalist writers. (Indeed, Josephson's more famous *The Robber Barons* was largely based on Myers' book.)

In truth, the guns were in perfect working order and, more to the point, Morgan was only peripherally related to the transaction: he loaned

money to one of the principals in the deal. When his loan was repaid, Morgan's brief involvement in the affair was concluded. The Myers account of the affair is breathtaking in its level of distortion. Naturally then, Myers's has acquired a reputation as a historian whose "method was one of exhaustive and patient research summed up in a straightforward narrative which let the facts speak for themselves."[16]

Regarding Rockefeller, perhaps his most effective critic was Ida Tarbell, whose *History of the Standard Oil Company* was well documented and filled with useful information. She assailed Rockefeller for (among other things) both the rebates he received from the railroads and for allegedly intimidating smaller refineries into selling out to Standard Oil. The Rockefeller she painted was a ruthless competitor unconcerned with the "ruin" he brought on others. For example, speaking of the dreams of the independent Pennsylvania oil producers, she wrote: "But suddenly at the very heyday of this confidence, a big hand reached out from nobody knew where, to steal their conquest and throttle their future. The suddenness and the blackness of the assault" she blamed, of course, on the supposedly iniquitous Rockefeller.

The truth – and the full truth? Rockefeller received large rebates – special discounts for shipping – from the railroads. This was a common practice of the time; it existed before Rockefeller went into business; it was perfectly legal during the days of Rockefeller's rise; other shippers – including Rockefeller's competitors – also received large rebates; and they constituted voluntary, generally secret, agreements between shippers and carriers. The practice was denounced for decades and eventually prohibited by law. Those opposed to rebates, then and now, generally hold that railroads, as common carriers, must provide one rate for all, and declare it unjust to practice discriminatory rate policies, especially ones that favor large shippers over small. To be blunt, the little guy should get the same rate as the big guy.

But why? If Standard shipped vastly more oil than most of its com-

petitors, as it did, why is it immoral for the railroad to give it a lower rate? The railroads were in competition for the heaviest shippers and offering the largest discount was one means for them to win business. Such a practice, constituting good business sense and fully understandable, goes on routinely and uncontroversially in other fields. For example, if a baker has as customers a local grocery store, a chain of hotels and the United States Army, he does not give them the same price. Presumably, he charges the hotels less per unit of bread than he does the grocer and the Army less still. The greater the volume of business the customer brings, the lower rate per unit he is charged. There is no injustice involved to the little guy. The provider charges his larger customer less per unit but makes significant profit on the greater volume.

Further, as one American historian stated: "So long as the railroads provided the service for which they were paid and at *the rate agreed upon with each party to a contract,*" there was no element of injustice involved. To legally restrict individual shippers and carriers from voluntarily negotiating freight rates agreeable to both parties is to violate the rights of each.

Additionally, because in practice the railroads gave the largest discounts to the customers who brought them the heaviest volume, Standard received its fattest rebates only after it had achieved its status as the largest shipper of oil. King-sized rebates were not the first cause of Standard Oil's rise.

Some of Rockefeller's smaller competitors understood this point. In 1872, when Robert Hanna of Hanna and Baslington asked the president of the Lake Shore Railroad to give his company the same rate as Standard's, he was asked how many barrels of oil he shipped. "One thousand a day," he replied. "Mr. Hanna, do you expect that a shipper who gives us one thousand barrels a day can get as low a rate as a shipper who gives us five thousand barrels a day?" "No," said the oil refiner. "I don't suppose he can."

In the fall of 1871, Rockefeller joined an alliance of oil refiners

and railroads known as the South Improvement Company. Under this arrangement, the railroads would raise general shipping rates, then not only give member refiners rebates on the oil they shipped but also give them an equivalent amount of money based on what non-members shipped. In brief, member refiners received a large portion of the higher shipping rates paid by their competitors.

The resulting uproar put South Improvement out of business before one gallon of oil was shipped under its plan. But in the two month period between the time South Improvement's plan became public knowledge and the time the company went up in smoke, Standard Oil was able to absorb most of its Cleveland competitors in oil refining. The accusation was and remains that Rockefeller stressed to his competitors that they would be ruined under the South Improvement's plan – and that their only viable alternative was to sell out to him.

Did Rockefeller lean on his competitors for all he was worth? Although he vigorously denied it to the end of his long life, it is certainly possible. But in the welter of claims and counter-claims surrounding this issue, several factual points are clear. One is that hard economic times had many Cleveland refiners reeling. Intense competition among the dozens of refiners had helped push the price of kerosene inexorably downward.

Kerosene prices had fallen an average of 25 percent between 1869 and 1871 while the average price of crude oil in 1871 rose "12 percent above that for 1870." Kerosene, selling for 58 cents a gallon in 1865 and over 30 cents in 1869, was going for around 22 cents in 1872 and approximately 11 cents by late 1874. Many firms were "forced to sell, since they were small, marginal, non-integrated refiners who could not lower costs as quickly as the market lowered prices." Based on the extraordinary efficiency of Rockefeller and his team, their company still made a profit when many of their competitors struggled badly. Because of this, Rockefeller's firm enjoyed a superior reputation with the banks.

A second important point is that Rockefeller had long planned to expand and had begun his process of buying out Cleveland refiners "fully six weeks before the public knew about the South Improvement Company." The first company he bought in this way was Clark, Payne and Company, "the Standard's strongest Cleveland competitor," but a firm that had been losing money. Having absorbed its largest rival first, Standard was in a very strong bargaining position, especially given "the heavy losses most refiners had suffered during the past two years."

It is possible that Rockefeller's aggressive expansionist policy might have threatened his rivals – certainly the situation was threatening – but the bottom line truth is that under the chaotic, relentlessly competitive and often depressed conditions of the early oil industry it made sound economic sense for many of the struggling firms to merge with one as efficient as Standard Oil. This is the main reason for Rockefeller's "conquest of Cleveland," not any intimidatory use he allegedly made of his standing in the South Improvement Company.[17]

Furthermore, it was the moral right of railroads to enter into any voluntary business agreements with shippers that they chose. Nor would the preferential agreements of the South Improvement Company necessarily leave non-members at the mercy of members. It was the right of non-members to band together, boycott the railroad, scream to the public regarding the perceived inequities of the arrangement, make their case to the press, seek to convince other shippers and the general public of the danger and to join the boycott, search for alternative forms of transportation, make clear to entrepreneurs and potential investors that there was now sufficient business to financially justify a new railroad, etc. On a free market, where men are free to act in the face of adversity, the most common outcome would be that competition for the "offending" railroad would be encouraged. Additionally, negative publicity is damaging for companies who must satisfy their customers on a competitive marketplace; bad press and falling revenues will cause profit-seeking companies

to alter their policies.

The anti-capitalist writers have also been mistaken in their treatment of Carnegie. For example, there is the legend of the "worthlessly defective" armor plate the Carnegie Corporation allegedly sold the U.S. Navy in 1893, an inaccuracy which springs from erroneous and lurid newspaper accounts of the day. The fertile imagination of Gustavus Myers seized on this story and it has been accepted uncritically by numerous subsequent authors. The truth is that the Secretary of the Navy, Hilary Herbert, stated his satisfaction with the Carnegie steel in no uncertain terms: "The Department was very much gratified to find...that the armor was all good, and in all cases the steel was of the best quality..." Captain William Sampson, Chief of the Bureau of Ordnance, added, "Every plate was above the requirements."

The U.S. government fined the Carnegie Corporation, in part, not because the steel was defective – it was assuredly not – but because while one batch of armor was "twenty percent better than specifications demanded," the rest was only five percent better. Not understanding that the vagaries of steel manufacturing at that time precluded a precise uniformity of product, the government reasoned that if Carnegie's firm was capable of turning out armor that was 20 percent above the norm required, then armor only 5 percent above the standard could not represent the company's best effort.

Henry Clay Frick, one of Carnegie's most talented lieutenants, eloquently summed up the meaning of such twisted logic: if one batch of steel had exceeded the Navy's standards by 100 percent, he said, and the rest by only five, then presumably the company would have had to refund all its payments and given Uncle Sam the armor besides. "What could be better calculated to suppress any efforts to experiment or to make improvements?"

However, the company was, in fact, guilty of serious infractions regarding its method of making the armor. Because company executives consid-

ered government inspectors arbitrary, meddlesome and utterly ignorant of steelmaking, beliefs no doubt true, they falsified results regarding government specifications they considered irrelevant and gratuitous. They believed that as long as the armor was good, the government should keep its ignorant nose out of the steelmaking processes required to produce it. However justified the company's estimate of the government inspectors, it was properly punished for violating the specific terms of its contract.

But the armor was indeed good — not defective, as Gustavus Myers and subsequent historians claimed.[18]

The bloody 1892 strike at Carnegie's Homestead plant may be used as a final example. Despite the claim that he was the "cruelest taskmaster in American industrial history," Carnegie's record in dealing with his workers in the years leading up to the Homestead disaster was quite respectable. Carnegie was one of the first to experiment with the method of producing steel by means of three 8-hour shifts, rather than by two 12-hour work periods. He recognized labor unions and avoided strife when violent strikes wracked heavy industry during the 1880s. Starting in 1886, he spent millions to modernize the Homestead plant, innovations that greatly increased labor's productivity, generating high wages for his skilled workers. He pushed for a sliding scale as the form of compensation fairest to both workers and the company – one that permitted wages to rise indefinitely when the steel industry boomed, but prevented them from falling below an agreed-upon minimum during business slumps.

When the men at his Edgar Thompson mills went out on strike in the winter of 1887-88, Carnegie neither met their demands nor attempted to operate the struck plant with replacement workers – "strikebreakers," to the unions' non-objective way of thinking . Instead, he shut the doors and waited the men out. In May, the union capitulated, met the company's demands, and the men went back to work. Carnegie believed that the way to avert labor violence was to refrain from operating plants that were struck. He believed that he already possessed the finest labor

force, so that it was senseless to import new steelworkers. Further, the men had to eat, he reasoned; hence, eventually they had to work.

Henry Clay Frick, a superbly able man but of a more pugnacious school of thought in dealing with labor unrest, was chairman of the Carnegie Steel Company in 1892. Frick believed that Carnegie's method of dealing with labor disputes was "soft." Before leaving the country for cooler climes, as he did every summer, Carnegie recommended that Frick shut the Homestead plant down in case of a strike. This Frick did not do. He fortified the plant grounds as a prelude to hiring workers as individuals, not as union members. Thousands of workers – union and non-union men alike – then rose up and seized control of Carnegie's mills. Instead of appealing to the Governor of Pennsylvania for troops to regain control of the company's property, Frick made the mistake of introducing 300 hated (by union members) Pinkerton guards into the tense situation.

When the Pinkertons attempted to disembark from the barges carrying them and land on company ground, one of the strikers fired a shot. The Pinkertons blasted back with full force, the strike became a. large-scale riot, and men on both sides were killed. When the Governor finally did send 8,000 soldiers, the strikers relinquished company property without a hand "raised in hostility." In the end, months later, the company won its demands and broke the union. But the haunting specter of lethal violence hung over a leading center of American productivity.[19]

Although Carnegie's earlier policy of not operating struck facilities may avoid labor violence in the short run, there is a moral principle that must be understood. The plant belongs to the company. Its officers have the moral right to staff it with non-union workers and operate it if they so choose. Union supporters claim that men have "a right to their jobs." As stated, this belief is crucially, centrally, tragically false. A man has a right to a job if and only if an employer voluntarily chooses to hire him. If an employer chooses not to hire or to fire or – at contract's end – to

replace him, he has no right to the job.

Consider: if an employer claimed a right to a man's labor without his consent, such a policy would be properly identified as advocacy of slavery. But the converse is equally true; if an employee claimed a right to a position without the owner's consent, he is guilty of violating the employer's right to run his own property as he thinks best. It is the unions' belief that their men have a right to their jobs that causes their moral outrage when companies hire independent workers during strikes – and that accounts for the self-righteous attitude with which they subsequently permit themselves to commit the most heinous acts of violence.

The union was dead wrong throughout the Homestead strike. Frick was well within his moral rights to hire non-union workers. He had the right to bring in Pinkerton guards to protect the company property. He had the right to appeal to the Governor for soldiers to do the same. By contrast, the union men had no right to seize Carnegie's property. They had no right to physically oppose the landing of the Pinkertons on company grounds. Above all, they had no right to riot and commit murder. Carnegie was certainly responsible for the actions of Frick, his man. But Frick, hard and recalcitrant as he was, was morally blameless throughout the affair. His error of bringing in Pinkertons rather than appealing for troops was a tactical, not an ethical, one. The first cause and prime mover of the hideous brutality was the union: as soon as its men seized Carnegie's property, they thereby initiated the use of force and established a context of violence. The unions' generalized belief in their men's inalienable right to their jobs is responsible for their chronic – and sometimes lethal – violence against workers independent enough to cross picket lines during strikes.

But to this day, writers on the topic condone the union and condemn Carnegie. For example, Peter Krass, Carnegie's most recent biographer, depicts the sharp contrast between Carnegie's enormous wealth and the crushing poverty and brutal work conditions of the steelmaster's laborers.

He reiterates the long-standing claim that Carnegie's fortune was founded on severe exploitation of his workers.[20]

Too often, anti-capitalist writers approach such questions with a
combination of fiery moral outrage and invincible economic ignorance.
A series of tough questions must be asked of these writers — and then
rationally answered.

Question: Why were thousands of workers willing to take these horrible jobs and literally fight to the death to retain them from other men,
i.e., "strikebreakers," who wanted them? Answer: Because in the early
days of American industrialization, not 30 years after the conclusion of
the Civil War, the country was still poor by 21st century standards, and
such jobs were generally superior to the other jobs available to these men.

Question: Why did so many European immigrants, including the
Hungarians and Poles at Carnegie's mills, emigrate to America, accept
these back-breaking jobs, and not return to their native lands? Answer:
Because in their judgment such industrial jobs were superior to the pervasive destitution of their non-capitalist homelands.

Question: Why was there such widespread and severe penury that
these ghastly jobs were the best available to thousands of workers?
Answer: Because not even capitalism can effect Biblical-style miracles. It
takes decades, even in a free country, even during the Inventive Period, to
raise general living standards from destitution to prosperity.

Question: Why was the market level of monetary wages appallingly
low? Answer: Anti-capitalists hold what may be termed the "Scrooge
Theory" of wage rates. On this view, employers who are nice guys pay
higher wages, and those who are miserly skinflints lower ones. But in fact
the relative benevolence or malevolence of respective employers is irrelevant. Wages, the price of labor, are set by supply and demand, as any
other price. In impoverished nations or eras, hordes of penniless workers
seeking whatever employment they can find inevitably drive down the
price of labor.

Question: Why were real wages so low? Answer: Real wages rise because of one factor only — increased productivity. Levels of productivity were very low prior to the Technological and Industrial Revolutions of the Inventive Period. Consequently, supply of goods was limited and prices were high relative to wages. What constituted state-of-the-art technology in the 1890s was primitive by the standards of a century later. Productivity was low by subsequent standards (though rising dramatically).

Question: What happened to real wages during the Inventive Period? They rose by 20 percent, exactly as would be expected given the increasing rates of productivity.

Question: Who or what was fundamentally responsible for such increases? Answer: Those inventors who developed the revolutionary technologies and the risk-taking entrepreneurs who deployed them in their manufacturing plants.

Question: Given all of this, was Andrew Carnegie friend or foe of the workingman? Answer: It was the enormous output of Carnegie and his fellow industrialists that was fundamentally responsible for raising the real wages of American workers — so that before World War I, the United States was already the wealthiest nation of history.

Question: Why these endless charges against Carnegie and his peers? Answer: Because the Great Disconnect is too much with us. Peter Krass, as but one example, admires Carnegie for his philanthropy, not for his productiveness; as if giving wealth away is a virtue, but creating it is morally neutral.

As has become evident, two philosophical errors permeate the general anti-capitalist theory. One is the death morality of self-sacrifice that decries a man's selfish pursuit of his own values. The other is the failure to recognize the fundamental role of the mind in creating wealth. Given an understanding of these two points, it is clear that Carnegie's genius was the first cause and prime mover of his vast steel-producing empire,

and that his enormous contributions to the productive process earned him his huge fortune; a fortune not earned by his less-productive colleagues and employees; a fortune that rightfully was his. The philosophical issues are the real points of difference between capitalism's supporters and its critics, not the real wages of steelworkers during the 1890s or the relative culpability of the union or of Frick's Pinkertons for the violence at Homestead.

Even so brief a discussion of unjust accusations against the Productive Geniuses cannot be concluded without remembering the charges directed against E.H. Harriman by President Theodore Roosevelt. According to Roosevelt, the man who rebuilt the outdated Union Pacific, Central Pacific and Southern Pacific Railroads, and transformed them into the most gigantic and productive railway network the world had seen, was an "undesirable citizen," an "enemy of the Republic," and a character of "deep-seated corruption." Harriman was, in Roosevelt's view, the worst of big business's "malefactors of great wealth." The contrast between Harriman's achievements and Roosevelt's insults was so stark that the only proper response is to question the altruist-collectivist-statist code that gives both rise and respectability to the anti-business smears.[21]

But the endless, at times gross and outrageous inaccuracies in the specific moral accusations against the Productive Geniuses is the minor problem with the anti-capitalists' case. The major problem is a much more global error in their reasoning. For research may very well reveal moral breaches committed by the great producers during their lifetimes. Suppose that such is the case. What it establishes is that they were not morally perfect. But men do not have to be morally perfect in order to be achievers on a grand scale.

Heroes sometimes have moral flaws. For example, an individual may spend years of scrupulous, exhausting effort and discover a cure for cancer – and at the same time be unfaithful to his wife. Men are not always flawlessly consistent. The point – in justice – is not that the heroic

achievement mitigates the moral breach – it does not; rather, it is that the moral breach does not diminish the heroic achievement. In such a case, both the injustice committed to the wife and the glorious achievement are actual occurrences; each is part of reality. Although the dishonesty is to be deplored, the supreme accomplishment – and the sedulous devotion to its attainment – are to be celebrated.

That the Productive Geniuses created enormous value in service of man's life on earth is not to be doubted. That their lives were scrupulously devoted to the arduous task of producing wealth – the indispensable goods and services upon which human survival and prosperity depend – is clear. But the purveyors of the Robber Baron thesis deny this fundamental truth and focus almost exclusively on the producers' flaws – and when they can't find real examples, invent fictitious ones.

When we recognize that human life depends on achievement – on growing food, curing diseases, producing steel and oil, etc. – then we will understand that, though the wicked must be punished, it is far more important to reward the good. The good, the creative, the productive, the life-giving – these are significant. A negative emphasis on men's moral flaws – even if real – and a sweeping, dismissive neglect of their virtues and accomplishments, is in itself an act of injustice. If the Productive Geniuses committed actual moral transgressions, then those must be acknowledged and condemned. But such would in no way vitiate the enormity of their achievements. The time is long past to drop the misconceived "Robber Baron" thesis and to recognize and honor the men to whom we owe so much.

The answer to the question that initiated this Chapter is clear: when judged by the standard of man's life, the creative activities of the Productive Geniuses are recognized as a supreme virtue.

The distinguished historian, Louis Hacker, understood this point. He wrote:

> The "Robber Barons" were not the despoilers we have

been led to believe. The United States of the post-Civil War period, a developing country, was transformed in not more than a single generation into the greatest industrial nation of the world...A complete transportation net, the beginnings of the generation of electrical power and its transmission, the creation of new industries, the modernization of farm plant: all these were accomplished in this brief time. In consequence all sectors of the economy benefited.

Professor Hacker went on to ask: "What were those circumstances in the America of the post-Civil War years that were so favorable to the astounding growth and development of the United States?...First, government and the American people rarely placed obstacles in the way of a freely-operating private enterprise system or imposed any important restraints or penalties on its practitioners."[22]

The deeper point is that the Great Disconnect is operative here. The foundation of the critics' argument is an anti-egoist approach to ethics, an altruist-collectivist-statist theory that holds selfless service to others as the criterion of virtue. On such grounds, any profit-driven activity represents a moral breach and is to be viewed with suspicion. Any moral code repudiating egoism as a virtue, necessarily condemns the pursuit of profit. Consequently, if Carnegie, Rockefeller, et al., made hundreds of millions of dollars, it is logical to conclude — irrespective of the specific facts — that their primary means were fraud and exploitation.

The exponents of altruism are unable to identify, much less honor, the enormous productiveness of these men. Their conceptual framework makes it virtually impossible for them to apprehend capitalism's true nature; they see it in a form distorted by the prism of the moral theories through which they view it. Their moral code is profoundly in error and woefully inadequate for the task of properly evaluating the Productive Geniuses. A proper evaluation of the great producers requires a moral code upholding both man's life as the standard of value and its logical

corollary of rational egoism. Until the altruist-collectivist-statist doctrine is supplanted by the more rational code, the Great Disconnect between facts and evaluations will continue to dominate discussion of this issue.

It is for the same reason that statist intellectuals generally muster only a comparative fraction of outrage for the true "robber barons" of the era: the paragons of graft at Tammany Hall and the other big city political machines. While prominent businessmen of the Inventive Period created wealth, prominent politicians plundered it. Perfect examples were William Marcy "Boss" Tweed, Richard Croker, John Kelly and George Washington Plunkitt. Tweed's ring stole roughly $50 million before being caught (approximately $500 million in today's value).

Plunkitt, a leading Tammany figure for decades around the turn of the 20th century, was a colorful character. He boasted of becoming a millionaire by means of "honest graft," was an unabashed and vocal champion of the "spoils system," was expert in getting out the vote—living and dead—and could strongarm recalcitrant supporters with the best.

In a series of speeches he gave, Plunkitt was "compellingly honest about the true lure of politics — first and foremost, the desire to hold and wield power." As one contemporary economist writes: "Plunkitt's motto...would undoubtedly be well-known to generations of American high-schoolers if a captain of industry had ever said it: 'I seen my opportunities and I took 'em!'"

Why an inverted standard of evaluation that incessantly excoriates productive businessmen as plunderers but fails to engender a similar degree of outrage regarding counter-productive, plundering politicians? Such a travesty is based on the intellectuals' altruistic ethics that makes it possible for them to condone the corrupt political bosses who provided spoils for their slum-dwelling supporters while reviling the corporate "fat cats" who made millions for themselves. On an anti-egoistic ethics, earning and enjoying wealth is a moral transgression; stealing it and distributing it among poverty-stricken followers is morally superior.[23]

Robber Barons or Productive Geniuses

One final point needs to be established regarding this period of American history. Historians often contrast "the Gilded Age" with the 18th century American Enlightenment. They recognize the period of Franklin, Jefferson and Paine for what it was – an era of supreme intellectual attainments, with an emphasis on rationality, science, the rights of man, liberty and progress, i.e., the application of critical intelligence to the material betterment of human life. The "Gilded Age" they view as a period rejecting these virtues – an era whose leading figures renounced rationality for mindless, rapacious greed and the rights of man for callous exploitation. These are the years, they claim, in which America lost its way and relinquished the great promise with which she was born. To them, the era's "social philosophy, which it found adequate to its needs, was summed up in three words – preemption, exploitation, progress...Premption meant exploitation and exploitation meant progress. It was a simple philosophy and it suited the simple individualism of the times. The Gilded Age knew nothing of the Enlightenment; it recognized only the acquisitive instinct."[24]

Such a theory could not be further from the truth. The essence of the Enlightenment was the application of rational intelligence to the practical problems of man's life on earth. The *philosophes* dearly, desperately wanted to both free men from political tyranny and elevate them above the tragic recurrences of famine, disease and the most hideous penury. They recognized that innovation, invention, technological progress and industrialization were invaluable means to achieving their goals.

Chapter Three showed the close relationship between the Enlightenment and the Industrial Revolution. In light of that insight, it can be concluded that the Inventive Period – with its outpouring of technological advances resulting in vast material improvements in the quality, quantity and longevity of human life – fitted the program of the *philosophes* exactly. The Inventive Period, and the creative efforts of the Productive Geniuses, was the direct historical and historic descendant of the 18th century Enlightenment. The *philosophes* hungered for human progress –

[437]

and in the realms of health, wealth, living standards and life expectancies, the great minds of the Inventive Period gave it to them in doses the size of which were historically undreamed of.

Notes

Introduction: The Great Disconnect

1. Thomas Sowell, *Race and Culture* (New York: Basic Books, 1994), pp. 186-196. Dinesh D'Souza, "We the Slaveowners: In Jefferson's America Were Some Men Not Created Equal?" *Policy Review* (Fall 1995, Number 74).
2. Stephane Courtois, et al., *The Black Book of Communism: Crimes, Terror, Repression* (Cambridge, Mass.: Harvard University Press, 1999), pp. 565-575. W. Stanley Mooneyham, *Sea of Heartbreak* (Plainfield, N.J.: Logos International, 1980), pp. 3-92 and *passim.* Nguyen Qui Duc, *Where The Ashes Are: The Odyssey of a Vietnamese Family* (New York: Addison-Wesley Publishing, 1994). www.boatpeople.com
3. Henry Grady Weaver, *The Mainspring of Human Progress* (Irvington-on-Hudson, NY: Foundation for Economic Education, 1953), pp. 11-12.
4. Gerald O'Driscoll, et al., *The 2001 Index of Economic Freedom* (Washington, D.C.: the Heritage Foundation and the *Wall Street Journal*, 2001), pp. 1-5. Kim Holmes and Melanie Kirkpatrick, "Freedom and Growth," *The Wall Street Journal*, December 16, 1996
5. *The Black Book of Communism, op. cit.*, pp. 457-641 and *passim.* Paul Johnson, *Modern Times: The World From The Twenties To The Nineties* (New York: HarperPerennial, 1992), pp. 544-565. Richard Pipes, *Communism: A History* (New York: Modern Library, 2001), pp. 132-135. Ronald Segal, *Islam's Black Slaves: The Other Black Diaspora* (New York: Farrar, Straus and Giroux, 2001), pp. 199-223. Samantha Power, "Bystanders to Genocide," *The Atlantic Monthly*, September 2001.
6. Angus Maddison, *Phases of Capitalist Development* (New York: Oxford University Press, 1982), pp. 4-7.
7. *The Black Book of Communism, op. cit.*, pp. 463-500, 547-564, 577-635.

Modern Times, op. cit., pp. 548-551.

8. *The Index of Economic Freedom, op. cit.,* pp. 1-5.
9. *The Black Book of Communism, op. cit.,* pp. 562-563, 690-695.
10. Karl Marx and Friedrich Engels, *The Communist Manifesto* (New York: Washington Square Press, 1964), pp. 61-62.
11. Quoted in Ayn Rand, *Capitalism: The Unknown Ideal* (New York: Penguin, 1966), pp. 297-298.
12. Richard Hofstadter, *The American Political Tradition* (New York: Vintage Books, 1948), pp. 164-165.

Part One: History

1: What is Capitalism?

1. Wheaton J. Lane, *Commodore Vanderbilt: An Epic of the Steam Age* (New York: Alfred A. Knopf, 1942), pp. 10-11.
2. *Ibid.,* pp. 34-35.
3. Burton W. Folsom, *The Myth of the Robber Barons* (Herndon, Va.: Young America's Foundation, 1991), pp. 2-5.
4. Mark Skousen, *The Making of Modern Economics* (Armonk, NY: M.E. Sharpe, 2001), pp. 52-53.
5. Joseph Schumpeter, "The Creative Response in Economic History," in *Essays on Entrepreneurs, Innovations, Business Cycles and the Evolution of Capitalism,* ed. Richard Clemence (New Brunswick, NJ: Transaction Publishers, 1989), pp. 221-231; *idem., Capitalism, Socialism and Democracy* (New York: Harper and Row, 1942), pp. 81-86. For the best presentation of how innovative thinkers promote progress in a free society, see Ayn Rand's seminal novel, *The Fountainhead* (New York: Penguin Books, 1943).
6. Quote and paraphrasing from Ayn Rand, *Capitalism: The Unknown Ideal, op. cit.,* pp. 18-19.
7. Quote and paraphrasing from *Ibid.,* p. 320.
8. Quote and paraphrasing from *Ibid.,* pp. 321-322.
9. *Ibid.,* p. 322.
10. *Ibid.,* p. 46.
11. Ayn Rand, *Atlas Shrugged* (New York: Penguin Books, 1957), p. 1083.
12. Quote and paraphrasing from Ayn Rand, *The Ayn Rand Letter* (Gaylordsville, Ct.: Second Renaissance Inc., 1979), p. 109; quoted in *The Ayn Rand Lexicon,* ed. Harry Binswanger (New York: New American Library, 1986), p.

Notes

13.

13. Ayn Rand, *Capitalism: The Unknown Ideal,* op. cit., p. 19.
14. Gabriel Kolko, *The Triumph of Conservatism* (New York: The Free Press, 1963), pp. 2-5, 57-60, 255-278 and *passim.* Walter Williams, *The State Against Blacks* (New York: McGraw-Hill, 1982), pp. 109-113. Raghuram Rajan and Luigi Zingales, *Saving Capitalism From the Capitalists* (New York: Crown Publishing Group, 2003), pp. 1-3, 209-210, 226-246.
15. John Locke, "Second Treatise of Civil Government," in *Two Treatises of Government* (New York: New American Library, 1963), Sections 4-15, pp. 309-318. See also W.T. Jones, *A History of Western Philosophy,* vol. 3 (New York: Harcourt, Brace & World, 1969), pp. 266-269.
16. Leonard Peikoff, *The Ominous Parallels* (New York: New American Library, 1982), pp. 109-110.
17. Carl Becker, *The Declaration of Independence, A Study in the History of Political Ideas* (New York: Vintage Books, 1922), p. 41.
18. Peter Gay, *The Enlightenment: An Interpretation,* vol. 2, *The Science of Freedom* (New York: Alfred A. Knopf, 1969), pp.128-131.
19. Carl Becker, *The Declaration of Independence,* op. cit., pp. 42-46.
20. Peter Gay, *The Science of Freedom,* op. cit., p. 3.
21. *Ibid.,* pp. 6-7, 24, 27-29. Ernst Cassirer, *The Philosophy of the Enlightenment* (Boston: Beacon Press, 1955), pp. 3-10.
22. Peter Gay, *The Enlightenment: An Interpretation,* vol. 1, *The Rise of Modern Paganism* (New York: Alfred A. Knopf, 1966), pp. 182-183, 364, 366; vol. 2, *The Science of Freedom,* op. cit., pp. 46 and 83. Will and Ariel Durant, *The Story of Civilization,* vol. 9, *The Age of Voltaire* (New York: Simon and Schuster, 1965), pp. 633-649.
23. Daniel Boorstin, *The Discoverers* (New York: Vintage Books, 1985), pp. 446-455, emphasis added. Peter Gay, *The Science of Freedom,* op. cit., pp. 152-156.
24. Carl Becker, *The Heavenly City of the Eighteenth-Century Philosophers,* second edition (New Haven: Yale University Press, 2003), pp. 58 and 33-70 *passim.*
25. Robert Whittemore, *Makers of the American Mind* (New York: William Morrow and Company, 1964), pp. 73-81.
26. *The Writings of Thomas Jefferson,* edited by Albert Ellery Bergh, 20 volumes. (Washington: Jefferson Memorial Association, 1903), VI, pp. 258-261. Robert Whittemore, *Makers of the American Mind,* op. cit., pp. 139-152. Phillips Russell, *Jefferson, Champion of the Free Mind* (New York: Dodd, Mead, 1956), pp. 4-6, 8-11, 17-18, 20-24, 30-37, 40-41, 46-49, 57-58, 66, 73-76, 80, 95-97, 98, 113, 145-148, 153-154 and *passim.* Saul Padover,

Jefferson: A Great American's Life and Ideas (New York: Mentor, 1970), pp. 20-46.

27. *The Life and Works of Thomas Paine*, ed. William Van der Wyde, 10 Volumes. (New Rochelle: Thomas Paine National Historical Association, 1925), VIII, pp. 1 and 5; quoted in Robert Whittemore, *Makers of the American Mind, op. cit.*, pp. 85 and 93-103. Jefferson quoted in Harry Hayden Clark, "Introduction," *American Century Writers, Thomas Paine* (New York: Hill and Wang, 1961), pp. cxvii-cxviii.

28. Leonard Peikoff, *The Ominous Parallels, op. cit.*, pp. 108 and 110. Joseph Blau, *Men and Movements in American Philosophy* (Englewood Cliffs, NJ: Prentice-Hall, 1952), pp. 44-46.

29. Peter Gay, *The Science of Freedom, op. cit.*, pp. 555 and 558.

30. John Locke, *Two Treatises of Government, op. cit.*, Section 27, pp. 328-329.

31. Adam Smith, *The Wealth of Nations*, ed. Edwin Cannan (New York: The Modern Library, 1994), p. 140.

32. *Ibid.*, pp. 12 and 629. Mark Skousen, *The Making of Modern Economics, op. cit.*, pp. 13-43.

2: The Pre-Capitalist Political-Economic Systems

1. Friedrich Engels, *The Condition of the Working Class in England*, trans. W.O. Henderson and W.H. Chaloner (Stanford, CA: Stanford University Press, 1968), pp. 10-11.

2. J.L. and Barbara Hammond, *The Skilled Labourer 1760-1832* (New York: Harper and Row, 1970), pp. 1-3.

3. Cecil Driver, *Tory Radical: The Life of Richard Oastler* (New York: Oxford University Press, 1946), pp. 36-57, 164-177 and *passim*. Robert Hessen, "The Effects of the Industrial Revolution on Women and Children," in Ayn Rand, *Capitalism: The Unknown Ideal, op. cit.*, p. 114. "Evidence of Richard Oastler on 'Yorkshire Slavery,'" http://dspace.dial.pipex.com/town/terrace/adw03/peel/oastler.htm.

4. William Cooke Taylor, *The Factory System*; quoted in W.H. Hutt, "The Factory System of the Early Nineteenth Century," in F.A. Hayek, ed., *Capitalism and the Historians*, (Chicago: University of Chicago Press, 1954), p. 176.

5. J.L. and Barbara Hammond, *The Skilled Labourer 1760-1832, op. cit.*, p. 4. Friedrich Engels, *The Condition of the Working Class in England, op. cit.*, pp. 151 and 156. See also T.S. Ashton, "The Treatment of Capitalism by Historians," in F.A. Hayek, ed., *Capitalism and the Historians, op. cit.*, p. 36.

6. W.H. Hutt, "The Factory System of the Early Nineteenth Century," in F.A.

Notes

Hayek ed., *Capitalism and the Historians, op. cit.*, p. 157. Ludwig von Mises, *Human Action: A Treatise on Economics*, third revised edition (Chicago: Henry Regnery Company, 1966), p. 618.

7. Nathan Rosenberg and L.E. Birdzell, *How the West Grew Rich* (New York: Basic Books, 1986), p.172. Fernand Braudel, *The Wheels of Commerce* (New York: Harper & Row, 1979), pp. 506-510.

8. J.B. Black, *The Reign of Elizabeth, 1558-1603* (Oxford: Oxford University Press, 1959), p. 255.

9. George Reisman, *Capitalism: A Treatise on Economics* (Ottawa, Ill.: Jameson Books, 1998), p. 332.

10. Angus Maddison, *Phases of Capitalist Development, op. cit.*, p. 7.

11. M. Dorothy George, *London Life in the Eighteenth Century* (New York: Capricorn Books, 1965), pp. 22-25.

12. *Ibid.*, pp. 28-29.

13. *Ibid.*, pp. 27, 34, 38, 40.

14. T.S. Ashton, "The Treatment of Capitalism by Historians," in F.A. Hayek, ed., *Capitalism and the Historians, op. cit.*, p. 47.

15. Mark Skousen, *The Making of Modern Economics, op. cit.*, pp. 16-19.

16. M. Dorothy George, *London Life in the Eighteenth Century, op. cit.*, pp. 42-45.

17. *Ibid.*, pp. 72-73.

18. *Ibid.*, pp. 77, 85 and 101. F.A. Hayek, ed., *Capitalism and the Historians, op. cit.*, p. 47. Will and Ariel Durant, *The Story of Civilization*, vol. VIII, *The Age of Louis XIV* (New York: Simon and Schuster, 1963), p. 260.

19. M. Dorothy George, *London Life in the Eighteenth Century, op. cit.*, pp. 86-87. Mabel C. Buer, *Health, Wealth and Population in the Early Days of the Industrial Revolution* (New York: Howard Fertig, 1968), p. 88.

20. Stephen Coote, *Samuel Pepys, A Life* (New York: St. Martin's Press, 2000), pp. 180-183.

21. *The Diary of Samuel Pepys*, VI, 1665, ed. Robert Latham and William Matthews (Berkely, CA: University of California Press, 1974), p. 208.

22. *Ibid.*, VII, 1666, pp. 275-277.

23. Carlo Cipolla, *Before the Industrial Revolution* (New York: W.W. Norton and Company, 1976), pp. 152-154. J.J. Bagley, *Life in Medieval England* (London: B.T. Batsford, 1960), pp. 58-59. Frances and Joseph Gies, *Life in a Medieval Village* (New York: Harper & Row, 1990), p. 34. Will and Ariel Durant, *The Story of Civilization*, vol. VII, *The Age of Reason Begins* (New York: Simon and Schuster, 1961), pp. 89-90. John Dolan and William Adams-Smith, *Health and Society: A Documentary History of Medicine*

(New York: The Seabury Press, 1978), pp. 77 and 91. Paul Slack, "The Response to Plague in Early Modern England: Public Policies and Their Consequences," in John Walter and Roger Schofield, ed., *Famine, Disease and the Social Order in Early Modern Society* (Cambridge: Cambridge University Press, 1989), p. 167. Anne Roberts, "The Plague in England," www.education.guardian.co.uk/higher/humanities/partner/story/0,9885,58 5086,00.html.

24. M. Dorothy George, *London Life in the Eighteenth Century, op. cit.*, pp. 116-117.

25. *Ibid.*, pp. 121-122. Thomas Sowell, *Conquests and Cultures, An International History* (New York: Basic Books, 1998), pp. 64-66, 68. Mike Cronin, *A History of Ireland* (New York: St. Martin's Press, 2001), pp. 86-90.

26. J.J. Bagley, *Life in Medieval England, op. cit.*, pp. 57-59, 156-159. Mabel Buer, *Health, Wealth and Population in the Early Days of the Industrial Revolution, op. cit.*, pp. 104-105.

27. J.B. Black, *The Reign of Elizabeth, 1558-1603, op. cit.*, pp. 235-236, 255.

28. Maurice Ashley, *England in the Seventeenth Century* (New York: Harper & Row, 1980), pp. 23-25.

29. Andrew Appleby, *Famine in Tudor and Stuart England* (Stanford, Cal.: Stanford University Press, 1978), pp. 1-16, 95-154. Fernand Braudel, *The Structures of Everyday Life: Civilization and Capitalism, 15th-18th Century*, trans. Sian Reynolds (New York: Harper and Row, 1981), pp. 73-78, emphasis added. Arthur Herman, *How the Scots Invented the Modern World* (New York: Crown Publishers, 2001), p. 9. Peter Laslett, *The World We Have Lost Further Explored: England Before the Industrial Age* (New York: Charles Scribner's Sons, 1984), pp. 122-152. John Walter and Roger Schofield, ed., *Famine, Disease and the Social Order in Early Modern Society, op. cit.*, pp. 1-61. E.A. Wrigley and R.S. Schofield, *The Population History of England, 1541-1871* (Cambridge, Mass.: Harvard University Press, 1981), pp. 340-342.

30. Angus Maddison, *Phases of Capitalist Development, op. cit.*, pp. 4-7. Joyce Burnette and Joel Mokyr, "The Standard of Living Through the Ages," in Julian Simon, ed., *The State of Humanity* (Cambridge, Mass.: Blackwell Publishers, 1995), p. 136. Mark Skousen, *The Making of Modern Economics, op. cit.*, p. 15. Angus Maddison, "Poor Until 1820," *The Wall Street Journal*, January 11, 1999.

31. Will and Ariel Durant, *The Story of Civilization*, vol. 9, *The Age of Voltaire, op. cit.*, pp. 33-36, 630-644. W.T. Jones, *A History of Western Philosophy*, vol. 2, *The Medieval Mind* (New York: Harcourt, Brace & World, 1969), pp. 60-

Notes

69.

3: The Enlightenment and the Industrial Revolution

1. Addison, Voltaire and Hume quoted in Peter Gay, *The Science of Freedom, op. cit.*, pp. 49-51; Samuel Johnson in Paul Johnson, *A History of the American People* (New York: HarperPerennial, 1999), p. 676. Mabel Buer, *Health, Wealth and Population in the Early Days of the Industrial Revolution, op. cit.*, p. 37.
2. Peter Gay, *The Science of Freedom, op. cit.*, pp. 50-51.
3. Arthur Herman, *How the Scots Invented the Modern World, op. cit.*, pp. 161-191.
4. Abraham Wolf, *A History of Science, Technology and Philosophy in the Eighteenth Century*, vol.1 (New York: Harper Torchbooks, 1961), pp. 34-35.
5. Peter Gay, *The Science of Freedom, op. cit.*, p. 9.
6. T.S. Ashton, *The Industrial Revolution* (New York: Oxford University Press, 1997 ed.), p. 15-16. Arthur Herman, *How the Scots Invented the Modern World, op. cit.*, pp. 274-275.
7. Arthur Herman, *How the Scots Invented the Modern World, op. cit.*, pp. 93-137.
8. Arthur Herman, *How the Scots Invented the Modern World, op. cit.*, pp. 271-272. Peter Gay, *The Science of Freedom, op. cit.*, pp. 3-55.
9. Arthur Herman, *How the Scots Invented the Modern World, op. cit.*, pp. 274 and 278. David Daiches, ed. *A Hotbed of Genius: The Scottish Enlightenment 1730-1790* (Edinburgh: Edinburgh University Press, 1986), pp. 24-34, 116-117. Samuel Smiles, *Brief Biographies* (Boston: James Osgood and Company, 1876), pp. 14-15, 25. Robert Schofield, *The Lunar Society of Birmingham: A Social History of Provincial Science and Industry in Eighteenth-Century England* (Oxford: Oxford University Press, 1963), pp. 19, 66-67, 75. Mark Skousen, *The Making of Modern Economics, op. cit.*, pp. 30-31. James Buchan, *Crowded with Genius, The Scottish Enlightenment: Edinburgh's Moment of the Mind* (New York: HarperCollins, 2003), pp. 290-299.
10. Peter Gay, *The Science of Freedom, op. cit.*, p. 10.
11. Arthur Herman, *How the Scots Invented the Modern World, op. cit.*, p. 274.
12. *Ibid*, pp. 279-280. Henry and Rodney Dale, *The Industrial Revolution* (Oxford: Oxford University Press, 1992), p. 26.
13. Samuel Smiles, *Selections from Lives of the Engineers*, ed. Thomas Parke Hughes (Cambridge, Mass.: M.I.T. Press, 1966), pp. 173-285.
14. Arthur Herman, *How the Scots Invented the Modern World, op. cit.*, p. 280. Henry and Rodney Dale, *The Industrial Revolution, op. cit.*, pp. 27-28.

15. Abraham Wolf, *A History of Science, Technology and Philosophy in the Eighteenth Century, op. cit.*, vol. 2, pp. 565-568. Samuel Smiles, *Selections From Lives of the Engineers, op. cit.*, pp. 57-73, 136-161, 330. Jacob Bronowski, *The Ascent of Man* (Boston: Little, Brown and Co., 1973), pp. 260-262.

16. Samuel Smiles, *Selections From Lives of the Engineers, op. cit.*, pp. 330, 349-358. Abraham Wolf, *A History of Science, Technology, and Philosophy in the Eighteenth Century, op. cit.*, vol. 2, p. 568. Paul Johnson, *The Birth of the Modern* (New York: HarperPerennial, 1992), pp. 179-192. Arthur Herman, *How the Scots Invented the Modern World, op. cit.*, pp. 9, 281-283.

17. Arthur Herman, *How the Scots Invented the Modern World, op. cit.*, p. 281-283. Samuel Smiles, *Selections From Lives of the Engineers, op. cit.*, pp. 410-417.

18. Robert Schofield, *The Lunar Society of Birmingham, op. cit.*, pp. 3, 35-39, 75-82, 189-366. Jenny Uglow, *Lunar Men: Five Friends Whose Curiosity Changed the World* (New York: Farrar, Straus and Giroux, 2002), pp. 26-34, 70-84, 93-104, 107-121, 243-257, 275-276 and *passim*. Brooke Hindle, *The Pursuit of Science in Revolutionary America 1735-1789* (Chapel Hill, N.C.: the University of North Carolina Press, 1956), pp. 91-92. Jacob Bronowski, *The Ascent of Man, op. cit.*, pp. 259-288. T.S. Ashton, *The Industrial Revolution, op. cit.*, pp. 55-58. Brooke Hindle and Steven Lubar, *Engines of Change: the American Industrial Revolution 1790-1860* (Washington, D.C.: the Smithsonian Institution Press, 1986), p. 31.

19. Peter Gay, *The Science of Freedom, op. cit.*, pp. 10-12.

20. Arthur Herman, *How the Scots Invented the Modern World, op. cit.*, pp. 276-279.

21. Ernst Cassirer, *The Philosophy of the Enlightenment, op. cit.*, pp. 7-8. James Buchan, *Crowded with Genius, op. cit.*, pp. 273-287.

22. Henry and Rodney Dale, *The Industrial Revolution, op. cit.*, pp. 36-41. Paul Johnson, *The Birth of the Modern, op. cit.*, pp. 188-189, 580-583. Samuel Smiles, *Brief Biographies, op. cit.*, pp. 55-70. T.S. Ashton, *The Industrial Revolution, op. cit.*, pp. 10, 53.

23. Paul Johnson, *The Birth of the Modern, op. cit.*, p. 188.

24. H.W. Brands, *The First American: The Life And Times of Benjamin Franklin* (New York: Anchor Books, 2000), pp. 12-16.

25. Brooke Hindle, *The Pursuit of Science in Revolutionary America 1735-1789, op. cit.*, pp. 1, 77-78, 190-192.

26. *Ibid.*, pp. 121-126, 136-140, 190-215, 368-379. Abraham Wolf, *A History of Science, Technology and Philosophy in the 18th Century, op. cit.*, vol. 2, pp. 550-

Notes

551.

27. Paul Johnson, *A History of the American People, op. cit.*, pp. 308-310. Brooke Hindle and Steven Lubar, *Engines of Change, The American Industrial Revolution 1790-1860, op. cit.*, pp. 227-228.

28. James Boswell, *Life of Johnson* (Oxford: Oxford University Press, 1980), under March 22, 1776, p. 704.

4: The Industrial Revolution Brings Advance

1. T.S. Ashton, *The Industrial Revolution, op. cit.*, pp. 58-61. Henry and Rodney Dale, *The Industrial Revolution, op. cit.*, pp. 6-15, 48-54. Paul Johnson, *A History of the American People, op. cit.*, pp. 307-308.

2. T.S. Ashton, *The Industrial Revolution, op. cit.*, p. 127.

3. George Reisman, *Capitalism: A Treatise on Economics* (Ottawa, IL: Jameson Books, 1998), p. 618.

4. R.M. Hartwell, *The Industrial Revolution and Economic Growth* (London: Methuen and Company, 1971), pp. 314-316.

5. J.L. Hammond and M.R.D. Foot, *Gladstone and Liberalism* (London: English Universities Press, 1952), pp. 46 and 66. Nick Elliott, "John Bright: Voice of Victorian Liberalism," in Burton Folsom, ed., *The Industrial Revolution and Free Trade* (Irvington-on-Hudson, NY: Foundation for Economic Education, 1996), p. 28. J.H. Clapham, *An Economic History of Modern Britain*, vol. 1, *The Early Railway Age* (Cambridge: Cambridge University Press, 1926), pp. 559-560. See also pp. 128 and 601-602.

6. R.M. Hartwell, *The Industrial Revolution and Economic Growth, op. cit.*, pp. 328-337, 356-360.

7. J.H. Clapham, *An Economic History of Modern Britain*, vol. 1, *The Early Railway Age, op. cit.*, pp. 548-561.

8. Peter Lindert and Jeffrey Williamson, "English Workers' Living Standards During the Industrial Revolution: A New Look," *The Economic History Review*, 2nd Series, 36 (Feb. 1983), pp. 4-7.

9. Peter Lane, *The Industrial Revolution: The Birth of the Modern Age* (New York: Harper and Row, 1978), p. 249. T.S. Ashton, *The Industrial Revolution, op. cit.*, p. 127.

10. Ludwig von Mises, *Human Action, op. cit.*, p. 621. See Mises's full discussion of capitalism's enormous benefits to the workingman, pp. 615-623.

11. Peter Lindert and Jeffrey Williamson, "English Workers' Living Standards During the Industrial Revolution: A New Look," *op. cit.*, pp. 1-2, 23-24.

12. *Ibid.*, p. 24. Jeffrey Williamson, *Did British Capitalism Breed Inequality* (Boston: Allen and Unwin, 1985), pp. 7-33. Clark Nardinelli, *Child Labor*

[447]

and the Industrial Revolution (Bloomington, IN: Indiana University Press, 1990), p. 156. For an enlightening debate between pessimistic and optimistic thinkers regarding the effects of the Industrial Revolution – and one showing their contrasting cognitive methods – read: E.J. Hobsbawm, *Labouring Men: Studies in the History of Labour* (Garden City, NY: Anchor Books, 1967), pp. 75-147 and R.M. Hartwell, *The Industrial Revolution and Economic Growth, op. cit.*, pp. 313-360. The reader can judge for himself whose case is grounded more firmly in facts and rational argumentation and whose in ad hominem attacks, unsupported assertions, distorted statements, exaggerated "straw man" formulations and an emotionalist tone.

13. T.S. Ashton, *The Industrial Revolution, op. cit.*, pp. 60-61; *idem*, "The Treatment of Capitalism by Historians," in F.A. Hayek, *op. cit.*, p. 51; *idem*, "The Standard of Life of the Workers in England, 1790-1830," in F.A. Hayek, *op. cit.*, pp. 129-131.

14. Joyce Burnette and Joel Mokyr, "The Standard of Living Through the Ages," in Julian Simon, ed., *The State of Humanity, op. cit.*, pp. 135-145.

15. R.M. Hartwell, *The Industrial Revolution and Economic Growth, op. cit.*, pp. 324-325.

16. George Reisman, *Capitalism, op. cit.*, pp. 76-78.

17. T.S. Ashton, "The Standard of Life of the Workers in England, 1790-1830," in F.A. Hayek, *Capitalism and the Historians, op. cit.*, p. 136; *idem*, *The Industrial Revolution, op. cit.*, pp. 53-54.

18. Paul Johnson, *A History of the American People, op. cit.*, pp. 674 and 679; *idem*, *The Birth of the Modern, World Society 1815-1830, op. cit.*, pp. 755-756. Mabel Buer, *Health, Wealth and Population in the Early Days of the Industrial Revolution, op. cit.*, p. 109. Otto Bettman, *The Good Old Days – They Were Terrible* (New York: Random House, 1974), pp. 47 and 51.

19. Joseph and Suzy Fucini, *Entrepreneurs, The Men and Women Behind Famous Brand Names and How They Made It* (Boston: G.K. Hall, 1985), p. 236. "The Story of Schweppes," http://members.tripod.com/~mikesheridan/schweppes1.htm.

20. Paul Johnson, *A History of the American People, op. cit.*, pp. 674-679.

21. Mabel Buer, *Health, Wealth and Population in the Early Days of the Industrial Revolution, op. cit.*, pp. 100-102.

22. *Ibid.*, pp. 76, 77, 102, 107-108.

23. "Drinking Water in the 19th and 20th Centuries," www.awwa.org/pressroom/BHIST-3.html.

24. "The History of Chlorine," http://c3.org/chlorine_knowledge_center/history.html. Stephen Gold, "The Rise of Markets and the Fall of Infectious

Notes

Disease," in Burton Folsom, ed., *The Industrial Revolution and Free Trade, op. cit.*, p. 84.

25. Lawrence Wright, *Clean and Decent: The History of the Bathroom and the W.C.* (London: Routledge and Kegan Paul, 1960), pp. 163-165, 176, 191-192, 218, 240, 242 and 245.

26. T.S. Ashton, "The Treatment of Capitalism by Historians," in F.A. Hayek, *Capitalism and the Historians, op. cit.*, p. 37. M. Dorothy George, *London Life in the Eighteenth Century, op. cit.*, pp. 60-61. Mabel Buer, *Health, Wealth and Population in the Early Days of the Industrial Revolution, op. cit.*, p. 60.

27. Joseph and Suzy Fucini, *Entrepreneurs The Men and Women Behind Famous Brand Names and How They Made It, op. cit.*, p. 221. www.pg.com/about_pg/overview_facts/history.jht.

28. Joseph and Suzy Fucini, *Entrepreneurs The Men and Women Behind Famous Brand Names and How They Made It, op. cit.*, pp. 84-86. www.americanstandard.com/history2.html.

29. Donald Boudreaux, "Cleaned by Capitalism," *Ideas on Liberty*, February 2000, pp. 4-5.

30. T.S. Ashton, The Industrial Revolution, *op. cit.*, pp. 3-4. Kenneth Hill, "The Decline of Childhood Mortality," in Julian Simon, ed., *The State of Humanity, op. cit.*, pp. 39-41.

31. E. A. Wrigley and R.S. Schofield, *The Population History of England, 1541-1871* (Cambridge, Mass.: Harvard University Press, 1981), pp. 230, 234-236, 528-529. Pat Hudson, "Preface" (1997 edition), T.S. Ashton, *The Industrial Revolution, op. cit.*, p. viii. Julian Simon, *The State of Humanity, op. cit.*, pp. 8-9; Samuel Preston, "Human Mortality Throughout History and Prehistory," in *ibid.*, pp. 30-32. R.M. Hartwell, *The Industrial Revolution and Economic Growth, op. cit.*, p. 338.

32. E.A. Wrigley and R.S. Schofield, *The Population History of England, 1541-1871, op. cit.*, pp. 208-209, 213-215, 402-426.

33. Milton Friedman, *Free to Choose, op. cit.*, p. 34. Michael Sanera and Jane Shaw, *Facts, Not Fear* (Washington, D.C.: Regnery Publishing, 1996), p. 65.

34. E.P. Thompson, *The Making of the English Working Class* (New York: Vintage Books, 1966), pp. 331-349.

35. Clark Nardinelli, *Child Labor and the Industrial Revolution, op. cit.*, pp. 1-4. W.H. Hutt, "The Factory System of the Early Nineteenth Century," in F.A. Hayek, *Capitalism and the Historians, op. cit.*, pp. 159-160. Friedrich Engels, *The Condition of the Working Class in England, op. cit.*, pp. xvii-xxv, 192.

36. M. Dorothy George, *London Life in the Eighteenth Century, op. cit.*, pp. 215-218.

37. William Cooke Taylor, The Factory System, quoted in W.H. Hutt, "The Factory System of the Early Nineteenth Century," in F.A. Hayek, *Capitalism and the Historians, op. cit.,* p. 176. Carlo Cipolla, *Before the Industrial Revolution, op. cit.,* p. 151. Fernand Braudel, *Capitalism and Material Life 1400-1800* (New York: Harper & Row, 1967), p. 38.

38. M. Dorothy George, *London Life in the Eighteenth Century, op. cit.,* p. 219.

39. *Ibid.,* pp. 227-236.

40. J.L. and Barbara Hammond, *The Town Labourer, 1760-1832* (New York: Longmans, Green and Co.,1919), pp. 144-146. Robert Hessen, "The Effects of the Industrial Revolution on Women and Children," in Ayn Rand, *Capitalism: The Unknown Ideal, op. cit.,* p. 112.

41. Lawrence Reed, "Child Labor and the British Industrial Revolution," in Burton Folsom, ed., *The Industrial Revolution and Free Trade, op. cit.,* pp. 62-63.

42. Clark Nardinelli, *Child Labor and the Industrial Revolution, op. cit.,* pp. 88-89. See also Nardinelli's footnote 73 on p. 176.

43. *Ibid.,* pp. 60-61, 72-73, 75.

44. *Ibid.,* pp. 59, 108, 110, 111, 122, 144. W.H. Hutt, "The Factory System of the Early Nineteenth Century," in F.A. Hayek, *Capitalism and the Historians, op. cit.,* pp. 168, 174, 176.

45. Pamela Horn, "Child Workers in the Pillow Lace and Straw Plait Trades of Victorian Buckinghamshire and Bedfordshire," *Historical Journal* 17 (December 1974), pp. 779-96.

46. Nathan Rosenberg and L.E. Birdzell, *How the West Grew Rich, op. cit.,* p. 173. Rondo Cameron, *A Concise Economic History of the World* (Oxford: Oxford University Press, 1997), p. 189.

47. Clark Nardinelli, *Child Labor and the Industrial Revolution, op. cit.,* pp. 108-110.

48. *Ibid.,* p. 144 and 149. Robert Hessen, "The Effects of the Industrial Revolution on Women and Children," in Ayn Rand, *Capitalism: The Unknown Ideal, op. cit.,* pp. 112-113. Ludwig von Mises, *Human Action, op. cit.,* p. 622.

49. "Child Labor Cures are Often Worse than the Problem," www.ncpa.org/pi/internet/index11.html.

50. www.childreach.org.

51. Angus Maddison, *Phases of Capitalist Development, op. cit.,* p. 4, emphasis added.

52. Johan Norberg, *In Defence of Global Capitalism* (Stockholm, Sweden: Timbro, 2001), pp. 197-209.

Notes

53. For the profound errors of economics involved in Marx's conception of "exploitation," his iron law of wages, his labor theory of value, and his theory of surplus value, see: George Reisman, *Capitalism, op. cit.*, pp. 603-613; Thomas Sowell, *Marxism: Philosophy and Economics* (New York: William Morrow and Company, 1985), pp. 189-195; and Henry Hazlitt, "The Legacy of Karl Marx" in Burton Folsom, ed., *The Industrial Revolution and Free Trade, op. cit.*, pp. 43-50.

5: The Inventive Period

1. Matthew Josephson, *Edison: A Biography* (New York: John Wiley and Sons, 1959), pp. 107-124, 159-174, 176-267, 384-403, 407-423, 435-436 and *passim*. Jonathan Hughes, *The Vital Few: American Economic Progress and Its Protagonists* (Boston: Houghton Mifflin, 1966), pp. 149-213.

2. L. Sprague de Camp, *The Heroic Age of American Invention* (Garden City, New York: Doubleday and Company, 1961), pp. 156-167. Ira Flatow, *They All Laughed...From Light Bulbs to Lasers: The Fascinating Stories Behind the Great Inventions That Have Changed Our Lives* (New York: Harper Collins, 1993), pp. 71-84. Jonathan Hughes, *The Vital Few, op. cit.*, pp. 170-171.

3. Daniel J. Boorstin, *The Creators: A History of Heroes of the Imagination* (New York: Vintage Books, 1992), pp. 536-548. Paul Johnson, *A History of the American People, op. cit.*, pp. 554, 570-577. Louis Hacker, *The World of Andrew Carnegie: 1865-1901* (New York: J.B. Lippincott Company, 1968), pp. 350-351.

4. David McCullough, *The Great Bridge: The Epic Story of the Building of the Brooklyn Bridge* (New York: Simon and Schuster, 1972), pp. 21, 39-53, 195-214, 231-247, 286, 289-308, 315-321, 353, 462-464, 467, 475-478, 484-485, 493, 502, 545, 551, 556, 561-562 and *passim*. Michael Pollak, "Brooklyn Bridge Online."

5. Edwin Locke, *The Prime Movers, Traits of the Wealth Creators* (New York: American Management Association, 2000), pp. 83-84. L. Sprague de Camp, *The Heroic Age of American Invention, op. cit.*, pp. 104-113.

6. L. Sprague de Camp, *The Heroic Age of American Invention, op. cit.*, pp. 99-101, 212-214. Edmund Fuller, *Tinkers and Genius: The Story of the Yankee Inventors* (New York: Hastings House, 1955), pp. 273-283.

7. Ruth Brandon, *A Capitalist Romance* (New York: J.B. Lippincott Company, 1977), pp. 44-52, 100-140. John Steele Gordon, *The Business of America* (New York: Walker Publishing Company, 2001), pp. 52-56.

8. L. Sprague de Camp, *The Heroic Age of American Invention, op. cit.*, pp. 71-75.

9. L. Sprague de Camp, *The Heroic Age of American Invention, op. cit.*, pp. 53-56. www.georgewestinghouse.com/wwcard.html.

10. Joseph and Suzy Fucini, *Entrepreneurs, The Men and Women Behind Famous Brand Names and How They Made It, op. cit.*, pp. 16-18.

11. Elizabeth Brayer, *George Eastman, A Biography* (Baltimore: The Johns Hopkins University Press, 1996), pp. 19-20, 26-28, 59-72, 204-05. Ira Flatow, *They All Laughed...From Light Bulbs to Lasers: The Fascinating Stories Behind the Great Inventions That Have Changed Our Lives, op. cit.*, pp. 45-51. www.digitalcentury.com/encyclo/update/eastman.html.

12. Burton Folsom, *Empire Builders: How Michigan Entrepreneurs Helped Make America Great* (Traverse City, Mich.: Rhodes and Easton, 1998), pp. 141-42.

13. Fred Howard, *Wilbur and Orville: A Biography of the Wright Brothers* (New York: Dover Publications, 1998), pp. 30-37, 327-334, 403-405 and *passim*. Charles and Mary Beard, *The Rise of American Civilization*, vol. 2 (New York: Macmillan, 1930), pp. 411-412.

14. Lawrence Lessing, *Man Of High Fidelity: Edwin Howard Armstrong* (New York: Bantam, 1969), pp. IX, 14-22, 77-98, 157-73, 258-270.

15. Daniel Stashower, *The Boy Genius and the Mogul: The Untold Story of Television* (New York: Random House, 2002), pp. 12-26, 28-42, 154-183 and *passim*.

16. Lawrence Elliot, *George Washington Carver: The Man Who Overcame* (Englewood Cliffs, NJ: Prentice-Hall, 1966), pp. 5-26, 145-185 and *passim*.

17. Mark Twain, *A Connecticut Yankee in King Arthur's Court* (Berkeley, Cal.: University of California Press, 1979), p. 4.

18. Maury Klein, *The Change Makers* (New York: Henry Holt and Company, 2003), pp. 160-162.

19. Richard Hofstadter, *The American Political Tradition* (New York: Vintage Books, 1948), pp. 16, 164-167, emphasis added.

20. Matthew Josephson, *The Robber Barons* (New York: Harcourt, Brace & World, 1934), pp. vi and 101.

21. Richard Hofstadter, *The American Political Tradition, op. cit.*, pp. 164-65. Rondo Cameron, *A Concise Economic History of the World, op. cit.*, p. 228. Louis Hacker, *The World of Andrew Carnegie, op. cit.*, pp. 120-121, 157-158. Henry Hazlitt, *Economics in One Lesson* (Westport, Ct.: Arlington House Publishers, 1946), p.140.

22. Jonathan Hughes, *The Vital Few, op. cit.*, p. 215.

23. Andrew Bernstein, "The Inventive Period," *Ideas on Liberty*, April 2001, pp. 10-16.

Notes

24. Ayn Rand, *The Fountainhead, op. cit.*, p. 679.
25. Richard Hofstadter, *The American Political Tradition, op. cit.*, p. 164.
26. Ayn Rand, "Faith and Force: the Destroyers of the Modern World," in *Philosophy, Who Needs It* (New York: Bobbs-Merrill, 1982), p. 79.
27. Nathan Rosenberg and L.E. Birdzell, *How the West Grew Rich, op. cit.*, p. 265.
28. On this theme, see Ayn Rand's novelette, *Anthem* (New York: Penguin Books, 1995).

Part Two: Philosophy

6: The Nature of the Good

1. Immanuel Kant, *Foundations of the Metaphysics of Morals*, ed. R.P. Wolff, trans. L.W. Beck (Indianapolis: Bobbs-Merrill, 1969), pp. 16-17. Arthur Schopenhauer, *On the Basis of Morality*, trans. E.J.F. Payne (Indianapolis: Bobbs-Merill, 1965), pp. 139-140, 141-142, 165. Both quoted in Leonard Peikoff, *The Ominous Parallels, op. cit.*, pp. 76, 85-86.
2. John Dewey, *John Dewey: The Later Works, 1925-1953*, vol. 3, 1927-1928, ed. Jo Ann Boydston (Carbondale, Ill.: Southern Illinois University Press, 1984), pp. 219, 228-229. George Counts, *The Soviet Challenge to America* (New York: John Day, 1931), pp. 306-307, 314-315, 316. Both quoted in Diane Ravitch, *Left Back: A Century Of Failed School Reforms* (New York: Simon & Schuster, 2000), pp. 205-207, 210-214.
3. Charles Beard, "The Myth of Rugged Individualism," *Harper's Magazine*, March 1931. Quoted in Jim Powell, *FDR's Folly* (New York: Crown Forum, 2003), p. 2.
4. Jamie Glazov, "Frontpage Interview: In Denial," www.frontpagemagazine.com, emphasis added.
5. Quotes and paraphrasing from Ayn Rand, *The Virtue of Selfishness* (New York: Penguin Books, 1967), pp. 13-14.
6. Paraphrasing of *Ibid.*, pp. 14-15.
7. Quote and paraphrasing from *Ibid.*, pp. 15-16.
8. Paraphrasing of Leonard Peikoff, *Objectivism: The Philosophy of Ayn Rand* (New York: Penguin, 1993), pp. 192-193.
9. Paraphrasing of *Ibid.*, p. 209.
10. Ayn Rand, *The Virtue of Selfishness, op. cit.*, p. 16.
11. Quotes and paraphrasing from Leonard Peikoff, *Objectivism: The Philosophy*

of Ayn Rand, op. cit., pp. 209-211, 212.

12. Quotes and paraphrasing from Ayn Rand, *The Virtue of Selfishness, op. cit.*, pp. 16-17.
13. Quotes and paraphrasing from *Ibid.*, p. 17.
14. *Ibid.*, pp. 23-24.
15. Leonard Peikoff, *Objectivism: The Philosophy of Ayn Rand, op. cit.*, p. 231.
16. Ayn Rand, *The Fountainhead, op. cit.*, p. 680.
17. Ayn Rand, *The Virtue of Selfishness, op. cit.*, pp. 18-19. Leonard Peikoff, *Objectivism: The Philosophy of Ayn Rand, op. cit.*, p. 231.
18. Leonard Peikoff, *Objectivism: The Philosophy of Ayn Rand, op. cit.*, p.231.
19. Leonard Peikoff, *Objectivism: The Philosophy of Ayn Rand, op. cit.*, p. 232.
20. Quotes and paraphrasing from *Ibid.*, pp. 234-235. Ayn Rand, *Atlas Shrugged, op. cit.*, p. 681.
21. Quotes and paraphrasing from Leonard Peikoff, *Objectivism: The Philosophy of Ayn Rand, op. cit.*, p. 235.
22. *Ibid.*, pp. 235-236.

7: The Mind as Man's Instrument of Survival

1. Quote and paraphrasing from Leonard Peikoff, *Objectivism: The Philosophy of Ayn Rand, op. cit.*, p. 194.
2. Paraphrasing from Ayn Rand, *The Fountainhead, op. cit.*, p. 680.
3. Ayn Rand, *Atlas Shrugged, op. cit.*, pp. 938-939, 940.
4. Frederick Copleston, *A History of Philosophy*, vol. 7, pt. II (Garden City, New York: Image Books, 1965), pp. 77-84. W.T. Jones, *A History of Western Philosophy*, vol. 4 (New York: Harcourt, Brace, Jovanovich, 1975), pp. 188-190. Leonard Peikoff, *Objectivism: The Philosophy of Ayn Rand, , op. cit.*, p. 33.
5. Paraphrasing of Ayn Rand, *Atlas Shrugged, op. cit.*, p. 387.
6. Paraphrasing of Ayn Rand, *The Virtue of Selfishness, op. cit.*, pp. 20-21.
7. Burton J. Hendrick, *The Life of Andrew Carnegie* (London: William Heinemann, 1933), p. 408.
8. Ayn Rand, *Atlas Shrugged, op. cit.*, pp. 940 and 944; *idem., The Virtue of Selfishness, op. cit.*, p. 25, emphasis added.
9. Quote and paraphrasing from Ayn Rand, *The Virtue of Selfishness, op. cit.*, pp. 25-26.
10. Paraphrasing of Leonard Peikoff, *Objectivism: The Philosophy of Ayn Rand, op. cit.*, pp. 293 and 294.
11. Ayn Rand, *Atlas Shrugged, op. cit.*, p. 946; *idem., The Virtue of Selfishness, op. cit.*, pp. 26-27. Leonard Peikoff, *Objectivism: The Philosophy of Ayn Rand, op. cit.*, pp. 292-303.

Notes

12. Paraphrasing of Ayn Rand, *Atlas Shrugged, op. cit.*, p. 962.
13. Leonard Peikoff, *The Ominous Parallels, op. cit.*, pp. 45-67.
14. Quote and paraphrasing from Ayn Rand, *The Virtue of Selfishness, op. cit.*, pp. 94-95.
15. Ayn Rand, *Capitalism: The Unknown Ideal, op. cit.*, p. 17.
16. Quote and paraphrasing from Leonard Peikoff, *Objectivism: The Philosophy of Ayn Rand, op. cit.*, pp. 313-314.
17. Quote and paraphrasing from Ayn Rand, *Atlas Shrugged, op. cit.*, p. 949.
18. Quotations and paraphrasings from Ayn Rand, *The Virtue of Selfishness, op. cit.*, p. 95.
19. Quote and paraphrase from Ayn Rand, *The Virtue of Selfishness, op. cit.*, p. 108.
20. Quote and paraphrasing from Ayn Rand, *The Virtue of Selfishness, op. cit.*, p. 109.
21. *Ibid.*, p. 109.
22. *Ibid.*, p. 107.
23. Quotes and paraphrasings from Leonard Peikoff, *Objectivism: The Philosophy of Ayn Rand, op. cit.*, p. 363.
24. Quotes and paraphrasings from Leonard Peikoff, *Objectivism: The Philosophy of Ayn Rand, op. cit.*, pp. 366-367. Ayn Rand, *The Virtue of Selfishness, op. cit.*, p. 112.
25. Paraphrasing of Ayn Rand, *The Virtue of Selfishness, op. cit.*, p. 114.

8: Capitalism as the Embodiment of Rational Philosophical Principles

1. Ayn Rand, *Atlas Shrugged, op. cit.*, p. 1083.
2. Will and Ariel Durant, *The Story of Civilization*, vol. IX, *The Age of Voltaire, op. cit.*, pp. 633-649.
3. *The Black Book of Communism, op. cit.*, pp. 19, 167-168, 513-538, 591, 803. Richard Pipes, *Communism: A History* (New York: Modern Library, 2001), pp. 62-72, 132-135. Paul Johnson, *Modern Times* (New York: HarperPerennial, 1992), p. 655. Eugene Lyons, *Workers' Paradise Lost* (New York: Funk and Wagnalls, 1967), pp. 301-319.
4. Meghnad Desai, *Marx's Revenge: The Resurgence of Capitalism and the Death of Statist Socialism* (New York: Verso, 2004), pp. 1-11, 44-45.
5. Ayn Rand, *Atlas Shrugged, op. cit.*, pp. 985-993.

Part Three: Polemics

9: War and Imperialism

1. Ayn Rand, *Capitalism: The Unknown Ideal, op. cit.*, p. 37.
2. *The Black Book of Communism, op. cit.*, pp. 565-575. Doan Van Toai, *The Vietnamese Gulag*, trans. Sylvie Romanowski and Francoise Simon-Miller (New York: Simon and Schuster, 1986), pp. 99-142, 209-275 and *passim.* Michael Lind, *Vietnam: The Necessary War* (New York: Touchstone Books, 1999), pp. 148-156, 240-245. William Duiker, *Ho Chi Minh: A Life* (New York: Hyperion, 2000), pp. 474-481.
3. Gerald O'Driscoll, Kim Holmes and Melanie Kirkpatrick, *2001 Index of Economic Freedom, op. cit.*, pp. 209-210, 233-234.
4. Michael Ledeen, *The War Against the Terror Masters* (New York: St. Martin's Griffin, 2003), pp. 10-28 and *passim.* Richard Perle and David Frum, *An End To Evil: How To Win the War On Terror* (New York: Random House, 2003), pp. 41-60, 97-145. Benjamin Netanyahu, *Fighting Terrorism: How Democracies Can Defeat The International Terrorist Network* (New York: Farrar, Straus and Giroux, 2001), pp. 78-80 and *passim.* Bernard Lewis, *What Went Wrong? Western Impact and Middle Eastern Response* (New York: Oxford University Press, 2002), pp. 151-160. Martin Kramer, *Ivory Towers on Sand: The Failure of Middle Eastern Studies in America* (Washington, D.C.: The Washington Institute for Near East Policy, 2001), pp. 44-57, 61-80.
5. *The Black Book of Communism, op. cit.*, pp. 549-550. Laurie Mylroie, *The War Against America: Saddam Hussein and the World Trade Center Attacks* (New York: HarperCollins, 2001), pp. 28-32, 106-118, 251-257 and *passim.* Stephen Hayes, *The Connection: How Al Queda's Collaboration with Saddam Hussein Has Endangered America* (New York: Harper Collins, 2004), pp. 45-61 and *passim.*
6. *The Black Book of Communism, op. cit.*, pp. 39-215, 463-546, 577-635. Miron Dolot, *Execution by Hunger: The Hidden Holocaust* (New York: W.W. Norton, 1985), pp. 177-231 and *passim.*
7. David Lamb, *The Africans* (New York: Vintage Books, 1987), p. 78.
8. Ayn Rand, *Capitalism: The Unknown Ideal, op. cit.*, p. 37, emphasis added.
9. *Ibid.*, p. 35.
10. *Ibid.*, p. 38.
11. *Ibid.*, p. 38.
12. Karl Marx and Friedrich Engels, *The Communist Manifesto, op. cit.*, p. 64.
13. Robert Heilbroner, *The Worldly Philosophers* (New York: Touchstone Books,

Notes

1972), p. 185.

14. J. A. Hobson, *Imperialism* (Ann Arbor: University of Michigan Press, 1965), pp. 51-61. Wolfgang Mommsen, *Theories of Imperialism*, trans. P. S. Falla (Chicago: University of Chicago Press, 1980), pp. 11-19.

15. V.I. Lenin, *Imperialism: The Highest Stage of Capitalism* (New York: International Publishers, 1939), pp. 12-14, 62-67.

16. John Ridpath, "Integration and Human Life: Say's Law," tape lectures (Gaylordsville, Ct.: Second Renaissance Books, 1995).

17. Louis Hacker, *The World of Andrew Carnegie, op. cit.*, pp. 211-212.

18. Thomas Sowell, *Marxism: Philosophy and Economics* (New York: William Morrow, 1985), pp. 213-215. V. I. Lenin, *Imperialism, op. cit.*, p. 64.

19. George Reisman, *Capitalism, op. cit.*, pp. 553-554.

20. Thomas Sowell, *Classical Economics Reconsidered* (Princeton, NJ: Princeton University Press, 1974), p. 11. Ludwig von Mises, *Omnipotent Government* (Spring Mills, Pa.: Libertarian Press, 1985), p. 104. Marc Ferro, *Colonization: A Global History* (Quebec: World Heritage Press, 1997), p. 15.

21. Will Durant, *The Story of Civilization*, vol. 1, *Our Oriental Heritage* (New York: Simon and Schuster, 1954), pp. 265-273, 352-355; vol. 3, *Caesar And Christ* (New York: Simon and Schuster, 1944), pp. 475-477; vol. 6, *The Reformation* (New York: Simon and Schuster, 1957), pp. 178-187, 702-707. Ibn Warraq, *Why I Am Not a Muslim* (Amherst, New York: Prometheus Books, 1995), pp. 198-222. Donald Morris, *The Washing of the Spears: The Rise and Fall of the Zulu Nation* (New York: Da Capo Press, 1998), pp. 40-67. Walter Sulzbach, *Capitalistic Warmongers: A Modern Superstition*, Public Policy Pamphlet No. 35 (Chicago: University of Chicago Press, 1942), p. 33.

22. Ludwig von Mises, *Omnipotent Government, op. cit.*, pp. 19-39, 103-104. Thomas Pakenham, *The Scramble for Africa: White Man's Conquest of the Dark Continent From 1876 to 1912* (New York: Avon Books, 1991), pp. 201-217, 276-296, 346-357, 606. Thomas Sowell, *Conquests and Cultures* (New York: Basic Books, 1998), pp. 116-117. Eugene Staley, *War and the Private Investor* (New York: Doubleday, Doran and Company, 1935), p. 99. William Langer, *The Diplomacy of Imperialism* (New York: Alfred Knopf, 1968), pp. 427-442.

23. Ludwig von Mises, *Omnipotent Government, op. cit.*, p. 101. Thomas Pakenham, *The Scramble for Africa, op. cit.*, pp. 11-23, 239-255, 434-451, 585-601, 656-668. Adam Hochschild, *King Leopold's Ghost* (New York: MacMillan, 1998), pp. 34-46, 167-177 and *passim*. George B.N. Ayittey, *Africa Betrayed* (New York: St. Martin's Press, 1992), pp. 83, 87-89. Peter Schwab, *Africa: A Continent Self-Destructs* (New York: Palgrave, 2001), pp.

14-15.

24. Nick Elliott, "John Bright: Voice of Victorian Liberalism," and John Chodes, "Richard Cobden: Creator of the Free Market," both in Burton Folsom, ed., *The Industrial Revolution and Free Trade, op. cit.,* pp. 28, 38-40. J.L. Hammond and M.R.D. Foot, *Gladstone and Liberalism* (London: English Universities Press, 1952), pp. 46 and 66. Nicholas Edsall, *Richard Cobden: Independent Radical* (Cambridge, Mass.: Harvard University Press, 1986), pp. 1-2.

25. Burton Folsom, ed., *The Industrial Revolution and Free Trade, op. cit.,* p. 29. J.L. Hammond and M.R.D. Foot, *Gladstone and Liberalism, op. cit.,* pp. 56-59, 73, 93. W.E. Williams, *The Rise of Gladstone to the Leadership of the Liberal Party* (London: Cambridge University Press, 1934), pp. 20-21. Goldwin Smith, *England: A Short History* (New York: Charles Scribner's Sons, 1971), p. 345.

26. W. E. Williams, *The Rise of Gladstone to the Leadership of the Liberal Party, op. cit.,* pp. 23-24, 27, 29-32. Nicholas Edsall, *Richard Cobden: Independent Radical, op. cit.,* p. 333.

27. Anthony Wood, *Nineteenth Century Britain, 1815-1914* (London: Longmans, 1960), pp. 289-290, 292, 296, 297-298, 307-309, 311-312, 322-324. J.L. Hammond and M.R.D. Foot, *Gladstone and Liberalism, op. cit.,* pp. 4, 56-59, 131, 138-139. Goldwin Smith, *England: A Short History, op. cit.,* pp. 363, 367-368. Robert Blake, *Disraeli* (New York: St. Martin's Press, 1967), pp. 655-679.

28. Lionel Robbins, *The Economic Causes of War* (New York: Macmillan, 1940), pp. 80-83. William Langer, *The Diplomacy of Imperialism, op. cit.,* pp. 75 and 95.

29. Ludwig von Mises, *Omnipotent Government, op. cit.,* p. 103.

30. Eugene Staley, *War and the Private Investor, op. cit.,* pp. 55-70, 178-195. William Langer, *The Diplomacy of Imperialism, op. cit.,* pp. 629-647. Lionel Robbins, *The Economic Causes of War, op. cit.,* pp. 46-57. Walter Sulzbach, *Capitalistic Warmongers: A Modern Superstition, op. cit.,* pp. 1-35.

31. Robert Endicott Osgood, *Ideals and Self-Interest in America's Foreign Relations* (Chicago: University of Chicago Press, 1953), p. 46.

32. Ayn Rand, *Capitalism: The Unknown Ideal, op. cit.,* p. 38. Robert Endicott Osgood, *Ideals and Self-Interest in America's Foreign Relations, op. cit.,* pp. 32-39, 44-47. Charles Beard, *A Foreign Policy for America* (New York: Alfred Knopf, 1940), pp. 39-44, 46-50, 56, 71-73. Michael Malone, *James J. Hill, op. cit.,* pp. 161, 195, 269. Andrew Carnegie, *Autobiography of Andrew Carnegie* (Boston: Houghton Mifflin Co., 1920), pp. 346-353. Burton J. Hendrick, *The Life of*

Notes

Andrew Carnegie (London: William Heinemann, 1933), pp. 656-672. Carol Gelderman, *Henry Ford: The Wayward Capitalist* (New York: The Dial Press, 1981), pp. 59 and 92.

33. Burton Folsom, *The Myth of the Robber Barons, op. cit.*, pp. 1-2. Ayn Rand, *Capitalism: The Unknown Ideal, op. cit.*, pp. 102-109; *idem.*, "The Money-Making Personality," *The Objectivist Forum*, February 1983.

10: Slavery

1. Thomas Sowell, *Race and Culture* (New York: Basic Books, 1994), pp. 186-196, 201. Thomas Sowell, *Conquests and Cultures* (New York: Basic Books, 1998), pp. 13-14, 109-112, 133, 140-141, 153. Donald Widener, *A History of Africa South of the Sahara* (New York: Vintage Books, 1962), pp. 45-47, 55-58, 62, 71-72, 75-78. Reginald Coupland, *East Africa and its Invaders From the Earliest Times to the Death of Said in 1856* (New York: Russell and Russell, 1956), pp. 34-35. Dinesh D'Souza, "We the Slaveowners: In Jefferson's America, Were Some Men Not Created Equal?" *Policy Review* (Fall 1995, Number 74.) Joseph J. Ellis, *Founding Brothers: The Revolutionary Generation* (New York: Random House, 2000), p. 100. David Brion Davis, *Slavery And Human Progress* (New York: Oxford University Press, 1984), pp. 32-33. Orlando Patterson, *Slavery and Social Death: A Comparative Study* (Cambridge, Mass.: Harvard University Press, 1982), p. viii.

2. Orlando Patterson, *Slavery and Social Death, op. cit.*, pp. 13, 105-122. David Brion Davis, *Slavery And Human Progress, op. cit.*, pp. 11 and 107.

3. Peter Gay, *The Science of Freedom, op. cit.*, pp. 407-408. Frank J. Klingberg, *The Anti-Slavery Movement in England: A Study in English Humanitarianism* (New Haven, Ct.: Yale University Press), pp. 47-49. David Brion Davis, *Slavery And Human Progress, op. cit.*, pp. xvii, 107, 112, 129-130. James Boswell, *Life of Johnson* (Oxford: Oxford University Press, 1980), p. 878; under September 23, 1777. Joseph Ellis, *Founding Brothers, op. cit.*, pp. 85 and 111. Dinesh D'Souza, "We the Slaveowners," *op. cit.* Arthur Ekirch, *The Decline of American Liberalism* (New York: Atheneum, 1967), p. 110.

4. Peter Gay, *The Rise of Modern Paganism, op. cit.*, pp. 21-22; *idem.*, *The Science of Freedom, op. cit.*, pp. 407-423. Frank Klingberg, *The Anti-Slavery Movement in England, op. cit.*, pp. 22-58. Joseph Ellis, *Founding Brothers, op. cit.*, pp. 81-119. Carl Becker, *The Declaration of Independence, op. cit.*, pp. 212-213. Henry Hayden Clark, ed., *American Century Writers: Thomas Paine, op. cit.*, pp. lxxxii-lxxxvii.

5. Thomas Sowell, *Race and Culture, op. cit.*, p. 186. Orlando Patterson, *Slavery and Social Death, op. cit.*, p. 27. Dinesh D'Souza, "We the Slaveowners," *op.*

cit. Paul Johnson, *The Birth of the Modern, op. cit.*, p. 303.

6. David Brion Davis, *Slavery And Human Progress, op. cit.*, p. 129.

7. Dinesh D'Souza, "We the Slaveowners," *op. cit.*

8. Frank Klingberg, *The Anti-Slavery Movement in England, op. cit.*, pp. 25, 28, 31-34, 43-47. Thomas Sowell, *Race and Culture, op. cit.*, p. 210. Donald Widener, *A History of Africa South of the Sahara, op. cit.*, p. 73. Reginald Coupland, *Wilberforce: A Narrative* (New York: Negro Universities Press, 1968), p. 256. David Brion Davis, *Slavery And Human Progress, op. cit.*, p. 130. Paul Johnson, *The Birth of the Modern, op. cit.*, pp. 291-303, 308.

9. Reginald Coupland, *The British Anti-Slavery Movement* (New York: Barnes and Noble, 1964), pp. 159-218. Thomas Sowell, *Race and Culture, op. cit.*, pp. 210-214. Thomas Sowell, *Conquests and Culture, op. cit.*, pp. 91-95. Andrew Coulson, *Market Education: The Unknown History* (New Brunswick, N.J.: Transaction Publishers, 1999), p. 93. Paul Johnson, *The Birth of the Modern, op. cit.*, p. 322.

10. *The Black Book of Communism, op. cit., passim.* Aleksandr Solzhenitsyn, *The Gulag Archipelago 1918-1956*, trans., Thomas P. Whitney (New York: Harper & Row, 1973). Robert Conquest, *Kolyma: The Arctic Death Camps* (New York: The Viking Press, 1978), pp. 49-66, 214-231 and *passim.* Dmitri Volkogonov, *Lenin: A New Biography*, trans. Harold Shukman (New York: The Free Press, 1994), pp. xxvi-xxvii, 233-245, 330, 340-41. Harry Wu, *Laogai: The Chinese Gulag*, trans., Ted Slingerland (San Francisco: Westview Press, 1992); also Harry Wu and Carolyn Wakeman, *Bitter Winds: A Memoir of My Years in China's Gulag* (New York: John Wiley & Sons, 1994). Regarding slave labor in Cuba see Armando Valladares, *Against All Hope: A Memoir of Life in Castro's Gulag* (San Francisco: Encounter Books, 2001).

11. David Brion Davis, *Slavery And Human Progress, op. cit.*, pp. 5-8. Thomas Sowell, *Conquests and Cultures, op. cit.*, pp. 154-155. Thomas Sowell, *Race and Culture, op. cit.*, p. 208. Marc Ferro, *Colonization: A Global History, op. cit.*, pp. 183-184.

12. Ronald Segal, *Islam's Black Slaves: The Other Black Diaspora* (New York: Farrar, Straus and Giroux, 2001), pp. 199-223. Dinesh D'Souza, "We the Slaveowners," *op. cit.* Francis Bok, *Escape From Slavery* (New York: St. Martin's Press, 2003), pp. 23-32 and *passim.*

13. www.iabolish.com.

14. Dinesh D'Souza, "We the Slaveowners," *op. cit.*

15. David Levy, *How The Dismal Science Got Its Name* (Ann Arbor: The University of Michigan Press, 2001), pp. xiii-xv, 3-28, 41-57; *idem.*, "150 Years and Still Dismal!," *Ideas on Liberty*, March, 2000. David Levy and

Sandra Peart, "The Secret History of the Dismal Science: Brotherhood, Trade and the 'Negro Question,'" www.econlib.org. Ludwig von Mises, *Socialism, op. cit.*, pp. 522, 528-529.

16. David Levy, *How The Dismal Science Got Its Name, op. cit.*, pp. 22-23, 147, 158-197 and *passim*.

17. Eric Williams, *Capitalism and Slavery* (London: Andre Deutsch, 1964), pp. v-vi, 51-84, 98-107. Thomas Sowell, *Race and Culture, op. cit.*, pp. 214-215. Roger Anstey, "The Volume and Profitability of the British Slave Trade, 1675-1808," *Race and Slavery in the Western Hemisphere: Quantitative Studies*, ed. by Stanley Engerman and Eugene Genovese (Princeton: Princeton University Press, 1975), pp. 22-24. David Brion Davis, *Slavery And Human Progress* (New York: Oxford University Press, 1984), p. 108. Paul Johnson, *The Birth of the Modern, op. cit.*, pp. 328, 330-331, 334-335.

18. Adam Smith, *The Wealth of Nations, op. cit.*, pp. 92-93, 417-419. John Elliott Cairnes, *The Slave Power* (New York: Harper and Row, 1969), pp. 44-47. Ludwig von Mises, *Human Action, op. cit.*, pp. 628-634.

19. Thomas Sowell, *Markets and Minorities* (New York: Basic Books, 1981), p. 92.

20. Robert William Fogel and Stanley Engerman, *Time on the Cross: The Economics of American Negro Slavery* (Boston: Little, Brown and Co., 1974), pp. 67-94, 191-196.

21. Jeffrey Rogers Hummel, *Emancipating Slaves, Enslaving Free Men* (Chicago: Open Court, 1996), pp. 37-60.

22. Thomas Sowell, *Markets and Minorities, op. cit.*, pp. 83-102.

23. Norman Angell, *The Great Illusion* (New York: G.P. Putnam's Sons, 1910), pp. 30-62. J.D.B. Miller, *Norman Angell and the Futility of War* (London: Macmillan, 1986), pp. 25-52.

24. Booker T. Washington, *Up From Slavery* (Garden City, NY: Doubleday and Company, 1901), pp. 17-18.

25. L. Sprague de Camp, *The Heroic Age of American Invention* (New York: Doubleday and Co., 1961), pp. 104-111.

26. Quoted in J.D.B. Miller, *Norman Angell and the Futility of War, op. cit.*, p. 28.

Part Four: Economics

11: The Great Laboratory

1. Werner Keller, *East Minus West Equals Zero* (New York: G.P. Putnam's Sons,

1962), pp. 195-201.

2. Stephane Courtois, et al., *The Black Book of Communism, op. cit.*, pp. 4, 13-14, 78.

3. *The Black Book of Communism, op. cit.*, pp. 39-268 and *passim.* Anne Applebaum, *Gulag: A History* (New York: Doubleday, 2003), pp. XXXIX, 92-115 and *passim.* Robert Conquest, *Kolyma: The Arctic Death Camps* (New York: The Viking Press, 1978), pp. 49-66, 214-231; *idem., The Great Terror: A Reassessment* (New York: Oxford University Press, 1990), pp. 308-340 and *passim.* Miron Dolot, *Execution By Hunger: The Hidden Holocaust* (New York: W.W. Norton, 1985), pp. VII-XII, 203-231 and *passim.*

4. Werner Keller, *East Minus West Equals Zero, op. cit.*, pp. 213-214. Stephane Courtois, *The Black Book of Communism, op. cit.*, pp. 111-112. Antony Sutton, *Western Technology and Soviet Economic Development, 1917-1930* (Palo Alto, CA: Hoover Institute Press, 1968), p. 345. On the similar privations of the Stalin era, see Sheila Fitzpatrick, *Everyday Stalinism, Ordinary Life in Extraordinary Times: Soviet Russia in the 1930s* (New York: Oxford University Press, 1999), pp. 40-66 and *passim.*

5. Antony Sutton, *Western Technology and Soviet Economic Development 1917-1930, op. cit.*, pp. 4-5, 185, 345. Robert Hessen, "Review of Western Technology and Soviet Economic Development, 1917-1930," *The Objectivist* (Gaylordsville, Ct.: Second Renaissance Books, 1993), pp. 777-783.

6. Antony Sutton, *Western Technology and Soviet Economic Development 1917-1930, op. cit.*, pp. 67, 185, 310-313, 345. Werner Keller, *East Minus West Equals Zero, op. cit.*, pp. 213-214.

7. Antony Sutton, *Western Technology and Soviet Economic Development, 1917-1930, op. cit.*, pp. 16-20, 23, 25, 46, 51-52. Werner Keller, *East Minus West Equals Zero, op. cit.*, pp. 216, 219, 220-221.

8. Antony Sutton, *Western Technology and Soviet Economic Development, 1917-1930, op. cit.*, pp. 95-97. Werner Keller, *East Minus West Equals Zero, op. cit.*, pp. 216-221.

9. Werner Keller, *East Minus West Equals Zero, op. cit.*, pp. 226-229. Antony Sutton, *Western Technology and Soviet Economic Development, 1930-1945* (Palo Alto, Cal.: Hoover Institute Press, 1971), pp. 177, 181, 184.

10. Antony Sutton, *Western Technology and Soviet Economic Development, 1930-1945, op. cit.*, pp. 62, 74-77. Werner Keller, *East Minus West Equals Zero, op. cit.*, pp. 229-232.

11. Antony Sutton, *Western Technology and Soviet Economic Development, 1930-1945, op. cit.*, pp. 12, 185-190. Werner Keller, *East Minus West Equals Zero,*

op. cit., pp. 233-235.

12. Antony Sutton, *Western Technology and Soviet Economic Development, 1917-1930, op. cit.*, pp.202-205. Werner Keller, *East Minus West Equals Zero, op. cit.*, pp. 236-238.

13. Werner Keller, *East Minus West Equals Zero, op. cit.*, pp. 225-239.

14. Antony Sutton, *Western Technology and Soviet Economic Development, 1917-1930, op. cit.*, p. 267. Stephane Courtois, et. al., *The Black Book of Communism, op. cit.*, p. 123.

15. Antony Sutton, *Western Technology and Soviet Economic Development, 1917-1930, op. cit.*, pp. 95-97. Werner Keller, *East Minus West Equals Zero, op. cit.*, pp. 216-217, 240-241.

16. Stephane Courtois, et. al., *The Black Book of Communism, op. cit.*, pp. 124-126.

17. Eugene Lyons, *Workers' Paradise Lost* (New York: Funk and Wagnalls, 1967), pp. 136-137.

18. Stephane Courtois, et al., *The Black Book of Communism, op. cit.*, pp. 105-107.

19. Werner Keller, *East Minus West Equals Zero, op. cit.*, pp. 221-222. Antony Sutton, *Western Technology and Soviet Economic Development, 1917-1930, op. cit.*, pp. 97-100, 180.

20. Antony Sutton, *Western Technology and Soviet Economic Development, 1917-1930, op. cit.*, pp. 86-91.

21. Werner Keller, *East Minus West Equals Zero, op. cit.*, pp. 262-268. Antony Sutton, *Western Technology and Soviet Economic Development, 1930-1945, op. cit.*, pp.167-168, 198-199, 206, 217, 220-221, 335.

22. Antony Sutton, *Western Technology and Soviet Economic Development, 1945-1965* (Palo Alto, CA: Hoover Institute Press, 1973), pp. 5-11. Edith Efron, "Review of East Minus West Equals Zero," *The Objectivist Newsletter* (Gaylordsville, Ct.: Second Renaissance Books, 1993), p. 48. Robert Nisbet, *Roosevelt and Stalin: The Failed Courtship* (Washington, D.C.: Regnery Gateway, 1988), pp. 6, 26-27, 73.

23. Werner Keller, *East Minus West Equals Zero, op. cit.*, pp. 268-281. Antony Sutton, *Western Technology and Soviet Economic Development, 1930-1945, op. cit.*, p. 275. Robert Nisbet, *Roosevelt and Stalin: The Failed Courtship, op. cit.*, p. 10.

24. John Earl Haynes and Harvey Klehr, *Venona: Decoding Soviet Espionage in America* (New Haven, Ct.: Yale University Press, 1999), pp. 116-163, 287-330 and *passim*; *idem.*, *In Denial: Historians, Communism and Espionage* (San Francisco: Encounter Books, 2003), pp. 141-192 and *passim*. See also by the

same authors: *The Secret World of American Communism* (New Haven, Ct.: Yale University Press, 1995), and *The Soviet World of American Communism* (New Haven, Ct.: Yale University Press, 1998). Christopher Andrew and Oleg Gordievsky, *KGB: The Inside Story of its Foreign Operations from Lenin to Gorbachev* (New York: Harper Collins, 1990), pp. 279-290, 367-402.

25. Werner Keller, *East Minus West Equals Zero, op. cit.*, pp. 281-290. Antony Sutton, *Western Technology and Soviet Economic Development, 1945-1965, op. cit.*, pp. 30-32, 119-121, 139-140, 193-196, 261, 325-327.

26. Hedrick Smith, *The Russians* (New York: Ballantine Books, 1976), pp. 72-74, 75-79, 83-84. Hedrick Smith, *The New Russians* (New York: Avon Books, 1990), pp. 3-4, 6, 22-24, 249 and *passim*. Eugene Lyons, *Workers' Paradise Lost, op. cit.*, pp. 143, 150-151, 153. Tara Smith, "Forbidding Life to Those Still Living," in Robert Mayhew, ed., *Essays on Ayn Rand's We The Living* (New York: Lexington Books, 2004), pp. 317-332. David Horowitz, *The Politics of Bad Faith* (New York: the Free Press, 1998), pp. 98-103.

27. John Clark and Aaron Wildavsky, *The Moral Collapse of Communism: Poland As a Cautionary Tale* (San Francisco: Institute for Contemporary Studies Press, 1990), p. 117. Daniel Yergin and Joseph Stanislaw, *The Commanding Heights: The Battle Between Government and the Marketplace That Is Remaking The Modern World* (New York: Simon and Schuster, 1998), pp. 266-273.

28. Eugene Lyons, *Workers' Paradise Lost, op. cit.*, pp. 148-149.

29. Meghnad Desai, *Marx's Revenge, op. cit.*, pp. 42-43.

30. Eugene Lyons, *Workers' Paradise Lost, op. cit.*, pp. 295-299.

31. *Ibid.*, p. 298.

32. Stephane Courtois, et al., *The Black Book of Communism, op. cit.*, pp. 647-665. Armando Valladares, *Against All Hope: A Memoir of Life in Castro's Gulag* (San Francisco: Encounter Books, 2001), pp. 1-156 and *passim*.

33. Gerald O'Driscoll, et al., *2001 Index of Economic Freedom, op. cit.*, pp. 143-144. Peter Brimelow, "The High Cost of Castro," *Hoover Digest*, 1998 No. 3. William Ratliff, "Cuba: Semper Fidel," *Hoover Digest*, 2001 No. 4. Jonah Goldberg, "Potemkin Village in Cuba," www.nationalreview.com. "Freedom and Growth," *The Wall Street Journal, op. cit. The World Factbook 1999.*

34. Miguel Faria, M.D., *Cuba in Revolution: Escape From a Lost Paradise* (Macon, Georgia: Hacienda Publishing, 2002), pp. 177-194.

35. Robert Levine and Moises Asis, *Cuban Miami* (New Brunswick, NJ: Rutgers University Press, 2000), pp. 3-6, 93-105. Carlos Seiglie, "Cuba's Road to Serfdom," *The Cato Journal*, Vol. 20, No. 3 (Winter 2001), pp. 425-430. Marcelo Stiles, "Income Differentials in the U.S.: Impact on Latino Socio-Economic Development," ISRI Working Paper #33, The Julian Samora

Notes

Research Institute, Michigan State University, 1997. Albert Camarillo and Frank Bonilla, "Hispanics in a Multi-Cultural Society: A New American Dilemma?" in *American Becoming: Racial Trends and Their Consequences*, vol.1, ed. Neal Smelser, William Julius Wilson and Faith Mitchell (Washington, D.C.: the National Academy Press, 2001), pp. 103-134. Herbert Hill and James E. Jones, eds., *Race in America: The Struggle for Equality* (Madison, WI: University of Wisconsin Press, 1993), pp. 222-225.

36. Peter Stein, "Sweden: From Capitalist Success to Welfare-State Sclerosis," www.cato.org. *The World Factbook 1999*. Gerald O'Driscoll, et al., *2001 Index of Economic Freedom, op. cit.*, pp. 289-290, 347-348.

37. Daniel Yergin, *The Prize: The Epic Quest For Oil, Money and Power* (New York: Simon and Schuster, 1991), pp. 667-670.

38. Peter Stein, "Sweden: From Capitalist Success to Welfare-State Sclerosis," *op. cit.*

39. Stephane Courtois, et al., *The Black Book of Communism, op. cit.*, pp. 547-564. Kang Chol-Hwan and Pierre Rigoulot, *The Aquariums of Pyongyang: Ten Years in the North Korean Gulag* (Basic Books, 2001), pp. 47-104 and *passim*. Andrew Natsios, *The Great North Korean Famine* (Washington, D.C.: United States Institute of Peace Press, 2001), pp. 37-88 and *passim*. Daniel Yergin and Joseph Stanislaw, *The Commanding Heights, op. cit.*, pp. 169-175. Gerald O'Driscoll, et al., *2001 Index of Economic Freedom, op. cit.*, pp. 229-232. "Freedom and Growth," *The Wall Street Journal*, Dec. 16, 1996.

40. Milton Friedman, "The Hong Kong Experiment," *Hoover Digest*, 1998 No. 3. Daniel Yergin and Joseph Stanislaw, *The Commanding Heights, op. cit.*, pp. 210-212. Gerald O'Driscoll, et al., *2001 Index of Economic Freedom, op. cit.*, pp. 197-198. Milton and Rose Friedman, *Free To Choose* (New York: Harcourt Brace, 1980), p. 34. "Freedom and Growth," *op. cit.*

41. Daniel Yergin and Joseph Stanislaw, *The Commanding Heights, op. cit.*, pp. 175-181. Gerald O'Driscoll, et al., *2001 Index of Economic Freedom, op. cit.*, pp. 131-132.

42. Stephane Courtois, et al., *The Black Book of Communism, op. cit.*, pp. 487-497. Daniel Yergin and Joseph Stanislaw, *The Commanding Heights, op. cit.*, p. 196. Paul Johnson, *Modern Times* (New York: Harper Collins, 1991), pp. 550-551.

43. Daniel Yergin and Joseph Stanislaw, *The Commanding Heights, op. cit.*, pp.198-199, 202-204, 206-210, 214. Gerald O'Driscoll, et al., *2001 Index of Economic Freedom, op. cit.*, pp. 127-129.

44. Eric Hobsbawm, *The Age of Extremes: A History of the World, 1914-1991* (New York: Pantheon Books, 1994) pp. 495-499. David Horowitz, *The*

Politics of Bad Faith, op. cit., pp. 17-26, 190.

12: Capitalism as the Economic System of the Mind

1. Jean-Baptiste Say, *A Treatise on Political Economy*, trans. C.R. Prinsep (New York: Augustus Kelley, 1971), pp. 134-139. Richard Salsman, "The Invisible Hand Comes to Life: Economics in Atlas Shrugged," tape lecture (Gaylordsville, Ct.: The Ayn Rand Bookstore, 1997). John Ridpath, "Integration and Human Life: Say's Law," tape lecture (Gaylordsville, Ct.: the Ayn Rand Bookstore, 1995.) Mark Skousen, *The Making of Modern Economics, op. cit.*, pp. 54-57.
2. John Steele Gordon, *The Business of America* (New York: Walker and Company, 2001), pp. 219-223.
3. Ayn Rand, *The Fountainhead, op. cit.*, pp. 679-686.
4. George Reisman, *Capitalism, op. cit.*, p. 269.
5. *Ibid.*, p. 269.
6. *Ibid.*, pp. 137, 272.
7. *Ibid.*, pp. 269-270.
8. *Ibid.*, p. 137.
9. *Ibid.*, p. 270. Regarding the complexities of the economic calculation issue, see: Ludwig von Mises, *Economic Calculation in the Socialist Commonwealth* (Auburn, Alabama: the Ludwig von Mises Institute, 1990), pp. 3-50; *idem.*, *Socialism* (Indianapolis: Liberty Classics, 1981), pp. 110-130; *idem.*, *Human Action*, 3rd rev. ed. (Chicago: Henry Regnery, 1966), pp. 698-710. F.A. Hayek, *Individualism and Economic Order* (Chicago: University of Chicago Press, 1948), pp. 119-147.

13: Refuting the Economic Fallacies About Capitalism

1. Ayn Rand, *Capitalism: The Unknown Ideal, op. cit.*, pp. 104-105. Burton Folsom, *The Myth of the Robber Barons, op. cit.*, p. 22. Oscar Lewis, *The Big Four,* (New York: Alfred A. Knopf, 1938), pp. 354-412 and *passim.*
2. Michael Malone, *James J.Hill* (Norman, Ok.: University of Oklahoma Press, 1996), pp. 204-206. George Kennan, *E. H. Harriman: A Biography*, vol. 1 (New York: Houghton Mifflin Company, 1922), pp. 109-184. Maury Klein, *The Life and Legend of E.H. Harriman* (Chapel Hill: University of North Carolina Press, 2000), pp. 130-161. Regarding the damage done by government support of railroad construction, see Clarence Carson, *Throttling the Railroads* (Indianapolis: Liberty Fund, Inc., 1971), pp. 30-37.
3. Ayn Rand, *Capitalism: The Unknown Ideal, op. cit.*, p. 68.

Notes

4. *Ibid.*, pp. 68-69. Caleb Hornbostel, *Construction Materials: Types, Uses and Applications* (New York: John Wiley and Sons, 1991), pp. 26-27. Alton Brown, *Alton Brown's Gear For Your Kitchen* (New York: Stewart, Tabori and Chang, 2003), pp. 208-209. Thomas Jester, ed., *Twentieth Century Building Materials: History and Conversation* (New York: McGraw Hill, 1995), pp. 47-49.
5. Ayn Rand, *Capitalism: The Unknown Ideal, op. cit.*, p. 68.
6. Burton Folsom, *Empire Builders* (Traverse City, Mich.: Rhodes & Easton, pp. 93-94.
7. *Ibid.*, pp. 94-99.
8. Milton and Rose Friedman, *Free To Choose, op. cit.*, pp. 236-237. George Reisman, *Capitalism, op cit.*, pp. 144-145. Clarence Carson, *The War On the Poor* (Birmingham, AL: American Textbook Committee, 1991), pp. 117-157; *idem.*, *Organized Against Whom: The Labor Union in America* (Alexandria, VI: Western Goals, 1983), pp. 13-15, 47-60. Henry Hazlitt, *The Conquest of Poverty* (Irvington-on-Hudson, NY: The Foundation for Economic Education, 1996), p. 133. Hans Sennholz, ed., *American Unionism: Fallacies and Follies* (Irvington-on-Hudson, NY: The Foundation for Economic Eduction, 1994), pp. 1-10, 87-96.
9. Henry Hazlitt, *Economics In One Lesson, op. cit.*, p. 135.
10. Milton and Rose Friedman, *Free To Choose, op cit.*, pp. 237-238.
11. *Ibid.*, pp. 236-237.
12. *Ibid.*, pp. 234-235. H.G. Lewis, *Unionism and Relative Wages in the United States* (Chicago: University of Chicago Press, 1963), pp. 4-5.
13. Henry Hazlitt, *What You Should Know About Inflation* (Princeton, NJ: D. Van Nostrand Co., 1960), p. 123.
14. George Reisman, *Capitalism, op cit.*, pp. 580 and 582.
15. *Ibid.*, pp. 584 and 658. Henry Hazlitt, *Economics In One Lesson, op. cit.*, pp. 150-151.
16. Henry Hazlitt, *What You Should Know About Inflation, op. cit.*, p.1.
17. *Ibid.*, p. 138.
18. *Ibid.*, pp. 138-39.
19. *Ibid.*, p. 139.
20. *Ibid.*, p. 141.
21. *Ibid.*, p. 140.
22. *Ibid.*, p. 141.
23. *Ibid.*, pp. 16 and 141-42.
24. George Reisman, *Capitalism, op. cit.*, pp 504-505.
25. Thomas Sowell, *Basic Economics: A Citizen's Guide to the Economy* (New York:

Basic Books, 2000), p. 226.

26. George Reisman, *Capitalism, op. cit.*, pp. 504 and 954.

27. Henry Hazlitt, *What You Should Know About Inflation, op. cit.*, pp. 37-38.

28. *Ibid.*, pp. 26-27. George Reisman, *Capitalism, op. cit.*, pp. 219-220, 503-506, 920-922; *idem.*, "Gold: The Solution To Our Monetary Dilemma," *The Intellectual Activist*, October 1st and November 1st, 1980. Murray Rothbard, *What Has Government Done to Our Money?* (Auburn, AL: The Ludwig von Mises Institute, 1990), pp. 55-89. Murray Rothbard, *The Case for a 100 Percent Gold Dollar* (Auburn, AL: The Ludwig von Mises Institute, 1991), pp. 19-51 and *passim*. Murray Rothbard, *The Case Against the Fed* (Auburn, AL: The Ludwig von Mises Institute, 1994), pp. 20-57. Mark Skousen, *Economics of a Pure Gold Standard* (Irvington-on-Hudson, NY: The Foundation for Economic Education, 1977), pp. xii-xiii, 82-91.

29. Burton Folsom, *The Myth Of The Robber Barons, op. cit.*, pp. 103-120.

30. Richard Salsman, "The Cause and Consequence of the Great Depression," *The Intellectual Activist*, June 2004. Jim Powell, *FDR's Folly: How Roosevelt and His New Deal Prolonged the Great Depression* (New York: Crown Forum, 2003), pp. 42-45. Gene Smiley, *Rethinking the Great Depression* (Chicago: Ivan Dee 2002), pp. 4-7. Burton Folsom, ed., *The Industrial Revolution and Free Trade, op. cit.*, p. 4.

31. Gene Smiley, *Rethinking the Great Depression, op. cit.*, p. x. Faustino Ballve, *Essentials of Economics* (Irvington-on-Hudson, NY: The Foundation for Economic Education, 1963), pp. 57-58. Benjamin Anderson, *Economics and the Public Welfare* (Indianapolis: Liberty Press, 1979), pp. 182-185, 196, 197-198. Murray Rothbard, *America's Great Depression* (Auburn, Al: The Ludwig von Mises Institute, 2000), pp. 9, 91-93 and *passim*. Ludwig von Mises, *Human Action, op. cit.*, p. 577.

32. Gene Smiley, *Rethinking the Great Depression, op. cit.*, p. 30. Jim Powell, *FDR's Folly: How Roosevelt..., op. cit.*, pp. ix, 30-32, 58-59.

33. Gene Smiley, *Rethinking The Great Depression, op. cit.*, p. 22. Jim Powell, *FDR's Folly: How Roosevelt..., op. cit.*, pp. 48-49. Paul Johnson, *A History of the American People, op. cit.*, pp. 740-741.

34. Benjamin Anderson, *Economics and the Public Welfare, op. cit.*, pp. 224-230. Murray Rothbard, *America's Great Depression, op. cit.*, pp. xv, 209-256. Paul Johnson, *A History of the American People, op. cit.*, pp. 739-742.

35. Lawrence Reed, "Great Myths of the Great Depression," www.mackinac.org. Paul Johnson, *A History of the American People, op. cit.*, pp. 749. Burton Folsom, "Franklin Roosevelt and the Greatest Economic Myth of the Twentieth Century," *Ideas on Liberty*, November 2002.

Notes

36. Benjamin Anderson, *Economics and the Public Welfare*, *op. cit.*, p. 225. Ayn Rand, *Capitalism: The Unknown Ideal*, *op. cit.*, p. 83. Jim Powell, *FDR's Folly: How Roosevelt...*, *op. cit.*, pp. ix-x.
37. Jim Powell, *FDR's Folly: How Roosevlet...*, *op. cit.*, pp. 207-220.
38. Lawrence Reed, "Great Myths of the Great Depression," *op. cit.* Benjamin Anderson, *Economics and the Public Welfare*, *op.˙ cit.*, pp. 331-337. Robert Higgs, "Regime Uncertainty: Why the Great Depression Lasted So Long and Why Prosperity Resumed After the War," *The Independent Review*, Spring 1997, pp. 561-590. Lester Chandler, *America's Greatest Depression, 1929-1941* (New York: Harper & Row, 1970), p. 132. Jim Powell, *FDR's Folly; How Roosevelt...*, *op. cit.*, pp. vii, 75-87. Richard Salsman, *Gold and Liberty* (Great Barrington, Mass.: The American Institute for Economic Research, 1995), pp. 67-69. Paul Johnson, *A History of the American People*, *op. cit.*, pp. 755-759. John Flynn, *The Roosevelt Myth* (San Francisco: Fox and Wilkes, 1948), pp. xi-xii, 39-44, 104-118.

Afterword: The Great Disconnect Revisited

1. Eric Hobsbawm, *The Age of Extremes: A History of the World*, 1914-1991, *op. cit.*, pp. 268-274.

Appendix: Robber Barons or Productive Geniuses

1. Vernon L. Parrington, *Main Currents in American Thought*, vol. 3 (New York: Harcourt, Brace & World, 1930), pp. 9-26. Charles and Mary Beard, *The Rise of American Civilization*, vol. 2 (New York: Macmillan, 1930), pp. 178, 198-204.
2. Jonathan Hughes, *The Vital Few*, *op. cit.*, pp. 215-219.
3. Burton J. Hendrick, *The Life of Andrew Carnegie* (Garden City, NY: Doubleday, Doran and Company, 1932), vol. 1, pp. 51-67, 82, 85-95, 105-109, 122-131, 137-138, 180-193 and *passim*; vol. 2, pp. 2-6, 13-23, 28-40. Joseph Frazier Wall, *Andrew Carnegie* (New York: Oxford University Press, 1970), pp. 73-74, 86-95, 102-106, 114-115, 124-125, 149-152, 166-167, 171-172, 177-179, 259-266, 637-638. Bernard Alderson, *Andrew Carnegie: The Man and His Work* (New York: Doubleday, Page and Company, 1909), pp. 19-22, 27-28, 34-37, 54-57. Louis Hacker, *The World of Andrew Carnegie*, *op. cit.*, pp. 337-362. Robert Hessen, *Steel Titan: The Life of Charles Schwab* (New York: Oxford University Press, 1975), pp. 21-27. Jonathan Hughes, *The Vital Few*, *op. cit.*, pp. 220-273. Paul Johnson, *A History of the American People*, *op. cit.*, pp. 550-555. Roger Donway, "The Steelmaster,"

The Objectivist Forum (New York: TOF Publications, 1993), vol. 6, June 1985, pp. 12-15. Arthur Herman, *How the Scots Invented the Modern World*, *op. cit.*, p. 342.

4. Allan Nevins, *Study in Power: John D. Rockefeller, Industrialist and Philanthropist* (New York: Charles Scribner's Sons, 1953), vol. 1, pp. viii, 1-19, 26, 33-34, 54-55, 60, 63-65, 70-73, 77-78, 81-91, 132-158, emphasis added; vol. 2, pp. 3-36. Jules Abels, *The Rockefeller Billions* (New York: Macmillan, 1965), pp. x, xiii, 5-18, 29, 38-58, 83-90, 97-100. Harold Williamson and Arnold Daum, *The American Petroleum Industry: The Age of Illumination 1859-1899* (Evanston, Ill., 1959), pp. 343-368, 509-519, 589-613, 630-661. Burton Folsom, *The Myth of the Robber Barons, op. cit.*, pp. 83-100. Burton J. Hendrick, *The Age of Big Business: A Chronicle of the. Captains of Industry* (New Haven, Ct.: Yale University Press, 1919), pp. 25-57.

5. Burton J. Hendrick, *The Age of Big Business, op. cit.*, pp. 18-24. Alvin Harlow, *The Road of the Century: The Story of the New York Central* (New York: Creative Age Press, 1947), pp. 186-212. John Stover, *American Railroads* (Chicago: University of Chicago Press, 1997), pp. 101-102.

6. Albro Martin, *James J. Hill and the Opening of the Northwest* (St. Paul, Mn.: Minnesota Historical Society Press, 1976), pp. 207-236, 366-398, 430-523. Michael Malone, *James J. Hill: Empire Builder of the Northwest* (Norman, Ok.: University of Oklahoma Press, 1996), pp. 64-150, 226-227. Burton Folsom, *The Myth of the Robber Barons, op. cit.*, pp. 17-39. David McCullough, *The Path Between the Seas: The Creation of the Panama Canal, 1870-1914* (New York: Simon and Schuster, 1977), pp. 459- 491.

7. Louis Hacker, *The World of Andrew Carnegie, 1865-1901, op. cit.*, pp. xxx-xxxi. Burton Folsom, *The Myth of the Robber Barons, op. cit.*, pp. 83-87. Ron Chernow, *Titan, The Life of John D. Rockefeller* (New York: Random House, 1998), p. 467.

8. Jonathan Hughes, *The Vital Few, op. cit.*, pp. 379-386. George Kennan, *E.H. Harriman: A Biography*, vol. 1 (Boston: Houghton Mifflin, 1922), pp. 286-339.

9. Jean Strouse, *Morgan: American Financier* (New York: HarperPerennial, 2000), pp. x-xii, 93-95, 230-234, 246-249, 251-253, 575-593. Frederick Lewis Allen, *The Great Pierpont Morgan* (New York: Harper & Brothers, 1949), pp. 1-7, 76-125, 239-266. John Winkler, *Morgan the Magnificent: The Life of J. Pierpont Morgan, 1837-1913* (New York: The Vanguard Press, 1930), pp. 125-199, 257-277. Robert Sobel, *Panic on Wall Street: A History of America's Financial Disasters* (New York: Macmillan, 1968), pp. 234-272,

Notes

301-321. Jonathan Hughes, *The Vital Few, op. cit.,* pp. 399-454. Michael Malone, *James J. Hill, op. cit.,* pp. 177-231. Paul Johnson, *A History of the American People, op. cit.,* pp. 546-548, 555-566. Clarence Carson, *Throttling the Railroads* (Indianapolis, IN: Liberty Fund, Inc., 1971), pp. 30-37.

10. George Kennan, *E.H. Harriman: A Biography* (Boston: Houghton Mifflin, 1922), vol. 1, pp. 109-184, 232-260, 311-339; vol. 2, pp. 1-29, 66-76, 88-173. Maury Klein, *The Life and Legend of E.H. Harriman* (Chapel Hill, NC: University of North Carolina Press, 2000), pp. 105-147, 254-291, 372-385. Jonathan Hughes, *The Vital Few, op. cit.,* pp. 362-398.

11. Jonathan Hughes, *The Vital Few, op. cit.,* pp. 400-403. Jean Strouse, *Morgan: American Financier, op. cit.,* p. 215.

12. Ayn Rand, *Atlas Shrugged, op. cit.,* pp. 387-391; *idem., For the New Intellectual* (New York: Penguin Books, 1961), pp. 88-94.

13. Gustavus Myers, *History of the Great American Fortunes* (New York: Modern Library, 1937), pp. 548-552, 596-597, 600 and *passim.* Ida Tarbell, *The History of the Standard Oil Company* (New York: Peter Smith, 1950), pp. 36-69, 99-103 and *passim.* Leon Wolfe, *Lockout: The Story of the Homestead Strike of 1892: A Study of Violence, Unionism, and the Carnegie Steel Empire* (New York: Harper and Row, 1965), pp. 28-152 and *passim.*

14. Matthew Josephson, *The Robber Barons, op. cit.,* pp. 104-105.

15. Burton J. Hendrick, *The Life of Andrew Carnegie, op. cit.,* vol. 1, p. 122 and *passim.* Josephson also tells a distorted version of J.P. Morgan's role in the Wall Street panic of 1901, as Jean Strouse, Morgan's most recent biographer, points out. Matthew Josephson, *The Robber Barons, op. cit.,* pp. 437-441. Jean Strouse, *Morgan: American Financier, op. cit.,* pp. xi-xii.

16. R. Gordon Wasson, *The Hall Carbine Affair: A Study in Contemporary Folklore* (New York: Pandick Press, 1948), pp. 77-92 and *passim.* Robert Hessen, *Steel Titan: The Life of Charles Schwab, op. cit.,* p. 309.

17. Ida Tarbell, *The History of the Standard Oil Company, op. cit.,* pp. 36-37. Allan Nevins, *Study in Power, op. cit.,* vol. 1, pp. 132-158. Ralph and Muriel Hidy, *Pioneering in Big Business, 1882-1911* (New York: Harper and Brothers, 1955), pp. 3-25, 649-651. Clarence Carson, *Throttling the Railroads, op. cit.,* pp. 53-54, emphasis added. For an excellent discussion of rebates and Standard Oil's absorption of smaller competitors that is written by an economist, not a historian or biographer, see Dominick Armentano's *The Myths of AntiTrust: Economic Theory and Legal Cases* (New Rochelle, NY: Arlington House, 1972), pp. 67-73.

18. Burton J. Hendrick, *The Life of Andrew Carnegie, op. cit.,* vol. 2, pp. 401-406. Robert Hessen, *Steel Titan: The Life of Charles Schwab, op. cit.,* pp. 42-58,

307-310. Peter Krass, *Carnegie* (Hoboken, NJ: John Wiley & Sons, 2002), pp. 306-311.

19. Burton J. Hendrick, *The Life of Andrew Carnegie, op. cit.*, vol. 1, pp. 365-413. Robert Hessen, *Steel Titan: The Life of Charles Schwab, op. cit.*, pp. 32-37.

20. Peter Krass, *Carnegie, op. cit.*, pp. ix-xi, 263-303.

21. George Kennan, *E.H. Harriman: A Biography, op. cit.*, vol. 2, pp. 174-227. Maury Klein, *The Life and Legend of E.H. Harriman, op. cit.*, pp. 8-9, 386-402.

22. Louis Hacker, *The World of Andrew Carnegie, op cit.*, pp. XXV-XXVI.

23. William Riordan, *Plunkitt of Tammany Hall* (New York: Signet, 1995), pp. x-xi, xv-xvii, xxiv, 3-16 and *passim*. Seymour Mandelbaum, *Boss Tweed's New York* (New York: John Wiley & Sons, 1965), pp. 67-86. Lawrence Reed, "The Forgotten Robber Barons," *Ideas On Liberty*, January 2003.

24. Vernon Parrington, *Main Currents in American Thought, op. cit.*, pp. 9-10. Charles and Mary Beard, *The Rise of American Civilization, op. cit.*, pp. 383-479. Louis Hacker, "The Anti-Capitalist Bias of American Historians," in F.A. Hayek, ed., *Capitalism and the Historians, op cit.*, pp. 77-79.

Annotated Bibliography of Liberty

The following is a partial list of books and essays that are important to understand the intellectual case for individual rights and capitalism.

Benjamin Anderson, *Economics and the Public Welfare*. Indianapolis, IN: Liberty Press, 1979. Anderson, an accomplished business economist, analyzes the origins of the Great Depression, arguing for the conclusion that government intervention in the economy was the decisive and disastrous first cause.

Anne Applebaum, *Gulag: A History*. New York: Doubleday, 2003. A current examination, based on newly-available Soviet archives, of the extensive slave labor camps run by the Soviet dictators for decades.

T.S. Ashton, *The Industrial Revolution*. New York: Oxford, 1968. The author, an expert on the Industrial Revolution, is one of the leading "optimistic" thinkers on the subject. His slender book shows many of the positive results of capitalism's early days.

Frederic Bastiat, *Economic Sophisms*. Irvington-on-Hudson, NY: The Foundation for Economic Education, 1996.

The Capitalist Manifesto

------------------, *Selected Essays on Political Economy*. Irvington-on-Hudson, NY: The Foundation for Economic Education, 1995. Two superb volumes of essays by Bastiat, a leading 19th century economic journalist and supporter of free trade.

P. T. Bauer, *Equality, the Third World, and Economic Delusion*. Cambridge: Harvard University Press, 1981. One of the leading development economists of recent years demonstrates the profoundly positive impact of Western Civilization and capitalism on starving, backward Third World nations.

Charles Beard, *A Foreign Policy for America*. New York: Alfred Knopf, 1940. Though Beard, the eminent American historian, is certainly no supporter of capitalism, he provides evidence substantiating the conclusion that politicians and naval officers, not businessmen, were generally responsible for imperialism.

Petr Beckmann, *The Health Hazards of Not Going Nuclear*. Boulder, Col.: Golem Press, 1976. The only book a reader will need in support of nuclear power by a professor of electrical engineering who also understands free market economics. Excellent on this topic.

Andrew Bernstein, "Black Innovators and Entrepreneurs Under Capitalism," *Ideas on Liberty*, October 2001. By showing the success of numerous black American entrepreneurs this essay disproves the claim that the elimination of racism is a pre-requisite for the success of a deprecated ethnic minority. Instead, what such individuals require is full capitalism, i.e., the consistent legal protection of their individual rights.

------------------, "The Welfare State Versus Values and the Mind," *The Intellectual Activist*, October 2001. The essay shows that the welfare state

clashes with the survival requirements of mankind and that this is the fundamental cause of the destruction it inevitably wreaks.

Fernand Braudel, *The Structures of Everyday Life*. New York: Harper & Row, 1981.

--------------------, *The Wheels of Commerce*. New York: Harper & Row, 1982. Braudel, the great French historian, provides abundant evidence establishing the miserable, widespread destitution of the pre-capitalist European workers and peasants.

Elizabeth Brayer, *George Eastman, A Biography*. Baltimore, MD: The Johns Hopkins University Press, 1996. The definitive biography of Eastman, one of the semi-overlooked originators of America's Inventive Period.

Mabel Buer, *Health, Wealth and Population in the Early Days of the Industrial Revolution*. New York: Howard Fertig, 1968. Buer's research reveals the unsanitary and unhygienec conditions of England prior to the Industrial Revolution, and the improvements wrought by the developing new technology of the 19th century.

Clarence Carson, *Organized Against Whom? The Labor Union in America*. Alexandria, Va.: Western Goals, 1983. Carson, an American historian, chronicles the government legislation and policies that have made possible coercive, monopolistic labor unions.

------------------, *The War On The Poor*. Birmingham, Al.: American Textbook Committee, 1991. Professor Carson details the extensive harm done to America's poorest citizens by government programs ostensibly designed to help them.

The Capitalist Manifesto

Ernst Cassirer, *The Philosophy Of the Enlightenment*. Boston: Beacon Press, 1955. A definitive examination of the philosophic thought of the Enlightenment by one of the leading scholars of the period.

Carlo Cipolla. *Before the Industrial Revolution: European Society and Economy, 1000-1700*. New York: W.W. Norton & Co., 1976. A distinguished recent historian documents the widespread European penury prior to the Industrial Revolution.

J.H. Clapham, *An Economic History of Modern Britain*, vol. 1, *The Early Railway Age*. Cambridge: Cambridge University Press, 1926. Clapham, one of the early optimists regarding the effects of the Industrial Revolution, uses statistical analysis to begin the gradual overturning of the conclusions reached by earlier pessimistic writers.

John Clark and Aaron Wildavsky, *The Moral Collapse Of Communism: Poland As a Cautionary Tale*. San Francisco: Institute for Contemporary Studies Press, 1990. Clark and Wildavsky argue that Communism's was fundamentally a moral collapse; that the economy failed primarily because of the pervasive denial of individual rights.

Robert Conquest, *Kolyma: The Arctic Death Camps*. New York: The Viking Press, 1978. A distinguished British historian tells the truth about the Stalin Holocaust.

------------------, *The Great Terror: A Reassessment*. New York: Oxford University Press, 1990. One of the leading Sovietologists analyzes all aspects of the atrocities committed during the Stalin era. Conquest's conclusions were disputed or denied by Western leftists for years, but were fully corroborated by recent research into the archives of the fallen Communist states.

Stephane Courtois, et.al., *The Black Book of Communism: Crimes, Terror, Repression.* Cambridge: Harvard University Press, 1999. Contemporary European Marxist intellectuals finally tell the truth regarding Communism in an 800-page tome filled with dispassionate descriptions of blood-curdling atrocities. Their research included access to archives of the fallen East European Communist regimes. An important and long-overdue book.

David Daiches, ed., *A Hotbed of Genius: The Scottish Enlightenment, 1730-1790.* Edinburgh: Edinburgh University Press, 1986. A series of essays describing the achievements of leading thinkers of the Scottish Enlightenment and, to a limited degree, their causal relation to the British Industrial Revolution.

L. Sprague de Camp, *The Heroic Age of American Invention.* Garden City, NY: Doubleday and Company, 1961. The author describes in the form of exciting stories the achievements of many of the pioneering thinkers of the Inventive Period.

Paul Driessen, *Eco-Imperialism: Green Power, Black Death.* Bellevue, WA: Free Enterprise Press, 2003. Exposes the ways in which the contemporary environmentalist movement, by attacking technology, industry, capitalism and economic progress, condemns to death countless penniless citizens of Third World countries.

Dinesh D'Souza, "We the Slaveowners: In Jefferson's America Were Some Men Not Created Equal?" *Policy Review* (Fall 1995, Number 74) A contemporary Indian-American scholar argues that the principle of individual rights implemented by the Founding Fathers led inevitably to the abolition of slavery.

Peter Duignan and L.H. Gann, ed., *Colonialism in Africa, 1870-1960*, Vol. 4, *The Economics of Colonialism*. Cambridge: Cambridge University Press, 1975. The contributors show the many economic benefits to Africa of European colonialism.

Miguel Faria, *Cuba In Revolution: Escape From a Lost Paradise*. Macon, Ga.: Hacienda Publishing, 2002. A brutal exposé of Castro's atrocities written by a Cuban émigré. The author is a physician who tells the ugly truth about the Communist state's vaunted health care system.

Sheila Fitzpatrick, *Everyday Stalinism, Ordinary Life In Extraordinary Times: Soviet Russia In The 1930s*. New York: Oxford University Press, 1999. A leading expert on modern Russian history shows how the Communist abrogation of freedom led to political repression and economic destitution for the overwhelming preponderance of the Soviet population.

Burton Folsom, *Empire Builders: How Michigan Entrepreneurs Helped Make America Great*. Traverse City, Mich.: Rhodes & Easton, 1998. Folsom tells the stories of such entrepreneurial giants as Henry Ford, Herbert Dow, Will Kellogg and others who helped build Michigan from an inconsequential backwater into an industrial power.

----------------, ed., *The Industrial Revolution and Free Trade*. Irvington-on-Hudson, NY: The Foundation for Economic Education, 1996. A collection of essays by numerous accomplished economists describing many positive results of capitalism's early days.

----------------, *The Myth Of The Robber Barons*. Herndon, Va.: Young America's Foundation, 1991. An accomplished American historian describes the extraordinary productive achievements of such maligned

business leaders as Cornelius Vanderbilt, John D. Rockefeller, James J. Hill and others.

Milton and Rose Friedman, *Free To Choose*. New York: Harcourt, Brace and Company, 1980. A popular, eminently readable statement regarding the virtues of capitalism by the distinguished economist and Nobel Laureate.

Joseph and Suzy Fucini, *Entrepreneurs: The Men and Women Behind Famous Brand Names and How They Made It*. Boston: G.K. Hall & Co., 1985. The fascinating, important and little-known stories of how many outstanding risk-takers started new companies to manufacture innovative products that, in time, enriched millions of customers. An ode to the great entrepreneurs.

Peter Gay, *The Enlightenment: An Interpretation*, vol 1, *The Rise of Modern Paganism*. New York: Alfred Knopf, 1966.; vol. 2, *The Science of Freedom*. New York: Alfred Knopf, 1969. A superb multi-volume study of Enlightenment thought, culture and influence by the greatest recent scholar of the 18th century.

M. Dorothy George, *London Life in the Eighteenth Century*. New York: Capricorn Books, 1965. Dr. George's research documents the horrifying conditions of English metropolitan life prior to the Industrial Revolution.

Louis Hacker, *The World of Andrew Carnegie, 1865-1901*. New York: J.B. Lippincott, Co., 1968. An outstanding study by a distinguished American historian of the productive achievements of Carnegie and other leading captains of industry during the Inventive Period.

R.M. Hartwell, *The Industrial Revolution and Economic Growth.* London: Methuen and Company, 1971. A series of essays by one of the leading "optimists" among British economic historians, arguing for the extensive benefits of 19th century capitalism and the Industrial Revolution.

F. A. Hayek, ed., *Capitalism and the Historians.* Chicago: University of Chicago Press, 1954. A series of invaluable essays arguing for the benefits of capitalism in its early days, written by leading economic historians, edited and with an introductory essay by Nobel Prize-winning economist, Hayek.

John Earl Haynes and Harvey Klehr, *Venona: Decoding Soviet Espionage in America.* New Haven: Yale University Press, 1999. Two American historians examine the de-classified Venona papers, the project by means of which U.S. intelligence broke the Soviet code. Their research documents the extensive Communist espionage that helped strengthen Soviet Russia at America's expense.

--------------------, *In Denial: Historians, Communism and Espionage.* San Francisco: Encounter Books, 2003. Haynes and Klehr dissect the anti-capitalist, anti-American historians who continue to deny the reality of Communism's evil and of the extensive Soviet espionage against the United States.

Henry Hazlitt, *Economics In One Lesson.* Westport, Ct.: Arlington House Publishers, 1979. The classic introductory text to free market economics written by a brilliantly lucid thinker and writer on the subject. Should be required reading in every high school and university in the country.

-----------------, *Man vs. The Welfare State.* New Rochelle, NY: Arlington House, 1969. A leading 20th century economist argues that the welfare

state exacerbates rather than cures poverty, and that it leads inexorably toward dictatorship.

————————, *The Conquest of Poverty*. Irvington-on-Hudson, NY: The Foundation for Economic Education, 1996. Hazlitt shows that statist programs cannot eradicate or even ameliorate poverty; only capitalism can achieve this. Includes a very good chapter on the harmful effects of coercive unionism.

Burton J. Hendrick, *The Life of Andrew Carnegie*, 2 vols. Garden City, NY: Doubleday, Doran and Company, 1932. Carnegie's life story told in detail by a Pulitzer Prize-winning author who understands and admires Carnegie's heroic achievements.

Arthur Herman, *How the Scots Invented the Modern World*. New York: Crown Publishers, 2001. The fascinating account by a contemporary historian of how the great minds of the Scottish Enlightenment were largely responsible for much of the progress attained in the last three centuries.

Robert Higgs, "Regime Uncertainty: Why the Great Depression Lasted So Long and Why Prosperity Resumed After the War." *The Independent Review*, Spring 1997, pp. 561-590. A contemporary economist examines the causes of the Depression's longevity and of post-War recovery. Not surprisingly, he finds the reasons for the upturn in the lesser degree of statism embodied in the Truman administration relative to FDR's.

Brooke Hindle, *The Pursuit of Science in Revolutionary America, 1735-1789*. Chapel Hill: University of North Carolina Press, 1956. An American historian studies the progress in science and inventiveness during the American Enlightenment.

Philip Howard, *The Death Of Common Sense: How Law Is Suffocating America.* New York: Warner Books, 1994. A contemporary lawyer describes in detail the way government bureaucrats, from the FDA to OSHA to the EPA, often impose arbitrary and counter-productive regulations on American entrepreneurs, workers and property owners to the detriment of both freedom and economic progress.

Jonathan Hughes, *The Vital Few: American Economic Progress and its Protagonists.* Boston: Houghton Mifflin, 1966. An economist analyzes the role of several distinguished inventors and entrepreneurs in promoting American economic progress.

Paul Johnson, *A History of the American People.* New York: HarperPerennial, 1997. A leading British historian chronicles the rise of America to greatness and acknowledges the positive role played by capitalism.

----------------, *Modern Times: The World From the Twenties to the Nineties.* New York: HarperPerennial, 1991. Paul Johnson examines the 20th century, paying careful attention to the rise of collectivist dictatorships in Russia, Germany and China.

------------------, *The Birth of the Modern: World Society, 1815-1930.* New York: HarperPerennial, 1992. Johnson analyzes the manner in which numerous distinctively-modern advances were born in this era, providing valuable information regarding the early days of capitalism and the Industrial Revolution.

Matthew Josephson, *Edison: A Biography.* New York: John Wiley and Sons, 1959. An outstanding biography of Edison by an author who admires inventors but who, in his book, *The Robber Barons,* reviled America's pioneering entrepreneurs and industrialists.

Annotated Bibliography of Liberty

Werner Keller, *East Minus West Equals Zero*. New York: G.P. Putnam's Sons, 1962. A German historian documents many of the ways in which Western capitalism helped build much of whatever industrial strength the Soviet Union had.

George Kennan, *E.H. Harriman: A Biography*, 2 vols. Boston: Houghton Mifflin, 1922. For almost 80 years, Kennan's was the only major biography of the "Little Giant's" life and work. An admiring look at an industrial giant who, at the turn of the 20th century, was properly recognized as the equal of Carnegie, Rockefeller and Morgan, but who, unfortunately, is scarcely remembered at the turn of the 21st. The other "Robber Barons" are merely reviled; Harriman has suffered a worse injustice: he is forgotten.

Martin Kramer, *Ivory Towers on Sand: The Failure of Middle Eastern Studies in America*. Washington, D.C.: Washington Institute for Near East Policy, 2001. The author, a Middle East scholar, tells the truth regarding contemporary Islamists and Islamic dictators who threaten America—and contrasts it with the fantasies presented by many current anti-Western Middle East scholars in the United States.

Jay Lehr, ed., *Rational Readings on Environmental Concerns*. New York: Van Nostrand Reinhold, 1992. A series of essays by scientists, physicians, engineers and economists highly critical of the pseudo-science employed by environmentalists in their crusade against industrialization and capitalism. Explores numerous issues from global warming to nuclear power to species extinction to many others. Particularly valuable is George Reisman's "The Toxicity of Environmentalism."

David Levy, *How the Dismal Science Got Its Name*. Ann Arbor: University of Michigan Press, 2001. A contemporary American economist tells the

fascinating story of how the 19th century free market economists fought for abolitionism against Britain's leading literary racists, slavery advocates and anti-capitalists Thomas Carlyle, John Ruskin and Charles Dickens.

Bernard Lewis, *What Went Wrong: Western Impact and Middle Eastern Response*. New York: Oxford University Press, 2002. A leading Middle Eastern scholar chronicles the decline of Islamic Civilization from its past glories, and helps explain the anti-Western sentiment that fuels contemporary Islamist aggression against America and its allies.

Oscar Lewis, *The Big Four*. New York: Alfred Knopf, 1938. Lewis's book shows that the Big Four who monopolized the California railroad industry for decades in the late-19th century gained their power from government enfranchisement, not by means of a free market.

Peter Lindert and Jeffrey Williamson, "English Workers' Living Standards During the Industrial Revolution: A New Look." *The Economic History Review*, 2nd Series, 36 (February 1983). Two comparatively recent economic historians provide more data showing the rise of real wages during the early days of the British Industrial Revolution.

Edwin Locke, *The Prime Movers: Traits of the Great Wealth Creators*. New York: American Management Association, 2000. Professor Locke analyzes the characteristics of many superb businessmen by means of which they created vast amounts of wealth.

Albro Martin, *James J. Hill and the Opening of the Northwest*. St. Paul: Minnesota Historical Society Press, 1976. A major biography of the legendary railroad builder who was so instrumental in building up the American Northwest.

Ludwig von Mises, *Human Action*, 3rd ed. rev. Chicago: Henry Regnery Company, 1966. Mises is considered the dean of the Austrian school of economics, and this is his comprehensive work on economic theory. A landmark work in the history of economic science.

------------------------, *Socialism*. Indianapolis, IN: Liberty Fund, 1981. A devastating economic critique of socialism by one of the great economists of history.

David McCullough, *The Great Bridge: The Epic Story of the Building of the Brooklyn Bridge*. New York: Touchstone Books, 1982. The in-depth story of one of the greatest engineering achievements of the Inventive Period.

--------------------, *The Path Between the Seas: The Creation of the Panama Canal, 1870-1914*. New York: Touchstone Books, 1977. Although the Panama Canal was a U.S. government project, the man who turned around the floundering construction job was John Stevens, one-time chief engineer of James J. Hill's Great Northern Railroad.

Charles Murray, *Losing Ground: American Social Policy, 1950-1980*. New York: Basic Books, 1984. This is the preeminent book, by a distinguished conservative social scientist, documenting the factual horrors of the welfare state in action.

Clark Nardinelli, *Child Labor and the Industrial Revolution*. Bloomington: Indiana University Press, 1990. An economist shows that, contrary to anti-capitalist propaganda, the Industrial Revolution did not cause or exacerbate child labor; it ended it.

Allan Nevins, *Study in Power: John D. Rockefeller, Industrialist and Philanthropist*, 2 vols. New York: Charles Scribner's Sons, 1953. This

major study of Rockefeller by an eminent American historian is highly respectful of the oil magnate's productive accomplishments.

Johan Norberg, *In Defense of Global Capitalism*. Stockholm: Timbro, 2001. A succinct and informative account of the many benefits of global capitalism. Includes an effective discussion of so-called "sweatshops."

Gerald O'Driscoll, et al., *The 2001 Index of Economic Freedom*. Washington, D.C.: The Heritage Foundation and the *Wall Street Journal*, 2001. The book examines 155 countries around the globe and finds stunning correlations between freedom and prosperity, repression and destitution.

Leonard Peikoff, *Objectivism: The Philosophy of Ayn Rand*. New York: Penguin Books, 1993. The definitive study of the entire theoretical structure of Objectivism—the only system of thought explaining and validating man's need of freedom—by Ayn Rand's leading student and intellectual heir.

——————————, *The Ominous Parallels: The End of Freedom in America*. New York: Penguin Books, 1983. A contemporary philosopher shows the frightening similarities between present day America and Weimar Germany—the culture that spawned National Socialism.

Jim Powell, *FDR's Folly: How Roosevelt and His New Deal Prolonged the Great Depression*. New York: Crown Forum, 2003. An exhaustive survey of the endless economic errors of FDR's New Deal and the way in which they unnecessarily prolonged the agonies of the Great Depression. Helpful in finally puncturing the untruthful hagiographies that surround Roosevelt's presidency.

Ayn Rand, *Atlas Shrugged*. New York: Penguin Books, 1957. The seminal novel in the process of promoting fundamental philosophical and social change. Ayn Rand presents a full, systematic, rational philosophy in the form of an epic mystery story. The single most important book in the battle for reason, egoism, individualism and capitalism.

----------, *Capitalism: The Unknown Ideal*. New York: Penguin Books, 1967. A brilliant series of essays by Ayn Rand and other contributors, arguing above all for the moral superiority of capitalism to statism.

------------, *The Fountainhead*. New York: Penguin Books, 1943. This book is simultaneously a landmark novel and an impassioned and brilliant statement in support of innovative thinkers, their requirement of freedom, their role in carrying mankind forward, and the struggle they face from those who will benefit most from their achievements.

-------------, *The Virtue of Selfishness: A New Concept of Egoism*. New York: Penguin Books, 1964. The lead essay, "The Objectivist Ethics," is of especial importance. In it, Ayn Rand develops the fundamentals of a revolution in moral philosophy. This is the work that lays the foundation for an intellectual validation of egoism, individualism and freedom.

George Reisman, *Capitalism: A Treatise on Economics*. Ottawa, Ill.: Jameson Books, 1998. A comprehensive work in support of free minds and free markets by a leading contemporary economist. Includes an excellent section refuting the anti-industrial, anti-capitalist claims of current environmentalists.

------------------, *Capitalism: The Cure For Racism*. Laguna Hills, Cal.: The Jefferson School of Philosophy, Economics and Psychology, 1992. Shows how the unfettered functioning of a free market militates against

racism and all forms of ethnic bigotry, and how statism fosters both.
Paul Craig Roberts and Karen LaFollette Araujo, *The Capitalist Revolution in Latin America*. New York: Oxford University Press, 1997. Shows how centuries of relentless statism has impoverished Latin America, and how capitalism is beginning to liberate and enrich it.

Nathan Rosenberg and L.E. Birdzell, *How the West Grew Rich: The Economic Transformation of the Industrial World*. New York: Basic Books, 1986. This is a scholarly book that shows the important role played by political freedom and scientific achievements in promoting the success of the Industrial Revolution.

Richard Salsman, "The Cause and Consequence of the Great Depression," *The Intellectual Activist*, June-September, 2004. A contemporary business economist presents an original and powerful case regarding the specific statist measures responsible for the worst depression of U.S. history.

Robert Schofield, *The Lunar Society of Birmingham: A Social History of Provincial Science and Industry in Eighteenth-Century England*. Oxford: Oxford University Press, 1963. Tells the story of the extraordinary group of scientists, inventors and industrialists whose devotion to technological advance and material progress helped promote the British Industrial Revolution.

Peter Schwartz, "The Philosophy of Privation," in Ayn Rand, *Return of the Primitive: The Anti-Industrial Revolution*. New York: Penguin Books, 1999. An excellent moral and philosophical dissection of the evils of environmentalism. Mr. Schwartz shows the virulently anti-man nature of this intellectual and political movement.

Annotated Bibliography of Liberty

Hans Sennholz, ed., *American Unionism: Fallacies and Follies*. Irvington-on-Hudson, NY: The Foundation for Economic Education, 1994. A series of articles by recent economists and historians analyzing the ills of American unionism made possible by governmental coercion.

Julian Simon, ed., *The State of Humanity*. Cambridge, Mass: Blackwell Publishers, 1995. A series of essays by economists, scientists and historians providing a plethora of factual data leading to an inescapable general conclusion: mankind is vastly better off after (and because of) the Industrial Revolution than it was before it.

----------------, *The Ultimate Resource*. Princeton: Princeton University Press, 1981. A leading American economist argues for an all-important and too-often-neglected truth: the ultimate natural resource is neither iron nor coal nor oil, but man's rational mind. Simon shows by application to myriad contemporary issues that rational thought, operating under conditions of political-economic freedom, is the solution to mankind's most urgent problems.

Mark Skousen, *The Making of Modern Economics: The Lives and Ideas of the Great Thinkers*. Armonk, NY: M.E. Sharpe, 2001. A readable intellectual history of the great economists and their theories written from a free market perspective by a contemporary economist.

Samuel Smiles, *Lives of the Engineers: Selections From Samuel Smiles*, ed., Thomas Parke Hughes. Cambridge, MA: The M.I.T. Press, 1966. Smiles, a 19th century author, wrote with supreme respect for the constructive achievements of the great engineers and here tells the stories of several leading builders of the British Industrial Revolution, including the superlative Thomas Telford.

Thomas Sowell, *Conquests and Culture: An International History*. New York: Basic Books, 1998. Excellent, among other virtues, for a discussion that combines an understanding of the general horror of conquest with a recognition of the benefits to culturally less advanced peoples of the uniquely British version of imperialism.

------------------, *Ethnic America: A History*. New York: Basic Books, 1981. An excellent analysis by a leading American economist of how various ethnic groups have generally fared in America. Tells the inspiring story of the economic rise of many different immigrant groups in history's freest nation.

------------------, *Markets and Minorities*. New York: Basic Books, 1981. An accomplished economist shows that, in case after case, freedom benefits racial minorities and governmental intervention generally harms them.

------------------, *Race And Culture: A World View*. New York: Basic Books, 1994. Includes an excellent discussion of slavery as a global phenomenon, and of abolitionism as a distinctively Western one.

Jean Strouse, *Morgan: American Financier*. New York: HarperPerennial, 2000. This latest biography of America's Wall Street titan describes all of his flaws but never loses an appreciation of his extraordinary financial achievements.

Antony Sutton, *Western Technology and Soviet Economic Development*, 3 vols. Palo Alto: Hoover Institute Press, 1968, 1971, 1973. A British historian exhaustively documents the extensive Soviet reliance on Western capitalism for whatever degree of industrialization the Communist state was able to achieve.

Michael Tanner, *The End of Welfare: Fighting Poverty in the Civil Society.* Washington, D.C.: Cato Institute, 1996. Makes a convincing case that the welfare state necessarily has been an utter failure; that it cannot be reformed, but must be eradicated, replaced by private responsibility, private charity and private enterprise.

Jenny Uglow, *Lunar Men: Five Friends Whose Curiosity Changed the World.* New York: Farrar, Straus and Giroux, 2002. The latest work examining the lives and achievements of the intellectual pioneers composing the justly-famed Lunar Society of Birmingham.

Walter Williams, *South Africa's War Against Capitalism.* New York: Praeger, 1989. A contemporary economist establishes that South Africa's racist regime necessarily imposed statist policies as a method of implementing apartheid. Capitalism was the solution to South Africa's problems.

--------------------, *The State Against Blacks.* New York: McGraw-Hill, 1982. Professor Williams argues powerfully that government intervention in the U.S. economy has hindered, in numerous ways, rather than helped, the economic advance of black Americans. Again, a free market is the solution to the difficulty.

Jeffrey Williamson, *Did British Capitalism Breed Inequality.* Boston: Allen and Unwin, 1985. A recent economic historian provides substantial statistical data showing the rise of real wages for numerous categories of British workers during the early days of the Industrial Revolution.

Abraham Wolf, *A History of Science, Technology and Philosophy in the Eighteenth Century*, 2 vols. New York: Harper Torchbooks, 1961. A scholarly examination of many of the advances reached during the 18th century.

The Capitalist Manifesto

Daniel Yergin and Joseph Stanislaw, *The Commanding Heights: The Battle Between Government and the Marketplace That is Remaking the Modern World*. New York: Touchstone Books, 1998. The authors examine the successful worldwide movement toward privatization and free markets that has taken place in the past three decades.

Index

Index